12/01
6

Israel Observed

Israel Observed

An Anatomy of the State

WILLIAM FRANKEL

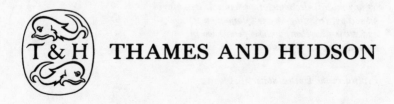
THAMES AND HUDSON

Contents

Introduction

'You're writing a book on how Israel works,' repeated my Israeli friend thoughtfully, and then, after a pause, 'That's brave.' 'Foolhardy,' I replied. 'Well,' he responded, 'there are rules even in a lunatic asylum,' and followed with this story:

A visitor to a mental home was taken to see a newly-installed swimming pool. To avoid what might have been awkward encounters with inmates, he was invited to view it from a fairly distant window. From that vantage point, he could see groups of patients around the pool, some jumping in or otherwise disporting themselves in their new amenity. The visitor expressed pleasure at the sight and remarked that the patients seemed to be enjoying themselves. 'That's true,' said his guide, 'and it will be even better when there's water in the pool.'

Israelis are as fond of telling these stories against themselves as they have been adept at adjusting their lives to the unfinished country in which they live. Not only are many material elements of Israel still in course of construction, but the institutions and infrastructure which the state either inherited or created are in a constant state of adaptation and revision. Entrenched establishments in, for example, political parties, the Labour Federation and governmental bureaucracies see in the maintenance of the *status quo* the retention of the source of their power, but the momentum for change is irresistible.

In Britain, despite vast changes, well-established institutions like Parliament, the monarchy, or 'the City', products of centuries of development, possess well-defined characteristics which can be described with some precision. In Israel, however, improvisation and temporary expedients (which may or may not become permanent) are the national way of life and their operations are much more difficult to pin down.

The object of this book is to describe the structure and workings of the main political and social institutions of Israel which determine national policies and influence the way Israelis live. Since the character of these institutions reflects the attitudes and personalities of the people who run them, I have also written about some of their leaders. This is not a history of Israel, though historical background has been given wherever it is essential to the understanding of existing situations. Nor is it – like so many books in the voluminous literature which has grown up about the Jewish State – an attempt to make out a case, for or against. Of course, as a Jew committed to the support of Israel, I am not impartial. But I have endeavoured to deal with my subject with as much objectivity as I can command.

I am aware that the intense emotional involvement in Israel of many Jews in the diaspora has created a certain intolerance of, and even resentment at, any criticism of the country. Israeli Jews, while addicted to habitual self-castigation (some would say they overdo it), are generally no less offended than their diaspora co-religionists at criticism from outside. It creates a kind of defensive reflex, illustrated by the response of an Israeli friend when I once casually remarked that I'd come from England to escape from the climate but that it was almost as cold in Jerusalem. He reluctantly admitted that, yes, it was cold just then, but triumphantly produced the excuse – 'It's because of the weather!'

Some Israelis believe in the existence of a national streak of paranoia and Professor Amnon Rubinstein, a lawyer and politician who appears on a number of occasions in this book, once wrote a caustic essay on this theme entitled 'All the world is against us'. And indeed such tendencies are understandable in the light of the Holocaust, of which so many Israelis are survivors, and of the continual state of war and tension under which the state has existed since its creation. Paranoia may be too strong a term for it. I have always thought that the Israelis' attitude towards their country is similar to that of parents towards their children; they themselves are free to be highly critical but they bridle when criticism comes from others.

In dealing with a variety of aspects of Israeli life, I have not omitted the seamier side. I hope it will not offend my Israeli friends. I know that the country is still in a state of siege and that its enemies abound. I am aware, too, of the danger that critical assessments are frequently taken out of context and used as ammunition in the incessant propaganda warfare against Israel. But I believe that Israel is now old enough and secure enough to accept, if not with gratitude, at least without rancour, the criticism of candid friends.

However, because this is my hope rather than a conviction, I have omitted from the acknowledgments which follow the names of a large number of Israelis who were kind enough to spend time with me and give me the benefit of their knowledge and experience in gathering material for this book. I would not want any of them to be embarrassed by my recording their contributions.

The material for this book comes from three main sources. Its foundations are the accumulated mass of information and impressions I have gained from innumerable visits to Israel over many years, from talking to many Israeli friends, both leaders and led, and from consistently following the news from that part of the world throughout my adult life. Secondly, in preparation for the book, I interviewed dozens of Israeli policy-makers, public servants, journalists, professional men and women, academics, soldiers and workers, from each of whom I gained much. The third source was the existing published material in books, periodicals and newspapers.

Necessarily, I have often had to paint with broad strokes of the brush, for to have entered upon much detail on each of the aspects of Israel with which I deal would have made the book impossibly long. Nor have I been entirely comprehensive, having omitted any systematic examination of areas like local government, science and technology, agriculture and the revival of the

Hebrew language, though some are referred to incidentally. On the other hand, I found it impossible to avoid a certain amount of repetition. Religion, for example, is dealt with both in the chapter on politics, because of the existence of religious political parties, and in the chapter on Judaism in practice. To make each of these chapters comprehensible without the need for frequent crossreference, I have, on occasion, referred to the same events in both.

I have also concentrated on the Jewish component of Israel, omitting any detailed consideration of the institutions of the non-Jewish minorities. Nor have I included any discussion of the occupied territories, their administration and problems, since they are not Israel proper. My excuse for these various deficiencies is that a book attempting to cover such a wide subject must necessarily be selective and my selection has been based on my perception of what would be of most interest and importance to the general reader.

And because this book is directed to the general reader rather than the specialist, I have not included references to sources and have restricted myself to a minimal number of footnotes. To help those who want more detailed information, I have added a bibliography and, as an aid to comprehension, a glossary of Hebrew names and terms, although most of them are explained at least once in the text.

Before I started on this enterprise, Anthony Sampson gave me valuable advice on the techniques of writing a book of this nature. Two American friends in London, Julie Leff and Jan Macdonald, assisted me during the hesitant early stages of preparation, while Betty Enoch, Keren Jacobs and Anne Lee performed nobly in transforming my indistinct calligraphy into a typed manuscript.

I owe a debt to the Jerusalem Foundation for hospitality at Mishkenot Sha'ananim. I stayed there in the spring of 1979 when I started work on this book and, on the frequent occasions when I felt daunted by the magnitude of my undertaking, I had only to look at the glorious views of Jerusalem from my apartment in the 'habitations of tranquillity' for my spirits to revive.

Finally to the *sine qua non*. This book owes its genesis and completion to Claire. She encouraged and prodded me into starting it and heartened me through numerous setbacks and disappointments as the work progressed. This book is dedicated to my wife in love and gratitude.

Chapter one

The Assembly of Parliament

Prologue: the shock of 1977

The general election in Israel on 17 May 1977 produced what was widely described in the world's press as a 'shock' result. It brought to power an outsider with a reputation as a political reactionary, a demagogue, a hard-line chauvinist. Moreover, Menachem Begin had, in the turbulent years leading to Israel's birth, headed the Irgun Zvai Leumi – a band of fighters or terrorists (depending on the viewpoint of the commentator) responsible for killings and acts of sabotage in the struggle with Great Britain.

Nor was it only the outside world that was startled and apprehensive at the election result. The Israelis surprised and shocked themselves by what they had done. Some were amazed by their courage and others by their folly. They had not really meant to bring Begin to power, but to express disapproval of the Labour Party.

Though the party name had undergone change as various sub-groupings hived off, divided and then came together again, the Labour Party had been the ruling group in Israel from the time of the nation's birth in 1948. The first Prime Minister, David Ben-Gurion, the father-figure of Israel, personified the party (although he later left its mainstream). Labour's long period in power had made it seem the permanent party of Government, and most observers assumed that it would again be victorious in the 1977 elections, even though it had entered the campaign with a considerably tarnished image.

Three main contenders in the elections, which took place six months earlier than the final date the law permitted, were the ruling Labour coalition, a conservative grouping called the Likud and a new force, the Democratic Movement for Change (DMC).

Leading Labour was Shimon Peres who, at 54, was still young by Israeli political standards. He had reached the top only four weeks before the election, when his predecessor, a former Chief of Staff and Ambassador to the United States, Yitzhak Rabin, stepped down as Prime Minister after his wife's conviction on a currency offence.

Menachem Begin, the long-serving head of the Likud, was ten years older than Peres and not in the best of health. Apart from a short period in the Government of National Unity which emerged through the Six Day War, he had never held Cabinet office. Peres, on the other hand, as a protégé of Ben-Gurion, had been at the centre of power for decades. Yet Begin was respected as a man of integrity and his rousing oratory made him a powerful force, more effective on the platform than Peres, whose speeches tended to be coldly logical and unemotional.

The Democratic Movement for Change had come into existence only a short time before the election. It was spearheaded by Labour dissidents and reflected the disillusionment felt by many with the corruption in the party after so many years in Government. At the head of the DMC was the attractive figure of Yigael Yadin. With a popular national reputation as a military leader in the War of Independence and international fame as an archaeologist, he possessed the additional advantage of being a new face, uncontaminated by any previous political involvement.

As in every earlier Israeli General Election, various lesser parties – nineteen of them, in fact – also put up candidates, the most important being the National Religious Party. But the real fight was between Labour and the Likud.

The election could not have come at a worse time for Labour. Just before the voters went to the polls, a series of public scandals culminated in the conviction of one of the most powerful figures in the Labour Party, Asher Yadlin, who was sentenced to five years' imprisonment and a fine of I£250,000 for accepting bribes and filing a false income tax declaration. What made it an even worse reflection on the competence and moral authority of the Government, then still headed by Rabin, was the fact that, at the time of his arrest, Yadlin was his party's nominee for the key appointment of Governor of the Bank of Israel.

While the Yadlin trial was still pending, an additional blow was the suicide of Avraham Ofer, the Minister of Housing, another major figure in the Labour Party. He had been the target of newspaper accusations of corruption, all of which he had denied. Finally came the affair of the Prime Minister's wife, Lea Rabin, who had infringed the foreign exchange laws by maintaining a personal dollar account at a bank in Washington.

Apart from the scandals, other adverse factors affected Labour. The first was the economy. Inflation was rising at a rate of 35 per cent, trifling compared with its gallop later, but high enough to make a serious impact on the poorer section of the community. In the main, these were the Oriental Jews, the immigrants from the Moslem countries of North Africa and the Middle East. They turned to the Likud not only on economic grounds but because it was seen as taking a harder line against the Arabs. Many entertained a deep animosity towards Arabs as a result of the inferior status accorded to them in the Moslem lands from which they had come.

To add to Labour's troubles, the President of the United States was making statements about the need for a Palestinian homeland. The fear that the Labour Party might find it politic to make too many concessions to the Americans also helped to drive votes to the right-wingers.

It was a time of almost palpable malaise in Israel's once idealistic society. Corruption, inflation, high taxation and a rising cost of living, declining immigration and increasing emigration all added up to a powerful indictment of the Labour Party. Whether or not the party had an answer to the accusations no longer seemed relevant. It had governed since the beginning and was held responsible.

The election result was a vote of no confidence in the Labour Party. The Likud won 43 of the 120 Knesset seats, making it the largest single party. Labour won only 32 seats (compared with 51 in the previous Knesset), reduced to 31 when Moshe Dayan resigned from the party, 'crossing the floor of the House' to become Foreign Minister of the Likud-dominated coalition.

The new Democratic Movement for Change did well to win fifteen seats, the National Religious Party (NRP) did as expected in retaining its twelve seats, while nine small parties shared the remaining eighteen.

Almost all the analysts had predicted another Labour victory, and the single Israeli public opinion poll which pointed to a Likud win had been ignored as an aberration. It was simply inconceivable that Labour would not continue to rule and that Menachem Begin, who seemed to be permanently and ideally cast in the role of opposition leader, could possibly become Prime Minister. However, Israel's democratic electoral system had proved that it could work to bring about change. The 1977 election did indeed signal the first major change of direction in Israeli politics as a whole and constituted a watershed in the history of the young nation.

The Knesset

Israel is a parliamentary democracy and, as in Britain, Parliament is supreme. Called The Knesset (meaning assembly – the same word is used in the Hebrew name for synagogue), it is composed of 120 elected members.

The solid building of the Knesset, Israel's Parliament house, sits squarely on high ground to the west of the Biblical city of Jerusalem. Impressive rather than beautiful, its elevated site commands sweeping views of the hills and valleys of Judea. The building was the munificent gift of James de Rothschild and was opened by his widow Dorothy, but the name of the benefactor is otherwise not associated with it, a rare phenomenon in Israel where so many buildings bear prominent plaques immortalizing the charitable.

Access, in these days of terrorism, involves the usual security routines. Armed soldiers stop all cars before the main gates and visitors are required to produce documents of identification at an entry lodge whose guardians hold a register of all expected callers that day. That stage successfully negotiated, the visitor is presented with a pass, the pass is rubber-stamped and first employed as a ticket of admission to a frisking cubicle – separate for men and women – which opens to the extensive and well-kept lawn leading up to the Knesset building.

Yet, undeterred by these protracted preliminaries, masses of visitors swarm over the building, with school parties predominating. They tour the ceremonial halls, admiring the Chagall tapestries and other art works before taking their seats in the visitors' section of the Chamber. It is a spacious, uncluttered auditorium, austere and modern. Each member has his own place at one end of the large curved tables facing the central podium. He sits in a comfortable swivel armchair and, when moved to intervene in the proceedings, need only lean over and talk into one of the microphones placed between every two desks. It makes interruptions easy, perhaps too easy.

The appearance of the Members indicates something unusual about this Parliament. There is so much variety. Many of the Labour people wear the standard open-necked shirt and slacks. Some of the more conventional (and not all of them are right-wing) wear business suits and ties. Women are colourful, though hardly fashionable, in skirts and blouses or simple dresses. More eye-catching are the bearded, black frock-coated, black skull-capped Members, many of them rabbis, representing the religious parties. Further diversity is contributed by the flowing robes of Arab and Druze members.

Speeches, as distinct from interruptions, are not delivered from the Members' desks but from the podium where the Speaker sits. They tend to be fiery and passionate in delivery, but the other Members appear unconcerned. They have heard it all before and, in any case, the speaker is really addressing the newspapers or the radio and television audience. The atmosphere is languid, relaxed. The Members in the Chamber, except on great occasions, write at their desks, read newspapers, chat with each other or walk about. They seem to do everything but listen.

Visiting groups (special visitors are accommodated elsewhere) sit in a rear section cut off from the inmates by a huge expanse of bullet-proof glass. During a normal sitting, the visitor is unlikely to become overexcited by what he sees and hears. The subject under discussion is more likely to be technical than interesting and the Members in the Chamber, possibly twenty or so, will be lounging nonchalantly in their well-upholstered seats.

The action, which the visiting groups do not see, takes place in the Knesset Members' cafeteria. From picture windows on one side, the low ceilinged room offers panoramic views of the dramatic scenery, but the splendid outlook is largely ignored, because everybody in the room is looking to see who else is there and what they are doing. About twenty tables seat some hundred occupants (with facilities for overflow), the green leather upholstered chairs tastefully colour-coordinated with the blue tablecloths. But the occupants are not interested in the aesthetics of the place either. Ministers have rooms in the building while ordinary Knesset Members have some office facilities which they say are inadequate. But even if they were perfect, Members would still congregate in the cafeteria, because they want to be seen and button-holed.

Like café life in Tel Aviv, like the habit in Israel of holding constant open house where people drop in unannounced, the Knesset cafeteria seems to express the Israeli rejection of privacy. Israelis prefer not to be alone; they seem to be afraid of solitariness. Perhaps it is a vestigial relic of the diaspora to feel more secure in the company of others.

Knesset Members like to be where everyone else is. Then they can chat with each other and with the journalists who happen to be around. The Foreign Minister holds court at a window table from which people come and go. At the next table, the Leader of the Opposition chats to colleagues, officials and reporters.

Wednesday is the only full working day at the Knesset, beginning at 11 in the morning and continuing until business is finished, which could be midnight or later. On Mondays and Tuesdays the sitting only starts at 4 in the afternoon, while none are held on Thursdays and Fridays. So Wednesday is the busy day in the cafeteria, when everyone is on parade, talking and being talked to, making deals or giving explanations, more usefully occupied than merely sitting in the Chamber.

How the Knesset works

What is described in the Basic Law as 'the elected Assembly of the State of Israel' took its Hebrew name from the Knesset Hagedolah, the Jewish Assembly, at the time of the Second Temple. The adoption of the name constituted a declaration that the Jewish State did not begin in 1948 but had its roots in an earlier sovereignty on the same soil.

Nevertheless, the structure and procedure of the Knesset owe less to remote Jewish history than to two much more recent influences. The close relationship with the British during the Mandatory period produced, not merely a series of conflicts, but also an exposure to the British parliamentary system which made a powerful and lasting impression on the mainly East European Zionist leaders. As a result, the Knesset is largely based on that British model, adapted and modified to local circumstances and incorporating some of the traditional procedures of the Zionist movement and its Congresses.

Above all else, Israel adopted from Britain the principle of the supremacy of Parliament. In Israel, the President, the courts and the executive are all subordinate to the Knesset. The President possesses no power to veto legislation, and the courts cannot declare any law passed by the Knesset unconstitutional. The laws passed by the Knesset are the source of all power and authority; but in practice this authority has rarely been exercised. Policy is made by the Prime Minister and his Cabinet and they come to the Knesset for *post-facto* approval. This has invariably been given, and never yet in Israel's history has a Government fallen as a result of a Knesset vote of no confidence.

The formative influence in shaping the organization, rules and general tone of the new Parliament was Moshe Rosetti. An immigrant from London, he had been a prominent figure in the Anglo-Jewish community. He had held senior posts in local government but his real interest was in the intricacies of parliamentary procedure, and when he was appointed the first Clerk to the Knesset (the British title was itself a tribute to Rosetti's essential British-ness; it was later changed to Secretary-General) he established himself as a creative authority, setting a pattern which still prevails.

Following British procedure, the first task of each newly elected Knesset is to elect a Speaker who, as at Westminster, is responsible for the conduct of proceedings. The second influence, that of Zionist Congresses, brought about the institution of a presidium consisting of the Speaker and his deputies, a group representing the major parties roughly in proportion to their strength in the House. That presidium determines the agenda for the plenary meetings which are normally held on Mondays, Tuesdays and Wednesdays during the two annual parliamentary sessions. In special cases they may take place on other days, but plenary meetings are usually avoided on Sundays and Fridays, the Christian and Moslem days of rest. Saturday is, of course, the Jewish and national rest-day.

The actual seating of Members in a semicircular chamber provides a contrast to the face-to-face confrontation of Government and Opposition in the House of Commons. It does not appear to have inhibited heckling, for Members can so easily interrupt through the microphones to hand; but the cut and thrust of debate at Westminster is lacking, possibly because the disputants are not facing each other. The actual number of Members' seats in the Knesset is 12 more than its elected 120 members because Cabinet Ministers are entitled to sit in the Chamber even though they may not have been elected to membership of the House.

Bills go through the British parliamentary procedure of three readings, but with a variation. At Westminster, first readings are formal; second readings debate the principles of the proposed legislation and then, after the committee stage where the wording is gone over, the Bill reappears for the third reading when it is voted on clause by clause. But in the Knesset, the first reading debates principles, the committee stage comes next and the second reading deals with the wording. The final stage, the third reading, is limited to voting on each clause.

Of growing importance and popularity in the Knesset is another British institution, question time. At Westminster every Minister must face direct questioning on his area of responsibility – an important method by which the legislature can try to control the executive. In Israel it took a long time for the system to begin working properly because, while a British MP will ask questions largely based on his mail from constituents, his Israeli counterpart has no constituency and little or no relationship with individual electors. So Israel's MPs asked far fewer questions which were far less specific than the British variety, and Israeli Ministers tended to give most of their answers in writing. Possibly because the present Prime Minister, Menachem Begin, is what is known in Westminster as a 'good House of Commons man', question time became more interesting after his accession to power.

A Member of the Knesset who wants to speak does not engage in the subtle and mysterious Westminster procedure of 'catching the Speaker's eye', for in the Knesset each party is allotted a fixed time for its participation in the debate and the party nominates the Member or Members who will utilize that time. But Ministers are not bound by a time limit, while the Leader of the Opposition can take fifteen minutes more than the time allotted to him. Speakers generally keep within the limit and those who exceed it are summarily requested to desist, but there are exceptions. When President Sadat addressed the Knesset on the historic occasion in November 1977, the Labour Party was given thirty-five minutes. Its leader, Shimon Peres, kept to his time but when the ex-Prime Minister and Grand Old Lady of the Knesset, Golda Meir, rambled on for seventeen minutes, substantially exceeding the party allocation, not a word was said.

The official languages for speeches are Hebrew and Arabic with simultaneous translation available, but on rare occasions permission may be obtained from the Speaker or presidium for another language to be spoken. One such was the Sadat visit. Because the Egyptian President had addressed the legislature in English, Begin sought and received permission to do the same.

Responsibility for the smooth running of the Knesset rests with the Secretary-General, Netanel Lorch, who has held this office since 1972. A genial, experienced civil servant, he combines an evident love of the institution he administers with a sometimes sardonic awareness of its weaknesses. He is responsible for the personnel in the building, controls its budget and ensures the smooth flow of legislation and documentation. Lorch is proficient in the rules, precedents and usages of the Knesset and his advice on these matters is frequently sought.

But most of his time goes in administration. In the absence of an equivalent to the British Ministry of Works, Lorch is responsible for the maintenance of the Knesset building and the provision of its necessary services which include the maintenance of the gardens, the running of an independent electricity supply and the telephone system.

He recalls, as the most notable event in his tenure of office, the dramatic occasion of President Sadat's visit. He was informed on Thursday evening that the Egyptian President would be addressing the Knesset on Sunday. Only 48 hours remained to prepare for the event. It seemed to him as though 100,000 VIPs from Israel and the Jewish world were clamouring for one of the 800 available seats. Arrangements had to be made for the hundreds of visiting journalists, for TV crews and their equipment and for the reception of the visiting party. No sooner had the work begun, than Lorch was asked to give an assurance to the religious authorities that not a stroke of work would be done on Saturday, the Jewish Sabbath. He concluded, 'If we'd had two months to plan, it would have been a disaster, but with only 24 hours, it all went like clockwork.'

Knesset powers and privileges

The most important function of the Knesset is to make the nation's laws, which it does through the legislative process previously described. After going through all its stages, a Knesset Bill becomes law when it has been signed by the President, the Prime Minister and the Minister of the Department which will have the duty of implementing it. But the President does not have to sign any Bill affecting his own office. Although theory permits private Bills to be introduced, in practice the Government keeps a tight grip on legislation and the individual Member must content himself with the hope of influencing legislation by the introduction of amendments in committee.

The Knesset's authority to approve the Budget and to impose taxes is theoretically the most important of its powers. It also has the prerogative of ratifying treaties with foreign States and of electing the President. However, the real debate and the real seat of decision in all these matters is within the governing coalition. Knesset Members very rarely take an independent position on issues decided by their party representatives in the Cabinet and a majority in the Knesset to implement all the decisions made by the Cabinet is automatic. All the political crises in Israel have come about from divisions within the coalition, not in Parliament.

It is rare for the Knesset ever to be given a free vote. Rabin's Government never took this step. But Begin tried to raise the stature of the Knesset by giving his coalition supporters a free vote on the Camp David agreement and the Egyptian peace treaty. This vote produced a unique and piquant situation. While Likud members exercised a free vote on the peace treaty ratification, the Labour opposition, to emphasize that (unlike Likud) it was totally in support of the territorial concessions, imposed party discipline on its MKs to support the Government!

Although the sovereign powers of the Knesset are rarely manifested in actual practice, the privileges granted to its Members are very real indeed. One of the earliest acts of the Knesset on its own behalf was the Knesset Members (Immunity, Rights and Duties) Law of 1951. In the title of this piece of legislation, the word 'duties' seems to have been chosen to suggest some semblance of balance between rights and obligations. In fact, the object of the law is to confer immunities and privileges.

Members of the Knesset are not only free from legal liability in the performance of parliamentary duties, but also from all other administrative actions which could restrict their liberty of action. So comprehensive is the law that it protects a Member from prosecution for any criminal offence, whether or not related in any way to his parliamentary functions; and proceedings can be instituted against a Member only if the Knesset first votes to remove his or her immunity.

An MK's non-parliamentary immunity – his parliamentary immunity is irrevocable – can be removed only if this step is recommended to the Knesset by the appropriate Committee, which must have given the Member concerned the opportunity to state his case. The right to apply for the withdrawal of immunity from prosecution is vested exclusively in the Attorney General. That procedure was followed in the case of Flatto-Sharon, a Member of the Knesset who was charged in 1979 with a number of violations of electoral law.

No Parliament in the world gives its members such wide immunity. The Israeli public became aware of this when, in answer to a question in the Knesset to the Minister of the Interior, it was revealed that more than 900 tickets for traffic offences given to Knesset Members in 1978 were cancelled. Motoring is beset by so many irritations in Israel, and so widespread are traffic violations, that the information that MKs could drive as illegally as they pleased provoked a sharp public reaction.

A minority party leader, Professor Amnon Rubinstein, promoted a Private Member's Bill in June 1979 to end the Knesset immunity in the case of a traffic offence where the offender has the option of a fine. Because it was opposed by the Likud, its defeat was assured, and only a small number of Members of the Knesset bothered to attend what was purely an academic debate. Rubinstein made the point that the specific question of traffic offences was of itself of no real moment. What concerned him was that it represented what he termed one of the basic problems of Israeli society: 'How to avoid the anarchistic situation in which every group exploits its power to get what it wants without regard to the rights and feelings of others.'

The Government spokesman, replying to the debate, argued that it was right for Members of the Knesset to possess this immunity so as to preclude the possibility that the authorities might trump up charges to prevent any Member from performing his duties. But, whatever the weaknesses of Israel's form of government, no examples were given in the Knesset debate of any attempts by the executive to use police power to 'frame' any legislator. On the other hand, it was pointed out that many Members of the Knesset have abused their immunity not alone in traffic offences but in the more serious areas of bribery and defamation.

The Rubinstein Bill was, predictably, defeated by a vote of 23 to 17 but, embarrassed by the surrounding publicity, the three largest factions in the Knesset agreed to form a committee to study parliamentary immunity. Nevertheless, cynicism persisted. There was no precedent in the past for the members of that club voluntarily abandoning any of their privileges.

These privileges go beyond immunity. In a comment on the Rubinstein Bill, the *Jerusalem Post* referred to MKs 'voting themselves munificent salaries, pension rights and other perks.'

The Knesset Members Emoluments Law of 1949 provided that members are entitled to payment made up of a basic salary plus family allowance. The salary of MKs is related to the basic salary of members of the Government, and the House Committee of the Knesset fixes the proportion and also rates of travel and lodging expenses for MKs when attending meetings. It may also reimburse MKs for expenses 'for recreational purposes'. All these grants and payments are exempt from income tax and are linked to the prices index.

Pension arrangements are attractive. They are given to all ex-Members over 45 (40 for women) who have served at least ten years. For those who have served at least six years, pensions are given to those over the age of 50 (45 for women). Ex-Members not entitled to a pension may receive a grant. The basis of pension calculation is complicated but, broadly speaking, the basic pension scale is 4 per cent of the MK's basic salary for every year of service. The pensions and grants extend to the next of kin of Members who, at the time of death, would have been entitled to them, and pensioners continue to benefit from the telephone allowance and medical facilities.

The electoral system

A General Election for the Knesset must be held at least every four years and, although it can be dissolved earlier by a decision of the Knesset itself (neither the President nor the Prime Minister has the power of dissolution), the tendency has always been for each Knesset to complete its full term.

OFFICIAL SALARIES AND BENEFITS
(Converted into US Dollars per month as at January 1980)

	Prime Minister	Ministers	Deputy Ministers	Speaker	MK
1 Basic Salary	555	472	400	555	400
2. Cost of Living Increment	514	514	514	514	514
3. Cars	All provided with official cars and drivers				Car allowance between 280–415 depending on home base
4. Meal Allowance	—	—	—	—	Between 7–12 per day
5. Hotel	MKs living outside Jerusalem are allowed two nights hotel expenses in Jerusalem when the Knesset is in session.				
6. Telephone	20,400 free calls per annum				
7. Medical	Free hospitalization and medical care for themselves and close family.				

Only the Prime Minister and Foreign Minister are provided with an official residence while in office.

The principles governing Knesset elections are set out in Article 4 of the Basic Law of the Knesset 1958. This provides that the Knesset shall be elected 'by general, national, direct, equal, secret and proportional elections'. The two most important of these adjectives are 'national' and 'proportional' because they record the victory of all the other parties over Mapai (the forerunner of the Labour Party). Mapai wanted to follow the British system and divide the country up into constituencies, each of which would elect its own representatives. But the minor parties calculated – quite rightly – that they would lose out that way and succeeded in retaining the system of proportional representation which had operated in the World Zionist Organization and in Israel since the first election, with the whole country serving as a single national constituency.

At elections, the voters do not vote for individual candidates, but for party lists, and all voters in the whole country have the same lists before them. They can vote only for the lists as published. It is not possible to 'write in', delete, or change the order of any of the names. There are no by-elections; vacancies are filled by the next name on the party list.

Any group of 750 Israelis eligible to vote may submit a list. (This applies only to a new party; any party which was represented in the outgoing Knesset can offer a list of candidates without this requirement.) In addition to 750 signatures, a new party must also deposit with the election authority I£40,000 (about $1,100 in 1980), which will be forfeited if it fails to win one seat.

A system of proportional representation encourages small groups, or even individuals, to seek election. If, for example, the total number of valid votes cast were 1,200,000 (the figure in the 1977 election was actually about

MEMBERS OF THE NINTH KNESSET ELECTED 1977

	Likud	Labour	NRP	Other	Totals
1. AGES					
20–29	1	—	—	1	2
30–39	3	1	4	2	10
40–49	13	10	3	8	34
50–59	16	11	1	8	36
60–69	7	4	2	8	21
70+	—	—	1	—	1

(Some MKs do not list their ages in the official directory)

2. ORIGINS: WHERE BORN	Likud	Labour	NRP	Other	Totals
Israel (Palestine)	25	15	2	17	59
W. Europe/USA/S. Africa	1	2	1	3	7
E. Europe	16	9	6	9	40
N. Africa/M. East	3	6	3	2	14

(Arabs are included under Israel)

3. UNIVERSITY EDUCATION	Likud	Labour	NRP	Other	Totals
	24	15	8	14	61

4. OCCUPATIONS	Likud	Labour	NRP	Other	Totals
Lawyer	11	3	4	7	25
Teacher	6	5	6	4	21
Farmer	5	2	1	3	11
Journalist	2	2	—	3	7
Business	5	3	1	3	12
Politician	14	13	3	8	38

Notes
1) There are, in addition, a poet, a locksmith, a building labourer and an author.
2) Some are listed under two categories, e.g. Begin both as lawyer and as politician.
3) Included under politicians are those like Begin and Abba Eban who, although listed under another category, are fully engaged in politics to the exclusion of other regular occupation.

5. BACKGROUND	Likud	Labour	NRP	Other	Totals
Ex-kibbutz	2	10	1	4	17
Ex-army	4	2	—	5	11

1 ¾ million), each of the 120 Knesset seats would require 10,000 votes. It is infinitely less difficult to pick up 10,000 votes over the whole country, than to win a majority of votes in any one constituency. This accounted for the success of the controversial Shmuel Flatto-Sharon (see p. 29) in the 1977 elections. At the same time, however, and more constructively, the system also made it possible for an invaluable maverick like Shulamit Aloni to gain a seat in the Knesset.

The signature requirement and the monetary deposit were introduced to inhibit the proliferation of splinter groups and crank candidates. On the face of it, the deterrent appears to have been ineffectual for, although the amount of the deposit has been continually increased to keep pace with inflation, the number of lists has also risen from 16 (when the deposit was first increased) to 22 in 1977.

A more effective obstacle to splinter groups is the provision that lists which gain less than one per cent of the total number of valid votes cast cannot participate in the allocation of seats. So, in the example above, a list would have had to receive at least 12,000 votes to gain its first seat; 20,000 votes would have given it two seats, with an additional seat for every extra 10,000 votes.

Each of the lists presented to the voters may contain up to 120 names, and the larger parties do put up as many candidates as there are seats in the Knesset. The important names are those that appear in the top half of the list. The bottom half is padding, offering some kind of status or prestige to the people listed, who have little or no hope of being elected. The manoeuvring for the top places in the list is the most important power game within the parties, and the place of an individual in the list is a guide to his or her growing or declining favour with the leadership.

This was traditionally the case in the compilation of the Labour list. Shulamit Aloni, for example, first became a Member of the Knesset in 1965 on the Mapai list. But her impatience with party discipline brought her into conflict with Golda Meir, who was then the Secretary-General of the Labour Party. As a result, she was dropped so low on the list for the 1969 election that her non-election was assured. She came back four years later with her newly-formed Citizens' Rights Party.

An even more striking example was the case of Dov Joseph, a Zionist veteran born in Canada who settled in Jerusalem in 1921. He became a distinguished lawyer, an intimate of Ben-Gurion, a leader of the Labour Party and a Cabinet Member when the State was formed. In the split between Ben-Gurion and the Labour Party in 1965, he sided with Ben-Gurion. The displeasure of the Party leaders was demonstrated when the list for that year's Knesset elections was published. Golda Meir, who was chairman of the nominating committee, ensured that Joseph was demoted from 8th place on the list to 118th!

Every citizen over 18, male or female, has the right to vote except those who have been deprived of that right by a competent court. In fact this form of disqualification is not widely practised; on the other hand, convicts or suspects in prison do not have the opportunity to vote, even though there is no legal justification for their exclusion.

Election candidates must be 21 years of age or over and any citizen may stand as a candidate for the Knesset (again with the proviso that the right has not been withdrawn by a competent court). Ineligible to stand as candidates are the holders of these offices: President of the State; the country's Ashkenazi and Sephardi Chief Rabbis; State judges and judges of the religious courts; the State Comptroller; the Chief of the General Staff; State-employed clergy; senior civil servants and army officers.

As an act of mercy towards the electors, ballot papers do not contain the names of all candidates, but only letters of the alphabet representing each of the various parties. The elector may vote for any one of the lists represented by an alphabetical letter.

Every encouragement is given to the electorate to exercise the vote. Election day is a public holiday – on full pay for wage earners – and free travel is available to those who are on an electoral register away from their homes.

Electoral reform and coalitions

Israel's electoral system – the whole country as one constituency and proportional representation – has been the subject of debate ever since the State was established. The substantial literature on the subject stands in inverse proportion to the action which has been taken to change the situation – none so far, because of the interest of the parties in maintaining the status quo.

Under the present system, a Knesset Member owes his election to the party leaders who have put him high up on the list. He has no practical reason to keep in contact with the voters, as do constituency members. The latter need to keep in touch with constituents if for no other reason than winning their votes at the next election.

For their part, the Israeli voters have no Congressman or Member of Parliament to whom they can go with their problems. On both sides, therefore, the present system precludes that relationship between the electorate and the elected which should be one of the most valuable instruments of a democratic system of government. In Israel, members of the Knesset are deprived of the constant flow of information and opinion from constituents and have no real inducement to get to the grass roots.

The party leaders, who draw up the lists, will try to attract voter interest by putting their most alluring names at the top. In 1977, for example, the Labour Party was headed by Shimon Peres as leader of the Party, and he was followed by Yigal Allon, Abba Eban, Yitzhak Rabin and other names with wide electoral appeal. Below them followed mostly colourless party men and women, people who could be depended on to give no trouble and accept the Party line. Under these conditions, party loyalty tends to become the main qualification for the candidates of the main parties. Moreover, since the candidate is dependent on the party leaders and party machine to ensure his re-election, he will not be inclined to act in such a way as to jeopardize his position in those quarters.

Probably the most far-reaching consequence of the PR system is that it works to prevent any one party from gaining an overall majority. In a constituency system, a party can achieve a landslide success without even winning a majority of the votes. In Israel, however, no party can expect to get more than the number of seats justified by the number of its votes.

In no election in Israel (the 1977 election was the ninth) has any party won an overall majority. The result has been a series of coalition governments. Until 1977 they were all led by Labour; in 1977 the key party of the coalition was the Likud. Putting a coalition together is a complex process involving tough bargaining. The more the main coalition-former needs partners, the higher the price those partners will ask in terms of policies, portfolios and patronage.

In the result, no Government has been able to pursue its own political line. All have had to make compromises in the course of coalition-building, thus weakening their effectiveness and diminishing their appeal to the political idealists. Throughout the whole of the twenty-nine years of its dominance, the Labour Party was compelled to compromise its ideals of civil liberties and civil rights because of the concessions it made to the religious parties to gain their votes in the Knesset.

In an interview published in the American magazine *Moment* in 1979, Yigal Allon succinctly encapsulated the greatest danger of coalition governments. Regretting that the Government had not produced a peace plan after the Six Day War, he related that, in 1968, at the height of Israel's prestige after the brilliant victory of the previous year, the then Prime Minister, Levi Eshkol, visited President Johnson at his Texas ranch. President Johnson asked Eshkol: 'What kind of an Israel do you want?' Whereupon poor Eshkol had to say: 'Mr President, I lead a national coalition which has decided not to decide, so I can't tell you what kind of an Israel I want.'

Allon concluded with the comment that 'the Government contained such divergent viewpoints that every position was cancelled out from within; it was a paralyzed Government.'

Not only have coalitions tended to negate strong government policies in favour of the lowest common factor among the partners; they have also promoted inefficiency and waste. Redundant ministries (e.g. the Ministry of Development) have been kept in existence because they were useful pay-offs to be bargained for in coalition negotiations.

The major party in office, whether Mapai or the Likud, will always keep the important portfolios of Foreign Affairs, Defence and Finance in its own hands; at the same time, it tries to diminish the power of the Ministries handed over to its lesser coalition partners. The result is that vital matters of social policy which should have been tackled by the minority-controlled Ministries have been accorded only low governmental priorities.

The supporters of the present system argue that it is well suited to Israel's particular needs and that Israel is too small a country to be divided into constituencies. They also claim that constituencies would mean that petty local interests would receive disproportionate emphasis to the detriment of national interests. It does not matter, they say, if voters do not have a local

MK to whom they can address themselves. The country is so small and intimate that every MK knows what is going on and every voter knows someone on the inside he can approach with his problems.

In extenuation of the undemocratic selection of candidates on the lists by party caucuses, it is argued that no ideally democratic way of selecting candidates has yet been devised. In the differing systems of the USA and Britain, party machines generally select the candidates while the voters usually vote for parties and not for an individual.

Nor are the PR protagonists discouraged by the fact that the system always produces coalition governments. Israeli coalitions have generally been stable and, if compromises have had to be made for coalition partners, that is democracy in practice, avoiding the excesses and extremes which one powerful party in office could impose on a large minority (or even a majority) which did not support it.

The issue of electoral reform was an extremely important one in the 1977 election. Labour had long advocated some form of constituency system while the strongest group in the Likud had always opposed a change, fearing it would be to the advantage of Labour. This time, however, a small Liberal grouping in the Likud managed to include in its platform a proposal for moderate electoral reform. The new and exciting DMC strongly emphasized the need for a change in the electoral system and made the issue almost the justification for its existence. It entered the 1977 election insisting that the first task of the ninth Knesset would be to change the electoral system, after which it should dissolve itself and elect a new, truly democratic tenth Knesset.

Early in 1977, the Labour group came to an agreement with the Likud, then the major opposition party, to introduce a change in the electoral system. It was agreed that 80 of the 120 Knesset Members would be elected from 16 constituencies into which the country would be divided, with five members from each constituency. The remaining 40 MKs would be elected on a PR system. The intention in retaining the 40 on a central list was to ensure that the party leaders and some party officials would become Knesset Members without having to face the possibility of defeat in constituency elections. Everything fell to the ground, however, when the eighth Knesset was precipitately dissolved and the political complexion of the country transformed in the elections which followed. Nothing more has been heard of that particular plan.

Variations were discussed in the negotiations which led to the NRP, and later the DMC, joining the Begin coalition government. All were based on a division of 80 seats from constituencies and 40 from central lists, but agreement could not be reached on the number of constituencies. The NRP wanted only 6, while the DMC demanded 24. The smaller the number of constituencies, the closer the result would come to proportional representation. By electing ten or more MKs from each constituency, the weaker parties would still achieve some representation. On the other hand, a larger number of constituencies, each electing a few MKs, could wipe out the small parties and provide an opportunity for an overall majority by one party.

With the entry of both the NRP and DMC into the Government, a committee was set up to prepare for change in the electoral system. It was, appropriately, to have finished its work in nine months but the gestation period passed without a happy event.

Few political leaders are sanguine about the prospects of a change in the electoral system in the foreseeable future. One of them, Shimon Peres, gave a succinct reason. It was 'because the people elected under the present system don't want to change it.' Another gave me the estimate that some 50 per cent of the members of the Knesset owed their seats to internal party manoeuvring alone and could never win an election under a constituency system.

The cost of elections

As an experiment, Israel introduced state financing of Knesset elections in 1969. The experiment was deemed to have succeeded and four years later it became a permanent feature of political life.

Before 1969, under a complex arrangement, employers deducted from wages a 'party tax' in addition to trade union fees. It was a voluntary tax and workers could avoid payment only by objecting in writing to the employer. Obviously many did object, for in 1969 the tax yielded only I£3.8 million instead of the estimated I£11 million.

The new state financing notwithstanding, deduction of 'party tax' continued, with rather better results. In 1973, the trade union organization, the Histadrut, to which employers paid the party tax, transferred to the election funds of the various parties a total of almost I£12 million. The distribution was made in proportion to the representation of the parties within the Histadrut – the 'party key' – and the Labour Party naturally received the lion's share.

State financing had been brought in as a 'one-off' deal for the situation in 1969 when elections for both the Knesset and the local authorities were pending, involving a specially heavy drain on party funds. The Election Financing Law then introduced met two main objectives: to provide money for the party compaigns, and to limit campaign costs.

The 1969 Law authorized the Treasury to provide a total budget of I£14,880,000 to finance the forthcoming elections, the figure being based on a sum of I£120,000 for each of the 120 Members of the Knesset. In addition, the parties were permitted to spend up to I£40,000 of their own money for each of their MKs. That was to be the limit of campaign expenditure.

To sell the idea to a cynical public which might suspect the parties and their officials of feathering their own nests at the taxpayers' expense, the law stipulated that the whole system was to be subject to the financial supervision of the State Comptroller. That office is one of the most respected in Israel, where the bureaucracy and officialdom are widely regarded with something less than adulation. And public concern was, to some extent, allayed when the State Comptroller reported after the 1969 election that, while there had been some excessive expenditure, it had not been serious enough to warrant any action being taken.

The 1969 experiment having worked, the parties were anxious for it to continue, and ensured that it would by means of the 1973 Law for the Financing of *Parties* – not simply elections. Not surprisingly, the new Law was so popular with the parties that the Knesset passed it with an unusually overwhelming majority of 78 to 7. The main innovation in this law – still in force today – is that it not only finances election campaigns but also the activities of the parties between elections.

But what constitutes a party in a political system where individuals or small groups frequently leave the party on whose list they were elected to the Knesset and form new factions? Is each such grouping, faction or even individual to be regarded as a new party entitled to public financing? The law defines with some particularity what constitutes a recognized party. In simple terms, it stipulates that parties represented in an outgoing Knesset and with at least one Member in a new one are recognized for the purposes of state financing. New parties have to be expressly recognized as such by the appropriate Knesset Committee.

This Committee does not appear always to exercise its function on exclusively judicial criteria. Like almost everything else in Israel, decisions can be affected by party considerations. For example, a leading right-wing Likud MK, Moshe Shamir, left that party in 1979 in protest against the ratification of the peace treaty with Egypt – he thought that Begin had betrayed Likud principles. He applied for the status of a one-man party, but the Knesset Committee denied the request on 15 May 1979, offering instead the sop of recognition as a single Knesset Member. All that did for Shamir was to make it possible for him to address the Knesset, because speaking time is divided among the parties, recognized factions and recognized non-faction MKs. What he did not get, which was presumably the purpose of his request, was Government money.

However, the Committee had come to quite a different decision on similar facts earlier in the same year. The split in the Democratic Movement for Change, Yigael Yadin's new party, had left one member, Assaf Yaguri, unhappy with both of the two new groups into which the DMC had divided. He applied for one-man party status – and obtained it. The formal reason given for that decision was that Yaguri was not a defector, but had simply been left high and dry when the party broke up. But in fact both the major parties, the Likud and Labour, supported his claim, because both hoped to receive his support.

One-man party status brings the MK a monthly allowance, various Knesset services and, when they come round, finance for election campaigns. Since 1975, the amount allocated for these purposes has been linked to the consumer price index to offset the effect of the rapid inflation. In 1977 a figure of I£72 million was allocated for that year's election and I£44 million for general-purpose party financing. At that time, the Israeli lira stood at approximately 10 to the US dollar. The budgeted figure for financing parties in 1978/79 – not an election year – was I£164.7 million, although by then inflation had reduced the lira to about 20 to the dollar. In 1979, by which time the rate had fallen further to 24 lira to the dollar, the budgeted figure amounted to about I£45,000 per month per MK.

The 1973 Law continued the 1969 precedent of setting a ceiling for direct election expenses by the parties and of limiting their income. These figures are also index-linked. Everything is under the scrutiny of the State Comptroller but, as in all formulations of this nature, there are bound to be loopholes. For example, do political advertisements by corporations count as election expenditure? (The Comptroller decided that they *might* be prohibited contributions.) And what of the many enterprises and subsidiaries of political parties which keep their own accounts and render services of various kinds to the parties, but are not subject to the Comptroller's scrutiny?

In fact, the State Comptroller's reports since 1973 have not disclosed any major infringements of either the spirit or the letter of the Election Law. But he did say in his 1977 report that the Law required comprehensive revision, and implied that there were abuses he could not get to because, in his words, 'the law in its present form allows only for a very limited audit.'

The parties have tended to become greedy. For example, after the 1978 municipal elections, the three major parties, the Likud, Labour and the NRP, on two occasions promoted retroactive legislation to cover their deficits at the taxpayers' expense. Their combined voting strengths ensured the passage of what were disguised, to avoid too much public attention, as amendments to the Local Authorities Election Financing Law. The State Comptroller has attacked this retroactive legislation in restrained language as doing 'no good to the status of the law or to respect for it.' More forcefully, one of the minor parties (a part of the DMC after the 1978 split) characterized the process as the parties 'slipping their hands into the pockets of the public to cover their extravagant election expenses.' They charged, not without justification, that the Likud, Labour and the NRP had regularly combined 'to pass whatever electoral legislation suited them.'

Before the introduction of party financing from public funds, the parties had been none too scrupulous about the ways in which they went about fund-raising, or spending for political purposes. Before statehood and in Israel's early years, a good portion of these funds came out of contributions received from abroad for the development of the Jewish National Home. It was doubtful whether those who made gifts for this purpose also intended them to subsidize the country's political parties, yet that is how the fund managers manipulated these gifts.

Every now and then a scandal would break, revealing the tip of an iceberg of malpractices. In 1954, in a well-publicized case, two leaders of the National Religious Party were charged with receiving foreign currency (at that time, all foreign exchange had to be sold to the Government) for the election campaign of Mizrachi (a religious political party). They were acquitted, but the evidence presented in court made it clear that this was not the only occasion on which a party had received funds from abroad for internal political purposes and that Mizrachi had not been the only party to do so. In addition no detailed accounts of expenditure were ever made available to the overseas or, for that matter, the local donors.

Ten years after this case, when a senior civil servant was convicted of receiving a 'kick-back' from contractors for a new hospital, it was claimed in court that the bribe had gone to the election funds of the NRP.

The most serious case of all, because it had a direct bearing on the 1977 election, was that of Asher Yadlin in February of that year. This top Labour Party leader and Governor-designate of the Bank of Israel was convicted and sentenced to five years' imprisonment on a bribery charge. In his defence he claimed that the whole of the bribe, amounting to I£80,000, had gone to the funds of the Labour Party and that this had long been a normal method of raising funds for the party.

Yadlin was released from prison in February 1980 after serving 3½ years of his sentence. In a newspaper extract from his book *Testimony* which appeared soon after his release, Yadlin charged that methods of financing the Labour Party when it was in power were 'so varied as to include foreign currency from abroad and money passed on to the Party illegally by the many Histadrut financial and industrial complexes.' One of his specific allegations was that Solel Boneh, the Histadrut's building enterprise, on one occasion contributed $250,000 to the Labour Party and was repaid by government export subsidies amounting to five times that sum.

The case of Flatto-Sharon

One of the quirks of the 1977 election, more relevant to party financing than to party politics, was the election to the Knesset of Shmuel Flatto-Sharon, who put himself up on a one-man list.

Flatto (which was his name before arriving in Israel) was born in Poland in 1930 and, surviving the Holocaust, settled in France. There he accumulated considerable wealth as a financier. His financial activities eventually led to charges of fraud, involving hundreds of millions of francs, being made against him by the French authorities. Flatto, experiencing coincidentally a surge of Zionist idealism, decided that he would be happier in Israel and arrived there in 1972. Israel's Law of Return assured him of instant citizenship.

To remove the threat of extradition which was hanging over him, he decided to seek the immunity which would be his were he a Member of the Knesset and stood under the rubric of 'Flatto-Sharon – the lonely man to the Knesset'. He made no secret at all of the fact that the purpose of his seeking election was to avoid extradition to France.

Despite his background and his virtual ignorance of the Hebrew language, Flatto-Sharon gained enough votes throughout the country to have given him *two* seats had he put another name on his list. Certainly his momentary popularity owed much to the current unpopularity of French policy towards Israel and to Flatto-Sharon's perceived position as a victim of French anti-Semitism. But his success was probably more directly the result of his wealth and the expertise of his campaign manager, Yaakov Halfon.

Halfon knew a great deal about running election campaigns. He had been the head of the Control Institute of Mapai and had had a very close relationship with Pinchas Sapir, the most successful fund-raiser and fund-disburser that powerful party machine had ever had.

In a speech at Bar Ilan University in Ramat Gan early in 1977, while the Yadlin trial was proceeding, Halfon declared publicly that Israel's political parties had received 'under the table' no less than 'between three and four hundred million Israeli pounds [i.e. 30 to 40 million dollars] to finance their election campaigns.'

During and after the election, allegations were widely disseminated – with much detail in private but more generally and circumspectly in public – that Flatto-Sharon had 'bought' votes. Not that such suggestions were new. They had been made about various parties in previous elections.

It took a little while, two years in fact, before the accusations against Flatto-Sharon resulted in any official action. In May 1979, the Attorney-General decided to prefer charges. Flatto-Sharon, Halfon and another adviser were charged on five counts of contravening the election law and one count of conspiracy. The detailed allegations included promises made at election meetings to provide apartments for young couples, and the actual payment of money to individuals for their votes and for the votes of their families and friends – payments were alleged to range from I£150 to I£300 ($15–30) per vote. Another charge referred to a plan to buy votes via the leaders of ethnic groups.

But nothing could be done until Flatto-Sharon's Parliamentary immunity had been removed, and this action was finally taken in August 1979 by a Knesset vote of 61 to 31. The removal of his immunity did not open the door to Flatto-Sharon's extradition to France. Under existing procedure, it was removed only so that he could be tried for the specific offences with which he was charged by the Attorney-General.

What is of wider interest than the fate of Flatto-Sharon personally is the light the case threw on the less appealing aspect of Israel's political rough-and-tumble. The fact that thirty Knesset Members voted in favour of Flatto-Sharon's retention of immunity was attributed by the *Jerusalem Post* to their 'fear of having some of their own parties' shadier practices exposed in the course of the trial.'

But even before the charges against him were heard, Halfon, who does not appear to object to his description as a 'vote contractor', said in a broadcast that he had done similar work for the large established parties in previous elections and would prove it.

The impact of the Flatto-Sharon case, at a time of heightened public sensitivity to corrupt practices in the aftermath of the Yadlin, Ofer and Rabin affairs, fortified the request of the State Comptroller for a thorough revision of the existing election laws, particularly in relation to finance.*

Knesset effectiveness and status

Whatever may be the balance of advantage between a constituency system and the national lists of Israel, one of the unquestionable drawbacks of the

---

* Flatto-Sharon returned to the headlines in 1980 in the bizarre context of a police hunt in the Sinai desert. Large numbers of expensive cars stolen in Israel had, he said, been sold in Egypt. To hide them en route, they had been buried in the sand-dunes until the (metaphorical) heat was off. MK Flatto-Sharon had a personal interest in leading the hunt, for among the stolen vehicles was his own $86,000.00 Mercedes, replete with television, radio-telephone and bar.

latter is that it diminishes the vitality and effectiveness of the elected representatives. Since the MK owes his election to his place on the list, his loyalty goes to the people who put him there – the party leaders. As Shulamit Aloni and Dov Joseph discovered (see p. 22), a lack of response to party requirements may result in a politically fatal drop in list-placing.

The Knesset has only the power that the ruling coalition gives it – and that is generally very little: it passes the necessary legislation, it debates Ministerial statements, it questions the executive. But the great majority of Knesset Members, particularly those supporting the Government, give their loyal support to the party which has given them a safe place on its list. They will vote both in the plenary assembly and in committees as the party instructs, rather than in accord with any independent opinions they may hold. Decision-making being the preserve of the party, the Knesset has become a debating society, the power given to it constitutionally having been effectively stripped away under the system developed by the Labour Party during its twenty-nine years in office.

It is often claimed in Israel that although MKs have no real power they do have the opportunity of exercising a decisive influence in committee. Many MKs describe this as marginal, though they do point to other positive elements in the present system. The first is that, although the independent individual is powerless in the Knesset, it provides a platform for ideas and offers the one- or two-Member parties a forum from which they can speak to, and be heard by, the people. Such mavericks as Uri Avneri and Shulamit Aloni have made good use of this facility.

Secondly, on legislation which does not involve major party political interests, Governments have been known to give way to reasoned and persuasive argument in the committee stage of a Bill. When, for example, the criminal law was substantially amended in 1978, the Government accepted a considerable number of changes in committee, particularly on the issue of rape.

The Likud Government was at first more brutal in using the steam-roller of its power because it was less experienced. Labour, having exercised power for fifty years, first in the Zionist movement and then in Israel, had acquired greater self-confidence; they were willing to listen, and felt the responsibility of founding fathers.

Although it carries little real power except in theory, membership of the Knesset is keenly sought after, though an increasing number of individuals of ability find it an unrewarding occupation. The present method of compiling lists of candidates gives a higher priority to party stalwarts than to the best and most thoughtful elements. To encourage turnover, the Labour Party instituted a weighting against those who had already served two terms in the Knesset. The lists had begun to look so boringly similar, election after election, with the same names in the same places, that an attempt was made in this way to introduce new faces. Some of the apparently indestructible stalwarts did disappear, but the new names and faces were, if anything, less exciting.

The new Knesset after the 1977 election was notable for containing no fewer than 50 new faces out of 120 members. But none of them emerged as new stars. The chamber filled for Begin mainly because he was the best speaker, an outstanding parliamentarian and Prime Minister. They listened in numbers to Peres, the Leader of the Opposition, and also to Dayan, Allon and Eban. But few others attracted MKs into the chamber. One of the Members told me, 'It's a small Parliament. After a couple of weeks we all know each other and have decided who is worth listening to.' Apparently not too many.

The decline in the prestige and public perception of the Knesset was not halted with the end of Labour's hegemony. When he became Prime Minister, Begin pledged himself to preserve and enhance the status and prestige of the Knesset and, in some instances, notably in relation to the peace with Egypt, he did so. He also addressed the Knesset more frequently than previous Prime Ministers and spent more time than they in his office in the Parliament building. But in spite of all this, the situation did not improve and, indeed, continued to deteriorate.

The image given to the Knesset, both nationally and internationally, by the election of Flatto-Sharon was particularly damaging. His election victory was greeted in Israel with a mixture of glee at having cocked a snook at the disliked French and shame that a fugitive from extradition on fraud charges should be a member of the legislature. With the passage of time, the embarrassed shame deepened as Flatto-Sharon performed no noticeable service as an MK, reserving his parliamentary activity for the protection of his personal interests.

Another 1977 MK did nothing to enhance the prestige of Parliament. Charlie Biton, formerly a leader of the 'Black Panthers'* was elected to the Knesset on the Communist Party list. Biton had been convicted on several criminal charges unrelated to his Black Panther activities and, from the early days of his membership of the Knesset, became involved in disruptive incidents in the legislature which further damaged its image.

More harm was done to the status of the Knesset by the awareness of its irrelevance during the course of the most far-reaching event in Israel's short history, the peace negotiations. Sadat did make a dramatic appearance in the Knesset and Begin did ask for Knesset approval of the agreements reached. But throughout the negotiations, neither the Knesset as a whole nor its Foreign Affairs and Defence Committee was informed of their progress. So frequent had been the leaks from this Committee, that the Government felt it could not take the risk of giving it confidential information in the course of the delicate bargaining.

The fact that Knesset debates and, to a lesser extent, committee meetings are covered by radio or television has been a mixed blessing. The Israel Broadcasting Authority, which is modelled on the BBC but lacks some of that body's safeguards against political interference, is free to select portions of a debate it wishes to televise. It will, on occasion, broadcast live a complete debate. The eight-hour debate in 1977 on the presentation of the

* A militant group of young Oriental Jews who organized demonstrations, sometimes violent, in the early 1970s, against the inequities suffered by their community in contrast to the inducements offered to new immigrants. Adopting the name of black militants in the USA, it was never a politically effective force but it did focus public opinion on Israel's 'two nations'.

new Cabinet attracted a peak audience, while an equally fascinated public followed the twenty-eight-hour marathon of the peace treaty debate. Committees are open to radio and to TV in limited cases and for special purposes.

This coverage, particularly on television, has made the Knesset much better known and, for better or for worse, has enhanced the interest of the electorate in that body. The public demand for open government has been supplemented by the interest of the media themselves in gaining greater accessibility to news sources, and these forces have combined to create a trend towards extending Knesset coverage.

On the other hand, there has been considerable adverse comment on the loss of spontaneity and purpose when speakers address themselves to radio, television or press audiences, rather than to the Knesset. Netanel Lorch made the same point in characteristically understated fashion in a report he presented in 1978 to the Inter-Parliamentary Union on 'Parliament and the Audio Visual Media'. He wrote, 'In Israel, awareness of television coverage may have contributed to a more dramatic performance by some Members,' and, 'it cannot be asserted unequivocally that the trend (towards greater coverage) has been wholly beneficial to the quality of Parliament and to the manner in which it conducts its business.'

Chapter two

The Party of Government

Origins of the Labour Party

The Israel Labour Party (formerly Mapai), until 1977 the country's dominant political party, suffered a shattering defeat in the election of that year. It had been the core of every previous Government coalition and, as Mapai, had been instrumental in creating the Jewish social and political institutions of Palestine in the pre-State era. These institutions, inspired and run by the Labour leadership and virtually constituting a State within a State, were smoothly transmuted into the Government when independence came in 1948.

Mapai began in 1929 as a merger of various socialist groups within the Zionist movement. The intention at that time was to create for Labour Zionism a strong, unified political arm parallel to the trade union arm, the Histadrut, which had been founded eight years earlier. The outlook of the new party was broadly that of the European Social Democratic parties, with which it established close ties through the Socialist International.

The grass-roots strength of Mapai lay in the two agricultural powers: the kibbutz movement of collective settlements and the moshav movement of cooperative small holdings. With them stood the unique and powerful Histadrut, which is not merely a trade union movement like the TUC in Britain or the AFL-CIO in the United States, but controls great industrial enterprises and acts as a social service agency for its members. The Histadrut was managed by the leaders of Mapai, and possession of this formidable economic and electoral power gave the party the means to control the Jewish Agency for Palestine and the World Zionist Organization, the main instruments for the building of the Jewish National Home in pre-State days.

When David Ben-Gurion, then the Secretary-General of the Histadrut, became Chairman of the World Zionist Executive in 1933, the leadership of Mapai effectively exercised control of the great financial resources raised from world Jewry. It was a situation which Mapai leaders never hesitated to exploit for party purposes.

Since the earliest days of Zionist settlement in Palestine, the party had found jobs for, housed, educated and protected the immigrants. In the course of this process the Zionist socialist groups and their offshoot, the Histadrut, virtually created a welfare state. Members of the Histadrut, always a majority of the population, were fully aware that Mapai and the Histadrut were run by the same people. Gratitude for the benefits conferred by the Histadrut was translated into votes for the Labour Party.

Paradoxically, one of the main architects of this system, Ben-Gurion, who had headed both the Labour Party and the Histadrut, also created the conditions for its contraction. When he became Prime Minister in 1948, Ben-Gurion pursued a policy of nationalizing the social services run by private organizations. The first to go was the Histadrut school system, which was merged into a State system. Then the Histadrut labour exchanges were replaced in 1959 by State labour exchanges.

Aware that the loss of these bases of power could have a serious effect on their electoral prospects, the Party leadership prevailed on the Government to change course and allow the Histadrut to retain its remaining functions, notably its health service. But there can be little doubt that Ben-Gurion's initial nationalizing policy weakened Labour's hold on some voters who had supported them as a thanks offering for services rendered, or possibly out of fear of loss of these services.

With the creation of Israel, Mapai and its leaders no longer seemed political partisans, but were identified with the State itself. The party that had brought the state into existence, that was bringing in new immigrants, finding them jobs, offering them trade union protection and the security of social services could, and in the early years did, confidently rely on the votes of those reaping these benefits. But such overwhelming superiority generated some of the Labour Party's later problems. It became a tightly-controlled party machine, an oligarchy perpetuating its own control and increasingly contemptuous of democratic principles.

Israeli political parties have always been characterized by processes of fission and fusion. Parties split on ideological or personal issues, and factions merge in the pursuit of a common interest. Mapai always had ideological factions, but its major split in 1965, when Ben-Gurion created a new party, Rafi, was concerned with power and personalities rather than with ideology. Three years later, however, Rafi returned to the fold in a new merger which produced the present Israel Labour Party.

Even then, in 1968, power in the Party remained in the hands of the old guard. Golda Meir, then Prime Minister, decided most issues with the aid of a small group of intimates known as 'Golda's Kitchen Cabinet'. They made the security and foreign relations decisions, while Party issues and domestic problems were handled by the Minister of Finance, the great 'fixer', Pinchas Sapir. The Knesset, indeed the Cabinet, were little more than rubber stamps. Criticism was barely tolerated, particularly in the most vital areas of security and foreign policy. Golda and her friends knew best.

It was the Yom Kippur War in 1973 that marked the beginning of the end of Labour's long rule. The election that year was too soon after the trauma of the war for its lessons to have seeped through to the voters. The need for fundamental changes, which emerged as a result of the war, expressed itself only at the next General Election, four years later.

The anxious questioning of the electorate following revelations of failings and ineptitude, and the complacent response of the Labour Party leadership is graphically illustrated by a passage from a report of a meeting at the end of 1973 between the Secretary-General of the Party (the same

Asher Yadlin who was jailed for corruption in 1977) and local Party
leaders:* 'Many of the local leaders reported "deep shock among the
people" and said that some people were "asking questions which reach the
sources of trust" . . . They listed as examples of the kinds of questions that
were being asked, "Where was our intelligence? Where were the reserves
and why weren't they mobilized sooner?" . . . Yadlin, representing the
views of top leadership replied, "The people will be wise. When the time
comes for them to vote, they will vote correctly."'

Yadlin was right, at least for a while. Although some votes were lost,
Labour still emerged as the major party in the December 1973 elections,
with 51 seats compared with the Likud's 39. Labour had lost 5 seats, but the
Likud had gained 13, a portent of things to come.

Still the old guard remained in control. Golda Meir remained Prime
Minister, but not for long. Growing protests over the mismanagement of
the war brought about her resignation four months later. The first
instinctive reaction of the Party leaders was to follow the precedents and
hand-pick their man, or woman, to be followed by the motions of a
democratic election. This failed because Sapir, the natural successor, did
not want the job.

In the absence of a workable alternative, there was no choice but to have
a real election within the Central Committee of the Party. The two
candidates were Yitzhak Rabin and Shimon Peres. Rabin won by 298 to
254 and became Prime Minister. But Peres had done so well that he
projected himself to the very top of the Party leadership and became
Minister of Defence in the new Rabin Government.

Rabin's brief leadership did little, if anything, to reinvigorate a declining
Party. He probably added to its demoralization by keeping the Party at
arm's length, rarely consulting its leaders on important issues. His three
years as Prime Minister were affected by the knowledge that his leadership
was insecure and would probably be challenged by both Peres and Yigal
Allon, his Foreign Minister. It did nothing to bolster his self-confidence or
his authority.

As expected, his leadership was again challenged at the Party conference
early in the fateful year of 1977. Again he beat it off, but even more narrowly
than on the previous occasion, with Peres gaining in strength and appeal.
When, four weeks before the General Election, Rabin resigned because of
the Washington bank account scandal, Peres was the obvious successor.

He took over a difficult and, as it turned out, impossible assignment. The
series of corruption scandals, high inflation, high taxes and labour troubles
all combined to turn voters away from Labour. But it was not a sudden fall
from grace. The election result was the cumulative effect of a process of
public disenchantment with an arrogant, self-serving, unresponsive
leadership, corrupted by fifty years of power.

---

*Quoted from *Power and Ritual in the Israel Labour Party* by Myron Aronoff, 1974.

Party organization

The Israel Labour Party (ILP) consists of three groups, now amalgamated –
but not entirely. Each of them retains some kind of inchoate identity. It is
generally known, for example, that Peres is Rafi and Yigal Allon was Achdut
Avoda, two of the groups which make up the ILP along with Mapai, the
senior partner. A fourth faction, Mapam, well to the left of the ILP and
Marxist in ideology, is affiliated to the ILP but still maintains its own
separate institutions. At elections, it joins in a combined list with the ILP
under the name of Ma'arach (Alignment).

The Party conference is the main legislative body of the ILP and, in
theory, as supreme in the Party as the Knesset is in the nation. In practice
the Party conference is a demonstration, a ceremonial, an opportunity for
thousands of Party key workers to meet together to draw comfort, and
possibly inspiration, from common endeavours and aspirations. In the
decision-making process, conference generally does little more than ratify
what has already been done or decided by the leadership.

Between conferences – they are supposed to be held every four years but
in fact have been taking place on an average about once in six years –
authority in the Party rests with the Central Committee which numbers
some 800 members. The members of the Central Committee are formally
elected by conference, though in practice this amounts to no more than
giving approval to names proposed by the leadership. As a result of this
procedure, a large proportion of the members of this (as of other important
ILP bodies) are party functionaries, safe supporters of the leadership since
many of them are dependent on the Party, or the Histadrut, for their
income. In preparing the election lists, the kibbutz and moshav
movements, considered as representing the idealism of the ILP, are given
special preference. The branches of these movements are permitted to elect
one delegate for each 72 members against the norm elsewhere of one for 120.

Such a tight management of internal affairs requires a high degree of
control over the elections to the various organs of the Party. In preparing
the list of nominees, the three factions, Mapai, Rafi and Achdut Avoda
(which in theory do not exist), ensure their representation in all these
organs.

An able, devoted, but troubled younger official of the Party confessed to
me that 'our process of elections is one of the most reactionary – only the
Communists are worse. All the others have more democratic systems than
does the ILP.'

The Central Committee generally meets monthly and less than half its
membership can be expected at routine meetings. Its business consists of
discussing, and usually ratifying, decisions made elsewhere. Elsewhere is
the Party Bureau (it is not often called 'politburo' to avoid comparison with
other systems), appointed by the Central Committee but selected by the top
Party leaders. The Bureau meets weekly and decides policy; the Central
Committee approves that policy or makes its own decisions but only on
issues on which the Bureau cannot agree.

One such was the decision to support the peace treaty with Egypt. ILP's

backing for the Begin Government was announced as a decision of the
Central Committee, ostensibly because it was a larger and more
representative body than the Bureau. In fact, the decision was made by the
Central Committee only because the Bureau was not unanimous.

The power system, focusing down from the conference of thousands,
through the Central Committee of 800, then through the Bureau, narrows
down still further to the Secretariat of the Bureau, which acts under the
direction of the two people who stand at the centre of the Party, its
Chairman, Shimon Peres, and its Secretary-General, former General Haim
Bar-Lev. The Secretariat, though not formally part of the constitutional
structure, is nevertheless a powerful body. Consisting of the heads of
departments of the national office, it deals with the daily business of Party
management and prepares the agenda for the meetings of the Bureau. Most
organization men agree that preparing the agenda for a meeting comes very
close to directing it.

Next to Peres and Bar-Lev in authority and power in the Party was Yigal
Allon until his unexpected death in February 1980. Close behind are the
Secretary-General of the Histadrut, Yeruham Meshel, the two leaders of
the kibbutz movements, Mussa Harif and Arik Nehamin, together with
Ya'acov Tsur who represents the moshavim. The inner power group is
completed by the secretaries of the three extremely powerful city party
machines in Tel Aviv, Haifa and Jerusalem, respectively Eliyahu Speiser,
Uri Agami and Uzzi Baram. With the backing of this group, the leader of
the Party can be certain of support by the Party as a whole.

The full-time staff of the party organization in 1979 consisted of 120,
some of them seconded by kibbutzim. In these cases, they continue to be
paid by their kibbutz and do not draw a salary from the Party itself.

Shimon Peres

The Chairman of the Israel Labour Party and the Leader of the Opposition
in the Knesset was born Shimon Persky in a small Polish town on 15 August
1923. He emigrated to Palestine in 1934, so he is clearly not a sabra (the
local label for somebody born in Palestine/Israel), but then he is also not,
except in the most formal sense, a diaspora Jew either, as were all his
predecessors except for Rabin. Peres represents the transition between the
East European Jew, worldly wise, witty and mordant, and the Israeli Jew,
tough, direct and aggressive, and he possesses many of the characteristics of
both.

His strong, regular features, an open engaging smile and a warm manner
(but only after a probationary period has led to the conclusion that the
acquaintanceship is one to be advanced) combine in a personality of
unusual vitality, charm and intelligence. *The New York Times* once reported
that he has the kind of features that come over well on television.

Peres' voice is low and deep while his style of speech is deliberate, coolly
assessing, interpreting, analyzing. He has a gift for the vivid phrase. In the
Knesset he described the protracted Israeli-Egyptian peace negotiation
which followed Sadat's visit to Jerusalem as 'a Hollywood script in reverse –

the happy ending came at the beginning.' And, 'the difference between a statesman and a prophet is that the latter doesn't have to fix any dates.' He enjoys writing poetry. One of his poems was set to music and popularized by folksinger Yaffa Yarkoni after the Six Day War.

His formal education stopped before university but it is rare to glimpse even a small gap in his educational background. He has been known, though infrequently, to exhibit the sort of inaccuracy which comes through having acquired knowledge from books rather than in collegiate contact with people. For Peres is largely an autodidact and remained a reader of books even during the most intense periods of political activity.

His office at the ILP's national headquarters in Hayarkon Street, Tel Aviv, is distinguished from that of most other politicians by the quantity of books it contains. They overflow in the large room, most of it taken up by a mammoth boardroom table. Low shelves around the room are full of books, possibly a thousand of them, while more are piled on desk and table.

At home, a spacious apartment in one of the high-rise blocks built by his brother near Tel Aviv University, Peres is a relaxed family man. His wife, Sonia, has made it a comfortable home; she is a quiet, diffident but attractive hostess. Rarely seen with him on political occasions, her obviously mature intelligence must make her a wise complement to her husband. As elsewhere in Israel, Friday night is home night for the Peres family, and there the Leader of the Opposition entertains his friends or visiting dignitaries with good food, wine and conversation. At his most expansive, he is a witty raconteur with an extensive repertoire of the foibles of some of his mentors and contemporaries.

Saul Bellow wrote of Peres, 'the shine of power is about him',* and it was a very apt description then. But that feature of the Peres personality has been less apparent since 1977. Until that devastating defeat, he had, with some hiccoughs, seemed to be permanently in occupation of some position of power.

His long experience of being at the centre of events, of rubbing shoulders with the great and famous, has given him a certain sleekness and urbanity. For a long time, these were regarded as characteristics of the apparatchik and Peres was dismissed as merely a technocrat. Opinions changed with his demonstration of toughness and persistence in fighting for, and winning, the Party leadership. In reviving the Party after the anguish of defeat he revealed qualities broader and deeper than those of a technocrat.

Peres' political career began when he became secretary of his kibbutz. When, at the age of 18, he received a leadership job in the Socialist youth movement, he was noticed by the Party chiefs. His first Government appointment came soon after the State was established, when Levi Eshkol (later Finance Minister and Ben-Gurion's successor as Prime Minister) was Director-General of the Ministry of Defence. It was a junior job, but brought him into contact with Ben-Gurion, who combined the office of Minister of Defence with the Premiership.

Ben-Gurion took to the young man, recognized his ability and sent him to

* *The Road to Jerusalem*, 1976.

the USA at the age of 27 as the head of the Defence Ministry's supply mission, a key post. Two years later, Peres returned to Israel to become Director-General of that Ministry.

Surrounded by implacable enemies, Israel's first priority was to ensure its capacity for self-defence. Although then, as always, the country was suffering from immense economic problems, the defence establishment was given practically a free hand and Peres was responsible for a huge part of Israel's national spending. To avoid total dependence on imports, he encouraged the expansion of domestic electronic, aviation and other defence-related industries. At the same time he had to find supplies abroad and was the architect of the invaluable arrangement with France, which came to an end with de Gaulle's veto in 1967. It was during this period of his life that Peres attracted the technocrat label, as well as the hostility of many important figures in Mapai who resented the power wielded by this young man and his closeness to the 'old one', Ben-Gurion.

For a complex series of reasons, but essentially as the consequence of his unyielding and pugnacious nature, Ben-Gurion decided in 1965 to leave Mapai and form his own party, Rafi. Two of his young protégés, Shimon Peres and Moshe Dayan, followed him.

It was a tough couple of years. Instead of the panoply and power of office and the control of vast budgets, Peres now held the post of Secretary of the new party, working from a tiny, dilapidated, almost foetid office in one of Tel Aviv's seamier areas. Gone were the official car and driver and the buffer of protective underlings who serve to segregate officials from the people. For the first time in his career, Peres experienced the pressures, irritations and discomforts of the unprotected masses. He later ruefully acknowledged that this had been a very positive period in his life.

In the aftermath of the tensions, fears, and then elation of the Six Day War, the opportunity arrived for healing the split in Mapai, and in 1968 Rafi joined the newly constituted Israel Labour Party and the Government. The old antagonisms initially kept Peres out of the Government, but his abilities and position could not be long overlooked. In 1969 he received his first Cabinet appointment as Minister of Immigrant Absorption. The following year he was moved to the Ministry of Transport and Posts, which he renamed Ministry of Communications. He stayed there until 1974 when, following the resignation of Moshe Dayan as Defence Minister after the criticism of his role in the 1973 Yom Kippur War, Peres succeeded him in this office under the new Prime Minister, Yitzhak Rabin.

He was the right man in the right place, rebuilding, reshaping and reequipping the Israel Defence Forces but, at the same time, never missing any opportunity to advance his claim to the leadership of the Party. After Golda Meir's resignation in 1974, Peres opposed the nomination of Rabin for the Party leadership and, in a secret ballot of the Central Committee, came close to winning, with 254 votes to Rabin's 298, a moral victory for Peres making him a key figure in the Party. Mutual antagonism between the two men deepened when, at the 1977 Party conference, Peres again challenged the incumbent and came very close to winning – a difference of a mere 41 votes out of some 3,600 delegates.

Rabin must have swallowed very hard when, after the bank account affair which led to his resignation, he telephoned Peres, inviting him to take over the office of Prime Minister and assuring him of support. Peres made it known that on the same occasion, Rabin asserted that he had no further ambitions. So, with the election only four weeks away, Peres succeeded to the leadership of a demoralized and divided Party.

He had fulfilled an ambition which had driven him hard in the tough and tortuous world of politics for three decades. Labour had led the Government after every previous election; Peres, like almost every other politician in Israel, assumed it would happen again. Labour would probably lose some seats, but his succession to the nation's highest office was now a certainty.

The country voted otherwise and, instead of leading a Government, Peres went on to lead the Opposition. It was a bitter disappointment – from which he quickly rallied. After conceding defeat he commented, 'We have taken a beating. I never expected it to be so hard, but we have to take it like men,' and, 'I expected the voters to give us a slap in the face–but not to cut our heads off.'

Peres' first task was to heal the wounds in the defeated Party. For the next year or two he patched up differences, minimized ideological and factional dissension and, to some extent, streamlined the Party machine. It was encouraging that, at the Histadrut elections which followed soon after the General Election, Labour kept control of that immensely powerful organization, even though the Likud gained something like 30 per cent of the vote. The Labour Party did well, too, at the municipal elections in November 1978.

All the public opinion polls in the mid-term samplings of the Begin Government disclosed a growth of support for the ILP, which owed something to the leadership of Peres as well as to the lacklustre performance of the Government. The most trying of the burdens Peres had to bear at this period was the continued sniping of Rabin, who had apparently not given up the hope of making a comeback. His autobiography, published in 1979 and containing strong and bitter criticism of Peres, probably went too far, alienating some of his diminishing group of supporters.

Peres went on strengthening his position in the Party by dint of application to his responsibilities. The important kibbutz movement came to his support although it had not been in his camp at the Party conference in 1977. His closest colleagues believe that if he wins the next election in 1981 or earlier, Peres will probably lead the Party for a generation, but that if he fails, he will find it hard to remain at the top.

Peres faces uncertainties with the optimism and resilience of the professional he is, but one of his weaknesses is a certain impatience. Had he stayed his hand and not openly challenged Rabin, but carried on as a successful and popular Defence Minister, the probability is that he would have stepped into Rabin's place effortlessly and without creating party divisions and personal antagonism. Secondly, some of his closest associates wonder whether he is tough enough for the top job. Has he the steel, the readiness to go for the jugular vein, or is he essentially too nice a man to act with the necessary ruthlessness of an effective leader?

Yitzhak Rabin

Blue-eyed, personable and well-built, Yitzhak Rabin, fifth Prime Minister of Israel, talks with intelligence and authority enhanced by his deliberate, unemotional and blunt style. His manner is quiet and low-key, so much so that he can appear flat and uninspiring on the platform and on television. He holds himself tightly; only his incessant cigarette smoking betrays what might be inner stress.

Rabin was born in Jerusalem in 1922 into a defence-orientated family. His father was an American volunteer in the Jewish Legion in World War I who settled in Palestine. His mother, of Russian stock, was the legendary 'Nurse Rose' who helped Jewish resistance during the 1920 Arab riots by smuggling arms to their self-defence units.

A good student at the Kadoorie Agricultural School in Tel Aviv, he became too involved in the Hagana, the Jewish defence force, to pursue a farming career and, in 1941, Allon recruited him for the Palmach, the Hagana's strike force. His rise was rapid. By 1947 he was a Palmach Commander, and in the War of Independence he led the famous Harel Brigade, which took part in the battle for Jerusalem.

Continuing his army career, Rabin became Chief of Staff in 1964 and was responsible for the planning which achieved the stunning victory in 1967. But two events deflected some of the glory from him. One was the appointment of the charismatic Dayan as Defence Minister just five days before the war began. Justifiably or not, much of the acclaim went to Dayan. The second was a consequence of Rabin's own personality. So keyed up and despondent was he about the Government's indecision in the protracted build-up to the war that, at the end of May 1967, two weeks before Israel struck, he suffered a nervous breakdown. His collapse was announced as being due to 'nicotine poisoning'.

His major contribution was nevertheless recognized, and Rabin was one of the generals who became national heroes. Politicians seized on their value as potential vote-getters and, as the generals retired from active service, they were snapped up for top political posts. A year after the war, Rabin became Israel's Ambassador in Washington, a plum diplomatic appointment. It was a post he filled with distinction, though not altogether happily since he was in constant conflict with his chief, Foreign Minister Abba Eban. Returning to Israel after his five-year stint, Rabin was disappointed not to receive the Cabinet post he had been promised by Golda Meir, the Prime Minister. However, he soldiered on, learning what Labour Party politics were about and was eventually given the reward of appointment as Minister of Labour.

When Golda Meir resigned after the Yom Kippur War, the two heirs-apparent, Dayan and Allon, were passed over by the kingmakers in the party. Their choice fell on Rabin, more because of his negative qualifications than any positive ones. He was too new in politics to have made important enemies, and he had not been involved in the 1973 war failures. This time, however, his nomination by the discredited Party leadership, unlike previous nominations, was not passively endorsed by the

Party. In the election held by the Party's Central Committee, he only narrowly defeated Shimon Peres, who stood against him. At 51, Rabin was the first native-born Prime Minister in Israel's history.

His three-year term of office was not highlighted by any major achievement in either the domestic or foreign spheres. But he proved himself a competent politician, coping adroitly with the complications of coalition-forming and of survival in the Knesset with a bare majority. He was never at ease in the Knesset and preferred to make important statements on television where he would not encounter interruptions. Only afterwards would he make a statement in the Knesset. The country's problems were immense. Losses in material and production during the Yom Kippur War and the costs of reequipment placed a very heavy burden on the economy. Sharply rising inflation produced stern fiscal measures, including the reduction of subsidies on staples, never a popular action in Israel. It was particularly tough for a Labour Government but Rabin grasped the nettle. Not that it achieved much; inflation and the cost of living continued to rise. Arab incursions into Israel were increasing and the Palestine Liberation Organization (PLO) was winning diplomatic successes.

Rabin entered the 1977 election campaign burdened not only by these problems but also by a depressingly long list of corruption scandals involving Party leaders. The conclusive blow was the successful prosecution of his wife, Lea, an articulate and independent lady. Rabin himself had been somewhat tarnished by the disclosure that, during his ambassadorial term in the USA, he had accepted substantial fees for making speeches which his predecessors had treated as part of their normal – and unpaid – functions. The public image of the Rabins was that they had been greedy.

A month before election day, he resigned as Prime Minister and Party leader. But, after a brief withdrawal from public activity, Rabin was much in demand as a commentator on current affairs for newspapers, radio and television. Curiously, although he had been neither popular nor respected as Prime Minister, he was accorded at this period the deference given to an elder statesman. With this new status, Rabin embarked on open and repeated criticism of the Labour Party, always directing his barbs at his successor, Shimon Peres. His autobiography of 1979 contained bitter and vitriolic references to his Party colleague and leader.

Rabin's standing within the ILP, his only political base, has suffered much from his vendetta against Peres. This open disloyalty to the Party leader has not endeared him to the rank and file, a factor of importance should he again offer himself as a candidate for the Party leadership.

The leadership group

The Secretary-General of the ILP, Haim Bar-Lev, is the Party machine man closest to the Chairman, Shimon Peres, and, by virtue of both his office and personality, a powerful figure in the councils of the decision-makers. Bar-Lev is in the mould of the ruling Labour elite. Born in Vienna in 1924, he arrived in Palestine fifteen years later and graduated from the country's most notable agricultural school, Mikveh Yisrael, in 1942.

He too exchanged agriculture for the fighting forces. In the year of his graduation he joined the Palmach, remaining in uniform for thirty years, with some breaks for studies. Many of Israel's top military commanders have been encouraged to study abroad both as in-service training and also to prepare them for redeployment after their normally early retirement. Bar-Lev not only attended university in Israel during his military service, but also a Staff College in Britain, and Columbia University in New York for a post-graduate course in economics and business administration.

It was a major turning point in his career when he was called in to assist Rabin, then wilting under the tensions of the waiting period before the Six Day War. Bar-Lev stepped into the breach. He became Deputy Chief of Staff and later Chief of Staff, bearing the responsibilities of the war of attrition between the two fighting wars of 1967 and 1973. He organized the complex and costly network of fortifications in the Sinai peninsula which came to be known as the Bar-Lev Line (and proved to be as vulnerable as its progenitor, the Maginot Line). His methodical, painstaking and imperturbable personality presented a comfortable and reassuring image to a country unaccustomed to the haemorrhage of small-scale and drawn-out warfare.

On his retirement from the Israel Defence Force in 1972, Bar-Lev, who had gained the respect and friendship of Golda Meir, was appointed Minister of Commerce. He accepted the Cabinet post knowing that real economic power rested exclusively with the towering figure of the Finance Minister, Pinhas Sapir. But that only confirmed the speculation that he was Mrs Meir's candidate for the succession and had been deliberately placed in an inconspicuous post to shield him from the limelight which engenders criticism.

But the prestige of the quiet ex-General was severely damaged by the ignominious failure of the Bar-Lev line in 1973 and, when the Party leadership was again open in 1974, he was regarded as being in the same boat as Mrs Meir and Moshe Dayan, who had resigned.

Since his appointment to the post of Secretary-General of the Party in 1979, Bar-Lev has become a respected and responsible administrator. He is rarely in the headlines, but his deliberate and thoughtful approach to problems has made him a valued adviser to Peres and other political leaders. He is now considered among the real policy-makers.

Bringing a special 'Anglo-Saxon' quality to the leadership of the ILP are two brothers-in-law, Abba Eban and Chaim Herzog. Their wives, Suzie and Aura (nee Ambache), are sisters and both are intelligent, attractive and sociable; ideal wives for men in public life.

Eban and Herzog achieved their positions in Israeli life largely through the spoken word, but in differing ways and at different times. Eban was, from his teens, a brilliant scholar and an accomplished public speaker. Born in 1915 into a deeply Jewish and Zionist family, Aubrey Eban (his friends still call him by that name rather than his adopted Hebrew version) joined the British Zionist youth and student movements. His gifts brought him effortlessly into positions of leadership.

He was already on the first rungs of the ladder of an academic career at Cambridge when Dr Chaim Weizmann, the outstanding leader of the World Zionist Movement and later first President of the State of Israel, persuaded Eban to join his staff. Eban followed his mentor on to the world stage when, in 1948, at the age of 34, he became Israel's representative at the United Nations, continuing in this post after his appointment as Ambassador to the United States. He became then, and has remained, Israel's most articulate voice to the outside world. His choice of language, wit and brilliant turn of phrase, combined with a clarity of expression (when he is not being deliberately obscure), have exhilarated audiences all over the world, in particular the Jewish community of the USA.

When told of his tremendous popularity among American Jewry, he ruefully remarks that, alas, they have no votes in Israel. For he has been so far less successful in domestic politics than as Israel's top orator. Returning to Israel in 1959 after his stint in the USA, he became Minister without Portfolio in the Ben-Gurion government. The following year he became Minister of Education. He was one of the three Ben-Gurion protégés in Mapai, the other two being Dayan and Peres. When Ben-Gurion broke away in 1965 to form his own party, Dayan and Peres joined him. Eban did not, remaining instead with the big battalions. Ben-Gurion found this unforgivable and lost no opportunity of denigrating Eban as an unprincipled office-seeker.

Eban served a lengthy term as Foreign Minister, from 1966 to 1974, with much greater success in articulating wise and moderate policies than in persuading his colleagues in the Cabinet to follow them. His effectiveness at the Foreign Ministry was diminished by the fact that the Prime Minister, Golda Meir, his predecessor as Foreign Minister, herself continued to dominate the country's foreign policy. While Eban was frequently opposed to her views, he rarely put up a fight for his. Within the Ministry he was known as an aloof man, establishing few intimate relationships. His senior officials complained of diminishing morale as the major decisions were made in the Prime Minister's office.

Nevertheless, Eban was occasionally named, and sometimes considered himself, as a candidate for the Prime Minister's job. In the world of politics, it is imprudent to talk of the impossible. But with Eban's negligible Party strength – his 'Englishness' still makes him something of an outsider – his chances of reaching the Party leadership appear remote.

From 1974, when Allon replaced him at the Foreign Ministry, Eban consolidated his position as No. 3 on the ILP list and, together with Peres and Allon, constituted the political inner cabinet of the Party. He continued writing and lecturing, and the freedom of opposition gave him even more opportunity of using his gift for the pithy phrase. The Begin Government, said Eban, 'have an extraordinary tactlessness about their settlement tactics. They are the only collection of bulls carrying around their own mobile china shops.'

Brother-in-law Chaim Herzog (his intimate circle continues to refer to him as Vivian) came into the front rank of Israeli leadership much later. Eban was already an international eminence when Herzog became a national figure in 1967 during the Six Day War. Called on by Israel Radio to comment on the gathering storm and, later, on the progress of the war, Herzog presented masterly and honest interpretations of the rapidly changing situation. They made him the single most effective prop of Israeli morale at that tense time.

Herzog's antecedents are distinguished. Both his parents were members of eminent rabbinical families and his father was the first Ashkenazi Chief Rabbi of Israel. (Israel has two religious Jewish communities. The Ashkenazim follow the German ritual, and the Sephardim preserve the traditions of Spain and Portugal. Each has its own Chief Rabbi.) Born in Ireland, Herzog emigrated with his family to Palestine in 1937. He went to England to study law, and was caught there by the outbreak of World War II. After gaining his LL.B. at London University and passing the Bar Final Examination, he joined the British Army and saw service in Europe.

Soon after his demobilization from the British Army and his return to Palestine, the War of Independence brought him back to arms. He spent the years from 1950 to 1954 as Military Attaché in Washington, after which he became Chief of Military Intelligence. On his retirement from the Israel Defence Force in 1961, he became the representative in Israel of Sir Isaac Wolfson, the notable British entrepreneur and philanthropist. A few years later he opened his own law office in Tel Aviv.

Far more to his taste and much more attuned to his abilities were his four years in New York as Israel's Ambassador to the United Nations from 1974 to 1978. He emerged as a powerful advocate for his country and his gregariousness and likableness made him a popular and successful representative.

He returned to Israel and his law practice, one of the most successful and respected in the country, continuing all the while his activities as a widely sought-after commentator. Peres brought him into the inner councils of the ILP. Herzog is affable, thoughtful, an excellent mixer and a popular figure in Israel. Hitherto denied a significant place on the ILP list, he has hopes of doing better next time and of assuring himself a place among his country's top politicians.

Two other men in the ILP, at present hardly known outside Israel, could become serious candidates for the Party leadership should Peres fail. But, whether or not they are presented with the opportunity to succeed to the top position, Moshe (Mussa) Harif, a kibbutz leader, and Jacob Levinson, a banker, are growing powers in the Party. Both are young men in Israeli political terms. Harif was born in 1933 and Levinson the following year. Both have a kibbutz background and both worked in the same Socialist youth movement where they became friends. But while Levinson was born into Israel's elite, Harif worked his way through the ranks after being brought to Palestine from Poland as an infant. His position of power stems from his secretaryship of one of the two major kibbutz movements.

Although he supported Rabin in the 1974 Party election, Harif has been firmly on the side of the new leader since Peres succeeded in 1977. Peres demonstrated his confidence by appointing him Chairman of Labour's permanent steering committee, which has considerable influence in Party appointments. His standing became even higher when, in 1979, he helped to bring about the merger of two of the three kibbutz movements.

Harif firmly believes in the kibbutz movement as the Socialist heart of the ILP, and in the need for the Party to end its internal dissensions and return to its Socialist ideology. On the issues of peace policies, he tends to be in the camp of the doves. Harif is youthful, almost boyish, in his appearance; bright-eyed, breezy and casual, he can quickly bridle when nettled. He is self-confident, has a good estimation of his own worth and of his capacity to succeed. The widespread public acknowledgment that he is a coming man has not diminished his self-esteem or his ambition.

Jacob Levinson is much more deliberate in manner, more formal in dress and more cautious in speech than his kibbutz contemporary. These characteristics reflect both his upper-crust background and his occupation as Israel's most dynamic banker.

He went through the customary progress of high school and army (not university, though), after which he became a member of Kibbutz Rosh Hanikra for ten years. He has described this as 'the most productive part of my life'. The death of his father, Gershon Levinson, who had for many years held the important post of Treasurer of the Histadrut, brought him out of the kibbutz with the responsibility of providing for his family. The Histadrut offered him a job in Hevrat Ovdim, the holding company of its great industrial and financial enterprises. He was a success and in 1970 was appointed Chairman of one of Hevrat Ovdim's undertakings, Bank Hapoalim.

Under his forceful and imaginative leadership, the Bank moved from dealing largely with the Histadrut's affairs to become one of the two largest banking operations in Israel. These successes put him in an authoritative place in the Histadrut, whose expert on the national economy's private sector he became. He was appointed to the Executive of the ILP.

In 1974 Rabin offered him the Ministry of Finance but Levinson declined on the ground that he was in the middle of his work at the Bank. At first reluctant to speak in public, he later, from 1978, began the practice of reprinting in pamphlet form the major speeches he had delivered in different parts of the world. In manner he is controlled, without being unfriendly. He looks the high-powered executive, knowing what he is about, tough, efficient, ambitious.

Every newspaper columnist writing about the future of the ILP inevitably refers to Levinson as its next Finance Minister. It is, apart from the Premiership, the hottest seat in the Government, and Levinson may well relish an attempt at the near-impossible – putting Israel on a sound economic footing.

Chapter three

Right-wing Federation

The making of the Likud

The Likud, the party which gained the largest number of seats in the Knesset elections of 1977 is, like its main opponent the ILP, a loose federation of parties, each maintaining some separate organizational structure – the word Likud means 'gathering together'. The four parties constituting the Likud were Herut, the Liberal Party, La'am and Achdut. Herut (Freedom), the hard core of the Likud, was only formed when Israel became a State, but its origins go back to the Zionist Revisionist Party and its militant offshoot, the Irgun Zvai Leumi (National Military Organization).

The Revisionist Party was created by one of the most colourful and dramatic figures in Zionist history, Vladimir Jabotinsky. A spellbinding orator and brilliant linguist, he was a dynamic personality who rebelled against the gradualism of Zionist leadership in the 1920s. Contemptuous of what he regarded as pussyfooting negotiations with the British Mandatory power for a few hundred more immigration certificates to Palestine, Jabotinsky urged that the most forceful pressure be applied for large-scale immigration and for the formation of Jewish military and police units. He founded the Revisionist Party in 1924, basing it on his conviction that the survival of Jewry would not be achieved by polite diplomacy but through the ability and readiness of Jews to fight for it.

Within a few years, the programme was crystallized into the aim of a self-governing Jewish commonwealth on both sides of the River Jordan. It was clear and uncompromising, but the polarization which ensued created tensions within the World Zionist Organization. The exasperated Jabotinsky took himself and his followers outside the movement in 1935, creating the 'New Zionist Organization'. Its youth movement, Betar, was even more radical than the parent organization, earning a reputation as ultra right-wing and militarist. Ben-Gurion even referred to Jabotinsky as a fascist.

Although damaged by suspicion of involvement in the 1933 assassination of Haim Arlozoroff, a Labour Zionist leader, the Revisionist movement became a strong force under Jabotinsky, who led the resistance to Britain's retreat from the obligation to create a Jewish national home in Palestine. By 1939, when a British White Paper signalled a virtual abandonment of the Zionist cause, the Revisionists had already created the Irgun Zvai Leumi, a clandestine fighting force for reprisals against Arab attackers. With the spread of the Nazi terror, the Irgun participated in the illegal immigration of Jewish refugees into Palestine, an activity which led to armed clashes with the British forces.

On the outbreak of World War II, the Irgun ended all action against the British. In 1944, after Jabotinsky's death, Menachem Begin became the commander of the Irgun. Under his leadership and with the ending of the war, the Irgun, disciplined, determined and ruthless, attacked British military targets, in the process creating a dedicated secret organization with its own loyalties and principles. The Irgun cooperated for some time with the recognized Jewish leaders in Palestine in the revolt against the British, but after the bombing of the King David Hotel in Jerusalem, which killed 91 and injured 45 others, it was denounced and outlawed by Ben-Gurion.

With the creation of the State, Begin formed the Herut Party. The Revisionist organization ceased to exist and so did the Irgun which, for a while, had been permitted to retain its separate units in the Israeli army.

The party label had been changed, but not the programme. Herut continued to claim the whole of 'historical' Palestine, on both sides of the Jordan River, as the Jewish State. On foreign affairs it has always adopted a pro-Western orientation, while its economic policy is capitalist, with encouragement for private enterprise. It has always been, on the whole, sympathetic to traditional Judaism. Its members are themselves unlikely to be observant, but the Party ideologists see orthodoxy as an expression of Jewish identification with the Holy Land. In more recent years, the militant wing of orthodoxy has come very close to Herut's nationalistic approach on territorial issues.

From the beginning, Herut concentrated on winning the support of the new immigrants, most of whom came from the Arab countries of the Middle East and North Africa in the early years of Statehood. With this support, Herut won 14 seats in the 1949 elections for the First Knesset. The second election in 1951 produced a drop in its representation to only 8 seats and Begin decided that the situation called for a much more militant policy of opposition to the Labour regime if Herut were to make any impact. In the third election (1955), Herut won 15 seats, making it the second largest party. It increased its representation to 17 in the 1959 and 1961 elections.

The merger between the Socialist parties led to a similar movement among the non-Socialist groups. In 1965, the Liberal Party came to an electoral agreement with Herut to form a joint parliamentary list with the name of Gahal (acronym for Gush Herut Veha-Liberalim, bloc of Herut and Liberals). That list won 26 seats in both the 1965 and 1969 elections.

A few days before the outbreak of the 1967 Six Day War, Gahal agreed to join a Government of National Unity. That government lasted for three years, during which six Gahal nominees held Ministerial portfolios. Begin himself was Minister without Portfolio for this period, his only experience of office before becoming Prime Minister in 1977. The Government of National Unity ended in August 1970, when Gahal left in protest against the decision to begin negotiations with the Arabs under UN auspices.

Gahal's taste of power had created an appetite for it and, back in opposition, the right-centre federation set about looking for additional partners which might enable it to command a majority. The religious groups were excluded as traditionally the supporters of Labour; this left as possibles the Independent Liberals with 4 seats, the Free Centre led by Shmuel Tamir, which had 2 seats, and the State List (a rump of the Rafi Party, the bulk of which had rejoined Labour) which had won 4 seats in the 1969 election. The differences between them presented obstacles but eventually, with the 1973 elections only a few months ahead, a new electoral bloc was created – the Likud. Its constituents (each of which would retain its own separate organization) were Herut, the Liberal Party, the Free Centre, La'am (successor to the State List) and Achdut (a one-man party breakaway from the Independent Liberals). The Independent Liberals remained independently outside Likud, while the Free Centre subsequently split and disappeared.

In the 1973 elections, postponed from October to December because of the Yom Kippur War, the profound changes brought about by the war received almost no expression. The population was too numbed to reassess traditional voting loyalties, and the elections left the Knesset virtually unchanged. The Likud did gain 8 seats, and Labour lost 5 but remained the party of Government.

Between 1973 and the next election, Likud made ground as the troubles of the Labour movement grew. Its territorial policy began to look more respectable and responsible as well-known national figures supported its major plank, the continuation of Israeli control in the occupied territories. The self-employed middle class, angry with the Socialist policies of the Government, found the free-enterprise policy of the Liberal component of the Likud to their taste. The poorer, mainly Oriental sections of the population, always traditional supporters of Herut, rallied in greater numbers as their economic situation suffered from higher prices and housing shortages. Recent immigrants from the Soviet Union provided a new accretion of strength. Disillusioned by Socialism and responsive to strong government, they were more attracted by the Likud than by Labour. The squabbling and corruption within Labour and the responsibility attached to it for the failures in the 1973 war additionally improved the chances of the main opposition grouping.

The right-centre Likud federation entered the 1977 elections with a real hope of winning, and the preparation of its list of candidates became a much more serious matter than usual. The Likud, like the other major parties, would be presenting a national list of 120 and would have to make a preliminary estimate of the number of seats it would be likely to win. The party had 39 members in the outgoing Knesset, so this figure could be regarded with certainty as the minimum. Thus the first forty names on the list could be assumed to be the 'real' ones. The next dozen or so places were still of importance as possible winners if the poll went exceptionally well, but the serious competition was for the 'real' places. The order of names in that part of the list indicated the candidate's importance in the party hierarchy.

The first four names on the Likud list were predictable: Begin; Simcha Ehrlich, Chairman of the Liberal Party; Yigal Hurvitz, representing La'am;

and Ezer Weizman, former commander of the Air Force and the Likud's campaign organizer. Of the remaining thirty-six safe places on the Likud list, seventeen went to Herut, eleven to the Liberals and seven to La'am. The remaining place went to Hillel Seidel, the one-man Achdut Party. In the event, Likud won 43 seats (Herut 20, the Liberal Party 14, La'am 8 and Achdut 1), becoming for the first time the largest party in the Knesset and the coalition-maker. The religious parties quickly joined. Equally quickly General Ariel ('Arik') Sharon, the hero of the Yom Kippur War and a political hawk, whose own party Shlomzion (Peace of Zion) had won 2 seats, joined Herut, increasing the Likud's seats to 45.

The figures showed that normal Labour voters in development towns and in the agricultural cooperatives had switched to the Likud. This defection from Labour could have been disastrous for the ILP if it happened again at the Histadrut elections a month later. Shimon Peres and Yeruham Meshel, the Histadrut Secretary, saw the danger, rallied their forces and organized a campaign which resulted in maintaining the ILP's hold on the organization. Even so, the Histadrut faction affiliated to Herut won a record 30 per cent of the vote.

At the start, the coalition led by the Likud had a mere 62 or 63 votes in the Knesset, but the accession of the Democratic Movement for Change (DMC) later in the year brought in an additional 14. A year later the DMC split, and only 7 of its MKs (who renamed themselves the Deomocratic Party) continued to support the Government. After the visit of President Sadat to Jerusalem in November 1977, the appeal of the Begin administration waxed and waned with the fluctuations in the peace negotiations. The new economic boom created by Simcha Ehrlich, the Liberal leader, who had become Finance Minister, freed the economy but aggravated the inflationary spiral. Labour supporters were gleefully observing that Ehrlich had made Rabinowitz (the much criticized finance Minister in the previous administration) look good.

Herut

The fact that Herut held 20 of the Likud's 43 seats in the 1977 Knesset was no measure of its importance. By far the most powerful component of the Begin Government, Herut was considerably under-represented. The Party was Begin's own creation, and he had remained its leader throughout, being reelected Party Chairman almost unanimously for the thirteenth time at the 1979 convention. Party national headquarters, in Bet Jabotinsky in Tel Aviv's King George Street, is a startlingly modern high-rise office block in an otherwise architecturally undistinguished thoroughfare. The base of the building is square, solid and massive, accounting for its popular description as 'Zeev Fortress' (Zeev was Vladimir Jabotinsky's Hebrew forename).

Completed in 1973, the building belongs to Keren Tel Hai, the Party fund administered by Herut (Tel Hai, in Galilee, was the place where Joseph Trumpledoor, a Revisionist hero, was killed by Arab marauders in 1920). Until 1977, the fund was deeply in debt, and the large and costly building was financed by borrowing and by letting most of it as office space to commercial and public institutions. But part of the building cost must have been raised in the traditional Zionist manner, because every door of the Herut offices, on the eighth and twelfth floors, bears a large plaque declaring the room to be 'in honour of' some named transatlantic sympathizer. Since 1977, when the Party went into government, capital debts have been repaid, while the grant received from the State covers the Party's running costs.

These are much lower than those of the ILP, the total central staff in 1979 numbering only thirty, about one-quarter of their chief rival's establishment. But Herut paid staff were augmented by full-time volunteers, one of them the then Chairman of the Executive, Avraham Schecterman.

The structure of the Party is cumbersome and complex although some streamlining has taken place since it gained power. Its policy-making body is the Central Committee, elected at the biennial Party conference and consisting of some 800 members. It meets about four times annually, and between meetings an Executive of some fifty members takes decisions. Day-to-day control is in the hands of a Secretariat consisting of twelve to fifteen members of the Executive, who head the various departments – organization, youth, finance, political, and so on. It is in the Secretariat that the real power lies.

In recent years, in response to pressure from local parties and younger members whose opportunities had been blocked by ageing office-holders, Herut has tried to effect a turnover of MKs. Political appointments in Israel generally, and not in Herut alone, have tended to be rewards for long service, and party leadership was in danger of becoming a geriatric occupation. In Herut, several veterans of the Knesset, including Schecterman himself, were persuaded to stand down in 1977, in favour of newcomers. In ensuring that Herut received its appropriate number of Ministerial portfolios, Begin was hampered not only by the claims of his coalition partners, but by the fact that so few of his senior colleagues had any experience of government or were of the required stature. The shortage of qualified personnel was also felt when the new Ministers considered to what extent they should follow the 'party key' system and staff the Ministries with their own Party supporters. The 'party key' system of patronage, which had existed in the Zionist movement before Statehood, had been continued in Israeli Governments. But as government developed its own cadres, party appointments were generally made only in senior posts when there was a change of Ministry. Herut, which could not call on enough qualified people, made a virtue out of that necessity by claiming credit for reducing patronage.

Of its Ministers, only two succeeded in making an early impact, placing themselves at the centre of Party power. They were Ezer Weizman, the Minister of Defence, and – unexpectedly – David Levy, the Housing Minister, who is of Moroccan origin. In the early days he had been the butt of Israel's 'Irish' or 'Polish' jokes, but by the second year of the Begin Government, there were no more jokes about Levy. Indeed, there was serious talk about him as a possible candidate for the Party leadership.

Within the Party, the managers of the machine included the bosses of the main urban sections. Haim Kaufman leads the central region and is head of the parliamentary Herut Party. Arye Kramer heads the Tel Aviv branch, and Haim Corfu the Jerusalem branch, as well as being Chairman of the coalition executive in the Knesset. Meir Cohen is also within the inner group of Party managers as leader of the Haifa branch, together with Israel Ben-Amitai of Beersheba, while Yoram Aridor, a Deputy Minister, is influential in the Secretariat.

They are the 'back room boys' of power, while in front, considered by the public as possible heirs to Begin (he announced his intention of retiring when he reaches seventy in 1983), are Weizman, Levy, and a man believed to be Begin's own choice, Yaakov Meridor. Outsiders include Professor Moshe Arens, the hard-line Chairman of the Knesset Foreign Affairs Committee, and Begin's 'favourite general', Ariel Sharon. Arens, born in Lithuania in 1925, gained degrees in aeronautics at MIT and CalTech, becoming Associate Professor of Aeronautical Engineering at the Haifa Technion. A Likud MK since 1973, he speaks well and is highly regarded. He is politically ambitious and was a strong candidate to succeed Moshe Dayan as Foreign Minister, but his criticism of Begin, whom he considered too compromising in the peace negotiations, probably weighed against him. He has been the competent chairman of a prestigious Knesset Committee, a stepping stone to higher things if Likud remains in power.

Menachem Begin

Israel's sixth Prime Minister is short, squat and balding and wears thick glasses, but awareness of these features fades quickly after the first few moments of conversation. Menachem Begin speaks quietly, persuasively and with conviction. He listens, too, but with almost imperceptible intimations that it is only out of politeness and not because he really wants to hear more than he has said. Begin is thoughtful and cultivated. His many years in opposition, free of the tensions and responsibilities of office, gave this naturally bookish man the opportunity to read and reflect. He has had ample time to think through his attitudes and, having reached conclusions, he believes them to be right and will not readily reconsider them. He gives the impression of possessing an implicit belief in his superior mental ability and rectitude.

He was the first Prime Minister with a positive attitude to orthodox Judaism, though he would not describe himself as orthodox. Rigid himself, he sees value in the strict discipline of orthodox observance. He tends to be formal, addressing people with their full style and title. Courteous almost to a fault, he will thank, almost profusely, the renderer of the smallest service. But he will respond sharply when he thinks he is being attacked or slighted, and invariably bridles when he is described as a former terrorist.

It is difficult to see in the courteous and considerate private *persona* of Menachem Begin the man described in a Palestine police warrant in 1946: 'A tall angular man with a thin lined face of a fanatic, jet black hair and myopic eyes behind thick lenses, he is the type of irresponsible, uncompromising rebel, thirsting for personal power.' But the description may become a little more credible during the demagoguery of a Begin public speech, for he is a fiery and rousing orator, fluent in many languages (some of his friends say he speaks ten). He enjoys displays of erudition and often garnishes his speeches with literary, historical and classical allusions.

Menachem Wolfovitch Begin was born in Brest Litovsk, on 16 August 1913, into an orthodox Jewish family and attended a Hebrew school of the Mizrachi, the religious Zionist party. His family background and his Mizrachi schooling gave him an understanding of, and sympathy for, the Jewish religious tradition. Although he never joined the Mizrachi, these early religious associations made him appear a more attractive coalition leader to Israel's religious parties than the ILP, with which they had been linked for the first twenty-nine years of the country's existence.

Under the influence of Jabotinsky, he was attracted to the Zionist Revisionist youth movement and became its last leader in pre-war Poland. Arrested in Soviet Lithuania in 1941 for Zionist activities, Begin was sent to prison camps in Siberia, where he remained until 1942. The Stalin-Sikorsky agreement of that year gave him the opportunity of release from Siberia to join the Polish army in what had, by then, also become Russia's war against the Nazis. Begin became a corporal in General Anders' army stationed in Palestine; his parents and brother became victims of Hitler's 'Final Solution'.

On arrival in Palestine, Begin established communication with fellow Revisionists and, in 1944, when it seemed certain that the war would soon end with an Allied victory, Begin deserted and went underground to become leader of the Revisionist Party's armed force, the Irgun. By that time its fortunes were at a low ebb, weakened by the opposition of the official Jewish leadership, by the death of its commander in 1941 and by its self-imposed quiescence during the war against Nazism. But it began to revive when Begin took over. His leadership certainly had something to do with this, but there were also two other factors. The first was that with the ending of World War II, the struggle for immigration and freedom could be pursued without hindering the major war effort. Secondly, many Jews deserted from the Polish army then stationed in Palestine and joined the Irgun. Like Begin, they were tough and had received military training. Many had lost their families in the Holocaust and had dedicated themselves to ensuring Jewish survival in the Land of Israel. They were invaluable recruits, determined, disciplined and apparently ruthless.

Begin headed the Irgun during the period of its greatest militancy, from 1944 until it was merged into the Israel Defence Forces in June 1948. The Irgun's attacks on British targets in Palestine made him the most wanted enemy, and a price of £10,000 was put on his head. He was reviled not only by the British, but also by the Arabs for his participation in the savagery at Deir Yassin, where 200 Arab villagers were massacred. Nor was he loved by many of his fellow Jews in Palestine who looked upon him as a hateful danger. Ben-Gurion – who became his most bitter antagonist – wanted him dead and declared: 'Irgun is the enemy of the Jewish people.'

As far as is known, Begin himself has never seen military action or participated in any violence. He does not even appear ever to have fired a shot at a living target. But he planned and directed the Irgun's most daring and ruthless actions, convinced that nothing would be achieved without force. The two grimmest were the bombing of the King David Hotel in Jerusalem in 1946 and the hanging of two British sergeants in August 1947, in retaliation for the hanging of a leading Irgunist. Begin was the 'Irgun thug commander' (as he was described in the House of Commons) who refused pleas for clemency. He had also ordered captured British officers to be whipped in retaliation for similar treatment of his men. He bore the execration heaped upon him with fortitude, in the knowledge that subsequently the whipping and hanging of Jews by the British was stopped.

With the creation of the State of Israel, Begin founded Herut and has led the party in the Knesset since its inception. During the early years, Begin and his Party were too busy settling into the strange role of loyal opposition in a Parliamentary democracy to be militant. Begin himself soon became distinguished as one of the most effective performers in the Chamber. His speeches always attracted attention, and he gave every evidence of relishing parliamentary debates and parliamentary procedure. But his progress towards recognition as a responsible democratic politician was retarded by the violence of his opposition to the negotiations with the government of West Germany for financial reparations. The decision, so soon after the horrifying events of the Nazi terror, to negotiate with the nation responsible for the deaths of six million Jews, understandably aroused the deepest emotions. But in 1951, Israel was in a desperate economic situation and German money could be of vital help in the absorption of hundreds of thousands of Holocaust survivors. The Government of Ben-Gurion agonized, but decided in the end to ask the Knesset to approve in principle.

Begin came very close to leading an insurrection against the government by the violence and bitterness of his opposition. He declaimed in the Knesset: 'There will be no negotiations with Germany. On less vital issues nations have gone to the barricades', and, 'this will be a war of life or death.' Herut demonstrators marched on the Knesset and it was not until Ben-Gurion called in the army that the mob was dispersed. Ben-Gurion remained firm and when the Knesset gave him their confidence on a vote of 61 to 50, Begin drew back, ended the demonstrations and quietly accepted his exclusion from the Knesset for fifteen months as the penalty for his incitement.

It took fifteen years before Begin emerged from the political wilderness. In May 1967, the Israeli public, fearful that the Eshkol Government was floundering in the face of the threat posed by Nasser, demanded a 'wall to wall' Government of National Unity. Begin called on the Prime Minister, Levi Eshkol, to hand over the country's leadership to Ben-Gurion, a remarkable act of political generosity towards the man who had been his bitterest antagonist. Ben-Gurion was not drafted, but a Government of National Unity was formed, including Gahal (the Herut-Liberal combination), and for the first time, and after nineteen years of opposition, Begin achieved office as Minister without Portfolio and Deputy Prime Minister.

Without a Department to run, Begin was able to take a broad view of the affairs of state. No longer a firebrand, he became conciliator, smoothing out differences among his colleagues. His advice was sought, and even experienced politicians like Eshkol, Golda Meir (who succeeded Eshkol as Prime Minister in 1969) and Moshe Dayan listened to him with respect. But he saw his main function in the Cabinet as preserving the new 'Greater Israel' which had come about through Israel's territorial gains in the 1967 war. When the Cabinet decided in 1970 to begin negotiations with the Arabs under the auspices of the UN negotiator, Gunnar Jarring, Begin saw it as demonstrating a willingness for territorial compromise. He withdrew Gahal from the grand coalition and went back into opposition.

But his two years in office had broadened him and given him a new stature in the nation. He had, at any rate, learned something of the restraints and responsibilities of power before he took office as Prime Minister in 1977. In response to the fears that Begin's hard line would kill whatever faint hope existed for peace with the Arabs, Ezer Weizman, the Defence Minister, said immediately after the elections: 'Give him time, and you will see him become more flexible than anybody believes.'

Yet in his early statements, Begin still insisted that Israel was entitled to the occupied areas and that the new settlements in the West Bank and Sinai would never be relinquished. In a speech one week after the elections, he said: 'I believe Judea and Samaria [Herut Biblical terminology for the West Bank] are an integral part of our sovereignty. It's our land. It was occupied by Abdullah [the King of Jordan] against international law, against our inherent right. It was liberated during the Six Day War, when we used our right of national self-defence. . . . You annex foreign land. You don't annex your own country.'

The policy of the Begin Government was outlined in the Knesset a month after the elections. 'The Jewish people has an eternal historic right to the Land of Israel, the inalienable legacy of our forefathers. The Government shall plan, create and encourage urban and rural settlement on the soil of the homeland.' Yet, even before the Sadat visit, Begin was giving signs of flexibility. To a group of American Jewish leaders, worried about the effects of his declared policies, he carefully explained, with talmudic skill, that Israeli sovereignty did not necessarily imply that these territories could never be relinquished. An owner of property, he told them, could give it away if he chose.

The protracted negotiations with President Carter and President Sadat in 1978 and 1979 tested his skill and resolution. But, though tough, he displayed a flexibility and a spirit of compromise which astounded all those who thought they knew him, and dismayed some of his colleagues. Haim Landau, Minister without Portfolio, who had been his closest friend since the Irgun days, opposed the peace treaty with Egypt, and the intimacy between them ceased. Apart from Landau, he had no close friends in the Cabinet, nor, like previous Labour Prime Ministers, did he create his own 'kitchen' of advisers. Probably closest to him was his personal secretary, Yechiel Kadishai, a cheerful man of about 60 and a former comrade-in-arms.

A trusted aide was the first Director-General of the Prime Minister's Office, Dr Eliahu Ben-Elissar, appointed Israel's first Ambassador to Egypt in January 1980, who was given responsibilities in the peace negotiations which a Foreign Minister more departmentally conscious than Moshe Dayan would not have permitted. Begin's friends outside the office are all political friends. He has never cultivated social friendships and, since becoming Prime Minister, has had neither the opportunity nor the inclination to do so. His early friends were either killed or have died. His closest associations of all are with his wife, children and grandchildren.

He has brought to the Cabinet his own style of courtesy, formality and legal precision. When Mr Begin is annoyed with a member of his Cabinet he refers to him as 'Adoni . . . . .' (i.e., Mr Minister). In a good mood, he refers to them by their first names outside the Cabinet room. The former Finance Minister, Simcha Ehrlich, was often and affectionately called 'Reb Simcha'. His old IZL lieutenant, Haim Landau, despite his open dissent from Begin's peace policies, remains Avraham, his underground code name.

Begin is an austere man. His indifference to material acquisitiveness gave him an added appeal in the eyes of the Israeli public, dismayed as it was by the corruption among the country's politicians. He lives simply, although he does apear to enjoy the society of some of the Israeli super-rich. Having achieved the highest office, Begin is now concerned with his place in history, and would like to surpass the achievement of his former adversary, Ben-Gurion, the man who created Israel, by being the leader who brought peace to the Jewish State.

It may have been concentration on the peace process that insulated him from the numerous other problems facing the State. Not that he had ever shown great interest in economic affairs – preferring to leave all that to the Finance Minister. However, as time went on he seemed to lose control of the direction of domestic affairs generally. This could have been partly due to his indifferent state of health, for he has a heart condition and has made a number of hospital visits for checks and rests. The constant feuding and bickering among his Ministers, both in and out of the Cabinet Office, gave the impression of a divided and inept government. One newspaper commented that, after two years, 'only the ban on smoking during sessions remains intact of Mr Begin's original list of don'ts to his ministers.'

Halfway through his government's term, the record was almost the looking glass image of what had been expected. Begin, of all people, gave back all the Sinai, including his beloved settlements, in return for peace with Egypt. Only Begin could have achieved it. Had it been proposed by another Government, Begin in opposition could have divided the country and issued another call to the barricades. He still talked of the West Bank and Gaza as belonging to Israel, but few doubted that he would make concessions in these areas too, were there a prospect of a durable settlement.

'Begin', one of his closest associates told me, 'is a far more sensitive man than people think, and although he is emotional, he keeps it tightly under control.' He retains one of the characteristics of a commander – he will reprimand a subordinate if necessary, but will always cover him in front of outsiders. He is also exaggeratedly loyal to his friends while at the same time not sparing them the unpleasant experience of his blistering tongue when he is irritated. In his loyalty to the Irgun, he often succumbs to the temptation to rewrite history by expanding its role in the creation of Israel at the expense of Ben-Gurion and the Hagana.

Weizman and Levy: two winners

Of the Herut representatives in the Begin Government the two most successful were also, perhaps, the most different from each other – the patrician Ezer Weizman, born into Israel's aristocracy, and David Levy, the deprived immigrant from Morocco.

Ezer Weizman, long thought of as a lightweight on the Israeli political scene, became Begin's Defence Minister, Sadat's 'my friend Ezer' and the leading candidate for succession to the leadership of the Likud. Tall, good-looking and breezy, he is the very model of the dashing Air Force Commander. His upper-class upbringing and financial security have given him something of the self-assurance, even to the point of arrogance, said to be characteristic of the old Etonian. Many object to what they regard as his swaggering cockiness; and this same self-confidence has enabled him to speak his mind and on occasion to be irreverent or flippant. Politics are a serious business in Israel, but Ezer Weizman can be light-hearted and sometimes hot-headed, characteristics not generally associated with conventional politicians. When asked what had changed since he left the Israel Defence Forces, he answered laconically: 'Longer hair, shorter skirts.' But the *enfant terrible* has been transformed into a responsible and popular national leader.

One of the second generation of top Israelis, Weizman was born in Haifa in 1924, the son of Yehiel Weizman, a wealthy merchant of that city and the brother of the great Dr Chaim Weizmann, the first President of the State of Israel. Ezer is fond of telling the story of his call on Ben-Gurion, when he was Israel's Prime Minister and Weizman was head of the Air Force. Paula, the Premier's forthright and eccentric wife, opened the door, asked the name of the visitor and yelled to her husband in another room, 'It's Weizman to see you – not the one who's dead.'

Weizman acquired his love of flying as a youth. He joined Britain's Royal Air Force at the age of 18 and was sent to Rhodesia for training as a fighter pilot. Service in North Africa and India was followed by aeronautical studies in England after the war. Returning to Palestine at the outbreak of the War of Independence, he played a major role in organizing the embryonic Israeli Air Force, while taking part in active operations. When only 26, he was appointed Air Force Chief of Operations and subsequently advanced to become its Commander in 1958.

His own audacity as a fighter pilot was transmitted to Israel's pilots and ground crews. Ezer Weizman was a tough leader, demanding high standards and giving the Air Force he was shaping his own brand of flamboyance and *panache*. Well before the Six Day War, he presciently claimed that six hours of a preemptive strike would be enough to wipe out the whole Egyptian Air Force and win a war.

The tough, uncompromising nationalism of Herut suited Ezer

Weizman's character and thinking. Although unable to participate in politics as a serving officer, his sympathies were known to be with that party, and when he retired from the Israel Defence Forces in 1969, he joined Herut and became a member of the Government of National Unity as Minister of Transport. It was a difficult assignment. He was thrown in at the deep end of a serious conflict with the dock workers, but successfully faced the problems with the same forcefulness and flair he had shown in the Air Force. His tenure of office proved him to be an able administrator and politician, and gained him popularity extending beyond his own Party.

Sharing Begin's hawkishness on the occupied territories, Weizman left the Government with him in 1970, when it seemed that the Labour majority was ready to relinquish the option of annexation which his Party favoured. The event did not affect his sense of humour. The Tel Aviv correspondent of the (London) *Jewish Chronicle* reported at the time the following conversation: Weizman: 'I'm very upset at the way you treated me in your paper after I resigned office.' Correspondent: 'But I don't recall having written anything bad about you.' Weizman: 'That's what I mean. You did not write about me at all.' He became a director of Maritime Fruit Carriers, a large and expanding shipping company headed by his relative by marriage, Yaakov Meridor, a leader of Herut and close associate of Begin.

Weizman was rapidly rising in the Party hierarchy and in 1970 was elected Chairman of Herut's Executive. But he was still not quite trusted by the veterans of the Party, to whom he appeared unreliable and volatile, an able but restless and mercurial personality, likely at any time to go his own way without paying too much regard to the views of the older heads in the Party.

A clash with Begin led to his resignation as Chairman of the Executive in 1972, but he was seldom out of the public eye and came back to the top rank of leadership when, against the advice of Party veterans, Begin chose him to organize the Likud's 1977 election campaign. His status in the Party was now such that he was given second place on Herut's election list and was a natural choice for the post of Minister of Defence when Begin formed his first Government.

Weizman believed the Sadat visit to be a historic breakthrough to the road towards peace (he had begun to reexamine his attitude to war when his son was severely wounded during Nasser's War of Attrition) and became the most eager advocate of concession and compromise. His conversion brought him a great deal of popular support in Israel and abroad, as well as acclaim in Egypt, but did little to improve his standing among the important Herut Party stalwarts, reviving early doubts about his reliability. They recognized his electoral assets, a natural charm and direct approach to which people responded, but they were nervous about his ideas which, in the words of a Party manager, 'were foreign to Herut.'

A succession of polls in 1979 showed him to be the Israelis' favourite as the next Prime Minister. But popular appeal has not enhanced his standing in the Party – indeed, it has bred resentments and suspicions. On the other hand, it is the business of parties and politicians to gain office and the Herut managers know how good a vote-getter he is. His position is fortified by the belief that the Liberals may not be willing to serve under anyone else than Weizman in the event of Begin's departure. But an image of irresponsibility is still attached to him and may assume greater significance when the moment of decision comes for the voters. One of the Herut managers, Haim Kaufman, who, it will be recalled, also heads the Parliamentary Party, had this to say of Weizman: 'Ezer has annoyed many people by some of his latest statements, but at the same time Herut really needs Weizman no less than he needs Herut. I would strongly recommend to those of his friends who have been urging him to go it alone to drop such ideas. We should start engaging in a mutual courtship.' But political courtship is alien to the character of the irrepressible and often flat-footed Weizman.

He had long chafed at what he regarded as the Begin government's slow motion on the implementation of the Camp David accords and repeatedly threatened to leave it. In a characteristically outspoken letter to Mr Begin, he finally tendered his resignation as Minister of Defence at the end of May 1980. But he remains a major political figure in Israel, unlikely to be out of power for long.

The political weakness of Weizman is that he lacks a power base; the strength of his colleague David Levy, the Minister of Housing, is his potential election-winning power base – the votes of the Sephardim, the poorer sections of Israel's Jewry originating from the Moslem lands of North Africa and the Middle East. The lower-paid Sephardi workers, as well as the young people, look on Levy as one of themselves. He has responded by becoming their voice in high places and this mutual recognition has given him self-confidence and stature. At the time of his appointment to the Cabinet, Levy was not held in high esteem. A typical joke of which he was the butt describes two men meeting and one asking: 'Do you want to hear the latest David Levy story?' The second man replies: 'I am David Levy.' 'OK', says the first man, 'then I'll tell it very slowly.' Another joke had it that when Levy was asked which had been the best five years of his life, he replied: 'The five years I spent in Grade 3.'

But within two years of becoming a Minister, Levy had established himself as an admired and respected leader – and not only by his own community. His meteoric rise was the success story of Herut in power. At the half-term Herut national convention, Levy was chairman of the important steering committee and was selected to propose Begin's re-election to the Chairmanship of the Party.

Born in Rabat, Morocco, in 1938, David Levy emigrated to Israel in 1957. Youthful, with an almost cherubic, open face, he has a warm smile, an engaging personality. In the directory of Knesset Members his occupation is listed as building labourer, but his record of public activity since his arrival in Israel suggests that his building was more political than manual. Like many other North African Jews, he was attracted to Herut because of its strong nationalistic emphasis and because of Labour's failure to deal with the economic and social problems of the underprivileged. His first major job for his party was as Chairman of the Gahal (Herut and Liberals) group in the Histadrut.

In government, Levy quickly emerged as something more than an ethnic spokesman. He became the voice of the proletariat in a predominantly middle-class administration. At a celebration of Herut's second year in power, he said that the Party always had to ask itself whether 'our promise to the voters has been fulfilled. We must remember that we would never have risen to power without the working classes.'

He was alone in the government in opposing the economic policies of the Liberal Finance Minister, Simcha Ehrlich. Many Ministers accepted those policies in principle while negating them in practice. Levy objected in principle, because those most harshly affected were the working classes, Herut's and David Levy's own constituency. Nor has he been afraid of differing in public from Begin. When the Prime Minister proposed an amendment to the law making it possible for the death penalty to be imposed on convicted terrorists, Levy was the lone abstainer in the Government.

Although a newcomer to the Cabinet, he was not content to take a back seat but fought to protect departmental interests where he thought his Ministry (originally Housing alone but later enlarged to include Immigrant Absorption) could do the job better. Such an issue arose in 1979 when Begin proposed to give the Jewish Agency full charge of absorption. Levy fought vigorously for the retention of this function, eventually persuading Begin to withdraw his original plan. It was said that Levy's strongest qualification for being Minister of Immigrant Absorption was that he practises what he preaches – the growth of Israel's population. In 1978, his wife gave birth to their eleventh child.

The top runners

While the two most popular Herut ministers, Weizman and Levy, improved their claims to the leadership, an uncompromising hard-liner on the right was making an appeal to those aspiring to a 'Greater Israel'. Ex-General Ariel (Arik) Sharon, the brash, swashbuckling war hero, was appointed by Begin Minister of Agriculture and Chairman of the Ministerial Settlement Committee. In the latter capacity he has gone ahead with settlements in the occupied territories, to the satisfaction of that section of the population which, distrustful of Arab attitudes, sees settlements as an essential security need. His policy also appealed to those who advanced religio-mystical claims for the retention of territories.

Largely futile attempts, notably by one of the Deputy Prime Ministers, Yigael Yadin, were made to restrain Sharon's enthusiasm for these controversial settlements, which were widely attacked outside Israel as obstacles to peace. However, the *Jerusalem Post* commented in September 1979 that 'the principle seems to have been accepted that, on settlements, whatever Arik wants, Arik more or less gets.'

Born in 1928 on a moshav (agricultural settlement) near Tel Aviv, Sharon joined the Hagana in his teens and later became one of the leading figures in the Israel Defence Forces. He led most of the reprisal actions between 1954 and 1956 and was in command of the paratroops who opened the Sinai campaign in October of that year. Promoted to the rank of

General in 1967, he was one of Israel's youngest senior officers. After the Six Day War, in which he established himself as a brilliant improviser, he was the successful military commander of the Gaza strip, neutralizing the terrorists who had been largely in control and ending the violence that had prevailed.

In the summer of 1973, Sharon had hopes of appointment as Chief of Staff, but this abrasive and individualistic commander had made too many enemies among colleagues and superiors, and he was passed over. In a huff, Sharon resigned his southern front command, announced that he would enter politics and joined the Liberal Party, which was then linked with Herut in Gahal. He immediately urged that if there were to be any chance of defeating the Labour Party, a wider right-wing coalition would have to be formed. As a popular hero – and a valuable political acquisition – Sharon carried weight, and his influence was decisive in the creation of the Likud. He became Begin's Number Two in the new alignment.

Hastily called back to the Army at the outbreak of the Yom Kippur War, Sharon was the initiator and commander of the Suez Canal crossing, a feat which gained him the description of 'the Israeli General Patton'. One of President Sadat's first questions after arriving at Ben Gurion airport four years later was, 'Is General Sharon here?' When introduced to him, the Egyptian leader said: 'I had hoped to catch you on the other side of the Canal,' to which Sharon replied: 'I'm more than glad to be welcoming you here.' After the Yom Kippur War, Sharon was elected on the Likud list but had no patience with what he saw as his Party's 'total divorce from the immediate political realities facing the nation' and resigned. Later he was appointed as an adviser by Yitzhak Rabin, the Labour Prime Minister, but resigned after a few months because he said the Prime Minister had rejected his advice too often.

In 1977, Sharon returned to politics and, finding some of his former colleagues in the Likud unenthusiastic about his return to that political fold, formed his own party, Shlomzion, which won 2 seats with 1.9 per cent of the vote. Almost immediately after the elections, however, the two Shlomzion members joined Herut, and Sharon himself was given Cabinet office. As a Minister he has been a turbulent and controversial figure, often helped out of hot water by the Prime Minister who admires his bounce and fearlessness. He is frequently described as 'Begin's favourite General'. Still boyish, despite his expanding paunch and silver thatch, Sharon radiates dynamic energy. A farmer at heart, he delights in showing off his 1,000-acre farm near Beersheba where he keeps sheep and grows melons. Like almost everything with which he is connected, his farm, too, became controversial. He was twice accused of being the only Cabinet member not to have complied with the rules against Ministerial conflicts of interest, under which he should have disposed of his estate. Criticism was not ended when, after almost three years in office, he 'leased' the farm to its manager.

His standing has not been enhanced in office, but his strong defence orientation and nationalism gave him a following among the most extreme sections of the population. This could become significant were the need for security seen to take precedence over the peace process.

Yaakov Meridor is often mentioned in considering the successor to Begin. He is looked on, at any rate in Herut circles, as a heroic commander of the Irgun. Today he is a business leader with considerable political experience and, having been out of party politics for some years, looks better than many of those who are in. He was born in Poland in 1913, went to Palestine at the age of 19 and joined the Irgun a year later. An intelligent and courageous operator, he participated in some of the most dangerous actions against the British in the pre-State struggle and became Begin's second in command. Captured by the British, he was sent to a detention camp in Africa, from which he escaped five times, the last occasion coinciding with the first day of Israel's existence. When Herut became a political party he was No. 2 on the list of candidates and the deputy leader of the Party in the Knesset, of which he remained a member for twenty-one years. But his heart was not in political factionalism and, in 1953, he and Mila Brener, a Russian Jewish ship's captain, joined forces to found what was to become the multi-million dollar international enterprise, Maritime Fruit Carriers Limited.

Beginning modestly in East Africa, which Meridor knew from the period of his detention, the partners developed the technique of shipping perishable cargoes in refrigerated vessels and eventually controlled a major part of the world's refrigerated shipping business. In 1973 Meridor and Brener were hailed as the 'saviours of British shipbuilding' when they placed orders with British shipyards totalling £500 million. But in 1976, the severe international slump hit them, and they were unable to meet loan repayments. Their indebtedness at the time was estimated at £65 million. MFC was bailed out of bankruptcy, and Meridor was obliged to relinquish control. But not for long. He returned six months later with the aid of Lonrho (a British company with substantial Arab holdings) and began, with signs of success, the long haul to recovery.

He has maintained his interest in Herut. In 1966, he was elected Chairman of the Party Executive and was Deputy Speaker of the Knesset until his resignation from that body in 1969. In that same year the Israelis spirited away from the Cherbourg shipyards five gunboats embargoed by President de Gaulle. Meridor is generally believed to have been the brains behind that skillful enterprise.

After the Begin Government came to power, he took no public part in politics — but he was clearly not forgotten by party colleagues. A contract was given to Meridor (no tenders had been invited) for the construction of homes for new settlers on the West Bank, the total value of which was said to run into millions of dollars. Whether because of sensitivity to criticism on that score, or his aversion to party politics, Meridor has continued his low profile. Party officialdom criticized him for his lack of interest – he has been out of politics for too long. However, with opinions divided about Weizman and Levy, the rank and file could well turn to the man who, because he has been remote, has created fewer enemies.

Yitzak Shamir, a cautious man, quietly established himself as a force in the Government. Appointed Speaker of the Knesset after the Likud victory, a post which is generally regarded as the culmination of a political career rather than as a stepping stone, he was Begin's choice to succeed Moshe Dayan as Foreign Minister. That, too, was surprising, for Shamir abstained, by reason of his hawkish convictions, from the Knesset vote on the Camp David accords. But he subsequently experienced a change of heart and publicly admitted the validity of the Prime Minister's approach and his admiration for Begin's achievement.

He was born in Poland in 1915 and came to Palestine at the age of 20. Two years later he joined the Irgun but left with Avraham Stern in 1941 to form Lehi (Lohamei Herut Israel – Israel Freedom Fighters). After the death of Stern, Shamir was one of the triumvirate who succeeded and, in effect, he became the Commander of the group. He was then arrested by the British, eventually receiving asylum in France and returning to Israel when the State was established.

In Israel, Shamir took no part in public life, and for a time was involved in the activities of the Mossad, Israel's Intelligence agency. He only joined Herut in 1970 and was first elected to the Knesset in 1973. As Speaker of the House, he enjoyed his parliamentary role and was effective in maintaining good order and decorum. Cheerful and optimistic in his general approach, his capacity for quiet and resolute action, his personality and Party loyalty were the probable grounds for his elevation, although he is untried in any senior political post. Were he to make a success of the Foreign Ministry, he would be a strong candidate to succeed Begin as Herut leader.

The Liberals: Ehrlich and Hurvitz

In the beginning, the Israeli Liberals were the General Zionists of the pre-State World Zionist organization. They were not really a party at all, but a vague grouping incorporating all those Zionists who were not committed to religion (Mizrachi), Socialism (Labour Party), or militant nationalism (Revisionist Party). The non-ideological General Zionists constituted for many years by far the largest section of world Zionism and, at the twelfth Zionist Congress in 1921, they accounted for 73 per cent of delegates. But, as the ideological parties became stronger, particularly through their practical achievements in Palestine, the General Zionists declined. In an effort to give themselves an ideological position, the organization split in 1935. The liberal wing became General Zionists A, and the conservatives General Zionists B.

With the creation of the State, the General Zionists A (with some small fringe groupings) became the Progressive Party, winning 5 seats in the first election. General Zionists B went to the polls without changing their name and gained 7 seats. Later they became the General Zionist Party, emerging as the party of the centre, conservative at home and pro-Western in foreign affairs. It gained strength, winning no fewer than 20 seats in the following elections, while the Progressives slipped to 4. But as the new State's political set-up crystallized into a broad division between Labour and the right-wing Herut Party, the General Zionists lost ground. By 1959 they had only 8 Knesset seats and the Progressives 6. The Progressives were on the whole sympathetic to the Labour Party's social welfare programme and were generally within the Government's coalition. So were the General Zionists for two brief periods in the 1950s.

By 1961, the Labour Party was at a low ebb, with Ben-Gurion's appeal seriously affected by his obsession with intra-party rivalries. The General Zionists and Progressives believed that this was the time to create a credible alternative to Labour and reunited to form the Liberal Party. In that year's elections the new party won 17 Knesset seats, the same number as Herut. Neither was strong enough to challenge Labour, and, inevitably, Herut and the Liberals moved together to form the political bloc called Gahal. But since Herut was too radical for some of the Progressives, they broke away to found the Independent Liberal Party. The rump Independent Liberals continued to support the Labour coalition, while Gahal, outside it except for its participation in the wall-to-wall coalition created by the Six Day War, constituted the effective opposition. Tarnished by their participation in the discredited Labour administration, the Independent Liberals were virtually wiped out in the 1977 elections, winning one solitary seat. The Liberal faction in Gahal, now the Likud, did much better. It was an important element in the Government and its leader, Simcha Ehrlich, became Minister of Finance, with the opportunity of putting into practice the free-enterprise concepts long advocated by his Party.

LIBERAL PARTY CHART

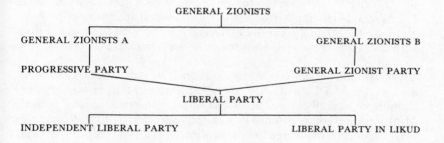

Ehrlich, who has led the Liberal Party since 1971, was born in Poland in 1915 and emigrated to Palestine in 1938. His first political office was as a member of the Tel Aviv Municipal Council, to which he was elected in 1955. He advanced in office and became Deputy Mayor, simultaneously moving up in the National Secretariat of the Liberal Party and becoming a member of the Executive Committee of Gahal when it was formed in 1965. At the same time, he was painstakingly building up his own business in optical instruments.

He was the obvious Minister of Finance for the Likud Government both because his economic principles coincided with the conservative approach of his Herut partners, and because of his own reputation as a sound and experienced man of affairs. Ehrlich did, indeed, free some of the bonds placed on the economy by his Socialist predecessors, but found that the essential corollary of expenditure cuts was effectively resisted by his Cabinet colleagues. Time after time he proposed economic measures intended to counter rapidly rising inflation, only to find sectional interests preventing their application.

By mid-1979, Ehrlich had become so closely identified with the sickness of the economy, that he himself realized he had become a liability to the Government. He offered his resignation to Begin, with whom he had established a friendship, probably the closest to intimacy the Prime Minister allowed himself with any of his colleagues. Begin refused at first to accept it, but as the economy continued to deteriorate, he did so some three months later. Ehrlich was succeeded by Yigal Hurvitz of the La'am faction, and the former Finance Minister retired to the Government sidelines as an additional Deputy Prime Minister.

One of the reasons the Liberal Party did not succeed in retaining the Finance portfolio for one of its other representatives was a split within the Party. The only other Liberal with a claim to the job was the Energy Minister, Yitzhak Modai, but he failed to mobilize enough support in his own Party to promote his candidature. A number of his younger fellow members wanted Hurvitz.

However, the dogged Ehrlich continued as leader of his Party. He had been a disaster as Finance Minister but there was widespread appreciation that his intentions had been frustrated by his blinkered Cabinet colleagues and also because of the unwillingness of the Prime Minister to take a strong line. Ehrlich remains a respected and trusted figure. Jovial and accessible, he has retained a simple style of living in his modest apartment in Tel Aviv. His business is being successfully managed by his wife, son and daughter while he continues to devote himself to the declining Liberal Party.

Yigal Hurvitz, the leader of the small La'am faction in the Likud federation and originally a Labour Party member, became Minister for Industry, Commerce and Tourism when the Begin Government was formed. Ministerial resignations on issues of principle have been uncommon in Israel, and Hurvitz emerged as a man of integrity when, in September 1978, he resigned because of his opposition to the peace treaty with Egypt, being adamantly opposed to the removal of the Israeli settlements in Sinai. But he remained a Member of the Knesset and, a year later, when it was obvious that Ehrlich had to go, a consensus emerged that Hurvitz would be the best man for the Finance job.

While he was driving up to Jerusalem to assume the stewardship of the Treasury, a taxi-driver whose vehicle stopped alongside his at a traffic light, called through the window: 'Mr Yigal, what's it to be, better or worse?' 'Worse,' he replied laconically. 'Very good,' responded the taxi driver, 'about time.'

Appointed by Begin in October 1979, Hurvitz assumed the responsibilities of Minister of Finance under daunting conditions. But he was virtually 'drafted' because the public – and the Prime Minister – recognized that, stubborn and honest as he is, he might be strong enough to overrule

Ministers, each fighting for more money for his own Department while supporting the idea of cuts in general. Hurvitz knew that the Government could not afford another Ehrlich and used the leverage of the political climate to impose himself on his colleagues. The public responded, and the early months of his appointment brought an improvement in the economic climate. A psychological success was his strong backing for Avraham Shavit, the newly appointed boss of El Al, who threatened to close the airline if grossly overpaid personnel did not accept wage cuts. The employees capitulated and firm handling was seen to bring results.

If Hurvitz were to prove able to handle state finance as he handled his own, the country could be optimistic. A farmer from a moshav, he took the opportunity afforded him to take over a bankrupt dairy farm in the 'sixties and, after only a few years, he achieved a tremendous success. In 1978, the turnover of his business – it is not a public company – was about US $35 million and the gross profit not less than three million. He achieved this result because he is obstinate, hard-working and decisive. He has strong views which he has developed himself and not acquired from books, for he has a limited education and little culture.

On the subject of the occupied territories and the need for Israel to retain them, he is a super hawk. His views were clearly publicized by his 1978 resignation and came to the fore again after his move to the Ministry of Finance. Asked about the vast proposed expenditure on settlements as being contrary to his general policy of Budget-cutting, he replied that there had to be money for 'vital purposes of state'. An abrasive personality, he undauntedly claimed that he was not in the job to be popular, but to save the country from an 'economic holocaust'.

Chapter four

Clericalists

The religious parties

Religion is important in many aspects of life in Israel and nowhere more so than in politics, where the religious political parties form the third of the three major party groupings. Apart from the first elections, they have not united to form a single list, like the components of the Likud and the ILP. They present themselves to the electorate on three lists, the National Religious Party (NRP) (in Hebrew, Mafdal, made up of the initials of Miflagah Datit Leumit), Agudat Israel and Poalei Agudat Israel. In the ninth Knesset (elected in 1977) the NRP had 12 seats, and the two smaller parties 4 and 1 respectively, a total of 17. While the vote for the secular parties has fluctuated, the religious parties have maintained their electoral support with a remarkable degree of stability. In every one of the nine Knessets, they have attracted between 12 and 15 per cent of the vote, bringing them between 15 and 18 seats.

All the religious parties profess orthodox Judaism, for Conservative and Reform Judaism are not strongly represented in Israel, and have never shown any interest in the formation of a specific political party. On the other hand, the 12 to 15 per cent who vote for the religious parties are not the total number of all observant orthodox Jews in Israel. How many there are is not known with any precision but the occasional polls conducted by the Israel Broadcasting Authority give a clue. These show that about 30 per cent of their regular audience do not listen to the radio on Saturdays, the Jewish Sabbath, when observant Jews would not operate any electrical equipment. The figure may be marginally increased by the zealots of the extreme right, Neturei Karta (Guardians of the City), who do not recognize the secular State of Israel, do not vote at all and probably never listen to the radio either.

The NRP was created in 1956 by a merger of two factions of Mizrachi, which had been the religious element in the Zionist movement since the beginning of the century. The pre-State slogan of Mizrachi was, 'The Land of Israel for the people of Israel according to the Torah of Israel' (Torah consists of the Biblical injunctions as interpreted and applied by Jewish religious leaders through the ages). The other two religious parties, Agudat Israel and its offshoot Poalei ('workers of') Agudat Israel differ from the NRP in being opposed to some aspects of Zionist ideology and in their more extreme attitudes on religious matters.

When the State of Israel was formed, the Mizrachi Zionist party combined with the Aguda groups to present a United Religious List for the first elections in 1949 and joined the first coalition government. Soon afterwards, however, the Aguda left both the United Religious List and the Government, while Mizrachi (later the NRP) stayed to become an almost permanent member of the Government.

That Israel was to be a secular state was made abundantly clear in the Declaration of Independence proclaimed on 14 May 1948. The new State would, in its words, be 'based on freedom, justice and peace as envisaged by the prophets of Israel . . .' It would, moreover, 'guarantee freedom of religion, conscience, language and culture.'

During the drafting of the Declaration, the religious representatives strongly urged that it contain at least a reference to the Deity. The secularist majority, intent to avoid any suspicion of a theocracy, would go no further than to insert a reference, in the last paragraph of the Declaration, to 'Placing our trust in the Rock of Israel' (the term 'Rock of Israel' is often employed in the Hebrew liturgy as a synonym for God).

Despite their commitment to a Jewish State based on Torah, none of the religious parties seriously advocates that Israel should be governed according to orthodox Jewish law. This is due not only to their minority position, but also to an uncomfortable (though unspoken) awareness that enormous changes would have to be made to the ancient laws before they could become applicable to the needs of a modern state. For the religious parties to admit this would be unthinkable. It is a heresy of the most fundamental kind, for orthodox Jewish doctrine holds that the laws of the Torah are immutable. But although the religious parties have, to all intents and purposes, abandoned the idea of a state *governed* by orthodox Jewish law, they have always promoted their idea of a state based on Torah.

To do so, they concentrated their efforts in two main directions – education and the Knesset. They reasoned that because a Jewish state based on Torah could only come about with the support of the majority of the population, their long-term programme must be to educate the young in the spirit of orthodox Judaism. For this purpose, they established a comprehensive network of schools and used their political weight to strengthen them.

Secondly, they acted to promote laws in the Knesset to preserve the status of orthodoxy as the only recognized form of religious Judaism and to legislate for specific religious interests, such as Sabbath observance. They also used their political power to prevent legislation which would directly conflict with orthodox Jewish law or interests, such as the introduction of civil marriage and divorce.

The considerable achievements of the religious parties in both these areas were made possible by the operation of Israel's electoral system. The effect of proportional representation, as we have seen, has been to encourage a multiplicity of parties represented in the Knesset and coalitions have become the norm. Until 1977, Labour led all the coalitions and the religious parties were its most constant partner, the NRP being in the Government since the State was created except for only two short periods. The first was in 1958–59 when the NRP left the Government on the 'Who is a Jew' issue, and the second, about six months in 1976–77, when they were excluded by Rabin for having abstained on a no-confidence motion in the Knesset. They came back as members of the Begin coalition in 1977. The participation of the Agudist groups in the Government has been erratic. After the 1977 election, Agudat Israel, with 4 seats, joined Begin's coalition while Poalei Agudat Israel, with its single seat, did not.

The religious parties, particularly the NRP with its substantial block of seats, are attractive coalition partners to the major party in power whose prime concerns are foreign affairs, defence and economic policy. An alliance with the religious parties gives coalition leaders a free hand on these issues and, in return, the Government supports special religious interests, which they regard as a reasonable price to pay.

Before the formation of every coalition, the leader of the largest group in the Knesset undertakes negotiations with all smaller groupings which could be possible partners. The minorities present their lists of demands, which become the basis for generally protracted negotiations. The terms the minority groups are able to secure depend on whether there is a seller's or buyer's market, for the weaker the major party, the greater will be the demands of the smaller parties in return for their votes.

The NRP and Aguda groups demanded a high price for their support of the Begin Government. The Likud had won 45 seats and could attract a few oddities like Flatto-Sharon (see p. 29), but to form a workable majority, Begin needed the support of one of the three large blocs, Labour with its 32 seats, the DMC with 15, and the 17 shared by the religious parties. Ideological differences and the resulting disagreements over policy put an alliance with Labour out of the question while DMC insisted on changes in the electoral system which Begin was not ready to concede. (Later the DMC did enter the Government, but not on its original terms.) He therefore had no choice but a coalition with the religious parties and they drove a hard bargain.

The 1977 coalition agreement

In terms of Israeli coalition-bargaining, the 1977 agreement did not take long to negotiate. It was signed between the Likud, the NRP and the Aguda on 19 June 1977, only a month after the election. The text of the agreement provided for an eight-member coalition executive to 'decide and direct the coalition activity and the voting of its members in the Knesset and its committees', to be made up of five Likud representatives, two of NRP and one from Agudat Israel. The document comprised forty-three paragraphs of varying degrees of significance, with the nub of the conditions of the religious parties in the following clauses (the numbered paragraphs are quoted from the agreement, parenthetical observations that follow are the author's):

6. The government will provide for the spiritual and social absorption of immigrants. Steps will be taken to facilitate the absorption of religious immigrants. Religious immigrants will receive housing in accordance with the usual privileges, in an environment suitable both regarding the services they require and a congenial religious atmosphere.

(This was designed to ensure the continuation and expansion of the orthodox residential enclaves and the availability of funds for this purpose.)

7. Enforcement of Paragraph 179 of the Criminal Law Ordinance 1936 will be strictly adhered to. The paragraph prohibits publication of pornographic pictures and their distribution, sale, exhibition etc. and the printing of pornographic literature, its distribution, sale etc. Should the existing law fail to achieve this aim, amendments to it will be legalised.

8. Since conversion is a Halachic concept, the Law of Return will be amended to establish that conversion is according to the Halacha. Knesset members of the coalition will table a Private Bill which will state that [the only] conversion [accepted will be carried out] according to the Halacha and that the Rabbinical Court will be the body authorised to approve the validity of any conversion certificate issued abroad. The Prime Minister will make every endeavour to mobilise a parliamentary majority for these bills. The former Minister of Internal Affairs [Dr Burg] said that, to the best of his knowledge, no non-Jew has been considered a Jew since the amendment to the Law of Return was passed seven years ago, and the Government will act similarly in the future.

(A long unresolved issue was the status *vis-à-vis* the Law of Return (see p. 208) of individuals converted to Judaism in Conservative and Reform synagogues in the diaspora. The orthodox do not regard these converts as Jews 'according to the Halacha' (Rabbinical Jewish Law) and they have endeavoured to achieve legislative sanction for their position. Previous governments had declined and, in this clause, Begin committed himself only to 'make every endeavour', etc. Whatever endeavour he may have made, by early 1980 no legislation had been presented to the Knesset on this issue.)

9. The Anatomy and Pathology Law (1953) will be amended to prohibit post-mortem examinations without written permission by the family even if the requirements set down by the present law have been met. If a person has objected in writing to a post-mortem being performed on his body, his wish shall be respected, even if his family agree to the operation.

(This sets out the Aguda attitude towards autopsies in which the NRP acquiesces. The subject has long agitated extreme orthodoxy which strongly objects to the mutilation of a corpse. Two years after this agreement, when neither this clause nor clause 19, which pledged an amendment to the Abortion Law, had been implemented, the Aguda threatened to leave the coalition unless appropriate legislation was passed. The Abortion Law was amended (see clause 19 which follows) but the autopsy situation remained in suspense and the Aguda continued to support the Government.)

10. Legislation will ensure that no person is to suffer discrimination in engagement, advancement and continuation at work due to his wish to observe the Sabbath.

12. Stoppage of public transport before the onset of Saturday or a public holiday will be ensured, as well as non-resumption of public transport before the end of Saturday or a holiday, maintaining the *status quo* on this subject.

(The *status quo* is a central dogma in Israel's religio-political attitudes. It is discussed in the next section.)

19. Since the penal code amendment 1977 [discontinuation of pregnancy] deviates from the religious *status quo*, it will be amended by rescinding paragraph 5 (a) (5) which permits discontinuation of pregnancy 'due to familial or social hardship of the woman or her environment'.

(Late in 1979, the Agudat Israel threatened to leave the coalition if this clause were not implemented. By applying the strictest party discipline, a bill was pushed through the Knesset, by a vote of 55 to 50, amending the Abortion Law by deleting the paragraph cited above. It did little for the popularity of religion in Israel, but kept the Government intact.)

21. Steps will be taken to grant equal rights to the legal independent school system, including all levels – pre-school, post-elementary and state educational seminars – at the same time preserving and ensuring educational autonomy. Steps will be taken to remedy malfeasance regarding construction of buildings for the independent school system and to bring buildings of the independent school system to a standard equal to that of buildings of the state educational system as soon as possible.

(This Clause obliges the Government to give money to Aguda schools without imposing any restrictions on their independent control.)

27. A girl who submits a declaration that a religious way of life or a religious family life prevent her from serving in the armed forces, and whose declaration is confirmed by a Rabbinical Court will be exempt from military service on the basis of her declaration alone, without any additional examination by any committee or other body.

(Considerable public outcry followed the announcement of this concession which was a potentially serious blow to the Women's Corps of the Army. Religious girls had previously been exempt, but some evidence of their religious commitment had been required. Since this agreement they have become exempted 'on the basis of her declaration alone'. This too is an issue more important to the Aguda than to the NRP.)

37. The government will show consideration for the special needs of the religious and observant public, as follows: Yeshivot, including Yeshiva students, Tora scholars and Metiftot, a Tora lesson network for adults and youth, hospitals, Mikvaot [ritual baths] and synagogues.

(The consideration to be shown was predominantly financial.)

To the participants in the negotiations, not the least significant area of negotiations was the portfolios to be allotted to them. The importance to Begin of NRP's support was demonstrated by the Ministries it gained. They were the Ministry of the Interior (combined with Police, which had previously been a separate Ministry) and the Ministry for Religious Affairs, both traditionally NRP spheres of interest. But this time they gained an important additional portfolio, the Ministry of Education and Culture.

The Ministry of the Interior maintains the registers of nationality, religious and marital status. Administratively, orthodox control of this Ministry has ensured that no person is registered as a Jew unless he is recorded as such by the orthodox controllers (see clause 8 of the Coalition

Agreement). The Ministry also controls the finances of local government and has been able to influence the use of these funds for religious and religious party purposes. The Ministry of Religious Affairs controls the rabbinical establishment and provides subsidies to religious institutions. NRP's gain of the Ministry of Education was a great achievement for the Party because of its intense religious involvement in education. Apart from the substantive advantages of achieving the implementation of party policies, control of a Ministry places in the hands of the party the gift of jobs, patronage and subsidies.

Agudat Israel was permitted by its spiritual authority, the 'Council of Torah Sages', to join the coalition but not to accept any Ministry. Nevertheless, all four Aguda MKs received other appointments. Two were made chairmen of Knesset committees, one of them, Finance, being probably the most important of all, and the other Welfare and Labour. Another Agudist became a Deputy Speaker of the Knesset, while the fourth became a member of its Foreign Affairs and Security Committee.

In local elections the system of proportional representation has made it difficult for a single party to win a majority of places on municipalities and local councils. They therefore follow the national pattern and form local coalitions in which the NRP almost invariably participates, whatever the political complexion of their coalition partners. It has most frequently been in alliance with Labour, but the NRP and Aguda have also participated in coalitions led by the Likud, the Liberals and even the very left-wing Mapam.

In each case, as on the national level, a coalition agreement is drawn up, and the pattern for that, too, has been standardized. It includes the appointment of a religious nominee as a deputy mayor, provision of jobs for NRP and Aguda supporters, the enactment of local ordinances on Sabbath observance and the dietary laws, and agreement on the amount of the grant to the local religious council.

The status quo

An unwritten, undefined, principle which has had a far greater influence on contemporary Judaism in Israel than any written or oral law of Moses is that of the 'status quo in religious affairs'.

Five days after the State of Israel was proclaimed and before any legislative machinery had been set in motion, the Provisional Council of State promulgated its first ordinance, that on law and administration. To avoid a legal interregnum between the ending of the British Mandate and the enactment of new laws by the State of Israel, the existing law courts were given authority to continue to function within their existing powers.

The Mandatory government had inherited from its predecessor, the Ottoman empire, what was called the 'millet system'. This gave all the religious communities in Palestine virtual autonomy in matters of personal status – marriage and divorce primarily – to be administered through their own court systems. The British Mandatory authority continued the system and the Israel ordinance of 1948 meant that personal status questions remained the province of the religious and not the secular authorities. That was the first and precedent-setting acceptance of the religious *status quo* which has prevailed throughout Israel's existence. It has been the base on which subsequent legislation has not only preserved the rabbinical courts and given them exclusive jurisdiction in personal status matters, but has maintained the rabbinic judges, rabbis and an extensive range of religious services at the public expense.

The *status quo* principle has been of immense benefit to orthodoxy in Israel and the concept, zealously protected by them, has been extended to local enactments and public services. In Israel today all public transport is prohibited on the Sabbath – except in Haifa where, during the Mandatory period, the powerful Mapai-controlled municipality, in the absence of a strong body of orthodox residents, insisted that the local bus service would operate. The *status quo* doctrine ensured that this pre-State arrangement was perpetuated.

Ben-Gurion who, as first Prime Minister of Israel, agreed to honour the *status quo* and sanctify it, explained in a newspaper interview that he felt, 'in the national interest, that it was wise to pay the comparatively small price of religious status quo.' Whether he equated 'national interest' with his own Party's interest in remaining in power or whether it was, as he regarded it, the avoidance of *Kulturkampf* (war of cultures) is open to dispute. But today the non-religious supporters of the *status quo* argue in its favour that it protects a threatened nation from the divisiveness of religious controversy.

As applied by the religious parties, the *status quo* has acquired a 'heads I win, tails you lose' quality. It has invariably been used to protect what already exists, but has never been invoked when further religious gains seemed possible. The religious parties edged forward in 1953 when the jurisdiction of the religious courts was extended to cover all Jews permanently resident in Israel. In Mandatory Palestine they had covered only Palestinian nationals and members of the Jewish community. The religious *status quo* was also breached when the Knesset extended religious legislation to cover the breeding of pigs and the sale of pig products (pigs are prohibited animals under the dietary laws) while the 1977 coalition agreement incorporated further extension of religious influence in the life of Israel.

At the same time, the *status quo* principle continued to be used to block what was regarded as anti-religious legislation. In 1979, the Minister for Religious Affairs won a vote in the Knesset to remove from the agenda a Private Member's Bill for the introduction of civil marriage. He argued that 'a delicate equilibrium had been observed by all Governments over the *status quo* in religious affairs . . . the Bill's sponsors want to damage the basic structure of Jewish life by upsetting that equilibrium.'

National Religious Party

The largest, most important and best organized of the religious parties in Israel is the National Religious Party (NRP), a merger of two groups, Mizrachi and Hapoel Hamizrachi. They had been parties in the World

Zionist Organization before the State came into existence. Both are dedicated to the religious life, but the Hapoel group is younger in its membership and social democratic in its policies. By the time of the merger in 1956, Hapoel Hamizrachi was the strongest religious party in Israel and became the dominant element in the NRP, although having to bide its time until the departure of the old leadership. In spite of the merger, each of the two groups maintains a separate existence and some independence.

The NRP has been notably stable in its share of Knesset seats and has been a regular member of Labour coalitions. After the Six Day War of 1967, the NRP for the first time moved into a situation of conflict with its ILP allies on a general political issue. Under the influence of its 'Young Guard', vigorous young leaders like Zvulun Hammer and Yehuda Ben-Meir, the NRP asserted, as did the Likud, Israel's claim to the occupied territories. Succumbing to the pressure of its younger extremists and with the old-guard leadership much weakened by the death in 1970 of the respected head of the party, Moshe Shapiro, the NRP as a whole opposed concessions in what it regarded as the God-covenanted land of Israel.

As this issue grew in significance, the position of the NRP in the government coalition became increasingly uncomfortable and the alliance eventually broke under the strain. The breaking point was comparatively trivial. On Friday, 10 December 1976, Israel received the first three F-15 fighter aircraft from the USA. Israelis, who had not had much to celebrate at that period, decided to make a fuss of their arrival and a distinguished welcoming committee, headed by Prime Minister Rabin, waited at the military airfield. Alas, the planes landed about twenty minutes late, and the ceremony ended only fifteen minutes before sundown when the Sabbath began. The result was that no visitor could return home without desecrating the Sabbath, since travelling is prohibited on the day of rest.

The religious parties were horrified at this official act of Sabbath-breaking and the Aguda proposed a motion of no confidence. Two of the three NRP Ministers were sufficiently sympathetic to abstain, and two days later, in an unusually decisive action, Rabin dismissed all the NRP Ministers. Since his coalition had no Parliamentary majority without them, the Prime Minister submitted his own resignation the following day.

To some extent, these events helped the NRP in the 1977 elections, for it could now present itself to the electorate as an opposition party, distancing itself from its erstwhile partner, the discredited ILP. To give itself an electoral face-lift, it expelled a powerful Party leader, Yitzhak Raphael, who had been tarnished by corruption allegations some years before. The Party had been uncomfortable with him ever since the allegations had been publicized, but he had nevertheless been able to remain at the top. His expulsion was a demonstration of the strength of the young party leaders, headed by Hammer.

As a Party, the NRP is fortified by a network of economic enterprises, including a bank, cooperatives and housing estates. Its religious school system is now State-maintained, but the Party sponsors its own higher education establishments, one of them being Bar Ilan University. It has its own kibbutzim and moshavim and has gained wide approbation for its youth movement, Bnei Akiva. Because of its permanent tenancy of the Ministry for Religious Affairs, the Party controls the Chief Rabbinate and the large rabbinical establishment. Its power of patronage is augmented by the jobs and finances available to religious institutions through the NRP occupancy of the Ministry of the Interior. Its supporters in the diaspora constitute a further source of strength to the party. Throughout the Jewish world, organized groups of Mizrachi members are affiliated to the World Mizrachi Movement, which is dominated by the NRP. The funds raised by these affiliates and the political pressure they can bring to bear are major assets to the Israeli political party.

Because it has shared the responsibility of government, the NRP tends to look at religio-political issues far more realistically than the Aguda groups, and as a result is constantly accused of compromising religious issues in order to keep positions in the Government. The NRP is, indeed, often battered between the pressure from its coalition leaders for collective responsibility and the attacks of the extremist religious groups, to whose charges of retreat from true orthodoxy the NRP is most sensitive.

The Party became well content with its position in the Begin Government. Its leaders were happier with Begin's attitude to the occupied territories than they were with Labour's but, above all, they approved of Begin's positive attitude to Jewish tradition. Their cup of happiness was filled when the Aguda joined the coalition because that meant the Aguda would in turn become identified with Government decisions and would no longer be able to attack the NRP from outside. But the situation also involved further finessing on the part of the NRP. One of its leaders has said: 'We don't publicly object to Aguda demands on abortion and about girls in the army because we can't afford to be seen as less interested in these religious issues than they are. But we don't work at it.'

The formal leadership of the party resides in a body of sixty called Hanhalat Hamiflagot (Executive of the Parties). Its members are elected (or more often nominated by agreement and without election) by the local parties. A few places are reserved for women and, as in the case of the ILP, a weighted proportion is allocated to the aristocracy of workers in each kibbutz and moshav affiliated to the party. The Parliamentary Party is officially bound by the decisions of the Hanhala but, in fact, it can do as it likes because the Parliamentary group has the power to interpret the decisions. And its combination of political and rabbinic expertise is capable of interpreting almost any decision out of existence. Political decisions, when the need for them arises, are also made by the Parliamentary Party, but on major issues it may call for the support or guidance of the Hanhala.

The unofficial inner cabinet of the Party consists of the three NRP Ministers, Dr Yosef Burg (Interior and Police), Aharon Abuhatzera (Religious Affairs) and Zvulun Hammer (Education and Culture), together with the party's Secretary-General, Danny Vermus, and Rafael Ben Natan of Hapoel Hamizrachi.

Ben Natan is the veteran NRP 'apparatchik', the backroom organization man, close to Dr Burg, the leader of the Party. He is the most powerful man in the Party machine and on one occasion told reporters, 'It doesn't matter even if they made me the switchboard operator, I'd still be running everything.' His political attitudes are those of the old-style, moderate leadership, epitomized by Dr Burg, ready to compromise in order to achieve gradual advances. He is uncomfortable with the uncompromising brashness of the new young troika of Hammer, Ben-Meir and Vermus, and believes that the NRP will eventually return to its centrist position.

Vermus is a much younger man than Ben Natan and his counterpart as the machine man of the NRP Young Guard. Appointed Secretary-General of the Party in 1978, he has proved to be a competent organizer and the *eminence grise* of the younger leadership who believe that the future of the Party rests with them. But as the militants of the 'sixties settled down into an establishment of their own, the competition between the Vermus and the Ben Natan groups became more evenly poised.

NRP Ministers

Yosef Burg is the most senior member of Israel's government, both in years and length of Ministerial service. Born in Germany in 1909, he was ordained a rabbi there and came to Palestine in 1939. Ten years later, after working through the political ranks, he became a Member of the Knesset, and he is still there. He obtained his first Cabinet post in 1951 as Minister of Health and, except during the short absences of the NRP from the Government, has held portfolios ever since.

He was the most seasoned member of the Begin Government and the most politically experienced leader of his Party. This pragmatic, deft politician has survived the virtual take-over of the Party by its younger leadership to become its most respected public figure. That situation owes a great deal to the personality of the man himself.

Jovial is perhaps the best word to describe him. A portly, stolid figure, never seen without the skull-cap of the orthodox Jew, Burg takes pride in his reputation as a wit and raconteur. His English is fluent and he is delighted when he can illustrate his proficiency in the language by playing with words. He loves telling stories, particularly those about the Jews of the southern Polish province of Galicia, who are the butt of many jokes, much as the Irish are in Britain. For, although Burg was born in Germany, his roots are in Galicia and he is much closer to the extrovert, jolly, rather crafty Galician personality than to the more solid qualities generally attributed to German Jews.

On religious issues, he tends to be a moderate, although always careful not to cross the line which would make his orthodoxy suspect to his more religiously fervent colleagues. His style of public speaking is witty and down-to-earth, interwoven with good stories, rabbinic homilies and the use of Yiddish. It has made him very popular with Jewish audiences in the English-speaking world and he spends much time on fund-raising tours. Impressed by his experience and flexibility as well as by his reliability in carrying out Cabinet decisions, Prime Minister Begin appointed Burg (over the head of the then Foreign Minister, Moshe Dayan, the obvious choice) as chairman of Israel's top negotiating team in the talks with Egypt on the nature of Arab autonomy in the occupied territories.

The NRP is loosely divided into three wings. On the right are the hawks, those who believe they are performing the Divine Will in retaining and settling the whole of the Biblical Land of Israel. This group is led by two Knesset members, Rabbi Haim Druckman (born in Poland in 1933) and Yehuda Ben-Meir (born in New York in 1939), both of whom are close to the powerful pressure group of Gush Emunim (Bloc of the Faithful). Zvulun Hammer is in their camp too. A second, small, doveish group, ready to relinquish post-1967 territory, is led by former Minister of Religious Affairs, Zerach Warhaftig (born in Poland in 1906), respected as an old-timer but with little influence, and Avraham Melamed (born in Lithuania in 1923). Both are MKs and lawyers. Dr Burg sees himself as the leader of the third, majority, grouping of middle-of-the-roaders.

Zvulun Hammer and Yehuda Ben-Meir have for some years been leaders of the 'Young Turks' of the NRP. Within the Party, the obstacle to the second generation's succession to the leadership was essentially Yitzhak Raphael, an experienced, though discredited, veteran in control of the Party machine. Hammer and Ben-Meir believed that if the Party were to be given new leadership and a new image, Raphael would have to go, and 1977 was the year in which they struck. By choosing a time when change was in the air and waiting until they had built up their strength in the Party, they succeeded in ousting Raphael from the electoral list. That achievement marked the two younger men as the coming powers in the Party.

They present contrasts in manner and appearance. Ben-Meir is saturnine and dark-jowelled. He often exhibits a scowl like a young Walter Matthau and talks with the rough forceful tones of an aggressive New Yorker. Hammer, whose English is halting, is altogether a softer personality. Born in 1935 in Haifa, he first became a Member of the Knesset in 1969 after service in the Six Day War as a tank officer. He studied at Bar Ilan University, qualified as a teacher and became a leader of the NRP youth movement, Bnei Akiva.

In the Knesset, the youthful Hammer was the leader of the young Party activists who chafed at the monopoly of power held by the old guard and objected to their compromises of principle induced by love of office. Hammer achieved his first success at the 1973 Party convention – he was then 38 – when his group, which had won 23 per cent of the vote, openly challenged the old leadership and achieved the passage of a number of resolutions calling for a tougher line on territorial and religious issues.

He is ideologically close to the Gush Emunim, but practical enough to know when the 'limits of the possible' have been reached. An affable man, his gentleness of manner and appearance belies a political manoeuvrer of the first order and, although he rode to power on the support of the extremists, he is political enough to recognize that future success will depend on his avoidance of diehard attitudes. Office has tempered Hammer. He has acquired the *gravitas* and moderation of a statesman. His views are not known to have changed but, as the first NRP Minister of Education and Culture, he has proceeded cautiously in introducing more religion into the non-religious schools.

The youngest of the three NRP Ministers in the Begin Government, Aharon Abuhatzera, was born in a small town in the Sahara area of Morocco in 1938 and came to Israel in 1949. In 1977, he and David Levy (the Likud Minister of Housing) became the first Moroccan Jews to reach Cabinet rank.

Moroccan Jews in Israel, an important group of voters, tend to be underprivileged and undereducated. The Minister for Religious Affairs is neither, for he was born into a distinguished family of rabbis. His grandfather, Yakov Abuhatzera, was a revered Cabbalist, and his tomb in Egypt is still a place of pilgrimage for both Jews and Moslems. Aharon, like many other Moroccan Jews, emigrated to Israel almost immediately after the State was declared; most of them pious and observant, they saw in the re-creation of the Jewish State the divine ingathering of the exiles.

In Israel at the age of 10, Aharon went to school and then Bar Ilan University, where he studied history. After graduation he became a teacher at the state religious high school in Ramla. When he was 31, he was elected Mayor of the town, the youngest in the country at that time; elected to the Knesset on the NRP list in 1973, he was reelected in 1977. As Minister for Religious Affairs, he occupies an austere office in one of the red civic buildings in Jerusalem's Russian compound. It is a typical run-down colonial administration office, linoleum on the floor, paint-smeared rather than painted, plaster walls, simple utilitarian furniture and a profusion of metal filing cabinets.

The Minister is youthful-looking, slim, dark-haired and thickly be-spectacled. An open, toothy smile smoothes over conversational gaps when his limited English becomes inadequate. Still a comparative novice as a Cabinet Minister and Party leader, he is overshadowed by his senior colleagues. However, his time will come, and his progress will be helped by his sense of humour. Like all his predecessors in office, he has been forced to contend with the problem of the two Chief Rabbis who do not speak to each other. 'Yes,' he said with a grin and his eyes brightened, 'I had to knock heads together. Being from a rabbinical family, I know how to handle rabbis – it's more delicate than politics.'

Aguda

The two wings of Agudat Israel (Association of Israel) came about in the same way as the division of Mizrachi into the party proper and a younger, more social democratic wing called Hapoel Hamizrachi. In Mizrachi, both wings eventually fused to form the NRP, but in the Aguda movement they have remained separate and occasionally go different ways. They did so after the 1977 elections. Agudat Israel, courted by Begin who needed their 4 Knesset votes, decided to join the coalition, but the Poalei Agudat Israel stayed out.

World Agudat Israel came into existence at a convention in 1912. It was a reaction by orthodox Jews against the secularization of Jewish life by the Zionists, and Agudist opposition was also directed at the religious Zionist movement, Mizrachi, which had been founded ten years earlier. The initiative and leadership of the Aguda movement came originally from the Westernized, neo-orthodox, anti-Zionist Jews of Germany, but by the outbreak of World War II it was receiving the bulk of its backing and leadership from the less sophisticated Jewish masses of Eastern Europe.

Although both Mizrachi and Aguda professed the same traditional Judaism, they differed on socio-economic lines. Much of Aguda's support came from the rabidly anti-Zionist Hassidic oligarchy, who vehemently rejected Zionism because of its irreligious leadership, but also for the movement's presumption in usurping the function of the Messiah. Aguda shared with Zionism a common desire to settle Jews in the Holy Land, but was expressly non-political. Those Agudists who went to live in the Holy Land did so because it was a *mitzva*, a religious obligation, and once there, they separated themselves from the Zionist pioneers and objected to the revival of colloquial Hebrew as a profanation of the holy tongue. Both in Palestine and the diaspora they conducted an intensive and bitter propaganda against Zionism and particularly Mizrachi.

The rise of Nazism and the realization that Palestine offered a refuge to its victims brought about a fundamental shift in Agudist policy. Heretofore, they had had no truck with those who were creating the agricultural settlements, industries, institutions and defence forces that were to be the foundations of a self-governing entity. Aguda had been content to build nothing but its own separate religious and educational establishments. Only as late as 1937 did it begin to support the claim to statehood. By then, through its workers' wing, it had begun establishing its own agricultural settlements, industrial enterprises, as well as its school system. In the process, practical cooperation with the Zionist authorities replaced the old animosities. Aguda joined the Provisional Council of State when Israel was declared an independent country and was represented in the first Israeli Cabinet.

Today Agudat Israel and Poalei Agudat Israel are intensely active in the political life of the country, both in the Knesset and locally. In one respect their separation from the general community continues: their own network of schools has remained independent of the state educational system. They have an enrolment of about 7 per cent of all elementary school pupils who receive traditional religious education from unassailably orthodox teachers. At least 85 per cent of the funding for the Aguda schools comes from the Government.

As a political party, Aguda's efforts follow three main directions. The first is to ensure that no legislation harms what it considers to be orthodox interests. Secondly, it is concerned to gain the greatest material support from the State and local authorities for its religious and educational institutions. Finally it is in keen competition with the NRP to gain influence in the religious establishment. So far it has not had much success, since the NRP occupancy of the Ministry for Religious Affairs has given that Party ascendancy in the local religious councils and in the rabbinate.

The structure of Agudat Israel is conventional. The Party conference representing local groups and called the Knessia Gedola (Great Assembly) chooses a council and central committee which are the administrative bodies. What distinguishes it from the other parties is the supremacy given to a council of rabbis called the Moetzet Gedolei Hatorah (Council of Torah Sages). This council has the power of a constitutional court, overruling the decisions of the organization's leadership if the Sages consider them contrary to religious law. The fifteen Sages of the Council are the heads of the Yeshivot (ultra-orthodox religious colleges) and leading Hassidic rabbis, generally combining to form a body of the utmost conservatism.

Directed by the Torah Sages, Aguda insisted, among the conditions for joining the Begin coalition, that legislation be introduced to revoke certain liberal provisions in the Abortion Law and to prohibit post-mortems without the express consent of the family of the deceased. When, after two years, neither item of legislation had been introduced the Sages instructed Aguda to inform the Government that it had two months in which to 'make progress', implying that otherwise Aguda might leave the coalition. The two months elapsed without progress, Begin explaining that he was finding it difficult, if not impossible, to muster the votes. The Council of Sages backed down, and Aguda stayed on in the Government. However, further pressure, at a time of government weakness at the end of 1979, brought about the Abortion Law change, though many doubted whether Aguda would have acted on the threat to leave the Government. The Sages, particularly those running Yeshivot, were well aware that they were receiving more money than ever before from the Government, especially since the Chairman of the Knesset Finance Committee was Agudist leader Rabbi Shlomo Lorincz.

Poalei Agudat Israel (abbreviated to Pagi) does not support the coalition nor does it accept the authority of the Sages. It is also becoming irrelevant to the political scene, losing its *raison d'être* as its social and political programme has come closer to that of the Zionists, particularly the NRP. It has therefore lost the support of the young militants of ultra-orthodoxy, while some of its own supporters moved to the Gush Emunim group, the religious nationalists on the right wing of the NRP. Until 1977, Pagi had generally won 2 Knesset seats, but in 1977 it lost one of them, and a measure of its decline is that this once vigorous and constructive party is represented in the Knesset by the Polish-born septuagenarian, Rabbi Kalman Kahana, a long-serving and undistinguished Party official.

The four Aguda MKs are also in or near the upper age-groups. Yehuda Abramovicz was born in Poland in 1914 and was made a Deputy Speaker by Begin; Shlomo Gross, born in Romania in 1908, was similarly appointed a member of the Foreign and Defence Committee. But the two most powerful politicians in the party are Rabbis Shlomo Lorincz and Menachem Porush, to whom went the Chairmanship of two Knesset Committees.

Shlomo Lorincz, grey-bearded, immaculately groomed, is the personification of the clerical politician. He wends his way through the Knesset building purposefully and with dignity, greeting those who merit recognition. He has been there a long time. Born in Budapest in 1918, he was educated at Yeshivot in Hungary and Lithuania and became a rabbi. Fortunate in getting out of Europe in 1939 and reaching Palestine, he involved himself in Aguda activities almost immediately, becoming one of its leading figures and first entering the Knesset in the election of 1952, its youngest member at the age of 34.

At the time, his party was a member of the coalition government. In September 1949 the Knesset had passed a law under which girls would be conscripted into the army for twelve months, with an exemption for those who brought evidence that they were religious. A later Bill provided that religious girls exempted from the army could be drafted for other work. Aguda was strongly opposed to this, believing that the duty of girls was in the home. Lorincz, in a speech soon after his election, warned that Aguda would leave the Government if the conscription of women continued. It did, and Aguda withdrew in November 1952.

Thereafter, he was continually active on religious political issues. In 1956 he complained that orthodox Jews could not accept a situation whereby trucks and lorries were allowed to carry passengers on the Sabbath but, being a realistic politician, he added: 'It is not my intention at this stage to call for a ban on the driving of private cars.' He agitated for a law to curb Christian missionary activity and vigorously promoted the other causes of Agudat Israel – an orthodox monopoly of religious conversions, opposition to autopsies and the observance of religious laws by State institutions.

His position in the Knesset coincided with an improvement in his own financial position and at one time suspicions existed that he had transgressed the secular laws. In 1954 the Attorney General asked for Lorincz's parliamentary immunity to be lifted to allow the police to investigate certain currency charges against him. The Knesset Standing Committee rejected the application by a vote of 12 to 4 and no more was heard of the matter.

When Aguda decided to join Begin's Government in 1977, one of its rewards was the Chairmanship of the powerful Knesset Finance Committee, which went to Rabbi Lorincz. This made him a most – if not the most – influential figure in the religious establishment, being the distributor of grants of public funds to Agudist and other religious institutions. The budget of the Ministry for Religious Affairs increased during the first two years of the Begin administration by 100 per cent, 40 per cent more than inflation, and Lorincz's hand was turning the tap. This was a strong incentive for remaining in the Government, and threats of resignation consequently lacked conviction.

His colleague Menachem Porush at the same time became Chairman of the Knesset Welfare and Labour Committee, a lesser but by no means insignificant post. Also a rabbi, Porush was born in Jerusalem in 1916 and became a member of the Knesset in 1959, after a period of intense activity in the separate Aguda school system. His public statements on religious issues have been more extreme in tone than those of Lorincz. He has denounced Reform Jews as 'haters of Zion' and in one Knesset debate threw the American Reform prayer-book to the ground and appeared to spit on it. He described the new Abortion Law of 1975 as 'worse than Pharaoh'. (In the Book of Exodus, Pharaoh had ordered the killing of the sons of the Hebrews.)

Rabbi Porush has become a hotel proprietor and his Central Hotel in Jerusalem is a lucrative operation. In 1971, he was sued by an American with gangsterdom associations for the return of $100,000 which the American said was meant to be invested in housing projects, but was used instead for financing the hotel. The action did not come to court.

Chapter five

Political Mavericks

Moshe Dayan

When Begin formed his Government in 1977, his first problem in building a team was the paucity of available talent and the inexperience of his own Party colleagues. He was also aware of his reputation abroad as a rigid and unyielding hawk whose announced policies might well have the effect of enlarging the Middle East conflict. He had his problems with world Jewry too. Communal leaders who had established long-standing relationships, and even personal friendships, with Israel's Labour rulers, knew little about the new men who had won power, and what they knew they disliked. In an inspired moment, Begin invited Moshe Dayan, one of the small top group of Labour leaders, to become his Foreign Minister.

It was a brilliant political stroke. Unlike every other Cabinet Minister of the new regime, Dayan was well known and respected abroad. Foreign governments knew him to be a clever and pragmatic politician, and his appointment offered some assurance that the new Government would not be totally dogmatic and uncompromising. It was equally welcomed by the Jewish diaspora, worried about Begin's image.

Dayan had long been one of Israel's most heroic figures, although his reputation was tarnished by his conduct of the Yom Kippur War. He had never been much of a party man and his defection from the Labour Party destroyed what little political power base he had left. He became the maverick in the Likud Government, with no party support (he showed no inclination to join any party), there by the grace and favour of Begin and bearing the stigma of a turncoat. But if this affected him in any way, he gave no sign of it.

Inside the Government, he became Begin's closest and most influential adviser during the formative stages of the peace process, though he angered some of the stalwarts by his frequent public criticisms of the Government's failings and often went off on his own tack, as when he met PLO supporters in the West Bank and Gaza. To the chagrin of prominent Herut leaders, however, Dayan remained in office during a crucial period because Begin needed him and knew that his Government would be seriously weakened internationally without this most original mind in Israel's political leadership.

From time to time, Begin made concessions to Dayan's critics by keeping him away from sensitive issues. It was in this spirit that Dr Burg, the NRP Minister of the Interior, was put in charge of the autonomy negotiations with Egypt over the head of the Foreign Minister who was the obvious

choice. Herut distrusted Dayan's pragmatism, whereas Burg's presence
was not only reassuring to Herut, but also pleased the religious parties on
whose parliamentary support Begin's coalition depended. For the normal-
ization of relations with Egypt, Begin set up a special committee under the
chairmanship of the Director-General of his own office. Prompted by the
indignation of senior Foreign Ministry staff at their exclusion from what
should have been their major concern, Dayan protested. Begin made no
changes but assured the objectors that the committee had been set up only
to prepare a working paper for the Foreign Minister.

Dayan himself had no regard for official or other prerogatives. Some of
his staff concluded that, after the shock of the Yom Kippur War, he had
become afraid of responsibility and was therefore not averse to shuffling it
off if other Ministers were ready to accept it. He even permitted the Defence
Ministry to deal with the Lebanese problem although, since it concerned
the United Nations, it was rightfully within the province of his own
department. A combination of his aloofness from his staff (he was close only
to the three aides he had brought with him when he took office) and his
passivity towards encroachments on the Foreign Ministry's preserves led to
an acute deterioration of morale in the Ministry during his tenure.

He operated very much as a loner, usually meeting his officials merely to
keep them informed, and rarely inviting their opinions or advice. Not a man
to engage in casual chats with colleagues, he responds thoughtfully to
specific questions, especially when they are put succinctly. He seems to
need yes-men, though he ignores their views.

Dayan has had little formal education but, as his books reveal, has
acquired a feel for words. His generally brusque manner suggests an
impulsive and wayward character, although in fact he rarely acts until he
has thought things out with great care. A former Labour Cabinet Minister
commented, 'Eban spends all his time studying what others did – and does
nothing himself. Dayan barely reads at all, but he thinks, sees clearly, then
acts.' He added that Dayan was not an easy man to work with, was critical
of most people, totally anti-social and often bad-tempered.

His irritability and moods could be partially attributable to the pain from
which he is seldom free. The loss of his left eye in 1941 (the black patch he
wears has become a trade mark), when he participated in a British action
against the Vichy regime in Syria, has been a constant source of distress to
him. And he has never fully recovered from a back injury sustained in an
accident on an archaeological dig.

Born in Degania, Israel's oldest kibbutz, on the shores of the Sea of
Galilee, Moshe Dayan was five years old when his home was burned down
by Arab marauders. The family moved to a moshav near Nazareth and, in
this centre of Arab population, he learned to speak Arabic and gained the
experience which later led to his reputation for knowing how to talk to the
Arabs. Joining the Hagana, the Zionist defence force, at the age of 14, he
became an instructor four years later and by the age of 22 was deputy to
Orde Wingate, the brilliant and eccentric British commander who organized Jewish commando units to fight the pillaging Arabs. In 1939, Dayan
was arrested by the British for carrying weapons without authority, tried,

convicted and sent to Acre prison. When World War II broke out and the British welcomed the Hagana as an ally in the fight against the Nazis, he was released.

After World War II, when the struggle for independence began, Dayan was directed by Yitzhak Sadeh, the revered head and founder of the Hagana, to organize its first mechanized infantry unit. In the War of Independence, that unit, commanded by Lieutenant Moshe Dayan, distinguished itself by capturing Lydda and Ramle, thus effectively countering the Arab threat to Tel Aviv. The action brought him to the notice of Ben-Gurion and marked the real beginning of his notable but turbulent career.

He has always seemed to be at the centre of Israel's great events. After the War of Independence, he represented his country in the armistice talks with Jordan and in 1948 was one of the negotiators with King Abdullah of Jordan in an effort to achieve a peace treaty which was aborted by the assassination of the King. Appointed Chief of Staff in 1953, when the Israel Defence Forces were at a low ebb, Dayan revised the system and gave a lead to the General Staff by taking parachute and commando courses. He was responsible for the rule that officers should lead personally in combat: the famous call of 'Follow me' which contributed incalculably to future successes.

Again at the centre of affairs, Dayan was a key figure in the Sinai Campaign of 1956. He commanded an impeccable operation, succeeding in his mission to destroy the Egyptian army, wipe out the terrorist bases in Gaza and break the Egyptian blockade of the Straits of Tiran.

On his retirement from the IDF in 1958, Dayan was elected to the Knesset and was appointed by Ben-Gurion to the Cabinet as Minister of Agriculture. It was a minor appointment, but Dayan tackled it methodically and efficiently, surprising those who thought that his reputation as an administrator was based solely on his military experience and therefore in a situation where orders were (more or less) unquestioningly obeyed.

Loyal to his mentor, Dayan resigned both his office and his membership of the Labour Party when Ben-Gurion decided to form his new party, Rafi, in 1965. Although he was elected to the Knesset on the Rafi list, he was never very much involved in either Party or Parliament. Public demand pushed him back into power when, days before the outbreak of the 1967 Six Day War, he was appointed Minister of Defence. While it was patent that the planning for this dramatic and overwhelming victory had been the work of others, Dayan's direction and operation decisions were widely believed to have been crucial, and his leadership improved both civilian and military morale. He emerged from that war with his reputation at its most glorious.

As Minister of Defence, he was responsible for the military government of the territories occupied as a result of the war. He wanted it to be the most humane occupation in history. The occupying forces were to be unobtrusive; Jordanian law would continue to be applied by Arab officials; the bridges to Jordan were to be kept open; Israeli grants were to be made to subsidize municipal budgets, and travel restrictions in both directions were to be gradually abolished. 'You may go anywhere you wish,' said Dayan to

Arab leaders, 'provided that you don't walk on my feet.' He talked of 'creating facts' and of learning to live together, but his attitude to the long-term future of the occupied territories was ambivalent.

The glamorous hero and enlightened statesman suffered his most grievous reverse in the wake of the 1973 Yom Kippur War. In his book on that subject, Chaim Herzog wrote: 'I personally feel that something snapped in Dayan when all the premises on which he had built as far as the army was concerned, failed to come up as he had expected. The result was that he went from one extreme to another.' Herzog accused Dayan of grave error in delaying full mobilization for 'five valuable hours on the morning of 6 October 1973', a delay which may have been responsible for loss of life. Dayan was exonerated by the Agranat Commission which was set up to enquire into the responsibility for what was so nearly a catastrophe, but public opinion was not so forgiving. Thousands of demonstrators denounced him as a murderer and criminal, and both he and the then Prime Minister, Golda Meir, finally bowed to the pressure and resigned together in April 1974.

The closest he came to a public explanation of his reasons for joining the Likud Government as Foreign Minister was a statement he made in an interview at the time: 'It may be true that the public is fed up with me and even that I am fed up with the public, but at this juncture, public opinion on the matter is not important.' He was more specific to one of his near-intimates, to whom he remarked that the question he had answered was: 'Is Begin with me a better Government than without me?'

As Foreign Minister, Dayan was generally upstaged by his Prime Minister in the dramatic events which led to the peace treaty with Egypt, but his presence was frequently crucial in rescuing the negotiations from deadlock. When the legalistic Begin could see no way out, Dayan's freedom from dogmatism discovered room for manoeuvre.

In his private life, Dayan's two passions have been archaeology and women. His villa in Zahala, a verdant suburb of Tel Aviv, is an archaeological museum. The sources of his collection have frequently been the subject of comment and, in a Knesset debate in 1971, he was accused of illegally excavating treasures and selling them. It was also alleged that his collection was worth £300,000. A subsequent investigation by the Attorney General cleared him, though the public remained unconvinced.

Dayan's first marriage at the age of 20 lasted until 1972, when his wife, Ruth, divorced him. A newspaper report that same year revealed to a not altogether unsuspecting public that Dayan was a man with a strong sexual appetite. *Ha'olam Hazeh*, a weekly magazine with an interest in the private lives of public figures, claimed in an article that Dayan had paid a young Tel Aviv dressmaker I£10,000 to buy off a threatened action for breach of promise, and published other lurid revelations of his sex life. Israeli public opinion seemed to regard Dayan's exploits as more a matter for applause than for condemnation, and his former wife commented drily: 'Security should try to defend Moshe not only against Arabs but also against such women making contact with him.' She described the girl named in the magazine as 'unsettled' and added, 'So were most of Moshe's other young girl friends.' After the divorce, Dayan married an old friend, Rachel Koren, a divorcee with two grown-up daughters.

The unpredictable Moshe Dayan ran true to form when he suddenly resigned as Foreign Minister in October 1979. He was out of sympathy with Begin's conduct of the peace process and unhappy with his own relegation to the sidelines. Although denying that he entertained any further political ambitions, Dayan's unique talents are such that he can always be counted on to enter the national reckoning at moments of crisis. The old guard of the Labour Party regarded party loyalty as the supreme virtue. Their successors are less intolerant and his return to that fold cannot be excluded. But whether he returns or contracts other political allegiances, Dayan remains a force in Israel's public life.

Two very independents

One of the merits of Israel's electoral system is that it permits the individual nonconformist to by-pass the constrictions of the established parties and to be elected to the Knesset under his or her own banner. Both Shulamit Aloni and Uri Avneri are one-member parties, but votes were cast for them because of who they are, not for the party labels under which they operate. Mrs Aloni represents the Citizens' Rights Movement and Avneri a party called Shelli.

Shulamit Aloni is a striking, handsome woman. Her strong face, dominated by a firm mouth and jaw, is topped by an unruly mop of reddish hair, which she combs with her fingers at moments of stress or excitement. And excitement is never far when she is about. She thrives on campaigns, issues and causes, communicating her own concerns in a rush of words. She seems most comfortable in casual clothes, sweaters or blouses and skirts, with an abundance of chains and necklaces.

Born in Tel Aviv (she does not supply the date for published records, but it is not likely to be distant from the mid-1920s) to Socialist-Zionist parents who had come from Poland, Aloni wanted to live on a kibbutz, but was persuaded by her parents to become a teacher. However, her training course over, she decided to become a lawyer instead, and studied at the Hebrew University. Her teaching qualifications helped her to work her way through her law studies, and she also found another outlet for her energies and enthusiasms by introducing and presenting a consumer programme on radio. When Ben-Gurion left the Labour Party in 1965 and formed the Rafi Party, an article by Aloni attacking him for his defection came to the notice of the then Prime Minister, Levi Eshkol. He was much impressed and invited her to join the Knesset on the Labour list.

She did so but found Party discipline increasingly irritating. As a result, the first instalment of her Parliamentary career was short and stormy. She was impatient of authority and took a certain satisfaction in cocking a snook at it. She angered the orthodox too when she appeared at the swearing-in wearing a low-cut dress. The straitlaced Golda Meir did not like it either, and a mutual distaste grew as Aloni presumptuously complained about the lack of democracy in the Party. That spelt the end of her career as a Labour

MK and in the 1969 elections her name was too low on the list for her to get a seat.

However, her four years in the Knesset had been valuable. They had given her experience of the running of the institution, and had provided her with a platform for her views. She emerged as a national figure and, for the next four years, while out of the Knesset, she continued to espouse the cause of civil rights. Deciding in 1973 that there was no hope of changing the Party from the inside, she left Labour and formed the Citizens' Rights Movement. The General Election of that year saw her back in triumph as the leader of a three-member party.

Labour had been returned with a slender majority. The Prime Minister, Yitzhak Rabin, initially unwilling to accept the terms demanded for its support by the National Religious Party, turned to the fringe groups. Aloni's 3 Knesset seats brought her into the Cabinet as Minister without Portfolio, only the second woman (the other was Golda Meir) to hold a Cabinet post. But it lasted for only four months. She left when the NRP came to terms with Rabin and entered the Government, for she felt that she could not possibly continue as a member of a Government inhibited by the religious establishment – her particular *bête noire*. At the following elections, in 1977, her party won only one seat.

Shulamit Aloni is the foremost champion of liberal causes in Israel. In the Chamber, in Knesset committees, on platforms, in the press, radio and TV, she has campaigned tirelessly for abortion law reform, equal pay for women and other women's rights, and has strongly opposed the orthodox religious control of marriage, divorce and other aspects of personal status. She advocates civil marriage, electoral reform and consumer protection, and played an active part in the creation and development of the Peace Now movement.

She is realistic about her comparative lack of effectiveness. She knows that the party machines – both Labour and Likud – will generally ignore her criticisms, but she regards it as important that an independent voice should be heard. She also believes that, as a member of the Knesset Legal Committee, she can influence legislation on technical questions where political issues are not involved. Asked by a reporter why a vote should be 'wasted' on her one-member party, she replied with characteristic pugnacity: 'Because you need me in the Knesset as a spokesman for all the right causes; someone who is guaranteed not to sell out and turn into a rubber stamp for the compromisers of coalition policies.'

Uri Avneri, publisher and editor of *Ha'olam Hazeh*, a popular weekly magazine, adds colour and spice to the staid Knesset. A compact man, his carefully trained grey beard and well-groomed grey hair with a quiff accentuate rather than detract from his youthful appearance. Avneri looks distinguished, not at all the scandalmonger and pornographer portrayed by his opponents. Experienced at giving interviews, he provides smooth answers and, to ensure that nothing has been missed, he has conveniently available a full biographical note.

Arriving in Palestine from Germany as a 10-year-old in 1933, Avneri left school at the age of 14. Soon afterwards, he joined the Irgun, but left when he was 18. He drifted in and out of jobs until 1947, when he decided to become a journalist and produced a booklet, the first fruits of his political thinking, entitled *War or Peace in the Semitic Region*. The title gives the clue to one of Avneri's continuing themes – the common interest of both Jews and Arabs as Semites. When the War of Independence broke out, Avneri joined the Hagana, at the same time writing for *Haaretz*, the leading Hebrew daily. After the war he joined the staff of the paper and his articles were widely read.

However, he saw no future in continuing as an employee and, in 1959, seized the opportunity to become his own master by buying *Ha'olam Hazeh* (This World), then a family magazine. Although his aim in acquiring it was political, he knew that it first had to be commercially successful and so decided to adopt the formula of sex and scandal which had sold magazines in other parts of the world. It worked in Israel too, and while puritanical Israelis were affronted by his pictures of naked ladies, the magazine became a moneymaker.

By 1965, *Ha'olam Hazeh* had gained a strong following, particularly among young Oriental Jews. Believing that a new anti-defamation law being mooted at that time was intended as an instrument to suppress his magazine, Avneri decided to launch his own political party to counter the real or imaginary threat. He gave the party the same name as his magazine, the only case known of a journal creating a political party, rather than the reverse. He was first elected to the Knesset in 1965 and in the following election in 1969 his readers' votes sufficed to gain him 2 seats. He lost both in 1973, but returned in 1977 as a member of Shelli, a loose alliance of peace groups, which won 2 seats.

Both *Ha'olem Hazeh* and its creator are provocative and irritating. Both have adopted highly unpopular political positions, which some Israelis have found so intolerable as to incite them to violence. In 1972, the magazine's offices were burned down and Avneri has been assaulted a number of times. Yet he enjoys a certain popularity in the Knesset, for he is an assiduous, hard-working Member, personally likable and accepted as a necessary gadfly, useful for keeping authority up to the mark.

He favours the creation of an independent Palestinian state on the West Bank and in the Gaza Strip, and maintains contact with the Palestine Liberation Organization through the Council for Israeli-Palestinian Peace, which is popular with the far left. His magazine has been zealous in exposing corruption, and its publication of the allegations against Labour Party leaders, in particular Yadlin and Ofer, was a factor in bringing down the Rabin Government. It is claimed that his 'hounding' led to Ofer's suicide, but Avneri indignantly denies the charge, saying that Ofer killed himself because he knew his Party had betrayed him. He favours the separation of church and state and advocates civil rights for 'Arabs, Sephardim and Israelis', as he puts it.

Avneri charges that not only Labour, but all the major parties, including the Likud, are corrupt. He traces this back to the receipt by the Zionist parties of large sums of money from the institutions, rather than from their members, who would have exercised closer supervision. Unusually for a reformer, he does not favour any change in the electoral system, believing that a constituency system would strengthen the established parties and exclude minority opinion from the Knesset. It would certainly be difficult for Avneri to gain enough votes in any one constituency to win a Knesset seat. He has no illusions about his powerlessness in the Knesset. However, he claims that the Knesset itself has no power either, although it provides a good platform for the propagation of ideas. His own ideas generally border on the eccentric, are unpopular and are sometimes attacked as being damaging to the country. But the Knesset would be a less interesting place without him.

Peace Now

No sooner had the peace talks with Egypt started in Jerusalem at the end of 1977, than they ran into difficulty and, a few days later, Sadat recalled his representatives. Begin, not to be deflected from his principles, continued to encourage settlement on the West Bank. The Labour opposition, still weakened by internal dissension, was feebly critical while the DMC, the Party of change and conscience, was hopelessly compromised by having joined the Government the previous October. Although many prominent Israelis were uncomfortable with Begin's handling of the situation, their criticism was muted for fear that it might aid what was still regarded as the enemy. Because of this tacit agreement not to rock the boat, Begin was able to refer to his negotiating positions and to his settlements policy as the 'national consensus'.

But in fact there was no such thing. A feeling that Begin might be letting the opportunity for peace slip by, powered the sudden, almost accidental, emergence of a popular movement called Peace Now. The catalyst was an open letter which appeared in the Israeli press in March 1978 signed by a group of reserve officers. They added their military ranks after their signatures to forestall comment that they were leftists or intellectuals, heretofore Begin's only public, though ineffectual, critics. That this representative, non-political group of army officers should express their disagreement with Government was sensational.

The letter received world-wide publicity. In Israel it came as a bombshell. The letter carried the suggestion that the forces upon which Israel's very existence depended might be subverted. The officers had written: 'A Government that prefers . . . the Land of Israel above peace would cause us grave difficulties of conscience. A Government that prefers settlements across the Green Line [i.e., on the West Bank] to the ending of the historic conflict . . . would raise questions for us about the justice of our cause.'

Publication of the letter opened the valve of the so-far suppressed apprehension of many Israelis that Begin did not share their strong desire for peace. There was public response also from abroad, initially from the United States, where a group of distinguished Jews, all known for their strong support of Israel, sent a message of encouragement. At the centre of Peace Now were the young, 23- to 35-year-old reserve officers, most of whom had fought in combat units in both the Six Day and Yom Kippur Wars. In organizing themselves they employed the IDF call-up system, with one person calling ten, those ten telephoning a hundred.

The first demonstration of the strength of the new movement was a mass meeting in Tel Aviv in September 1978 of some 100,000 supporters, on the eve of Begin's departure for Camp David. Israel had seen nothing like these numbers on such an occasion before and this was all the more impressive because the demonstrators were orderly, non-fanatical, respectable. One of the organizers, David Zucker, then a 30-year-old educationalist and a paratrooper in the reserves, revealed that Begin had written later to Amos Oz, the Israeli novelist, that he had walked along the Camp David pathways between the negotiating sessions, thinking about the great numbers of people who had participated in the Peace Now demonstration a few days before. The movement claimed that its demonstration had not only influenced Begin, but had also encouraged the Egyptians to pursue the cause of peace, knowing that the Israeli public was backing it, even though Begin appeared to be stalling.

With the achievement of the peace treaty with Egypt, Peace Now turned to the future of the West Bank. It was advocating two principles on which its followers were united. The first was a denial of Israeli sovereignty over the West Bank – 'Israel must not continue to rule over 1.1 million hostile Arabs.' Secondly, it urged that, whatever the political solution, Israel's security safeguards must include the complete and effective demilitarization of the West Bank and Gaza.

Its public activities were directed at organizing protests against Begin's settlements policy. By using its telephone call-up system, it was able to produce 'instant' demonstrations, notably at Eilon Moreh, a settlement of religious zealots on the West Bank started in June 1979 with Government support. A demonstration of 3,000 was organized at twenty-four hours' notice and this was followed by another with 30,000 supporters at the site a week later.

Peace Now is not a party. It deliberately has no paid officials, no big names at its head, no paraphernalia of organization. It remains a volunteer body run by a national council composed of representatives of its three big-city groups and delegates from the smaller towns and kibbutzim. Claiming 250,000 supporters, Peace Now has become a social as well as a political phenomenon. Whether it will be able to survive without sacrificing its precious innocence is questionable, but its growth has demonstrated the vigour of Israel's democracy and the survival of the idealism which the Democratic Movement for Change had so signally failed to maintain.

The Faithful

At the opposite end of the political spectrum from Peace Now, another pressure group, Gush Emunim, advocates an uncompromising stand on what it terms Judea and Samaria, the names of provinces of the ancient Jewish Kingdom, otherwise the occupied territory of the West Bank.

The Yom Kippur War was a climacteric for Israel in many respects. It ended the political domination of the Labour old guard, created the conditions which eventually led to the peace treaty with Egypt, and stimulated the formation of new political groupings to meet needs which the established parties were failing to fulfil. The religious parties were also affected by these stirrings.

To the more militantly nationalistic of them, the Land of Israel movement was too passive. Founded in the aftermath of the Six Day War, this movement declared that all the areas gained by Israel in the war were the inalienable possession of the Jewish people and should not be given up. It was not a party but a political lobby, and although including members of all parties, the participation of orthodox Jews was particularly strong. Yet the zeal of the group was appearing to wane and, as an instrument of political pressure, the Land of Israel movement was clearly having little effect.

The younger and more assertive religious elements decided upon a course of direct action. Forming themselves in 1974 into a group called Gush Emunim (Bloc of the Faithful), they began by organizing large rallies and demonstrations at biblical sites on the West Bank which, they believed, were part of the divine promise to the Children of Israel. With the support of the 'young guards' of the National Religious Party, they moved from demonstration to actual settlement on some of these sites. Small groups, without permission or warning, descended on biblical sites on the West Bank and set up encampments. The Government, Labour at the time, removed them, but many Israelis, not just the orthodox, admired the convictions of these young people who endured danger and hardship in settling on these inhospitable sites. Many saw it as a revival of the spirit of Zionist idealism – but their aura as pioneers was tarnished by the revelation that almost all of them retained their permanent residences elsewhere.

Gush Emunim attracted international attention in 1976, when it set up such a settlement at Camp Kaddum on the West Bank, renaming it Eilon Moreh after a place mentioned in the Book of Genesis. The local Arabs protested and the United States condemned the settlement as an obstacle to peace, while the Labour Government was divided on the issue. Undeterred, the handful of Gush Emunim settlers – nobody knew exactly how many there were – stayed at Eilon Moreh. A week after the 1977 elections, they were honoured by a visit from the new Prime Minister. Menachem Begin promised his elated audience: 'In a few months, there will be many Eilon Morehs. A Jew has every right to settle in these liberated territories of the Jewish land.' Two months after his first meeting with President Carter in Washington, Begin granted official recognition to Eilon Moreh and two other Gush Emunim settlements.

As the peace process unfolded and the West Bank settlements increasingly became an issue between Israel and both Egypt and the USA, Begin combined public admiration for what he termed 'the finest youth in the country' with private concern that they were endangering national interests. The need for peace and for good relations with the USA called for the exercise of restraint, a commodity which was not high among the Gush

Emunim's equipment. Begin and his closest advisers did what they could to keep the movement quiet. They gave it funds for its projects and sent some of its leaders on foreign assignments, but it was not to be deflected from what it considered a religious obligation.

In its early days, Gush Emunim leaned heavily on the advice of Rabbi Haim Druckman, who had occupied second place on the NRP election list in 1977. The movement also stayed close to New York-born Yehuda Ben-Meir, who succeeded to his father's seat in the Knesset in 1971. American influence in the Gush was by no means limited to Ben-Meir. Many of the young activists were of American origin and frequently appeared on television as its spokesmen. Women were also active in the movement, among them the militant American-born wife of Rabbi Moshe Levinger, a Gush leader described by Shimon Peres, leader of the Labour Party, as a public danger. Even one of his Likud friends said of Levinger: 'Of course the rabbi is fanatic. If such a man holds sway over working politicians and appeals to crowds, he can be a danger.'

No facts about the membership and financing of the group have been officially disclosed, apart from the government funds it has received. However, there is no doubt that the influence wielded by Gush Emunim was wildly out of proportion to the number of its activists, estimated at no more than 2,000 at the most. They presented a problem to Begin, for they constituted a pressure group he could not ignore, they were his own right wing. They were doing what he had always advocated and he found it admirable. But the world was urging him to do something about these fanatics, while, on the other hand, they were supported by the religious component of his own coalition which he could not afford to alienate. His compromise was to bar new settlements and hope that the energies of the Gush would be channelled into expanding those it had already set up.

Ordered by the Supreme Court at the end of 1979 to dismantle the Eilon Moreh settlement, the Government again succumbed to the pressure of the Gush and its supporters in the Cabinet and extended the deadline. The incident illustrated the power of this fringe group of mavericks and provided a preview of the difficulties that will eventually face a secular Israeli Government when it feels strong enough to stand up to the demands of the religious groups who owe allegiance only to a Higher Authority.

Secular Loyalists

While the religious component of the Land of Israel movement moved into the Gush Emunim, the secular nationalists found their political home in the Likud. However, as Begin adopted what appeared to be a more compromising posture on the future of the territories, the secular hawks came to feel that they had been betrayed.

One of the first to make the break with Begin on this issue was Moshe Shamir, a well-known writer and former stalwart of the Land of Israel movement who was elected to the Knesset on the Likud list in 1977. Resigning from the Party after the ratification of the Egyptian peace treaty, he formed his own one-man faction in the legislature. His example was followed by Geula Cohen, a termagant Likud MK, who achieved a certain notoriety when she heckled Begin during his speech to a world television audience on the occasion of Sadat's visit to the Knesset. Geula Cohen claims that she remains the true exponent of traditional Likud-Revisionist policies on territory; that she still stands where Begin once stood.

Both Shamir and Cohen dedicated themselves to fighting the Government peace policies at every stage and demanding the revision of the Egyptian treaty. They gained an intellectual partner and leader in the person of Yuval Ne'eman, one of Israel's ablest scientists. Born in Tel Aviv in 1925, Ne'eman graduated from the Technion, fought in the War of Independence and stayed on in the army to become a full colonel. Between 1952 and 1955 he was Director of Defence Planning in the Ministry of Defence and helped to mould defence thinking in Israel prior to the Six Day War. In the late 1950s he became military attaché in London, where he conducted research in physics at London University concurrently with his duties. He was successful both in acquiring a doctorate and in propounding a theory about sub-nuclear particles which was considered a major scientific advance.

Ne'eman gained international recognition in his further work on sub-nuclear particles with the Nobel Prizewinner, Professor Murray Gelman, at CalTech as well as in Israel at the Weizmann Institute. He turned to administration when he was appointed President of Tel Aviv University in 1971 but later returned to research at the Defence Ministry and at CalTech where he occupied their chair of physics.

Politically, Ne'eman began as a supporter of Rafi, Ben-Gurion's splinter from the Labour Party, but in 1971, when the then Prime Minister, Golda Meir, was being urged by doveish academics to undertake a peace initiative, he came to her support on the ground that it was a national necessity for Israel to retain the occupied territories. He gradually became more hawkish on territorial issues, resigning from the Defence Ministry after the disengagement agreement between Israel and Egypt, negotiated by the American Secretary of State, Henry Kissinger, which he thought contrary to Israel's interests.

He was prompted to take sterner political action by what he perceived as the Likud's 'softness' in the agreement with Sadat. Something might go wrong but Israel would have made irrevocable concessions. He feared that after Egypt had regained the whole of the Sinai and nothing had yet been done to solve the Palestinian issue, Egypt might renounce the treaty and rejoin the Arab world, leaving Israel again exposed on two fronts and without the defensive security the Sinai had afforded. In his opinion, because Egypt's economic illness is incurable ('Egypt is India on a small scale') it is also politically unstable and its rulers will continue to look for diversions.

Ne'eman says he is aware of the problems created by his hard-line position, but he believes that the best choice among the various evils confronting Israel is Israeli sovereignty over the West Bank and Gaza. This he considers to be the fulfilment of Zionism, which did not end when the State of Israel was created. The ingathering of the exiles is still incomplete and must continue, and the newcomers should be able to settle anywhere they like, Ne'eman says. He argues that the British Mandate created artificial borders and adds, 'I've as much justification for settling in the Golan [Heights area] as in the Mandate area.'

Hatehia (Revival), the new political party which he created in 1979, like almost all other groupings, claims the support of 'strong elements' from the prestigious kibbutz and moshav movements. He expected to gain support also from religious Jews dissatisfied with the machinations of the religious parties as well as from the elements to be found in all parties opposed to the Government's peace policy. Yet, in the beginning, there was little doubt that the major backing for the new party was coming from right-wing radical elements. Ne'eman is aware of the dangers facing his movement if it comes to be regarded as a right-wing extremist group of cranks and has been trying hard to include left-wingers.

Probably his best hope of avoiding the crank label is his own personality and standing. Ne'eman is not a populist or demagogue. He is diffident in speech, almost shy, although he marshals his facts with precision and expresses them forcefully. He is respected as a soldier and a scientist – in Israel an almost irresistible combination. But his expectation of winning 20 seats in the next General Election (due in 1981) has aroused no noticeable anxiety among the established parties. They feel the electorate has been disillusioned by the failed idealists of the DMC and is unlikely again to put any trust in a maverick fringe group.

A time for change

For a new political movement to emerge on the static Israeli political scene and, after only seven months of existence, to succeed in winning 15 seats in the 120-member Knesset, demonstrated the strength of idealism in the country. The decline and virtual demise of the Democratic Movement for Change (DMC) within only two years reflected some of Israel's less admirable characteristics.

The conditions which made the rise of the DMC possible can be traced back to two factors, both created by Israel's success in the Six Day War. The first was the conquest of the West Bank of the Jordan and the division of Israelis into hawks and doves on the issues related to the future of that territory. Should it be held or given up and, if the latter, to whom and under what conditions? How was security to be ensured? These were questions which were endlessly discussed and on which the policies of the Labour Government had resolutely remained irresolute. There was no agreement within the Labour leadership on a peace policy and even less so between Labour and their coalition partners. Growing disquiet with Government immobilism was particularly concentrated among the intellectual and professional segments of Israeli society, who later came together in the DMC.

The second factor was the economic upsurge which followed the war, widening the gap between the growing affluence of the nation as a whole and its underprivileged minority. Ten years after the war, one of the major planks in the DMC election manifesto was the closing of the social and economic gap.

But the immediate catalyst for the formation of the DMC was the Yom Kippur War in 1973. The failures and errors which had contributed to the success of the initial attack by Egypt and Syria and to the heavy Israeli death toll of almost 3,000 created widespread national depression. The established political leaders at that period seemed to be more concerned with party or personal considerations than the national interest, and the idealism which had created the Zionist movement and the Jewish State seemed all but stifled by party political machinations and the corruption of the consumer society.

Soon after the Yom Kippur War a group of twenty university professors came together under the leadership of Amnon Rubinstein, an expert in constitutional law. A professor of law at Tel Aviv University and former dean of its law school, Professor Rubinstein had never been the ivory-tower type of scholar. As a columnist for the country's leading independent newspaper, *Haaretz*, and in frequent television appearances, he had long expressed forthright views on the government of Israel.

A slight, intense man who talks so rapidly that his words fall over themselves, Rubinstein was not content to limit himself to verbal criticism. He concluded that the existing parties were beyond salvation and that a new political movement was essential. There was a ready response from among his peers. The new movement they formed (the very term 'political party' had, they felt, been debased) was called Shinui (Hebrew for change) and it gained support not only among the academics and professionals where it had begun, but also – and rapidly – from the middle class. Shinui called for a clean, uncorrupted, participatory democracy with policitcal parties financed by their members according to their means and not through Government subsidies. Fundamental to their plans for change was electoral reform and the introduction of a constituency system.

Shinui stood for clean politics at a time when the public was becoming increasingly disturbed by revelations of corruption. It was an idea whose time seemed ripe and less than two years after the announcement of its formation, a public opinion poll in the Tel Aviv evening newspaper, *Yediot Aharonot*, predicted that Shinui would win 9 Knesset seats. But while Shinui possessed the ideas and the idealism, it had attracted no household names, and Rubinstein believed it would not gain electoral support on a sufficient scale without well-known and respected public figures at its head. Providentially, it seemed, Yigael Yadin moved into the picture.

General Professor Yigael Yadin

Also a professor, Yadin was a far more eminent figure than Rubinstein. He was Israel's outstanding archaeologist, which alone made him a national figure in a country where archaeology is the national hobby. The subject attracts Israelis not only through its inherent interest, but because it emphasizes the continuity with the ancient Israelites, offering the new Israelis the reassurance of 'roots'. Leading archaeologists are national heroes, but Yigael Yadin had transcended local distinction, achieving worldwide fame through his excavations at Megiddo, Hazor and Masada and through his contribution to the unshrouding of the Dead Sea Scrolls.

The story of his early years parallels that of several other Israeli leaders. He was born in Jerusalem in 1917 and imbibed a love of archaeology from his father Professor Sukenik. (Yigael later Hebraized his name as was the fashion among Zionist; Ben-Gurion, for example, was born David Green.) Yadin was in the Hagana in his teens and during the War of Independence headed the Operations Division of the General Staff. His precise knowledge of the biblical accounts of ancient battles was put to good use in the operations he directed; he achieved the priceless element of surprise by moving his troops along routes known to the warriors of old but forgotten by contemporary strategists – unless they happened also to be archaeologists.

Immediately after the war, Yadin was made Chief of Staff, and was responsible for transforming the improvised military structure into the permanent organization of the Israel Defence Forces. Some three years later, General Yadin turned from military to academic discipline, eventually succeeding his father as Professor of Archaeology at the Hebrew University of Jerusalem. His eminence in this field, his splendid war record, his experience as a speaker and a certain flair for publicity ensured that he remained a popular figure and, despite his absence from the political scene, his name was continually mentioned as a future national leader. Many reports suggested that he had been Ben-Gurion's choice as his successor.

Even as late as 1967 Yadin was proposed as Minister of Defence to avoid conflict between the supporters of Dayan and Allon. But he declined all political offers and his resolution was generally attributed to the influence of his wife Carmella, daughter of Dr Arthur Ruppin, an eminent sociologist and one of the Zionist fathers.

After her death in 1976, Yadin began to take a more active interest in politics, with particular concern for the country's social problems. He felt that a system which had the effect of making half the population – those who had come from Arab countries – feel underprivileged had to be improved. In a television interview in 1976, which he described as a landmark for himself, he called for changes in the social system, reform of the electoral system and a clearer policy for the West Bank.

For five months after that, he toured the country to test the response to his views and learn how they could be advanced. Though he agreed with its foreign policy, he could not join the ILP because he held that Party responsible for turning productive people into welfare cases. Nor could he join the Likud because he could not accept its foreign policy. He came to the conclusion that a new party had to be formed and in May 1976, with seventy-five supporters, he formed the Democratic Party with the intention of contesting the General Election just one year later.

Democratic Movement for Change

Some six months after its formation, in December 1976, Yadin's Democratic Party and Rubinstein's Movement for Change decided to merge. The two groups had very similar aims, but more than that, the catalyst for the merger was that each needed the other. Rubinstein needed Yadin's name while Yadin lacked Rubinstein's organization. The two became the Democratic Movement for Change (DMC).

From the beginning, both sides entertained reservations about the match. Yadin had been warned by some of his advisers that the 'Change' people were protestors rather than positive politicians, while Rubinstein noted that, although he had brought many academics into his movement, not one Hebrew University professor had followed Yadin.

However, both worked together in the months leading to the election. The intensity of their activity and the stimulation of the support they were receiving smothered intimations of internal dissension. And the DMC certainly seemed to be a revivalist movement, renewing hope and idealism and bringing together large numbers of able and thoughtful Israelis, united about the need for change from the arid policies of the past.

Soon after the formation of the DMC, Yadin was joined by Shmuel Tamir, leader of an independent faction of two in the Knesset called the Free Centre, which had been part of the Likud. Then, together with key ILP people, Meir Amit, a powerful figure in the Histadrut, joined DMC. The bandwagon was rolling. Not all the new support was exclusively idealistic. For some of the experienced politicians who joined, DMC was an opportunity to reach higher positions of leadership than might have been open to them in the controlled hierarchical structure of the old parties. To the politicians were added some 38,000 individuals who became registered members of the DMC, activists who were invaluable as unpaid Party workers during the campaign. The Party list that was put before the electorate was intended as an earnest of the new moral stance, for the names on it were not the result of manipulations by Party leaders but of the democratic will of the Party members. 'We were purists at the time,' says Yadin.

Every member of the Party could put up candidates and some sixty or seventy nominations were received. A kind of primary election followed to determine in what order they would appear on the list. By prohibiting electioneering in this 'primary', an obvious advantage (whether intentional or not is unclear) was given to the names which were already well known. Yadin came first and Rubinstein second on what was a strong list with considerable vote appeal.

Yadin defined the aim of the DMC as seeking 'a radical change in the policies of Government, society and the economy.' The programme of the Party included improvement of the status of the underprivileged, a change in the economic system with less power to the unions, and – with much emphasis placed on it – reform of the electoral system. To the disappointment of many, the DMC did not publicly oppose religious legislation which affected the non-religious majority of the population for it was reluctant to alienate religious voters.

Differences of view within the DMC produced a certain ambivalence in its policy on the occupied territories and hesitations on its formulation. Eventually, only two months before the election, the DMC proclaimed its opposition to the PLO and to the creation of a Palestinian state. It proposed that the Palestinians should find their national expression within the state of Jordan, that the River Jordan should be Israel's security border and that, although Israel had a right to the occupied territories, concessions should be made in the search for peace. It hardly differed from ILP policy.

The 15 seats won by the DMC constituted a signal achievement for a new party. Even Ben-Gurion, a towering figure in Israel at the time, had won only 10 when he founded his Rafi Party. But if the DMC had hoped to hold the balance of power in the next coalition, the arithmetical division of seats militated against it.

Begin's Likud had won 45 seats, and the religious parties on whose support Begin could rely commanded 17, giving him a total of 62 plus the assurance that he could also count on the vote of Flatto-Sharon. That gave him a majority in the Knesset, but a slender one, and Israeli coalitions have traditionally sought a greater majority than they need technically.

As soon as his Government was formed, Begin initiated negotiations with the DMC to bring it into the coalition. Before the elections, Yadin had declared that the DMC would only join a Government which accepted its principles. But since its membership was not essential to the Likud Government, the DMC was not in a strong negotiating position. It could either stick to its principles and face a very uncertain future in opposition, or accept the possibility of a real influence on affairs as part of the Government, but at the cost of compromising on matters of principle.

Yadin was ready to compromise on various formulations but four months of negotiations ended in failure in September 1977 because the Likud would not commit itself to any acceptable change in the electoral system, which by then had become the symbol of the DMC's credibility. Begin, a shrewd and experienced politician, began by 'agreeing in principle' to electoral reform, with precise plans left to be devised by an all-party committee on a free vote. It sounded democratic but was disingenuous because even the merest tyro knew that the constituency elections demanded by the DMC would never be accepted by such a committee.

More detailed negotiations brought further concessions from the DMC. The new party agreed to leave one-third of the Knesset seats to be voted for under the existing system, but problems arose as to the number of constituencies from which the other two-thirds were to be elected. The National Religious Party (NRP), whose supporters are not evenly dis-tributed over the whole country but concentrated in a few areas, would have been decimated in constituency elections. It insisted on conditions which were virtually indistinguishable from the existing proportional representation. The negotiations failed because the Likud could not risk alienating their existing and reliable religious partners for the sake of the less dependable DMC.

But, says Yadin, 'as time passed, we were losing support. As far as public opinion was concerned, we either had to be an active opposition and be seen to be doing something, or be in the Government and exercising influence there. The public was getting impatient. In October 1977 I advocated going into the Government without conditions.'

Begin had left three Ministerial positions unfilled while negotiations were proceeding with the DMC but, after they broke down, it was clear that those portfolios would soon be distributed to other parties. Such an event held no terrors for Rubinstein, the conscience of the DMC, who urged patience and adherence to principle. But some of the experienced professionals, like Shmuel Tamir and Meir Amit, were bored by opposition and anxious to acquire positions of power. Their advice to Yadin was to take the three Ministries rather than be left out in the cold. A new party like the DMC, they felt, could only retain its electoral support by showing some achievement in power; in opposition it would disintegrate. The DMC nearly split on the issue, but Yadin, by a small majority, persuaded the Party to join the coalition. The 'Change' people were the main objectors but they democratically accepted the majority decision, though Rubinstein himself refused to be considered for a Cabinet post.

Yadin became Deputy Prime Minister. Meir Amit was appointed Minister of Transport and Communication, Shmuel Tamir Minister of Justice, and a fourth DMC member, Israel Katz, Minister of Labour and Social Betterment. The price they all paid was the near fatal damage to the idealistic image of the DMC; its top names had succumbed to the lure of power as much as the old party politicians they had attacked in their electoral campaign.

The party did not survive long after that. By August 1979, the original Shinui group were becoming restive and, together with Amit and his followers, urged the DMC to leave the Government. Yadin suggested waiting until October, the first anniversary of its entry but, when a vote was taken, Yadin lost. He refused to accept the majority decision and convened a breakaway council separating the DMC into its two constituent parts. Yadin remained in the Government as leader of a seven-member group called the Democratic Party, while Rubinstein's group of seven called Shai (Shinui v'Yosma – Change and Initiative) went into opposition.

Picking up the pieces

Yadin fell considerably in public estimation as a result of the DMC debacle. He believed that, as Deputy Prime Minister and acting Prime Minister during Begin's absences, he could exercise a moderating influence in the Government. He was patently content with his prestigious office, which others regarded as more ceremonial than effective. So far as DMC politics were concerned, the Party had placed a very high priority on electoral reform which, they considered, would create the conditions for a healthier democracy. In office, the DMC persuaded Likud to set up a committee on the cubject, but this was widely interpreted as a meaningless sop. The Shinui group felt particularly strongly about Yadin's abandonment of the central plank of the Party. It was, in Rubinstein's word, 'perfidy'.

Rubenstein later acknowledted that his search for prominent names had contained the seeds of the movement's destruction. Established political figures, he sadly learned, were more interested in office than in idealistic opposition.

Israelis tend to inflate their enthusiasms and to succumb to disillusionments with unusual rapidity. In the course of the coalition negotiations, when DMC began to waver from its proclaimed principles, members left by the thousand. The DMC vote in 1977 consisted in the main of the well-educated, high-income protest voters of Western origin and most of its gains had been at the expense of the Labour Party. Habitual Labour voters defected because of corruption within their Party and its failures in coping with the country's economic problems. The DMC intellectual leadership's interest in changing the electoral system meant little to the overwhelming majority of those who voted for the new party.

Yadin was on strong ground in asserting that 'nobody really doubts that it was us who brought down Labour.' But it was equally true that the election success of the DMC was a negative vote against Labour and not a positive desire of public opinion to start a third major party. The electorate voted, as Shimon Peres, the ILP leader, put it, to 'slap us in the face', and having done that, they returned to their traditional allegiances. A public opinion poll published halfway through the term of the Begin Government showed that, as against 11.6 per cent who voted for the DMC in 1977, only 2 per cent would have voted in 1979 for either of the two factions into which it had split.

Rubinstein claimed that he had learned that the new party, which he remained convinced was necessary, could only be established firmly by a slow process of growth, not by looking for the big names. On the initial evidence of the growth of his own post-DMC independent faction, it seemed that the process would be painfully slow, for there could be little doubt that the cause of electoral reform and the creation of a third major party must have been prejudiced by the DMC experience.

At the same time, the DMC saga encouraged those who maintain that, despite their high degree of professionalism and the power they possess, the established parties are not invincible. The Likud victory, because the DMC had split the left-wing vote, demonstrated to the voter that he could use his vote effectively and that the political structure in Israel was by no means as static and unchangeable as almost everybody had assumed before 17 May 1977. And because of the success of the academics in appealing to Israeli voters, the major parties became as hospitable to them as they had been to ex-generals.

Chapter six

Officers of State

The Presidency

The official head of the Israeli state is the President, 'Nasi' in Hebrew, and there have been five of them in Israel's history. The role of the President was defined almost casually, one of the lesser concerns of the infant State's tyro Government, and was one of the many subjects on which vastly differing views were held by Chaim Weizmann, the first President, and David Ben-Gurion, the country's autocratic first Prime Minister.

When Dr Weizmann arrived in Israel in 1948 as President of the Provisional Council of State, he envisaged something like the American type of Presidency with the head of state functioning as chief executive. He wrote at the time that, while an exact copy of the American Presidency would not suit Israel's conditions, the then French system, under which the President was merely a ceremonial figurehead, was no more desirable. He suggested as a middle course the Czech model, having in mind the role President Masaryk played in that country.

But Ben-Gurion had no intention of limiting his own authority by enhancing that of the President. The Presidency in Israel, he decided, had to be purely 'symbolic', a description which Weizmann regarded as insulting but, his protests notwithstanding, Ben-Gurion prevailed. The Israeli President was given a ceremonial role only and totally excluded from the decision-making process. Even Weizmann's request for Cabinet minutes was denied, and he had to content himself with a visit from the Cabinet Secretary after meetings, when he was informed of the decisions which had been taken. An essay by Richard Crossman on this period of Weizmann's life is entitled 'The Prisoner of Rehovot', a description which Weizmann himself used. His house at Rehovot, adjoining the scientific institute which bears his name, had become the President's official residence, and there he was immured, excluded from the power of the State he had done so much to establish.

President Truman once asked Weizmann why he had not acted to solve the Arab refugee problem and received the reply, 'I am only a constitutional President and it is outside my province. My handkerchief is the only thing I can stick my nose into. In everything else, it's Ben-Gurion's nose.'

Weizmann was succeeded by two elderly and respected scholar-statesmen, for whom the Presidency constituted an honourable retirement. Israel's fourth President, Professor Ephraim Katzir, was a distinguished scientist at the Weizmann Institute but he served only one term, finding the office too heavy on ceremonial for his taste and too light on content.

The President of Israel holds office for five years from the day he signs the declaration of allegiance. Any resident citizen (the office is not expressly limited to Jews) is eligible and may hold the post for no longer than two consecutive terms. He is not elected by popular vote but by the Knesset at an election which must be held between ninety and thirty days before the term of the outgoing President expires. If the office becomes vacant for any other reason than the normal expiration of the term, the election takes place not later than forty-five days after the vacancy occurs. The Speaker of the Knesset fixes the date for the election, of which he is required to give all Members at least twenty days notice. Within the first ten days of this period, any ten or more MKs may make a nomination in writing, accompanied by the written consent of the nominee. Not later than seven days before the election, the Speaker sends all members a list of the candidates with the names of those who have nominated them.

The election is by secret ballot at a special sitting of the Knesset. The procedure is that if no candidate receives a majority of the total number of voters, i.e., a minimum of 61 out of 120 Knesset Members, a second ballot is held. If there is still no absolute majority, a third ballot will decide the result by a simple majority of votes actually cast. The office may become vacant before the end of the regular term if the President resigns or dies, or if the Knesset decides by a three-quarters majority of the total membership that he should be ousted. It is easier if the President is deemed to be permanently unable to function for reasons of health; that can be decided by a simple majority. In fact, no President has so far been deposed under these provisions.

The Presidency is, of course, a grand and honorific position but the only legal privileges afforded to the incumbent are that he cannot be sued in any Israeli court and that he is exempt from any compulsory service – a less than meaningful benefit given the age at which Presidents usually assume office. His formal duties are hardly more significant. They are laid down in the Basic Law: State President 1964. Potentially the most important, though so far in Israel's history it has never been decisive, is the President's power, after consulting the various parties in the Knesset, to call on the leader of one of them to form a Government. He also accredits diplomats and appoints a number of senior officials, but these functions are totally formal and, in practice, are performed by approving the recommendations of the appropriate Ministers or committees. The President signs all laws and treaties, but has no share in framing them. He is given authority to grant pardons and reprieves, but that too is employed only on the recommendation of the Minister of Justice.

The fifth President

Itzhak Navon, Israel's fifth President, was elected in 1978. It was, in several respects, a singular appointment. In the first place, Navon is younger than any of his predecessors. He was a youthful 57 when he appeared before the Knesset and declared: 'I pledge myself to bear allegiance to the State of Israel and to its laws and faithfully to carry out my function as President of the State.' Secondly, he is the first Sephardi to hold that office and, to complete the singularities, he is a Labour man elected by a Knesset with a Likud majority.

He was born in Jerusalem in 1921 into a family with a history of many generations in that ancient city. From his parents he acquired a deep love for Jerusalem and for the traditions and customs of its old Sephardi community. Because he had studied Islamic culture at the Hebrew University and speaks Arabic, Navon was appointed to head the Arab department of the Hagana in Jerusalem immediately before the declaration of Statehood. Here he came into contact with Moshe Sharett, Israel's first Foreign Minister, whose political secretary he became after the War of Independence. Four years later, in 1952, he was appointed to perform the same duties for David Ben-Gurion, the Prime Minister.

Navon was at the centre of power and clearly relished the experience. Ben-Gurion could not have been an easy man to work for. Tempestuous, unforgiving and often wilful, Ben-Gurion needed a restraining influence at hand and Navon performed that function. He handled his boss with a sure touch, and became one of his most trusted advisers. Nor did he so submerge his personality as to become a faceless member of Ben-Gurion's entourage. Navon was his own man, and his sound common sense, sense of humour (Ben-Gurion had none) and sparkle as a raconteur made him a well-known and much-liked individual in political circles.

When Ben-Gurion left the Labour Party in 1965 to form his own faction, Navon joined him and became one of the ten Rafi MKs after that year's elections. He was a much-favoured candidate for the Presidency in 1973 when Labour was in power but, although the rank and file backed him strongly, the Party establishment headed by Golda Meir was hostile. Some suspect that it was because the elders of the Party thought he was too young; it was rumoured that Golda disliked the thought of having to stand up for someone of his age. More likely, his earlier Rafi associations were held against him. Golda and the old-timers had not completely forgiven the defectors and the appointment of Navon might have been taken as signalling the rehabilitation of Ben-Gurion, for which they were not yet ready. Nevertheless, Navon polled a respectable 221 votes in the Party Committee against 270 for the establishment candidate, Professor Katzir.

Although Katzir decided to stand down after only one term, Navon, then a member of the Labour opposition in the Knesset, was quite sure that he was out of the running, since Begin was expected to put in his own man. Begin had the same idea and, probably with the popular example of Navon in mind, announced that it would be symbolic and significant were a Sephardi appointed. But then he selected as his candidate a little-known Sephardi scientist, Dr Shaveh.

The more the politicos and the public saw and heard of Dr Shaveh, the less suitable he seemed, but the idea of a Sephardi President had received so general a welcome that more attention was focused on Navon. With Dr Shaveh looking more and more a loser, the Liberal contingent in the Likud put up their own candidate, a politician to whom Begin was implacably opposed. Realizing that his own man was hopeless and in order to block the candidature of the Liberal nominee, Begin had little choice but to turn to Navon who was also backed by the Labour Party, the DMC, some of the religious MKs and some members of Likud. The result was that he was elected by acclamation.

The President's official residence, Bet Hanassi (House of the President), is a low and unpretentious building of white stone. Entry is through automatically controlled gates in the geometrically sculptured palisade which surrounds it. The interior is simply decorated but without any style or grace – characterless, clinically impersonal. It could be a modern private hospital. Itzhak Navon's private office is quite different. Books in profusion, flowers, pictures on the walls and above all, the exuberant and warm personality of its occupant make it a comfortable, homely place. He is essentially the same convivial, reasonable and intelligent person who was Ben-Gurion's right hand twenty years before. Shortish, a little stockier than he was then, he welcomes visitors with unaffected pleasure in his job as Israel's first meeter and greeter.

He is aware that the Presidency lacks functions, and acknowledges that each individual can make something of it or, by acting strictly according to the book, pass much of his time idly. What he would like to make of it is to use his occupancy of the highest office in the State as an incentive to help the Sephardim to change their self-image. He illustrates what he has in mind by pointing to the example of many Ashkenazi national leaders who began with as few material advantages as most Sephardim. But they had the confidence and self-assurance to enable them to rise, while few Sephardim have, because they consider themselves to be inferior. A soldier, he explains, can be lazy under one commander and fight like a lion under another. He would like to be the proof to the Sephardi masses that everything in Israel is open and attainable to them. The example of a Sephardi President will, he hopes, encourage other Sephardim to raise their expectations.

So successful has Navon been in his public appearances (he did particularly well in his contacts with President Sadat) that many expect him to return to active politics eventually. If he completes two full terms, he will then be 67, by no means too old in Israel for political leadership. Some Likud supporters think him too political already and resented, as political campaigning, his walk-about in a Tel Aviv Sephardi slum, where he talked to residents about their problems. One Likud MK tabled a Private Member's Bill which would have instituted a mandatory four year 'cooling-off' period before a retired President could be elected to the Knesset, but it did not get very far. Navon himself, while remaining necessarily non-committal, has not ruled out the possibility of a return to active politics.

His first five-year term will end in 1983, the year Begin reaches the age of 70, when he has said he will retire. If the Labour Party at that time still suffers from leadership conflicts, Navon could well be a serious contender for the top job.

Centre of power: the Cabinet

One of the drawbacks of the Israeli system of coalition government is the inability of the Prime Minister to appoint the members of his Cabinet, who will share with him the responsibility of running the country. He can generally influence the appointment of members of his own Party to the Ministries allocated to the Party under the coalition agreement. But all the other parties in the coalition select their own nominees for the portfolios they have been allotted. When Begin put his coalition together in 1977, the agreement he made with the National Religious Party gave them the Religious Affairs, Interior and Education Ministries. The NRP, not the Prime Minister, nominated the individual office holders.

Nor can the Prime Minister dismiss any of his Ministers. The only way he can rid himself of a Minister who refuses to submit his resignation is to submit his own resignation together with the whole Cabinet. If he still has a Parliamentary majority, he will then be requested by the President to form a new Government. It is a cumbersome procedure and an academic one, because no coalition partner would permit the Prime Minister to dismiss one of its Ministers and, if persuaded that the Minister should go, the party would itself ensure that he did. A Cabinet reshuffle becomes in effect the construction of a new coalition, almost as difficult as the original negotiation and to be avoided at almost all costs.

One of the results of the Prime Minister's limitations in appointing or dismissing Ministers is that a divided Government continues in office. Ministers disagree and quarrel with each other, knowing that they cannot be forced to go. Ministers owe little personal loyalty to the Prime Minister nor, because of the system, are they necessarily the best and most able people. The only essential qualification for an Israeli Cabinet Minister is good standing within his own party.

Professor Benjamin Akzin, one of Israel's leading constitutional lawyers, has written: 'To use a simile, the Israeli Prime Minister is like the conductor of an orchestra whose members have been chosen by various behind-the-scenes groups, with these same groups deciding who will play which instruments. Yet the conductor is expected to produce a harmonious ensemble. No wonder if instead of a concert, we get cacophony.'

Negotiations towards the formation of coalitions conclude with elaborate agreements and the allocation of Cabinet posts. When the composition of the Cabinet is complete and it commands a majority in the Knesset, the new Government will be announced to that body, which will be asked for a vote of confidence. The Prime Minister himself is required by law to be a Knesset Member, but Ministers are not. Most of them in the past have been elected MKs but a Minister who is not a Member has the right to sit in the Chamber and indeed possesses all other membership rights save one – he is not allowed to vote.

One of the peculiarities of the 1962 Knesset Law is the provision that if a member of the Government votes against a Government motion or abstains without consent, he is considered to have resigned. It was intended as one of the means of maintaining discipline in a coalition system of government, as is another section of the law which imposes upon a Minister some responsibility for the voting of his group in the Knesset. If the group votes for a no-confidence motion or abstains on such a motion, the Ministers concerned are deemed to have resigned if the Cabinet, within seven days, decides that the vote or abstention involved a breach of responsibility.

The procedure has been adopted only once. In December 1976, when the Agudat Israel Party introduced a no-confidence motion on an issue related to Sabbath observance, two of the National Religious Party Ministers abstained. Prime Minister Rabin thereupon invoked the law and declared that the two offenders had resigned from the Government. The incident, because it resulted in a loss of Labour's majority in the Knesset, precipitated the 1977 General Election.

Much of the work of the Cabinet is performed by Ministerial Committees. They have proliferated during the Begin administration; by the middle of 1979, there were no fewer than fifty-five of them on the active list. They ranged from the Ministerial Security Committee (Chairman, the Prime Minister) to the Ministerial Committee for Emblems and Ceremonies, of which (somewhat curiously) the Minister of Energy and Infrastructure was the Chairman. The most important committees were:

Security Committee – Chairman: Prime Minister. Members: Deputy Prime Minister; Minister of Finance; Minister of Defence; Foreign Minister; Minister of Agriculture; Minister of Internal Affairs. Participant: Minister of Health.

Economic Committee – Chairman: Minister of Finance (Yigal Hurvitz). Members: Minister of Energy & Infrastructure; Minister of Construction & Housing; Minister of Agriculture; Minister of Internal Affairs; Minister of Industry, Trade & Tourism; Minister of Transport; Minister of Justice; Minister for Religious Affairs; Minister of Labour & Welfare; Minister without Portfolio (Moshe Nissim). Permanent Participant: Governor of the Bank of Israel.

Legislation Committee – Chairman: Minister of Justice (Shmuel Tamir). Members: Minister of Energy & Infrastructure; Minister of Education & Culture; Minister of Industry, Trade & Tourism; Minister Moshe Nissim. Permanent Participant: Legal Adviser to the Government.

Committee for Jerusalem – Chairman: Minister for Internal Affairs (Yosef Burg). Members: Deputy Prime Minister; Minister of Finance; Minister of Defence; Minister of Construction & Housing and Minister for Absorption; Minister of Health; Minister for Religious Affairs; Foreign Minister; Minister of Industry, Trade & Tourism; Minister of Agriculture; Minister Moshe Nissim. Permanent Participant: Mayor of Jerusalem.

Settlement Committee (with the World Zionist Organization) – Chairman: Minister of Agriculture (Ariel Sharon). Members: Minister of Finance; Minister of Defence; Minister of Construction & Housing; Minister of Transport; Minister of Industry, Trade & Tourism; Minister of Education & Culture; Minister Moshe Nissim.

Joint Government and World Zionist Organization Committee for Policy Coordination on Slum Renewal Projects – Chairman: Deputy Prime

Minister (Yigael Yadin). Members: Minister of Finance; Minister of Labour & Welfare; Minister of Construction & Housing; Minister of Education & Culture.

Committee for Negotiations with Egypt on Establishing Autonomy – Chairman: Minister for Internal Affairs (Yosef Burg). Members: Minister of Defence; Minister of Agriculture; Foreign Minister; Minister of Justice; Minister Moshe Nissim; Legal Adviser to the Government; Dr Meir Rosenne (Foreign Ministry).

Committee Preparing Proposals for Autonomy Negotiations – Chairman: Prime Minister. Members: Deputy Prime Minister; Minister of Finance; Minister of Defence; Minister of Health; Foreign Minister; Minister of Education & Culture; Minister of Agriculture; Minister of Justice; Minister of Internal Affairs; Minister Moshe Nissim.

Effective control of the Cabinet rests with the Prime Minister, who is solely responsible for drawing up its agenda. Ministers may suggest subjects for inclusion, but the Prime Minister decides on their merits and determines the order in which they are to be discussed. Regular meetings take place every Sunday morning but, in emergencies, additional meetings are held when necessary. Israel's Cabinet meetings tend to be leisurely affairs – they are regarded as short if they last less than four hours, and often continue throughout the day.

Confidentiality, except in security matters, has not been a conspicuous virtue of Israeli Cabinets. The official press release after meetings is generally only a small part of what is published. Ministers and Deputy Ministers invariably inform their party colleagues about what has transpired at the meetings and party colleagues tell the party press or their other journalistic friends. The result is that, within twenty-four hours of the meeting, every detail, almost every word uttered, is known and reported. The only way a Prime Minister can achieve any secrecy is by designating the meeting as one of the (enlarged) Security Committee, in which case disclosure of the proceedings becomes an offence. This often works – but not always (see the discussion of censorship in Chapter 8).

Under Labour Governments, the Cabinet usually considered issues which had already been decided by some kind of Prime Ministerial caucus. Golda Meir's so-called 'kitchen cabinet', an inner group of Ministers, met at her home on Saturday evenings to prepare for the following morning's Cabinet. Other Labour Premiers also worked closely with their circles of ministerial intimates. But Begin formed no such group. He has no intimate friends in the Cabinet, and the closest, Haim Landau, an Irgun colleague, fell out with him over the Egyptian peace treaty. But although nothing was settled in advance of Begin Cabinet meetings, he knew exactly what he wanted – at least he did during the first two vigorous years of his Premiership – and was firm in direction. The atmosphere changed after Begin's mild stroke in 1979. He was no longer so forceful, and the Cabinet became the forum for internecine quarrels, with the Prime Minister appearing to have lost effective control.

The procedure at Cabinet meetings requires any Minister who wants to speak to request the Cabinet Secretary to put his name on the list and the

Prime Minister calls on them in rotation. Begin tends to formality, and in the Cabinet room insists on formal modes of address. He is always referred to as 'Prime Minister' and addresses Ministers by their titles. Outside the Cabinet room he might address some of his colleagues by their first names or nicknames. The former Minister of Finance, Simcha Ehrlich, was usually 'Reb Simcha' and Arik Sharon was often hailed as 'mon general'.

Formally, the time limit for speeches in Cabinet is ten minutes – hopelessly optimistic, given the Israeli tendency to prolixity. But Begin is not strict in applying the rule. Occasionally, and with great politeness, he may mention that the speaker is exceeding the time limit but generally he lets the speaker continue, particularly if, in his opinion, he is talking sense. On important issues like the peace treaty, no time limit was applied.

All Ministers formally possess the same status and each has one vote. But their actual standing and influence will vary with both the importance of their Ministries and their own personal qualities. One of the standard methods of assessing Ministerial status is membership of the most important of the Ministerial Committees. Top of the list is the Security Committee, which also covers foreign affairs. Second only to the Prime Minister in Cabinet rank is the Minister of Finance. When Pinhas Sapir held that office under Labour, he was the virtual dictator in all the nation's internal affairs. He was the great 'fixer', determining who did what job, who was appointed, who was to receive benefits of one sort or another. Israel in some of its aspects resembles a 'shtetl', one of those Jewish townships in Eastern Europe from which Israel's early leaders sprang. Sapir continued the shtetl style, acting like the benevolent president of a synagogue, doling out the honours and the favours. This system had its drawbacks, but at least there was someone in charge who could get things done. His successors in the Begin Government, Ehrlich and Hurvitz, possessed no such power, and did not have the stature to assume it. But even without the personal authority of a Sapir, Finance Ministers, as the controllers of the national Budget, effectively decide how the country's internal affairs are managed.

The Prime Minister is the chief executive and *primus inter pares* among the Ministers. Using the instrument of the Cabinet agenda and the composition of the Committees, he effectively directs Government policies, but the principle is that of collective Cabinet responsibility. The policy of the Begin Government on this matter has been identical with that of all its predecessors. When the Prime Minister announced in 1977 that 'the Government will be established on the basis of collective responsibility of all its members and all the parties which form part of it', he was re-stating established practice. The one exception has been the stipulation of freedom of conscience on religious matters, which the National Religious Party has demanded of all the Governments in which it has participated.

Whatever their different characteristics, flavours or quirks, all Israeli Cabinets have been successful in totally dominating the Knesset, theoretically the sovereign authority. By controlling the Parliamentary agenda, by exclusively initiating all major legislation and by Ministerial control over the party factions in the legislature, the Cabinet asserts its supremacy over Parliament.

The unloved civil service

An old story which Israelis relate with a relish undiminished by repetition is of a foreign visitor arriving at a Government office in mid-afternoon. Walking through empty corridors and peering into unoccupied offices, he finally spies a cleaning woman whom he asks if anyone works there in the afternoon. She replies, 'You have asked the wrong question. They don't work in the morning. They don't *come* in the afternoon.'

The oft-quoted story catches the spirit of amused resignation with which many Israelis regard their bureaucracy. But not everyone is amused. In a hearing before the Supreme Court in June 1979, Chief Justice Sussman fulminated: 'No civilized country would tolerate our Government adminis-tration. Those officials who do not fulfil their tasks should be dismissed. There are officials who sit and do nothing and receive their salaries.'

Israel's bureaucracy is a creation of historical circumstance and the singular nature of the country's politics and policies. With the simultaneous departure of the British Mandatory administrators and the onset of the Arab invasion, the situation was not conducive to the calm and orderly planning of a civil service. As in many other areas of hurried creativity, the prescription was improvisation. Officials were hastily recruited to man Government agencies and a readily available reservoir was the Jewish Agency for Palestine, which had been set up under the Mandate to represent the Jewish people. The Jewish community in Palestine had also created its own representative body, the Va'ad Leumi (People's Council). Each had developed substantial administrative machines, with a number of departments which were embryonic Government ministries. It was com-paratively simple to translate this officialdom into government.

But the process brought with it inherent and serious drawbacks. The first was that these officials were, by and large, unaffected by the notion that they were servants of the public. Their approach to their jobs was either the disdainful unconcern of the Middle East official or the inflated self-importance of the East European bureaucrat. Moreover, standards of ability and efficiency were poor. The civil service could not attract able people because, in the Socialist egalitarian society which the Labour founders of Israel intended to create, salaries in the public sector were uniformly low. Nor was there the tradition and prestige of the British civil service to attract a public-spirited élite or even the heady inducement of wielding power, because Israeli politicians have always been reluctant to give their civil servants any real authority.

The ubiquitous politicization of the new nation compounded these problems. As a new Ministry was created, its political chief filled the jobs with his own party members – not totally irrespective of any possible merit, but merit was certainly lower on the order of priorities than payment for party favours received or anticipated. In an attempt to introduce order into this haphazard agglomeration and to mitigate some of the worst effects of the prevailing system, a Civil Service Commission was set up in 1951, and has brought about some improvement in recruitment. But the job patron-age for party members was too valuable a resource for the politicians to abandon completely. It still applies, though to a diminishing extent. The most persistent practitioner of the technique is the National Religious Party. To this day, practically every visible male at the Ministry of the Interior, long a preserve of the NRP, wears the small kipa (skull cap) which is the badge of the orthodox Jew in Israel.

A measure of the improvement that has taken place was that in the change-over of 1977, only one Minister, David Levy, the Minister of Housing whose first Cabinet post this was, brought in many of his own supporters to work in his department. Most other Ministers contented themselves with bringing in their own people for the most senior jobs only. The new Prime Minister retained the whole of the staff which had served his Labour predecessors, bringing with him only a Director General, Dr Eliahu Ben-Elissar (now Ambassador to Egypt), and his personal secretary, Yechiel Kadishai.

The Civil Service Commission was created by a Cabinet decision with the objects of setting out effective recruiting procedures, supervising the efficiency of the service and, with some specified exceptions, ensuring that it became politically neutral. After almost thirty years, the Commission remains one of the least known and least commented-on departments of government. It has little prestige, largely due to the fact that it is the whipping boy in the middle. Government departments will often justify their refusal of a particular course of action by attributing it to the restrictions imposed by the Commission. On the other hand, if the Commission accedes to a request, it is accepted as the right of the department concerned, which claims the credit for the decision. In many respects, it has become a convenient scapegoat for the whole of the much – and on the whole, justly – maligned bureaucracy.

The present Commissioner, Dr Avraham Friedman, is well aware of these problems. When he took office in 1979, he told his staff that his aim was to create conditions which would encourage them to be proud to say that they worked for the Civil Service Commission. At present, they still prefer to describe themselves as employees of the Ministry of Finance, under whose auspices the Commission operates, even though the small staff of 150 has substantial achievements to its credit, not least the institution of an efficient operating procedure. This owes much to the Commissioner, who came from the Hebrew University where he was Senior Lecturer in Business Administration.

At the University, Dr Friedman served as a faculty representative in staff negotiations with the administration and saw the other side of the job he now performs. Born in Tel Aviv in 1935, the Commissioner taught criminology before he moved over to business administration, receiving his doctorate in that field from the University of Chicago where he later served as Visiting Professor.

The Commission he now heads with the rank of Deputy Minister is the Government as employer. Its main duty is to set the wages of all the civil servants employed by the Government. There are about 120,000 of them, half of them bureaucrats and the rest teachers. Since Government rates of pay are followed by the rest of the public sector, the wage rates agreed by the Commission determine the incomes of more than 300,000 employees throughout the country.

These wage rates are achieved as the result of centralized national collective bargaining with the trade unions. Government departments are not permitted to negotiate with their own staffs, while public authorities and state-owned corporations are required to consult with the Commission and receive its approval for their wage negotiations. The Commission also plays a role in the setting of pay rates for the army and the various security agencies. When changes are contemplated, the Director-General of the Ministry of Defence and other military administrators are required to consult the Commission.

Wage negotiations are a leisurely business and, for the last decade, have been virtually a non-stop show in Israel. Agreements are intended to span two years, but they take about that time to settle and negotiations for the two-year period from April 1978 were expected to finish by April 1980, when it would be time to begin negotiations for the new agreement.

Next in importance after its functions in wage settlements, and not less difficult in practice, is the Commission's responsibility in the selection of employees. The Commission receives from each department of state a list of its establishment, that is, of all the jobs it offers and their grading. Generally the Commission approves the list – with or without modification – but there is provision in the State Service (Appointments) Law for an appeal to the Government against a negative decision of the Commissioner. When the need arises to fill an established post, the vacancy must be publicly announced and the Commission notified. The procedure is that the first announcement is within the office concerned and, if no suitable candidate is available from this source, the job is advertised. Applications are received by the Commission which sets up a selection board, according to a prescribed formula, to make the appointment.

The objects of this procedure are to ensure that the best applicant gets the job and to prevent the intervention of party or departmental influences. In these respects, the Commission has achieved only limited success. In practice, the opinion of the representative of the department in which the vacancy exists generally prevails, except in the rare cases where the unsuitability of the recommended candidate is manifest. The concept of open jobs openly arrived at is further impaired by the permitted procedure under which the department concerned may, without consultation, fill the vacancy for three months. About a quarter of all civil service vacancies are, in fact, first filled temporarily under this procedure. Approval is then sought (and almost invariably given) from the selection board.

Certain jobs are entirely excluded from this selection procedure. Among them are posts for which salaries are fixed by the Knesset or one of its committees: they include judges, defence personnel of certain ranks, and police and prison employees. Others are only exempted from the need for public announcement. They include the Civil Service Commissioner himself and the Directors General of Government Ministries and departments.

Dismissals of civil servants are rare and involve an exhaustive process. To succeed in obtaining approval for a dismissal both from the local workers' representatives in the same office and from the local Histadrut office, the offences of a civil servant will have to be of an extreme kind. Mere inefficiency will not suffice. The small number of employees who are dismissed will be compensated either by the immediate payment of a pension if close to retiring age, or by severance pay of one month's basic salary for each year of service.

Although some improvement has occurred in recent years, even members of the Commission's staff agree that there is still an intolerable amount of inefficiency. A law, pushed through the Knesset by an irate MK, requiring civil servants to reply in full to letters from the public within three months of receipt is widely disregarded, and nobody knows what to do about this situation. The shortcomings of the civil service owe much to the factors common today in all bureaucracies (only more so in Israel) – low wages resulting in poor quality, dogged conformity with established practices, no encouragement for personal achievement and no personal responsibility. In Israel too, inefficiency is compounded by bad manners. As one of the Commission's officials put it to me: 'In Israel you don't just get bad service; it is aggravated by a nasty look from the clerk. Maybe in another country you'd get the same lousy attention – but more politely.'

The State watchdog

Every May, Israeli officialdom of all varieties is weighed, assessed and given good or bad marks in the Annual Report of the Israeli State Comptroller. In the restrained, unemotional, measured terms of a pedagogue, the report passes judgment on the level of performance of Government agencies and other beneficiaries of public funds. Every newspaper gives extensive summaries, running into tens of thousands of words, of this annual balance-sheet of achievement and failure.

The office of the State Comptroller was instituted in 1949 to take the place of the audit department of the Mandatory Government. Appointed by the President on the recommendation of the House Committee of the Knesset, the Comptroller serves a five-year term which can be indefinitely renewed. He is responsible only to the Knesset and not to the Government, and while holding office, may not be actively engaged in politics or in any kind of business.

Bodies subject to the inspection of the Comptroller include every Government office and every State institution or enterprise, as well as all security establishments, political parties, universities, religious councils, the Health Fund of the Histadrut and cultural institutions which receive Government grants. Excluded from the Comptroller's scrutiny are legislative and judicial acts. The political parties came into his net when the Government began financing them in 1969. The Comptroller checks the use of Government funding and ensures that the parties do not receive donations from Israeli corporations. Since some of the parties by-pass the law by channelling donations through associated organizations, the Comptroller has asked for, but not yet received, an extension of his powers to inspect these associated bodies.

The Comptroller is given extensive powers to obtain all the necessary records for his inspection, which is directed towards issues of legality, efficiency, economy and probity. When completed, the Annual Report is presented to the Minister of Finance who, within twelve weeks, may make his observations and, with the agreement of the House Committee of the Knesset, decide to withhold from the published version any part of the report which might be damaging to security or internal relations.

Since 1971, the Comptroller's office has assumed an additional responsibility – investigating complaints from members of the public; for this purpose the title of Commissioner for Complaints from the Public was created. The first Commissioner was Gershon Avner, a former diplomat, but the office is now held by the State Comptroller, in which capacity he is now generally described as the Ombudsman. Since the institution was created, only two men have held the office of State Comptroller, Dr Siegfried Moses from 1949 to 1961 (he retired at the age of 75) and the present incumbent, Dr Yitzhak Ernst Nebenzahl, whose fourth term of office began in 1976.

The etymology of the word 'Yekke' is obscure, but one suggestion is that it derives from the German word for jacket and that it was used to describe German Jews because the stiffness and formality of the jackets they habitually wore distinguished them from the mass of casually dressed Israelis. Whatever its provenance, the word is still used in Israel as a synonym for German Jews (and occasionally for pedantic non-German Jews), sometimes applied pejoratively and at other times admiringly.*

When talking of the two Comptrollers, most Israelis will not fail to mention that they were both Yekkes, meaning that they are conscientious, reliable, meticulous in the performance of duty – lacking in imagination or humour perhaps, stiff in manner and possibly finicky but, above all, scrupulous and industrious.

Dr Nebenzahl possesses all the positive characteristics attributed to the Yekke. Born in the cultivated and exclusive neo-orthodox Jewish community of Frankfurt in 1907, he grew up in a strictly observant environment and was a member of Ezra, the orthodox youth movement. He studied law at various universities in Germany, and at the age of 25 became a lecturer in civil law at the University of his home town. A year later, he was one of the first to foresee that Germany, with the advent of Hitler, was no place for a Jew. He emigrated to Palestine, where he went into business.

With the emergence of the State of Israel, he had a brief fling in politics. In 1959, he was the National Religious Party's candidate for the Mayoralty of Jerusalem, but gave it up during the tortuous negotiations for the formation of a coalition. Before becoming Comptroller, he had held the important offices of Director of Planning for the Jewish Agency, Chairman of the Post Office Bank and membership of the executive of the Bank of

* In October 1979, the Israeli High Court ruled that use of the word 'Yekke' to denote a Jew of German origin was not derogatory. On the contrary, said the Court, the expression implied affection and respect. Two of the three judges were Yekkes.

Israel. When Dr Moses resigned as Comptroller in 1961, Nebenzahl was the NRP candidate, and prevailed in a contest with the Labour Party nominee. Nebenzahl had never really had his heart in politics and, even if there had been some political juggling in the course of his appointment, it left no lasting mark on the job, which is still one of the rare institutions in Israel universally accepted as non-political.

The personal probity of the Comptroller was, however, slightly tarnished when, ten years after his first appointment, his connections with the Ministerial Committee for the Jewish Quarter in Jerusalem brought him permission to purchase a plot of land facing the Western Wall, where he planned to build a house. The deal provoked a flurry of criticism, particularly as it was made before the Committee had agreed on an overall policy for the utilization of the area. Dr Nebenzahl published an apology in the press, explaining that his purpose was to build a house there so that his children and grandchildren, influenced by this holiest of Jewish sites, would grow up in a religious atmosphere. Public opinion was slightly mollified by the information that no price had been fixed but would be determined later in accordance with the Committee's general policy. The incident was generally considered a case of poor judgment rather than of moral turpitude.

Such criticism as there is of the office and its incumbent is directed at his reluctance to lean heavily on those who exercise the greatest power. He has been urged to name major offenders, but has never done so, contenting himself with analysis and criticism of the offence. The *Jerusalem Post*, after his 1973 report, commented sadly: 'Twenty-eight years of experience have shown that the measured reticence and purposeful understatement that have marked his *modus operandi* have not been successful in bringing about the desired results.'

Less arguable is the criticism that the Comptroller's inability to enforce any of his recommendations is a crippling weakness of the institution. But it would be inaccurate to regard his activity as simply a safety valve or window dressing, for the reports have a considerable influence on public opinion. Nebenzahl gave his own answer to the critics in a speech in Tel Aviv in June 1979, in which he said that the current demand for powers of enforcement was based on a misconception as to the distribution of functions in a democratic society. No institution like that of the State Comptroller would be able to function if it had an active part in the process of government. He asserted that the impact made by the publication of his reports showed that he was doing his job properly. The recurrence of certain offences could only mean that the responsible authorities were not doing theirs and the role of the Comptroller was to keep pointing that out.

Most of the 550 or so staff members of the Comptroller's office work at the main headquarters in Jerusalem. The branch in Tel Aviv concerns itself with the Defence Forces (the Defence Ministry is located there) and with the local councils, while the Haifa office supervises traffic projects and the northern local councils. The budget of the State Comptroller, which is fixed by the Knesset Finance Committee, amounted to approximately I£114 million (about US$6.7 million) in 1978.

The investigation of complaints from the public is also carried out by the Comptroller's staff and can include the activity of any authority, the major exclusions being complaints against courts or judges, for which other remedies are available, and political criticism. The Ombudsman will also not intervene if the complaint is delayed more than a year after the first occasion on which it could have been raised. In recent years, he has received between 5,000 and 6,000 complaints a year. About half of them were found to be justified, an extremely high proportion compared with the average 20 per cent in other countries with an analogous institution. The Ombudsman's report is contained in a separate document from that of the Comptroller and is published later in the year.

Eagle-eyed sleuths

The 29th Annual Report of the State Comptroller for Israel, published in May 1979, illustrates the wide-ranging nature of the office, both as the scourge of those who have erred or failed and as the upholder of national standards. Indeed, in his own unemotional way, Dr Nebenzahl wears the mantle of Israel's ancient prophets, castigating his people for their misdeeds and failings.

At the press conference which accompanied the publication of the 1,140-page report, the Comptroller was uncharacteristically passionate in his denunciation of the national malaise which he defined as a combination of cynicism and despair. The heart-searching which followed this cry of pain went far beyond the specific event which had prompted it, Operation Litani in Lebanon, launched in March 1978 in response to a terrorist attack on the coastal road a few days earlier. This was the first occasion on which the Comptroller had investigated the efficiency of the Israel Defence Forces in battle and passed judgment on the execution of a military operation, in which twenty-one soldiers lost their lives. All previous investigations had been related to maladministration, financial loss and bureaucratic excesses.

The blunders and mismanagement of the Litani Operation were the most sensational features of the Comptroller's 29th Report. What shocked the public most of all was his conclusion that the conditions which had brought the country close to disaster during the first stage of the 1973 Yom Kippur War still persisted in 1978. He found that the basic Intelligence data were not available to the troops and that what had been available was in considerable measure out of date. Vehicles from the depots were often defective. While it had been known that extensive mining was probable, there had been insufficient equipment to clear the routes, much of it in a state of disrepair. In the event, most of the Israeli casualties on the first day were caused by mines.

The Comptroller's investigation was detailed and meticulous, resulting in such findings as that, of the twenty-seven cases in which Israeli tanks had been 'neutralized' on the first day, twenty-one were due to the poor judgment of the tank commanders. Even the highly efficient Israeli system of mobilization had on this occasion been muddled. In the case of one brigade, the report found that 150 soldiers had not arrived on the eve of the operation because their call-up papers had not reached them and that, when it was decided to telephone them, the list of names was found to be out of date. And so the Report continued: errors, omissions, blunders. The strictures were devastating and alarming, all the more so since the army occupied such a high place in the estimation of Israelis generally. Whatever else could be criticized in Israel, it had always been thought that the army could be relied upon to function efficiently. The Comptroller's report shattered that complacency and brought a rapid response from the Prime Minister – the Cabinet would devote a special session to the discussion of the report! Begin added the well-nigh incredible comment that this would be the first time any Israeli Cabinet had devoted a session to one of the Comptroller's reports.

Although most of the public attention given to the 29th Report was concentrated on the Litani Operation, Nebenzahl and his staff had covered the complete range of national activity. A lengthy section examined the activities of the Finance Ministry, pointing to the deficit of I£12 billion in 1977/78 which had been financed by 'printing money', and to the increased cost of subsidies and administration which had far exceeded the rise in the cost-of-living index. The report analyzed the national debt, and the preparation of the state Budget was criticized as based on inaccurate facts. It was even more censorious of the commercial banks, delineating, with a mass of details, a large number of instances in which they had enriched themselves at the expense of the national exchequer.

But it was not all high policy and high finance. School attendance and the problem of truancy were among the subjects examined and the educational authorities were rebuked for the inadequacy of school shelters. The protection of schoolchildren against terrorist attacks is one of the abnormalities of life in Israel and found expression in the prosaic discussion of the subject in the Comptroller's Report.

Dozens of other matters investigated and censured included waste in the employment service, shortcomings in the car licensing bureau and the general ineffectiveness of the Tourist Authority in dealing with tourist complaints. The Broadcasting Authority's 'exaggerated and careless hiring of taxis' and the payment of car allowances to staff were subjected to critical comment – even the Prime Minister's Office did not escape. The Comptroller's eagle-eyed sleuths were everywhere and had discovered that, owing to an error in translation, an unspecified number of Independence Day posters were never used. It was not, apparently, an isolated occurrence, for about 18,000 other posters, costing about $10,000 and intended for use abroad, were found unused in the store rooms of the Prime Minister's Office – another contribution to the problems of the economy.

Chapter seven

Law and Order

A model judge

A visitor from Britain or the United States would feel at home and comfortable with Israel's lawyers and in Israel's law courts. He may not feel quite so much at ease with Israel's police, but there, too, would find a great deal about the system that was familiar.

The court system remains similar to that in Britain during the Mandatory period, while the law applied in Israel's courts still contains a substantial element of English law. Text-books on English law are still used, precedents contained in English law reports are cited in court and frequently followed for, although English law has no binding force, it has persuasive authority. The lawyers who set the pattern for Israel's legal system, when it began to operate independently in 1948, had been brought up in the English legal tradition and, indeed, many of them had qualified in England.

Justice Haim Cohn, Deputy President of the Supreme Court, is a notable exemplar of the independence, incorruptibility and competence of the Israeli judiciary and of its debt to the English model. Born into a religious German family in 1911 – both his grandfathers were famous rabbis in that country – Haim Cohn was himself destined for the rabbinate. When he left school at the age of 18 he was offered the choice of continuing his rabbinical studies either in Lithuania or in Jerusalem. He chose Jerusalem, and spent 1930 and 1931 at a Yeshiva there, although he was never ordained as a rabbi. His theological studies had led him to the legal sections of the Talmud and they fascinated him so much that he decided to become a lawyer.

His secular legal studies began in Germany but Hitler intervened and Cohn changed course. He moved to London and became a student at Lincoln's Inn where he was 'called' to the Bar (qualified as a barrister) in 1936. That permitted him to practise at the Palestine Bar, which he did for ten years until 1947. His rabbinic studies had given him a special interest in Jewish law, and he was summoned by the embryo Government of the nascent State of Israel to draft new laws in accordance with Jewish law. The relationship between the traditional religious law and the legal system of the secular state became an abiding interest with him.

A month after the new State was founded, Cohn became State Attorney, an office which, at that time, was similar to that of the Director of Public Prosecutions in England. Cohn had no experience of the criminal law, but Ben-Gurion brushed aside his objections with the exhortation: 'We're all soldiers now.' He later became the Attorney General and set the pattern for that important office.

Israel had inherited a system from the British Mandate, which in turn had inherited it from the Ottoman empire: each recognized religious community exercised exclusive jurisdiction in family matters (e.g. marriage, divorce, inheritance and so on) over its members. The secularists in the new Government wanted to abandon this arrangement, and proposed to transfer all legal jurisdiction to the ordinary civil courts. Cohn was instructed to draft the necessary legislation, but the opposition both of religious Jews and of Moslems was too great, and the Bill was permanently pigeon-holed. Many of his later judgments would have been unnecessary if the secularists had won the day.

His personal life was directly and disagreeably affected by the operation of religious law. When he decided to marry a divorcee, the rabbinical authorities refused to perform the marriage on the ground that, according to the law they were bound to apply, a 'Cohen', a descendant of the biblical priestly tribe (which Justice Cohn is), is forbidden to marry a widow or divorcee. Since Israel has no civil marriage, Haim Cohn and his bride, like many another couple unable to marry in Israel, contracted a civil marriage outside the country, which was recognized by Israeli law as a valid marriage.

Today, Justice Cohn personifies the unquestioned authority of the Supreme Court and the acceptance of the rule of law as a limitation of the power of both the secular and the religious arms of the State. His learned and liberal judgments have made invaluable contributions to Israeli jurisprudence and his personal bearing has enhanced the dignity of the institution he serves. Whether in the austere environment of the Supreme Court or in his modest apartment in Jerusalem's Rehavia district, Cohn radiates an aura of calm judiciousness. His manner is donnish and didactic and in his own small study, orderly but overcrowded with books, he will painstakingly expound his views, occasionally lightening his explanations with a darting humorous interjection. His manner is Germanic and his perfect English bears a trace of a German accent, but his legal approach is totally identifiable as English, and he could well be an English High Court Judge. With his domed head, fringed with grey, and his aquiline features, he even looks English.

The courts, the law and legal aid

Israelis go to court in large numbers not only because of a predisposition towards litigiousness, but also because the courts of law have established a high reputation. They are among the limited Israeli institutions trusted by Jew and Arab alike.

Israel has retained almost unchanged the three-tier civil court system which operated under the Mandate. In ascending order of seniority, the three categories of courts are the Magistrates' Courts, the District Courts and the Supreme Court, and all of them can deal with both civil and criminal cases. The jurisdiction of Magistrates' Courts is limited to minor criminal offences carrying a maximum sentence of three years' imprisonment, and smaller money claims of up to I£100,000. In 1977, the 105 magistrates (1979 salary $1,200 monthly) heard 368,346 cases, 101,906 of them civil claims and 266,386 criminal prosecutions. The 1978 Statistical Abstract of Israel records that the average time between the date of submitting a case to a Magistrates' Court and its verdict was 4.3 months in Jerusalem, 6.2 in Tel Aviv, and 5.3 in Haifa. Normally, cases are heard by a single magistrate, but the Chief Magistrates may direct that three magisrates should sit together to hear a particular case.

Appeals from Magistrates come before the District Courts, of which there are five: Jerusalem, Tel Aviv-Jaffa, Haifa, Beersheba and Nazareth. Each has a President and Vice-President, and their jurisdiction covers both civil and criminal matters exceeding the limits of the Magistrates' Courts. The seventy-nine District Judges functioning in 1977 (their salaries are the same as those of magistrates) carried a heavy workload. They heard 52,560 civil and 9,618 criminal cases, 2,772 of them appeals. Each case occupied an average of ten months of the court's time between the date the case was entered and the date it was decided. But this is not as protracted as would appear because Israeli judges, who organize their own lists, will frequently adjourn cases part-heard to accommodate the wish of litigants or lawyers for cases to be either delayed or expedited.

When sitting as a court of appeal, the District Court consists of a bench of three judges, as it does when dealing with serious crime as a court of first instance or in hearing other special cases at the request of the President of the Court. But, generally, as a court of first instance a single judge sits alone.

The full establishment of the Supreme Court normally comprises twelve Justices whose salary in 1979 was $1,400 a month. Its seat is in Jerusalem, and its jurisdiction is the whole country. As the highest appellate court, it hears appeals from the District Court, and its competence not only includes civil and criminal matters but also administrative and fiscal issues like infringement of Knesset election laws or income tax. It also acts as a court of first instance, then described as the High Court of Justice, where the interests of justice call for relief to be granted in questions which are not within the jurisdiction of any other court.

This power, which the Supreme Court has forthrightly used, has been of immense importance in curbing the activities of public authorities, including even the Cabinet. Probably its most notable exercise was the series of decisions imposing restrictions on Jewish settlement in the occupied territories. The High Court of Justice has the authority to exercise control over all the State authorities, subject only to the immunities granted by law (i.e., those of the State President and the Members of the Knesset). Among the authorities over which the Supreme Court may exercise control are the religious courts. (The use it has made of this power is discussed later.) Finally, the Supreme Court can act as an appeal court against its own decisions, if it decides that what is called a 'Further Hearing' is necessary. The Court will then consist of five or more Judges.

The court system is completed by a wide range of specialized courts and tribunals, the most important of which are the Municipal Courts, which deal only with petty criminal offences, Juvenile Courts and Tenancy and Labour tribunals. In all, twenty-one full-time judges are employed in these lower courts, with the same rank and salaries as magistrates. Military courts and courts martial deal with offences committed by soldiers and some security offences by civilians. Conducted by officers, they are under the jurisdiction of the Attorney-General.

For many years concern has been growing about the heavy workloads judges have to bear and the inadequacy of the facilities with which they are provided. The result has been long delays, both before cases come up and during the actual trial, often causing hardship to the parties involved. In 1979 Shmuel Tamir, the Minister of Justice, set up a committee under the chairmanship of Justice Moshe Landau, then deputy President of the Supreme Court, to examine the structure of the court system with a view to reform. Among the proposals it was considering was the abolition of the jurisdictional limits on the Magistrates' Courts so that they would be able to deal with all civil and criminal cases, leaving the District Courts free to hear only appeals. This change would, in turn, leave the Supreme Court freer to deal with the development of the law rather than the regular appellate business. The reforms have not yet been implemented, for the law, in Israel as in Britain, moves ponderously.

The Law which all Israeli courts apply – from the Supreme Court to the tenancy tribunals – is a strange amalgam, consisting, like an archaeological site, of layers of history. The Provisional Council of State, which exercised authority before the election of the first Knesset, had to ensure that the new State, born in war and still then at war, should be governed by some legal system. In those circumstances, the only practical course was to carry on as before, and the first constitutional ordinance promulgated by Israel declared that the law which had operated in Palestine as at 15 May, 1948 (the birth-date of Israel) would continue. That remains the position, and the law of Israel today consists of Palestine law prior to 1948, together with the new laws passed by the Knesset since Israel began. When there is any conflict between the two, the new law prevails. A great deal of legislation has been enacted in the thirty-two years' history of the State, but much of the pre-State Palestine law still operates.

Palestinian law before 1948 itself consisted of a variety of strands. When Britain acquired the Mandate for Palestine, it took over the Ottoman law, which was the system in force on the operative date of 1 November 1914 when Palestine was a province of the Ottoman empire. To make the story even more complicated, Ottoman law was itself an agglomeration of parts. Moslem religious law, with which it began, had been augmented by sections of the French Code Napoleon as well as by Jewish and Christian religious law on family matters. Although the Turkish elements in Israel's law have largely been replaced by subsequent legislation, some vestiges survive, and the long-suffering law student finds included in his syllabus the Ottoman Code of Civil Procedure 1879 as well as various other sections of the Majelle, the Ottoman Civil Code.

But the British influence on Israeli law was much stronger, composed in parts of Acts of Parliament expressly applied to Palestine, Orders in Council, Ordinances and various by-laws and regulations of the Mandatory authority. More far-reaching in its present-day application was the preservation of the influence of English common law and equity. The Palestine Order in Council of 1922, setting out the basis of government in the Mandated Territory, provided in Article 46 that lacunae (gaps) in the laws of Palestine should be filled by the application of the Common Law and the doctrines of equity in force in England. That Order in Council continues to enjoy statutory force in Israel and, with it, Article 46 which, on important issues, has been relied on by the Supreme Court. Almost every year a Bill is introduced into the Knesset to substitute 'principles of Jewish law' for 'English common law and equity', but so far they have failed.

In March 1980, the Knesset gave a first reading to a Foundation of Law Bill which, if passed through all its stages, will replace the famous Article 46 with a provision that Israeli courts faced with a lacuna in the law should act in accordance with 'the values of the Jewish heritage'. Patriotic sentiment favoured the change but it was strongly opposed by the lawyers who saw danger in the uncertainty of 'Jewish heritage', which is undefined. But in the debate on the first reading, the Minister of Justice emphasized that it was not the same as Jewish law, answering the critics who were afraid that the new Bill would bring in more religious orthodoxy by the back door.

Legal aid is provided in civil cases for those regarded as needy. Complicated regulations define who comes within that category but, as an example, a family of five whose total income is less than $250 monthly or a family of seven with less than $335 are entitled to legal aid. The law was extended in 1978 to include victims of terrorist attacks, new immigrants and women in respect of alimony. Another extension of the law ensures that all employees from whom national insurance contributions are deducted – in practice all employees – will receive legal aid in any claim they may make in the Labour Courts against the National Insurance Institute. In criminal cases the Mandate law of 1920 providing for defence of poor prisoners was incorporated into the Israeli criminal law.

Since 1966, the legal aid system has been operated by three district bureaux under the aegis of the Ministry of Justice, in Jerusalem, Haifa and Tel Aviv. Staff lawyers in these offices (these have an average of two each) sift the claims. Of those approved, 20 per cent are disposed of through out-of-court settlements. The rest are distributed among private lawyers who, if successful practitioners, are not very eager to accept these cases for which the permitted fees are very much lower than the commercial rate. The result is that, in practice, most of the private practitioners who accept legal aid cases are unlikely to be Israel's best.

A litigant who cannot afford the normal fees of a top lawyer may come to an arrangement to give him a share of the proceeds. Such an arrangement is called champerty and is unlawful in Britain; it is also frowned on in Israel, but in fact is widely practised. It has come to be a practical form of legal aid, for only in this way can an impecunious litigant acquire the services of one of the most competent lawyers. Although the Bar Association disapproves of the practice, it realistically recognizes that it exists and, on the whole, works satisfactorily. Some measure of regulation has therefore been attempted by insisting that the maximum share of the proceeds of litigation that may be retained by the lawyer is one-third.

The professionals

Israel is blessed – an adjective which is unlikely to attract universal approval in this context – with an abundance of lawyers. Over 9,000 of them have received licences to practise since the State began, and about 7,000 are working today, the majority in Tel Aviv, the country's commercial centre. Some 1,500 lawyers are salaried officials in the Government, army and police. The profession is said to be overcrowded. It is certainly difficult for a lawyer to join one of the large firms or, having started up on his own, to find business, for the competition is very keen. But somehow or other, the lawyers seem to make a living.

Prospective lawyers must (with extremely limited exceptions) have gained the Bachelor of Laws degree from a recognized Israeli university. The course for this degree lasts four years and the intending lawyer may, in his fourth year, begin his obligatory two-year apprenticeship (articles) with a lawyer already in practice. An immigrant lawyer with not less than two years' experience in his country of origin will have to serve an apprenticeship of one year. Both categories of applicant are required to take written and oral examinations which, if successfully negotiated, lead to a 'call to the Bar'. The nomenclature of the English Inns of Court is still used – no Hebrew word exists for Bar.

Once admitted, the new lawyer will apply for a licence to practise from the Bar Association. The annual intake is about five hundred and the fee, approximately $80, covers membership of the central organization and the district branch, of which there are four – Jerusalem, Tel Aviv, Haifa and Beersheba. But not all lawyers do pay and the Bar Association has never been particularly insistent about it. Since lawyers are allowed to practise even without a licence, many of them have no overwhelming incentive to make the payment.

The Bar Association sets examinations, arranges articles, admits new lawyers and enforces standards of professional ethics. A code of professional ethics sets the tone (e.g. 'an advocate will not advertise his office in any fashion or in any place except fixing his shingle over his office, to contain his name, address and degrees'). Outside the major firms, the code is not always followed with absolute dedication to its letter and spirit. To enforce the code, the Bar Association maintains disciplinary courts in each district, from which appeals by either side go to its national court which sits in Tel Aviv and, between 1975 and 1978, heard 183 appeals. In 1978, the local Jerusalem disciplinary court heard 134 complaints of which 80 were dismissed. In Tel Aviv, easily the biggest district with 4,500, lawyers, 3,387 complaints were made between 1975 and 1978. Most of them were thrown out during the preliminary screening process but, of the 226 complaints heard, 107 were found proved. Nearly all the complaints come from dissatisfied clients, and the Bar Association finds that the same lawyers are repeatedly involved.

Any lawyer charged with any offence in the national courts automatically comes before the Bar Association's disciplinary court, which has the power to disbar pending determination of the case. Generally, however, the penalty imposed on erring lawyers is a fine and very few have ever been disbarred.

The President of the Bar Association, a prestigious appointment, is Amnon Goldenberg, a Ph.D. of London University, born in 1934 and one of the country's outstanding practitioners. A Likud supporter, he would probably have been Minister of Justice had not the DMC joined the Government and been allocated that portfolio. Goldenberg is a partner in the Tel Aviv law firm of S. Horowitz and Co., probably the most highly respected in the country. Other top firms are those headed by Haim Zadok, Minister of Justice in the Rabin Government, Joshua Rotenstreich, a former Bar Association President, and Chaim Herzog, the Irish-born and British-educated former general and Ambassador to the UN. None of the superior firms is large, and few have more than a dozen lawyers.

Rewards for the top lawyers can be substantial. Members of the half-dozen or so prestige firms may earn between $50,000 and $100,000 a year, with a handful even approaching Wall Street standards of $200,000. But taxation takes a cut of 60 per cent for the top earners, although some of the less reputable among them with foreign business are believed to avoid tax by receiving payments abroad. The tax authorities are hard on lawyers – no car allowance, no telephone at home, and entertainment only if charged out to the client. Their only deductible expenses, lawyers relate with a deep sigh, are the actual expenditures for which the client pays, together with the expenses exclusively incurred in running a law office.

At the other end of the financial scale are the fledgling lawyers denied the family relationships and the connections which, for the fortunate few, offer entry to the top firms. They have the choice of joining struggling partnerships, starting out in practice on their own or taking jobs in government or industry. Those in industry, which generally are well paid, attract most applicants and the competition for them is naturally keen. But it is comparatively easy to find a legal job in government, particularly in the District Attorney's office. Since government salary scales are low, only non-breadwinners can afford to accept them. This is one of the reasons that most of these officials are women, and it is a common sight in Israel to see young (and often pregnant) women representing the State in both civil and criminal matters. In a way, the situation is a corrective to the power of the State because these young women prosecutors are generally inexperienced and (with exceptions) conscientious rather than brilliant. The defendant, on the other hand, has the opportunity of being represented by a top flight lawyer – if he has the required means.

The smaller firms, or practitioners on their own, cannot afford to specialize. Very few restrict themselves to advocacy alone, and forensic standards in the courts do not often reach the highest criteria. These lawyers gladly take whatever cases come their way. To reduce the expenses of a separate office, small firms or individuals frequently share a suite of offices either on a cooperative basis or by paying the main tenant a fixed sum for a room and the general facilities. For most of the less prosperous practitioners, even these overheads account for a high proportion of income – but they would be higher still if provided individually.

Under the Judges Law introduced in 1953, the system of appointment of all Israeli judges is uniform. All are appointed by the President on the recommendation of an Appointments Committee of nine representing all the major interests involved. Parliament is represented by two Members of the Knesset elected by secret ballot and holding office for an indefinite period until they leave the Knesset, or die, or are replaced by others elected by the Knesset. Two represent the Government – the Minister of Justice and another Cabinet Minister. The profession is represented by the President of the Supreme Court, two other Supreme Court justices and two elected representatives of the Bar Association – all these serve a three-year term.

The formal qualifications required for the Judiciary vary with rank. Magistrates must have been engaged in the practice of law for three years, a District Court Judge must either have been a Magistrate for four years or have been in practice for five, and a Supreme Court Judge must either have been a District Court Judge for five years or practised law for ten. But eminent jurists may be appointed to the Supreme Court without any of the above qualifications. One of its present members, Professor Menahem Elon, an authority on Jewish law, was appointed directly from the Hebrew University without having had any experience at the Bar. Political appointments are rare but have been made. One such was Justice Zvi Berenson, now retired, who was an unblushing Mapai Party appointment. He came to the Supreme Court directly from the legal administration, and had been legal adviser to the Histadrut. There is an unwritten convention that at least one Sephardi and one orthodox Jew shall be included on the Supreme Court.

The Judges hold office for life, with a retiring age of 70. They must be Israeli citizens and can be removed by the judgment of a Disciplinary Court, the composition of which is laid down in the Judge's Law, but so far no Judge has been thus disciplined. This, and other provisions of the law, are designed to ensure that a Judge is subject to no authority but the law. Israel's Judges in all grades have stoutly maintained their independence and, in return, they have gained the confidence of the public. Their salaries have always been low, but no Judge in the history of the State of Israel has ever been accused of taking bribes.

In 1979, the net monthly take-home pay of a Supreme Court Justice was approximately $800 ($1,400 gross), the only 'perk' being the use of a car for court purposes from the car pool. They all live very modestly. Some manage because they were German refugees and receive from that country either a pension or restitution payments. Others may earn small fees from writing or from occasional lectures. One Supreme Court Justice had a bank overdraft of over I£100,000 when he retired and was forced to capitalize his pension to repay it.

Magistrates and District Court Judges are an able and esteemed group in society, but the general public would probably be at a loss to name any of them. On the other hand, the Supreme Court Justices, by reason of the extraordinary powers they possess, are frequently in the limelight. At the present time it is an ageing court, many of the Justices having been appointed twenty-five years ago or more. Practically all of them have been sitting in some court or another for decades, and murmurs are occasionally heard that they are cut off from everyday living on their 'Mount Olympus'. The Supreme Court is sometimes, unkindly, described as being 2,500 feet above reality (Jerusalem is that distance above sea level). But even these critics agree that the legal acumen of the court is high and its integrity exemplary.

With all the publicity the Court receives and the investigative attention to which it has been subjected, no Justice's honour has ever been impugned. Nor is the public ever aware of the differences that must, at least on occasion, exist among them. They keep their squabbles to themselves like the gentlemen they are.

Of the Supreme Court justices, its Deputy President Haim Cohn has international juridical standing and is one of the 'characters' in the profession which, today, has few outstanding personalities. A man of liberal views, he is a great dissenter and takes a keen interest in penal reform. In 1968 he published a book entitled *The Trial and Death of Jesus*, a controversial revision of Jesus's trial which gained world-wide attention.

President of the Supreme Court is Justice Moshe Landau, who received international acclaim for his patient and judicious conduct of the Eichmann trial over which he presided. A sound lawyer with a German background, Justice Landau is also president of the court which decides internal constitutional issues for the World Zionist Organization and, by way of relaxation, is an excellent pianist. Born in 1912, he received his legal education in London and has served on the Supreme Court since 1953.

Meir Shamgar, a former Chief Judge Advocate of the army and subsequently Attorney General, is expected to be a future President of the Court. Born in Danzig in 1921, he fought with the Irgun and studied law after he was arrested in 1944 and detained for anti-British activity. Professor Barak, a young member of the court – he is in his 40s – became known to the public as the Prosecuting Counsel in the case against Mrs Rabin, wife of the then Prime Minister. Much admired by Prime Minister Begin, Barak accompanied him to the Camp David discussions, and his ingenuity gained him the respect not only of his own side, but of President Carter, too. Miriam Ben-Porat is the first, and so far the only, woman on the Supreme Court. With the reputation of possessing a prickly personality, her solid claim on grounds of professional competence overcame some personal objections and, as is the convention, she received the unanimous backing of all members of the Supreme Court before her elevation.

Law students regret that there is on the present court no follower of former Supreme Court Justice Eliahu Many. A Sephardi, he endeared himself to examination candidates by the brevity of his judgments which were frequently limited to the words, 'I concur.'

The power of the Supreme Court

In England, the Chancery Court and the system of law known as equity
were introduced to correct hardships and injustices brought about by the
strict application of the Common Law. We have seen that in Israel the
Supreme Court divides its functions in two – it is the highest court of appeal
and also the High Court of Justice dealing with matters in the first instance
which are not within the jurisdiction of any other court and where it
considers it necessary to give relief as a matter of natural justice. Under this
general authority, the Court has power to order Government agencies to
perform or to desist from a particular act. It also has the power to exercise
some control over the activities of the religious courts.

It has used these powers to such effect that it is the Supreme Court, more
than any other arm of the Israeli Government, which has acted, effectively
and responsibly, to preserve freedom of conscience and protect civil rights.
The Court has become the main protector of the Arabs against the
Government, in particular examining and often rejecting Government
efforts to acquire Arab-owned land compulsorily without due process of
law. No less important have been its liberal attitudes in correcting
inequities and hardships caused by the strict application of religious law –
and not only Jewish religious law.

A seminal case which established the principles on which the highest
court of the new State was intending to act occurred in 1953. The subject of
guardianship of children is within the jurisdiction of the Moslem Religious
Courts and in one such application, the court, in accordance with Moslem
law, refused to permit a woman to be a guardian. It was conceded that in all
other respects she would have been suitable for the appointment. She took
her case to the Supreme Court which held that, according to twentieth-
century concepts of natural justice, it was unacceptable to discriminate
between male and female with regard to the guardianship of infants. The
Supreme Court recognized that it did not possess the power either to apply
or interpret Moslem law – that was exclusively the right of the Moslem
courts – but what the Supreme Court did was to direct a civil court to deal
with the matter and appoint the woman since the Moslem Court was
unable to act in accordance with natural justice.

The next intervention of the Supreme Court in this area was directed to
the Rabbinical Courts in which, according to Jewish law, a woman is
ineligible as a witness. The Supreme Court, again on principles of natural
justice, declared that it would quash any judgment of a Rabbinical Court
where the evidence of a woman had been refused. This decision prompted a
rare instance of a change in rabbinical law, for thereafter women were no
longer barred as witnesses in any Rabbinical Court in Israel.

That began an important line of cases in the domestic field, in which the
Supreme Court has exercised control over the Rabbinical Courts without,
however, infringing the exclusive right of those courts to decide what the
Jewish law was. In 1953, the Court rejected a rabbinical ruling that Israel
would recognize only religious marriages of Jews and, in the Skornick case,
decided that a foreign marriage which was valid in the country in which it

was performed would be accepted as valid in Israel. Eight years later, the same principle was extended to cover a civil marriage in Cyprus between an Israeli Jew and a Christian girl.

An interesting example of the way in which the Supreme Court operates in these matters was in the 1964 case of Streit *v* Streit. The partners in that case had been married abroad at a civil ceremony. In Jewish law this was not a marriage at all, since the religious forms had not been observed and, when the husband, who wanted to remarry, went to the Rabbinical Court, it had no option under the law it administers but to declare the civil marriage a nullity. The wife petitioned the Supreme Court which, though it could not set aside the decision of the Rabbinical Court, exercised its power to ensure that the wife's rights would not be prejudiced. In a passage declaring the policy of the Court, Justice Sussman, quoting an English Equity Judge said, 'This is a case which shocks the conscience,' and continued, 'I can see no reason for interference with the determination by the Rabbinical Court of the Rabbinical Law in a matter of marriage. But while the proceedings of the Rabbinical Court may have been quite regular, the conduct of the husband was most reprehensible and in fact amounted to fraud. He chose to marry the petitioner in their country of origin in civil form, and after living with her in a normal marriage for thirty years, he applies to the Rabbinical Court for a declaration that his marriage is invalid and that he is at liberty to remarry. It does not matter to him that he hereby bastardizes his children and makes of his lawful wife a common mistress. Conduct such as this is contrary to public morals and will not be suffered. The fact that he succeeded in obtaining judgment of a court is quite irrelevant. Even now will this court intervene to prevent him making any use of the judgment in his hand.'

In a further development, the Court introduced the practice of giving directions to the District Courts to grant a divorce in specific cases not within the jurisdiction of the recognized religious courts. Today no couple in Israel can fail to be granted a divorce simply because Rabbinical law does not cover their situation. Several hundred such cases are dealt with every year by the Supreme Court and remitted with a direction to a District Court to hear the case and grant a divorce if warranted. Since there is in Israel no civil law of divorce, the District Court tries these cases on the basis of English law on the principle of Article 46 of the 1922 Order in Council that lacunae in Israeli law are to be filled by the law of England.* For all practical purposes, civil divorce now exists in Israel, not through legislation but by the creation of the Supreme Court.

In its approach to all these matters, the Supreme Court has used its statutory power to ensure that Rabbinical Courts apply their jurisdiction in marriage and divorce justly and fairly, on the presumption that the Knesset could not have intended that this jurisdiction should be exercised otherwise than in accordance with natural justice. They have therefore assumed the power to overrule decisions of Rabbinical Courts though without affecting the exclusive right of those courts to apply Jewish law as they define it.

* What the position will be if the 1980 Foundation of Law Bill is enacted is unclear. The English divorce law will be replaced by 'the values of the Jewish heritage'.

Of wider national and international importance has been the activity of the Supreme Court, in its High Court role, relating to the protection of the individual against the unrestrained exercise of the power of the executive. In the past few years the Court has issued a series of judgments prohibiting the authorities from expropriating Arab-owned land for the purpose of establishing Jewish settlements, the most far-reaching at the end of November 1979, in the case of the controversial settlement by the extremist religious nationalist group, Gush Emunim, at Eilon Moreh, near the West Bank city of Nablus.

In June 1979, a group of Gush Emunim settlers moved into a new site they had chosen for their permanent settlement amid the rugged hills of that part of the West Bank which they (and other nationalist elements, including Prime Minister Begin) called Samaria. There, with the aid of the army and air force helicopters, they erected several prefabricated buildings, and the small number of settlers, never more than a hundred and occasionally as few as three, announced that they had settled on this site under the biblical charter entitling the Jews to settle anywhere in the biblical land of Israel. Two days earlier, the local military commander had signed an order authorising the seizure of this land for military purposes. Seventeen Arab landowners petitioned the High Court for an injunction to stop work on the site and to cancel the seizure order.

According to the affidavits submitted to the Court by the Chief of Staff and the Secretary of the Cabinet, the initiative to establish the settlement had come from the Ministerial Settlement Committee headed by Ariel Sharon, probably the most hawkish member of the Cabinet on settlement issues. The Committee had chosen a number of sites in the area and the army had made the final choice, after which the decision of the Committee to seize the land was confirmed by the Cabinet.

Presiding Justice Moshe Landau, who delivered the main judgment, defined the issue before the Court as the legality of the seizure of private land for a civilian settlement. He noted that the Chief of Staff, General Rafael Eitan, had affirmed that the settlement on that site contributed to the regional defence of the area. However, applying the relevant article of the Hague Convention which permits the seizure of private property for the military purposes of the occupying army, he came to the conclusion that this had not been the real purpose of the settlement, but that its establishment was for Zionist reasons. In a unanimous decision, the five-judge Court revoked the seizure order, gave the state thirty days to remove the settlers and their possessions, including the buildings, from the site and awarded I£10,000 in costs to the plaintiffs.

The decision made headlines all over the world and was seen as a rebuff to the Begin Government settlement policy. The right-wingers raged, but despite the fulminations of Gush Emunim that they would not obey the Court order and would expect the Government to legalize the settlement, the Government quickly made it known that it would abide by the decision of the Court (although the deadline was modified), and eventually the settlers were removed. It was conclusive evidence of the independence of the Supreme Court on a highly sensitive political issue.

The police force

A Jew as a policeman! The idea would have been absurd to the down-trodden Jews of Eastern Europe for whom the police, like all other manifestations of officialdom, were the oppressor. But after the British left Palestine in 1947, one of the first of the new institutions that had to be created was a police force, and it had to be composed of Jews because the Arabs were then the enemy. The Mandatory police force had performed a quasi-military function, which had deepened the suspicion of the East Euro-pean Jews as well as their co-religionists from Arab lands, whose contacts with the police in their own countries had tended to be unpleasant. But the new police force had only the normal work of a constabulary and, in the course of time, was able to establish a better relationship with the public.

It may have become too good, for the old fear was replaced by an over-familiarity which induces Israelis not to take the police too seriously. Stopped by a police officer for any minor offence, the average Israeli is liable to enter into a prolonged discussion with the object of dissuading the policeman from pursuing the matter or, at least, settling for a lesser infringement. Israeli police are often persuadable in this kind of situation – after all, they are also Jews!

At the present time there are about 14,000 regular police, some 10 per cent of them Israeli Arabs or Druze and about another 10 per cent women. In addition, two units have been created with the special purpose of combating terrorism. One, the Civil Guard, is composed mainly of volunteers (about 100,000) stiffened by a leadership core of less than 1,000 professionals. The 'lightly armed' Civil Guard patrol conduct searches, man roadblocks and generally reinforce the army in defence against urban terrorism. A second force, the Border Guard, a small mobile unit with military training, assists in protecting the border zones against terrorist incursions and has recently been used against domestic hooliganism and in controlling potentially violent demonstrations.

Israel's police force is sophisticated, using advanced scientific apparatus in its numerous specialist laboratories and in its institute of forensic medicine. A research and development unit pursues experiments to improve internal security and law enforcement. One of the recent innova-tions for the Bomb Squad was a system for detecting clock mechanisms in suspicious objects, and the laboratories have developed a substance to detect traces of explosives on the hands of suspects. Its computer is claimed to be one of the most modern serving any police force in the world. The cost of all this in the year 1977–78 was about $130 million, qualified by an imprecise phrase in the Administration report – 'excluding sums derived from incomes from other bodies.'

The Inspector-General of the Israeli police force, Commissioner Haim Tabori, was born in 1920, and has come up through the ranks. Most police chiefs have been army men, but Tabori has been a policeman from the time he joined the British Mandatory Police Force in 1940. His qualities as a calm leader were particularly evident during his term as head of the Jerusalem sub-district, where he managed, with a distinctly low-key approach, to clamp down on the violence of the religious zealots in one of their forays against a sex shop. After a short period as head of the National Operations Department, he was appointed to his present post in 1976 and was due to be succeeded in 1980 by Herzl Shafir.

The police force comes within the responsibilities of the Ministry of the Interior and, in fact, the full title of Dr Burg, the incumbent in the Begin Government, was Minister of the Interior and Police. Every year the Inspector General presents a report to the Minister, which is then published in full in both Hebrew and English. Crammed with statistics, the report details the extent and variety of crime in Israel, and one table of particular interest makes a comparison with other countries. The data below are those for 1977 in Israel compared with the 1976 figures in London, West Germany and the USA. In each case the figure is the crime rate per 100,000 population:

	ISRAEL	LONDON	W. GERMANY	USA
Murder and attempted murder	5.3	3.4	4.5	8.8
Forcible rape	3.2	2.4	11.3	26.4
Robbery	10.3	72.3	31.6	195.8
Grievous bodily harm	13.7	160.9	80.9	228.7

In these figures the Inspector General attributes the abnormally high murder rate to the Middle East concept of 'family honour', pointing out that one-third of all murders occurred for family reasons other than jealousy or marriage breakdown. So far as the other serious offences are concerned, the Israeli record is a comparatively good one and, expressed as a percentage of the population, has shown comparatively little increase in the period of Israel's existence. The greatest cause for concern for the police and the nation was the revelation in recent years of the extent of organized crime. It is a phenomenon so much at variance with the idealistic roots of the Jewish national renaissance that, when the publicity given to organized crime coincided with the political scandals of 1976–77, the public reacted with genuine horror that this could be happening in the Jewish State.

Organized crime

Moshe Shamgar, who was Attorney General in 1971, was asked by the Labour Government of that year to conduct an investigation into the existence of organized crime in Israel following newspaper allegations. He came to the conclusion, which many thought disingenuous or at least ambiguous, that there was no organized crime in Israel in the sense in which the term is used in the United States.

Six years later, another series of articles appeared in the sober and respected daily *Haaretz* written by one of the newspaper's experienced investigative journalists, Avi Valentin. Naming names, Valentin gave detailed accounts of drug networks, smuggling, jewel thefts, protection rackets and even murder. The 'Mafia-like' group in Israel who ruled the organization, he alleged, maintained international associations and appeared to have contacts in the Israeli police force. In a subsequent libel action by one of the many individuals named by Valentin, the District Court judge found for the plaintiff on several counts. Judge Shulamit Wallenstein, while accepting that organized crime did exist and that *Haaretz* had an obligation to expose it, ruled that on the issues on which the plaintiff had succeeded, the newspaper had been at fault in publishing its allegations without any, or insufficient, proof.

Haaretz, which appealed against the decision, was legitimately gratified by the tenor of the Judge's general observations, which vindicated the overall accuracy of its articles. A typical example was: 'I have been convinced that Aharoni and Osheri [two of the names repeatedly mentioned in the Valentin article] are justly considered by the police as leaders of the "Karem Group" which is one of the branches of the Israeli-style organized crime. . . . The claimant denies any business contact [with Aharoni and Osheri]; I do not accept that denial. Aharoni and Osheri are not choosy about the type of offences they undertake, so long as there is a chance to make money. . . . I have been convinced that the claimant is friendly and has business contacts with the two but there was insufficient evidence in the articles to justify its [Valentin's] findings and conclusions.'

Almost simultaneously with the publication of the Valentin articles, the Cabinet set up a committee to study crime in Israel and, in record time, it submitted a long and substantial report – prefaced by a quotation from Psalm 104: 'Let the sinners disappear from the earth and let the wicked be no more.' The Shimron report (the strong committee was headed by a leading Jerusalem lawyer, Erwin Shimron) concluded that an organized underworld did exist in Israel and that it had achieved 'penetration into, and corruption of, Government agencies.'

While the causes of Israel's increasing crime rate are fundamentally the same as those affecting the affluent Western world generally, the report pinpointed a feature singular to Israel. More than half of the present Jewish population is composed of immigrants from Middle East or North African countries and their children. In the transition from the traditional paternalistic, closed societies of their countries of origin to the free and open environment of Israel, many of the young people have lost the values of their parents without acquiring new ones. The disadvantaged conditions under which many of them live have created, as the report put it, 'fertile soil for a life of crime', with street gangs of youths graduating into hardened criminals.

Without charging any individuals or further particularizing the organized underworld, the report meticulously analyzed the main areas of criminality: theft and smuggling at the port of Haifa included breaking into the new huge containers and even stealing complete units. At the Ben-Gurion Airport, 'the helplessness of the authorities in face of the diamond thefts which have been going on for years is a scandal.' The airport has also acquired a bad reputation for luggage thefts. The trade in soft and hard drugs imported illegally, which has 'all the earmarks of organized crime', is a big-money enterprise with vast international ramifications. The profits from drugs, extortion and smuggling have been invested in legitimate business so that they can be 'laundered'. At the same time, there has been heavy traffic in the other direction of the billions of Israeli lira amassed by legitimate business from the sale of agricultural produce, as well as by building contractors, diamond traders and a variety of other merchants, who engage in unrecorded cash transactions for the purpose of avoiding income tax. Some of this 'black' money undoubtedly finds its way into illegitimate enterprises.

It all made very sobering reading for the law-abiding mass of Israelis and many of the detailed recommendations of the Committee led to a re-examination of police organization. The complacency of the police estab-lishment, which had always denied the existence of organized crime 'on the American pattern', was shattered by the revelation that there was an Israeli pattern of which it had been unaware. It immediately conducted its own investigations and presented to the Ministry of the Interior what was described by the police as a 'comprehensive survey of organized crime, including names of people and their exact location in the criminal hierarchy.' But no prosecutions followed. Apparently evidence is difficult to come by.

The police are probably still hoping that the Government will implement the Shimron Committee's recommendation that the income tax laws be employed to track down the offenders. The Committee offered the example of 'the classic case of Al Capone, the Chicago gangster who managed to evade conviction on a multitude of charges and was eventually put behind bars for income tax evasion'. But the Begin Government, preoccupied with the pressing concerns of the peace process and the domestic economy, and torn by its own internal dissensions, seems in no hurry to introduce any measures to implement the Shimron report.

Almost two years after the report, Israel was shocked by underworld murders linked with some of the dramatis personae in the *Haaretz* articles. At the end of 1979, a reputed crime boss in the Mediterranean coast town of Netanya and his pregnant girl friend were shot and killed as they lay in bed. Ten days later, David Shulman, the owner of one of Israel's largest furniture businesses, was blown apart when a bomb wired to the ignition exploded as he started his car. The police reported that this was 'an act carried out by professionals, such as we have never known before in Israel. The murderer was a superb professional' and was assumed to have been imported from abroad for the purpose. He was not found.

The murdered man had given evidence on behalf of Bezalel Mizrachi, the plaintiff in the libel action against *Haaretz* based on the Valentin articles. In her judgment, Judge Wallenstein commented that he had 'given the impression of being a frightened witness who is not telling the truth.' Shulman had reason to be frightened. During the previous ten years, his furniture showroom had been burned down on three occasions and the police believed that this was because of Shulman's refusal to pay protection money to underworld extortionists. On each occasion, the store was rebuilt by a construction company owned by Bezalel Mizrachi. The police theory was that Shulman was killed because he had refused to comply with the latest demand for protection money.

The pressure was on Dr Burg, the Minister of Police, who at the time was

devoting himself almost entirely to his function as Israel's leading negotiator on autonomy. Both the public and police were critical of his apparent
lack of direction. Senior police officials claimed that Dr Burg had never
visited police headquarters. 'He receives documents and signs them in his
office. But he does not know more about current affairs than the average
citizen who reads newspapers,' they told the press. The outgoing police
chief called for a separate police ministry with no other responsibilities.

Prostitution has reached troublesome proportions. The police estimate
that in Tel Aviv, some 300 call-girls, the aristocrats of prostitution, operate
through a chain of contacts in bars and hotels. Most of them come from a
middle-class background and it is estimated that about half are of
Ashkenazi origin. These girls, unlike the more numerous streetwalkers, do
not usually maintain underworld contacts. But the girls on the streets, of
whom a high proportion are Oriental, are generally involved with pimps
and the centres of organized crime.

Death penalty

The five Books of Moses, the basic canon of Jewish law, contain what seems
a very harsh code with its extensive imposition of the death penalty for a
variety of offences. In practice, however, capital punishment in post-
biblical times was so ringed around with qualifications that it was rarely
applied. A brief discussion recorded in the Mishna (rabbinic interpretations of biblical law compiled about AD 200) quotes one rabbi as saying
that any Sanhedrin (Jewish court) which ordered one execution in seven
years was a murderous one. This is capped by another rabbi who extended
the period to seventy years, while a third declared: 'If we were members of a
Sanhedrin, no one would ever be put to death.'

In the short history of Israel, only one death sentence has ever been
imposed and carried out. After a four-months' trial in 1961, followed by an
appeal to the Supreme Court, Adolf Eichmann, the chief executive of the
Holocaust which annihilated six million of Europe's Jews, was sentenced to
death. To carry out the execution by hanging, a hangman had to be
imported.

Capital punishment for murder was abolished in Israel in 1954 except for
the murder of persecuted people during the Nazi regime. But Israel did not
repeal the Defence (Emergency) Regulations of the British Mandatory
Government, which imposed the death penalty for the illegal use and
carrying of arms and for membership of a group which illegally used or
carried arms. Although the death sentence has never been imposed by
Israel under these regulations, it still remains part of the law. After the Six
Day War, Israel issued a Security Regulation (valid under the Geneva
Convention) which made the possession or use of illegal arms in the
occupied territories a capital offence. However, the deep-rooted objections
to applying the penalty persisted and it has still never been implemented.
When the Security Regulation was approved by the Cabinet in 1967 (Begin
was a member of it at the time), it was accompanied by a direction to the
Attorney General that he should not ask for it at any trial.

In May 1979, after an Arab terrorist operation in Israel in which a father and his four-year-old daughter were murdered, the Cabinet decided – by a small majority – to revoke that direction. Begin insisted that he had not been provoked by the murders, but that he had favoured such a revision for several years. The Cabinet decision was challenged in the Knesset on a no-confidence motion, proposed by Uri Avneri, which was defeated by a vote of 50 to 14. It will now be theoretically possible for the prosecution to request courts to order capital punishment in cases of (in the words of the Cabinet resolution) 'terrorist crimes of inhuman cruelty'.

Within Israel, the change was received with approval by large numbers of the population, agonized by some ghastly acts of terror which have been perpetrated against innocent civilians. But most of the thoughtful comments were hostile. The arguments were generally twofold. The first was the moral objection to capital punishment, and the second that it would not deter fanatical terrorists but would make martyrs of them. The *Jerusalem Post* concluded its editorial on the subject with the dry observation that 'in view of the fact that our security forces have been successful in killing most of these murderers in armed confrontation on the field, it would seem best to permit [that situation] . . . to remain in practice.'

Under the Mandatory legislation which still governs this area, the death penalty is to be exercised by hanging. Begin has proposed that this be replaced by a firing squad, since it is 'not fitting for Israel to hang human beings'. But the Cabinet Secretary has stated that amending legislation would not be introduced immediately, but only 'if and when' a terrorist was sentenced to death. The event has not yet occurred.

Chapter eight

Communications

Press and broadcasting

Every day 75 per cent of Israelis read one newspaper, and more than a third read two or more. Most of Israel's highly publicized scandals and 'affairs' were unmasked by the press and, since MKs have no constituents to send them complaints, nearly all the questions raised in the Knesset are based on newspaper reports. The press, and to some extent radio and television also, constitute an extra-parliamentary opposition, as well as sources of information. They are followed avidly, for the precarious nature of Israel's existence has made its population ultrasensitive to news, assessments and opinions of their national concerns. Israel is a nation of compulsive radio listeners and, at times of crisis, the transistor becomes as much a part of the Israeli's accoutrements as his pocket handkerchief. Now television has overtaken even radio in popularity.

A wide range of newspapers, morning, evening and weekly, satisfy all tastes and interests – eighteen dailies, two evenings and no fewer than fifty weeklies. Hebrew is a difficult language and, even when they have learned to speak it, many immigrants are happier reading their native tongues, so in addition to those in Hebrew, daily newspapers also appear in Yiddish, English, Arabic, German, French, Polish and Hungarian, with the weeklies adding another half a dozen languages to the list.

With the major exception of *Haaretz*, the oldest and most important, the bulk of the other newspapers were founded by the Zionist political parties. It was axiomatic to these East European ideologues that the highest priority be given to a journal to express their political thinking and publicize party programmes. But in recent years, the Israeli party press has declined as costs of production soared, though finance is not the only reason. The smaller parties became less relevant as political alignments gradually coalesced into two loose federations of left and right in which ideologies mattered less. Israel seemed to be straining towards a two-party system with the emphasis less on political ideas than on the struggle for power.

Contributing to the decline of the minor dailies has been the rapid growth of the two evening papers, *Maariv* and *Yediot Aharonot*, neither of them politically affiliated. To describe them as 'evenings' is not quite accurate, because they are on sale in Tel Aviv at mid-morning, often as early as 10 a.m. (But then the morning papers are on the streets from about 6.) Together with *Haaretz* and *Davar*, they constitute the big four of Israel's daily press. The English-language *Jerusalem Post* is important too, but, as we shall see, for different reasons and in a different way.

Five radio programmes broadcast regularly. Three of them (two carry commercial advertising) are geared to the domestic public, including the Arab population, while a fourth broadcasts overseas in ten languages under the title of 'Kol Zion laGolah' (The Voice of Israel to the Diaspora). An army radio service combines the best of the three civilian networks with excellent programmes of its own. Television is transmitted on one channel, in black and white, and carries no advertising. Israeli listeners and viewers in some parts of the country have a free and unofficial bonus in being able to receive transmissions from Jordan and Lebanon.

Control of radio and television is vested in the Israel Broadcasting Authority (IBA) which was set up in 1965 on the model of the British Broadcasting Corporation. Until then, radio and TV had been directed from the Prime Minister's Office where, it was never seriously denied, policies were kept in line with those of the Labour Party. The Broadcasting Law of 1965 removed the media from the Prime Minister's direct control with the object of assuring independence.

However, like the Knesset, which follows the British Parliamentary model but with deviations, the IBA differed in two major respects from its British model. The Governors of the BBC are appointed by the Government generally non-politically, on grounds of ability and independence. Control of the IBA rests with a plenum of thirty-one members, which meets three times a year and a Board of seven members which meets weekly. The members of both are appointed by the government for a five-year term but on the basis of the 'party key'. This means that they are nominated by the major political parties in the proportion to which they are represented in the Knesset. The second crucial deviation from the BBC system is that the Director-General of the IBA is appointed by the Government and not the Board. The appointment of the Director-General by the Governors of the BBC makes it a professional choice; the Government's power of appointment in Israel is political.

The politicians who framed Israel's Broadcasting Law went further to ensure a measure of control by the Government. Since the governing bodies of the IBA hold office for five years, a change of Government during that period would mean loss of control. To avoid this situation, the Law provided that a minority of the governing bodies may appeal to the Minister of Education and Culture, the Ministry responsible for broadcasting, and so ensure Government control during a transition period.

After its electoral success in 1977, the Likud appointed Professor Reuven Yaron Chairman of the IBA Governing Board and, *ex-officio*, chairman of the plenum. Although a supporter of the Herut Party, the major component of the Likud, Yaron has neither the personality nor the career to suggest the doctrinaire party man. Amiable in manner, he looks the calm and judicious scholar he is, former professor of law and Director of the National Library. At the IBA (where only the Chairman and Vice-Chairman of the Board are stipendiary), he works with another Likud nominee, the Director-General, Yosef (Tommy) Lapid. The IBA chief executives under the Director-General are the Director of TV, Amnon Zuckerman, and the Director of Radio, Gideon Lev-Ari.

Television and politics

Lapid took office as IBA Director-General on 1 April 1979. It was clearly a political appointment intended to redress what the Israeli right-wing had long regarded as the domination of the IBA by the left. Lapid was a widely read *Maariv* columnist and his articles had frequently been critical of conventional liberal attitudes. He was close to the Herut Party but his experience of broadcasting was limited mainly to the army radio station.

Bulky, engaging and open, Tommy Lapid manages to be (almost) everyone's friend. He talks interestingly and well, his fluent English being the result of his twelve-year stint as *Maariv*'s correspondent in London. Born in Yugoslavia in 1931, he has been in Israel since 1938, where he began his journalistic career as a reporter for *Uj Kelet*, the Hungarian daily. In 1955 he moved to *Maariv* where he was successful and happy, becoming its managing editor in 1974. A diligent and probing reporter, he came to know everyone of importance in Israel and could generally be relied upon to produce an interesting or entertaining story about any of them.

At the time of the Likud election victory, the Director-General of the IBA was Yitzhak Livni. Younger than Lapid, he was born in Poland in 1935 and first made his mark as the Director of the Army radio station, giving it the present successful format of a round-the-clock mixed programme. His affection for the army radio continued after his appointment as Director-General in 1974 and every fortnight he took part in a hard-hitting exchange of views on current affairs with Lapid. The liberal political views he expressed in these discussions could well have contributed to the Likud's decision not to renew his contract when it expired in 1979. Lapid relates that his appointment to succeed Livni came about casually. Ephraim Kishon, the witty writer and playwright who was part of the 'Hungarian Mafia' on *Maariv*, had apparently mentioned Lapid's name to Prime Minister Begin. Lapid knew nothing about it until, at a diplomatic cocktail party, 'somebody' drew him into a corner where, glass in hand ('almost like a movie', he says), he was asked if he would be interested in the job.

The new Director-General of the IBA, who described himself as an 'old-fashioned liberal', gave immediate notice of a wind of change. In interviews after his appointment, Lapid expressed a certain lack of tolerance for 'bad news', with which he thought the public was surfeited, giving rise to the fear that he would try to 'balance' news reporting. Demonstrating his determination to establish himself as the man in charge, he lost little time in barring a notable TV and radio interviewer, ostensibly because his shows were 'tired', though few doubted that the motive was political. His refusal, soon afterwards, to renew the contract of the Director of Hebrew Programming, second in authority only to the Director of Television, raised a storm.

Mordechai Kirschenbaum, the dismissed official, a talented and out-spoken producer, had been responsible for an innovative and highly popular satirical show called 'Nikui Rosh' (Head Cleaning). Inspired by the national breast-beating which followed the Yom Kippur War, the show continued to run during the series of financial scandals, when subjects for satire were plentiful. Kirschenbaum clearly held left-wing sympathies, but all parties, not only the Likud, had writhed at some of his portrayals. The programme won Kirschenbaum the prestigious Israel Prize, an award which horrified *Maariv* and Tommy Lapid.

Within days of his appointment, Lapid had to decide whether to reappoint Kirschenbaum, whose three-year contract was expiring. On his recommendation, the Board of Directors decided not to do so. The decision was assailed in the press as political victimization, and a heated debate followed in the Knesset. Lapid's case was that Kirschenbaum was undoubtedly capable but 'he has a hostile attitude to the IBA and doesn't get along with people. You can't force me to work for the next three years with someone with whom I have no common language.' Labour politicians were outraged, or said they were. Eighty senior TV journalists and members of staff petitioned for Kirschenbaum's reinstatement asking, 'Is this a reactionary age in which one is judged not by one's abilities but by political considerations?'

Lapid seemed implicitly to agree that it had been a political decision when he told a reporter that he would be ready to have a satirical programme on Israeli life, 'but I'd want it done by someone on whom I could depend to aim his arrows at everyone.' His stand was staunchly supported by both the plenum and Board of the IBA as well as by the Minister of Education and Culture, Zvulun Hammer, who claimed, in the Knesset debate, that Lapid's aim was to prevent the politicization of the authority.

But sentiment at the time was perhaps more accurately expressed in the independent daily, *Haaretz*, in which a columnist observed: 'The struggle today is, without a doubt, over freedom of speech and expression in TV and radio. This is a bitter fight which must not be neglected, and whoever is doubtful about its importance may wake up one fine morning to discover the battle is lost.'

The press 'big four'

Haaretz (the Land), Israel's equivalent of *The (London) Times* owes its origins to the British. In 1918, the British Expeditionary Force in Palestine produced three newspapers, in English, Arabic and Hebrew. A licence to continue the Hebrew paper after the Force's departure was granted to I. L. Goldberg, a Russian immigrant. In 1935, he sold the paper to Zalman Schocken, a successful German Jewish department-store owner, a cultivated patron of literature and the arts, and a respected figure in the Zionist movement.

Schocken's eldest son, Gershom, joined the paper in 1937 and became its Editor in Chief in 1939. Now, more than forty years later, he is still the newspaper's overlord and one of the few survivors of the breed of editor-owners whose decisions are final, not on editorial policy alone but on all aspects of the paper's affairs. Portly, bald and shrewd, he sits Buddha-like in his large but simply furnished office in the Haaretz building in Zalman Schocken Street, Tel Aviv. A certain teutonic formality and brusqueness are frequently softened by a gentle smile or a flickering sparkle of the eye.

The paper is totally owned by the Schocken family and, with the passage of the years (Gershom Schocken was born in 1912), provision is being made for the succession. Gershom's son Amos, a graduate of Harvard Business School, has taken over the business side of the paper as General Manager, while Gershom's daughter, Rachel Edelman, has been placed in charge of Schocken Publications, the book-publishing subsidiary which produces between 20 and 24 new titles annually.

Haaretz is the prestige paper, sober, solid and sensible – a reflection of the Editor in Chief. It has probably the best news service of all the Israeli press, particularly from abroad, and tends to be liberal in politics (Gershom served briefly in the Knesset as a Progressive) with a commendable tendency to look critically at authority. It is unabashedly highbrow and its articles and editorials make few concessions to the ignorant or impatient. About 15 per cent of all newspaper readers in Israel read it. *Haaretz* has always been enlightened in its handling of journalistic staff, and has attracted some of the best talent in Israel by giving them the maximum independence and encouraging the free expression of their opinions.

Gershom Schocken has always fought for press freedom to expose injustice, crime and corruption, and he resigned from the Editors' Committee when it seemed to be acquiescing in restrictive practices. He sees one of his paper's functions as investigative and in 1977 he published a series of carefully documented articles revealing the existence of a network of organized crime in Israel. Although one of the individuals named succeeded in a libel action (subject to appeal, see Chapter 7), the judge affirmed the *bona fides* of *Haaretz* and the validity of the substance of the articles.

Even more dramatic was the *Haaretz* scoop in 1977, when its Washington correspondent's disclosure of the existence of Mrs Lea Rabin's illegal bank account in the United States led to the resignation of her husband, the Prime Minister. Schocken would not have published the story if Rabin had offered a reasonable explanation, but after it had been held for some days and all Rabin would say was that it was a 'personal matter', Schocken decided to print. Such responsibility is not a notable characteristic of the Israeli press generally.

The claimed circulation of *Haaretz* is 50,000 daily, increasing to 70,000 for the Friday (week-end) issue, and the paper has 400 on its payroll. With inflation rampant, the cover price of the paper increases every two or three months; so do advertising rates (classified advertising is shared with *Yediot Aharonot* and the *Jerusalem Post*) and the paper does make a profit although, since it is privately owned, figures are not available. It is read by 'the people who count', professionals, and the middle class and, in keeping with Schocken's conservatism, the paper has changed little over the years. 'I don't believe in gimmicks,' he says.

Nor does Hanna Zemer, the Editor of the other important morning newspaper, *Davar* (Word). Charming and attractive, her femininity gives her an unfair advantage with male politicians, some of her fellow-journalists good-humouredly complain. Her obvious competence and professional success have not given her that toughness which is such a marked feature of many career women and her unpretentious office on the top of the squat box of a building which houses *Davar* in Tel Aviv's commercial district, is that of a working journalist, unadorned, unglamorous.

Davar, founded in 1925, is second only to *Haaretz* in years and standing. Alone among the party press it has kept readership, prestige and influence. Amos Elon* gives a vivid description of *Davar* as 'a curious mixture of early Pravda and old style Quakerism, mouthpiece of the ruling Labour establishment and the abode of untiring watchdogs for purity of pioneering manners and ideology.' Although it is the official organ of the Histadrut (General Federation of Labour) and therefore of the Israel Labour Party which controls it, *Davar* has never been simply a Party mouthpiece. Particularly during the period after the Yom Kippur War, when everybody in Israel was asking where the country had gone wrong, *Davar* was not deterred by its political affiliation from publishing criticism of the Labour Government and some of its leaders. Golda Meir was very unhappy with the policy of the paper, which she thought too doveish. She had no particular liking for the Editor and was intensely irritated by one of its senior journalists, Danny Bloch, who particularly challenged her policies. Mrs Meir did not hide her disapproval, but *Davar* continued on its course.

Davar is owned by the Histadrut, which has the right to appoint, and also, presumably, dismiss, the Editor in Chief, though this has never occurred. Once appointed, the Editor has complete freedom – with the one exception that Histadrut trade-union policy is exempt from editorial criticism, though critical signed articles are acceptable. All the staff are appointed by the Editor, who is not required to maintain any formal regular consultation with the Histadrut or the Labour Party on policy matters. The Board of Directors, also appointed by the Histadrut, deals only with the newspaper's financial affairs.

It probably has a good deal to discuss, for *Davar* loses a considerable amount of money. Not having the economic incentives of an independent newspaper, *Davar* has never been aggressive in selling advertising space, and advertising accounts for only about a third of its income, compared with between a half and two-thirds, which most successful newspapers expect. It shares classified advertising with the evening paper, *Maariv*, and the income is divided between the two newspapers in proportion to their circulation.

In the true spirit of the Labour movement, the staff of *Davar* is involved in the direction of the paper through an editorial committee consisting of representatives of the working journalists and including Hanna Zemer's predecessor, Yehuda Gotthelf. It generally meets monthly to discuss questions of policy and any other matters which the Editor or any other member of the committee wishes to raise. The committee is entirely advisory, but Mrs Zemer takes its views seriously and generally respects them.

* *Israelis; Founders & Sons*, London/New York 1971.

Until 1977, the Histadrut was synonymous with the Labour Party in the same way as that Party was synonymous with the Government. The elections which put the Government under new management generated the fear, almost panic, in the Labour Party that the Likud might also win control of the Histadrut at its election soon after. In the event, the Likud received only 30 per cent of the vote and remained a minority, with Labour still in control. But had Likud done better, it might have taken over the Histadrut and, with it, *Davar*. Had that occurred, Hanna Zemer and her fellow Socialists on the staff would have resigned.

As it was, freed from the restraints of being the journal of the ruling Party, *Davar* became a more interesting paper. In opposition, it was more outspoken and objective, reflecting the personality of its Editor, and an interesting personality it is. Hanna Zemer was born in Czechoslovakia. Her age is not disclosed in works of reference, but the year of her birth was probably in the 1920s. She has worked for *Davar* for the whole of her professional life, beginning with *Omer*, the simplified paper, specially produced for new immigrants, which is an offshoot of *Davar*. Promoted to the main paper as a reporter, she became its Washington correspondent in 1958 and stayed for several years, enjoying and learning to know the United States. Her success in Washington led to top jobs at home, then to her appointment as Deputy Editor and finally Editor in 1970.

She immediately showed her mettle and her independence by standing up to the powerful Secretary-General of the Histadrut, Yitzhak Ben-Aharon. In 1971, she published an article which claimed that Ben-Aharon was involved in a conspiracy for a planned take-over of the Histadrut by the left wing. Ben-Aharon was furious but she refused to retract. The following year she published criticism of a strike which had received Ben-Aharon's blessing. He again reacted strongly, calling for her dismissal, but Hanna Zemer remained unrepentant. She gets on better with Ben-Aharon's successor and is well liked by most other political leaders.

Her classified advertising partner, *Maariv* (Evening), is a much later arrival on the Israeli newspaper scene and much more successful than *Davar* in both circulation and profitability. *Maariv* and its competitor, *Yediot Aharonot* (Latest News), are read by about 70 per cent of the population and each paper claims to have a larger circulation than the other. The situation appears to be that, until a few years ago, *Maariv* undoubtedly had the advantage, but *Yediot* moved up and now probably equals, if it has not overtaken, *Maariv*'s figures.

Tabloid in size, comfortably, at least for its proprietors, stuffed with advertising, *Maariv* is far more serious and of a far higher quality than any of the British or American tabloids. This popular evening paper was started in 1948 by a group of journalists led by one of Israel's most respected newspapermen, Dr Ezriel Carlebach, who broke away from *Yediot Aharonot*. Brilliant editorials and columns by Carlebach and a keen staff of young reporters combined to make an immediately favourable impact on the journalistic scene, then dominated by the solemn, heavy, politically orientated morning papers. Not that *Maariv* was apolitical. It was, and is, independent in the sense that it is privately owned and is not formally

affiliated to any party, but many of its senior editorial staff were supporters
or members of the Irgun.

Maariv offered a platform for all political opinions and retained the
loyalty and keenness of its journalistic staff by giving them their heads and
encouraging differing views on current affairs. But editorial opinion was
predominantly conservative on domestic affairs and hard-line on relations
with the Arabs. Though not a Likud paper, its editorials often reflect that
grouping's opinions.

Its editor in 1979 was Shalom Rosenfeld, one of Israel's most influential
journalists, not merely because of the position he occupied, but because of
his widely read and respected political column. He was one of the
journalists who followed Carlebach out of *Yediot* and has stayed with *Maariv*
ever since, first as head of the Jerusalem office, then as news editor and a
member of the Editorial Board. Somewhat incredibly, for both his appearance and exuberance of manner convey an impression of youthfulness,
Rosenfeld reached the age of 65 in 1980. He had previously announced his
intention of retiring at that age and, following the example of the *Jerusalem
Post*, two veteran members of the Editorial Board, Shmuel Schnitzer and
Moshe Zak, were expected to succeed as Joint Editors.

Maariv is owned by a private company in which half of the shares are held
by Oved Ben-Ami, who provided the original financial backing for Dr
Carlebach when the paper was formed. A soft-spoken industrialist and
local politician of right-wing views, he was the founder and first Mayor of
Netanya. The other half of the shares is held by a cooperative of senior staff
members.

Like other mass circulation newspapers elsewhere in the world, much of
the time and attention of *Maariv*'s directorate has been distracted from
journalistic concerns and devoted to the non-journalistic activities of
technical developments and labour relations. Shortly after he took over the
Editorship in 1974, Rosenfeld was thrown into a dispute with the printers
over the issue of photo-setting. He anticipated *The (London) Times* by five
years in writing to every member of the printing staff, assuring them all that
no jobs would be lost and offering those who wanted to leave voluntarily five
months' salary for every year of service. This was five times the minimum
severance pay. The transition was successfully accomplished.

Maariv is profitable, but under conditions of over 100 per cent inflation
figures are deceptive. Calculated as a return on investment, the profits are
small, *Maariv* concedes. Its main problems are how to keep up with rising
costs and overcome shortage of capital, a consequence of Israel's abnormal
conditions of existence. Because of the political situation, the newspaper
must keep a three-months' stock of newsprint, which involves tying up
something like a million US dollars. With Israel's astronomical interest
rates, the financial burden is a heavy one. Because of inflation, the cover
price and advertisement rates are raised every six to eight weeks and, in
consequence, future budgeting is very nearly impossible.

Despite its problems, *Maariv* responded vigorously to the challenge of its
competitor *Yediot Aharonot*, which had been successfully campaigning for
the younger readership. In 1978, *Maariv* realised, with immense shock, that

it was being overhauled by *Yediot*. A 'revolution' in *Maariv* brought about the introduction of three new weekly sections, all geared to youth, and even its former, typically Israeli, prudish attitudes have been abandoned to provide coverage of sex issues. As a result, circulation improved though competition continues unabated. *Maariv* expects hard times for the Israeli press and shares the view held by many that when commercial television inevitably comes to Israel, the newspapers will lose advertising revenue. However, when it does arrive, *Maariv* will make every effort to secure a stake and, given the continuance of a right-wing Government, its own political attitudes are likely to ensure it a sympathetic reception.

Yediot Aharonot succeeded in gaining the readership of young people, mainly from the Sephardi and Oriental segment of the population, by moving somewhat down-market and giving prominence to pop music and related interests. But it has not done so at the expense of serious features; and some of its contributors, notably Yeshayahu Ben-Porat, are respected and influential. An innovation which attracted the younger and more sophisticated readers was the irreverence of its Friday inside spread, a political satire called 'Fatah-Land'. So keen is the competition between the two evening papers that it has infected general relations between them, which are far from cordial. In fact, neither paper will mention the other unless for the purpose of denigration.

Like *Maariv*, *Yediot* leans politically to the right and it supported Begin while he was in opposition. It also takes the strongest anti-Soviet line in the Israeli press. Founded in 1939 by Yehuda Mozes, a Polish immigrant who provided the finance, and Dr Carlebach, who provided its contents, *Yediot* was an immediate success, although it suffered a reverse nine years later when Carlebach left to found *Maariv*. It recovered under the present owner, Noah Mozes, son of the founder, who was himself born in Poland in 1912. A retiring man, Noah Mozes is not prominent in politics or in any other aspect of public life. He concentrates on the paper and brings to it his own shrewd management and conciliatory attitudes. This unwillingness to become involved in damaging controversies, political or other, has not stifled the enterprise and independence of his regular journalists; the liveliness of their different views has made a major contribution to the newspaper's popularity. Mozes has been equally successful with his weekly popular magazine, *La-Ishna* (The Woman), which he launched in 1947 and which has become the most widely read magazine of its kind in Israel.

The Post

The *Jerusalem Post* has neither the largest circulation nor the greatest influence, nor is it the most prosperous daily newspaper in Israel. But because it is in English, the *Post* occupies a unique role as Israel's showcase to the English-speaking world. Ambassadors, journalists, distinguished foreign visitors and ordinary tourists read the paper. The professionals may, later in the day, receive translations from the Hebrew press but, to many, the *Post* is not simply the first, it is the only source of Israeli news and views.

Gershon Agronsky (later abbreviated to Agron), the founder of the paper, came to Palestine from the United States in 1927 as correspondent for the Hearst press. In 1932 he started *The Palestine Post* with the main object of providing an English-language platform for the Zionist cause which could be read by the officials of the British Mandatory power. From its beginnings, the *Post* was the voice of the Labour leadership of the Zionist movement in its fight against the British Government.

In a special supplement published on its fortieth anniversary in 1972, the *Post* wrote: 'From the very first issue and for the next 23 years until he was elected Mayor of Jerusalem, the story of *The Palestine Post* was to be very largely the story of Gershon Agronsky.' He set the pattern, the style and the tone, mobilizing from Labour political sources the financial backing without which the paper could not have survived.

Politically, the paper supported Labour, but Agron reacted against direct political pressure on editorial prerogatives. On the other hand, he was willing to perform what has been described by one of his close associates in the paper, Lea Ben Dor, as 'special favours for friends'. One of Agron's closest friends was Moshe Sharett, Israel's first Foreign Minister and second Prime Minister, who would occasionally drop in to look at, and sometimes correct, proofs. Agron gave the paper its serious tone. He liked the style of the *New York Times* and sought to give his paper the same dignity, despite the infinitesimally smaller scale of his resources. His policies were continued by Ted Lourie, another American, who succeeded Agron as Editor in 1955. Lourie's major contributions were the modernization of the newspaper's production and the introduction of its overseas weekly, which grew to reach the substantial circulation of 40,000.

During Lourie's editorship, the 'strong man' on the political end of the paper was Lea Ben Dor, its political correspondent, and after Lourie's death in 1974 it was she who became Editor. A formidable lady in her professional activities, she brooked few objections to her assessments and had little patience with equivocations. Direct and positive, she was intolerant of inefficiency or evasiveness in others. She possessed many of the characteristics of Ben-Gurion, whom she admired and whose partisan she became when he parted company with the Labour Party. It hardly endeared her to the official party leadership, but Lea Ben Dor suffered their annoyance with the sense of superiority inculcated by that most English of England's girls' schools, Roedean, where she had been a pupil. The paper's problems with Labour ended when Ben-Gurion's party returned to the Labour fold. But during the last months of Labour's rule, the *Post* was no less critical of the scandals which contributed to its downfall than was the Israeli press generally.

Lea Ben Dor's editorship had always been intended as a temporary arrangement, but there was some surprise at her abrupt departure in August 1975 after only one year in office. The two Assistant Editors, German-born Erwin Frenkel and Austrian-born Ari Rath were appointed to succeed her in tandem as Joint Editors, Rath also holding the post of Managing Editor. Many were the prognostications that the arrangement would fail because of the inherent likelihood of friction between two people of different character and temperament. In fact, it worked well, probably because they are so different that it was possible to establish a real division of functions.

Frenkel is the solid, hard-working journalist, happiest in running the editorial side of the paper, while Rath, an ebullient extrovert, enjoys the cocktail-party circuit and is a compulsive mixer and conversationalist. In general, Frenkel is the inside man and Rath the front man. Each sensibly keeps the other informed, ensuring that both are party to all major decisions.

Palestine Post Limited, the publisher of the newspaper (it has retained its pre-State name), is a private company, 26 per cent of its shares being held by the Histadrut, 25 per cent by the Israel Investors' Corporation (an American group led by the fund-raiser and investor, Sam Rothenberg, which has always had close ties with Israel's Labour leaders), and 19 per cent by senior employees, most of them also Labour supporters. The remaining 30 per cent is owned by some of the paper's pioneers or their heirs. Circulation is claimed to amount to 25,000 on weekdays and 44,000 for the Friday week-end issue. No newspapers are published on Saturdays in Israel. The weekly overseas edition is published by a separate company, Jerusalem Post Publications Limited, an arrangement which dates back to the 1960s, when the Israel Investors' Corporation wanted a separate company to benefit from the government's financial support to exporters. The paper is nowadays happy when it breaks even. The overseas edition, though profitable, has been badly hurt by the vast increase in postal rates since 1977.

Control of the business rests with a twenty-one member Board of Directors. Since Agron, it has had no permanent chairman and one of its members is elected to preside at each of the three or four meetings which take place every year. The executive body is a committee of six, made up of one representative each of the Histadrut, the Israel Investors' Corporation and the Jewish Agency, together with three senior members of the staff, at present Frenkel, Rath and Shalom Weiss, the Secretary-Treasurer of the company. The staff totals some 250 (including part-timers), of whom 55 are full editorial and about 75 full-time on the printing side. The modern, efficient plant on Jerusalem's outskirts is one of the largest enterprises in the city, with an annual turnover in excess of four million US dollars.

After the Likud's election win in 1977, the *Post* became almost non-party in its approach, and its mixed bag of writers expounded their personal views, some left, some right, some middle of the road. As a result, it had less trouble with the Begin Government than with some of its Labour predecessors. Rath would probably have plumped for a more clean-cut position, but Frenkel is temperamentally restrained and balanced, and the politically uncontroversial nature of the *Post* is of his making. 'Hebrew papers', he says, 'have a certain temper of hysteria about them. We're a little cooler by temperament. I think we're a little more judicious in our presentation of events.'

The Editors' Committee, leaks and censorship

The *Jerusalem Post* was created as a fighting paper – for Zionism and against the British. The Hebrew press was also in the fight and often in the van of the growing struggle for independence, as British support for the Jewish national home crumbled. To impose a measure of control, the Mandatory Government enacted a press ordinance in 1933 and introduced censorship three years later. The editors of the Zionist press – as all the Hebrew papers then were – set up what they called the Reaction Committee, deciding that they could achieve most in that situation by acting in concert. Each editor signed an undertaking that decisions of the Committee would be binding on them all.

Upon the end of British rule, the Reaction Committee was no longer 'agin the Government' and assumed a new role in cooperation with the Jewish authorities. It became the channel between the Government and the press, as well as the instrument for a working arrangement about military censorship with the security authorities. It was not a case of accepting arbitrary restrictions on the freedom of the press, because the need for censorship in Israel's beleaguered situation was unquestioningly and generally accepted.

In 1953, the Reaction Committee changed its name to the Editors' Committee and was officially registered as an independent association. Its functions, however, did not change, and it remained the voluntary partner of the General Staff of the IDF in the operation of a censorship code.

If all copy had to be submitted for censorship, the newspapers would be unlikely to meet their deadlines and vast numbers of censors would have to be employed. To avoid both these consequences, ground rules were agreed by both sides. The General Staff supplies the editors with a list of subjects connected with the security of the State, which is periodically up-dated. Material relating to these subjects is expected to be submitted to military censorship for prior approval. General guidelines, however, are not always easy to apply to specific cases, and it is the responsibility of a newspaper's editor to decide whether any particular story should be submitted. Sometimes an editor may err and, on occasion, may decide deliberately to publish an item clearly included on the list. In most such cases, the military censorship will be content with a warning telephone call. A second offence may provoke a more formal response, in the shape of a warning letter.

If defiance continues, the editor may be summoned to appear before a tribunal composed of military and journalistic representatives and a neutral chairman, who is generally a lawyer. The tribunal has power to suspend a newspaper and impose fines; but only once has a paper been closed. In 1973, *Kol Ha'am* (Voice of the People), the Communist paper, was shut down for a week for publishing an article on a security project without prior censorship. Any fines imposed go to the funds of the Journalists' Association, so it is all a rather cosy family affair.

On the whole, the system has worked reasonably well, censors act with moderation and the newspapers with a sense of responsibility. The reading public in Israel, very security-conscious, is highly critical of newspapers which may seem, for the sake of a scoop, to disregard national interests. This is another factor in making editors wary of sensational stories connected with sensitive security subjects.

Membership of the Editors' Committee is restricted to the daily newspapers, with the editor of the broadcasting news service as an affiliate. In practice, although not bound by an agreement, all the other news publications in the country follow the same procedure. The Arabic-language press on the West Bank is in a different category and, under Jordanian law to which it remains subject, submits everything to pre-censorship. But, security matters aside, the West Bank papers remain free to publish hostile material about Israel, and Arab journalists on the West Bank concede that no newspapers in the rest of the Arab world are as free as those for which they work. The East Jerusalem Arabic-language papers are also free to publish anti-Israel material, and make full use of this freedom.

The terms of the agreement between the editors and the General Staff apply only to security issues, but successive governments have on occasion tried to extend censorship to sensitive political subjects. In 1959, despite protests by the editors, the Government made censorship compulsory on the subject of immigration. At that time it could have been hazardous to disclose immigration facts concerning Arab or East European countries for Jews were often allowed to leave only on condition that nothing was said. At first, the press accepted this restriction on information as reasonable in the circumstances, but when the Government extended the area of censorship to cover all immigration, the editors successfully rebelled.

In some foreign policy areas which the Government regards as sensitive (the negotiations with President Sadat were an example), the cooperation of the press is achieved by Ministers meeting the Editors' Committee and briefing them with off-the-record information which usually buys their silence. Editors are aware that this is a technique to restrict freedom of information, but generally act sensibly and, when persuaded that national interests may suffer, restrain their journalistic zeal. Only Gershom Schocken, the Editor of *Haaretz*, has left the Editors' Committee, so as to protect his freedom of action.

Apart from the areas of security and the foreign policy issues connected with it, Israeli Governments, like most others, prefer to conceal their activities, except when they specifically want to reveal them. The business of the press is to penetrate that secrecy and, in Israel, one of the most effective methods is through the leak. In the circumstances of Israeli coalition Governments, leaks, even from the Cabinet, are both inevitable and, largely, irremediable.

Inevitable, because every Minister of a small party in the coalition is anxious to let his fellow party-members know what he is doing and, in particular, when he dissents from a Cabinet decision which in public he is bound to support on the principle of Cabinet collective responsibility. He will talk either to his own party press or to other journalists. Israel is a small country; everybody in and around the Government knows everybody else. They meet at parties, in corridors or at meetings and, in the course even of casual conversation, secrets are revealed.

Circumstantial reports of Cabinet meetings and who said what appear promptly in the press but, although Cabinet meetings are secret by law, no prosecution has ever been launched. The reason for this is that the source of every leak must be a Cabinet Minister, and political necessities determine that they cannot be disciplined. In one instance in 1957, Ben-Gurion resigned as Prime Minister because a leak from one of his colleagues had, as he put it, sabotaged the work of the Government. He could not dismiss the talkative colleague because he was a nominee of one of the coalition partners, not a member of Ben-Gurion's own party. In the event, Ben-Gurion came back to form a new Government, but only on condition that a new law was passed guaranteeing the secrecy of all Cabinet proceedings.

That was no cure either, but a recent technique has been more successful. In 1966, the Knesset defined the deliberations of the Cabinet Security Committee as 'state secrets', of which any unauthorized publication was condemned as 'severe espionage'. Golda Meir and Rabin instituted the practice of declaring the whole of the Cabinet a special session of the Security Committee, in this way achieving total secrecy. Mr Begin has habitually and successfully used the same method.

But widespread protests followed the decision of the Begin Government to include within the jurisdiction of the Security Committee the controversial political issue of settlements in the occupied territories. *Haaretz* described it as an undisguised attempt at political censorship, and the Editors' Committee has also protested, but without success. Most experienced journalists are prepared to bide their time, believing that the progress of the peace negotiations will reduce the security pressures which are at the heart of most of the conflicts between the needs of security and the right of the public to know.

Chapter nine

Education and the Arts

The educational system

Straggling crocodiles of schoolchildren shepherded by anxiously officious teachers are a ubiquitous sight in Israel. Occasionally the chatter is momentarily interrupted as the children stop on their educational hike to look and listen, or half-listen, to the teacher's commentary on one of the country's innumerable historical sites. The contrast between their freedom, exuberant vitality and educational opportunities and the restricted, often deprived, lives of most of their parents demonstrates one of Israel's high priorities. In no country in the world are children more carefully and devotedly reared by both parents and the State, and no country spends more on education in proportion to its total budget. Jewish parents, however poor, have always been accustomed to make sacrifices for their children's education and the Jewish State has continued the pattern.

Israel built on the educational structure which had been created by the pre-State organized community in Palestine. The Mandatory Government took over and largely maintained the predominantly Moslem Arab school system; Christian Arab children generally attended missionary schools. But although it contributed to and exercised some kind of nominal supervision over the Jewish schools, these continued to be maintained either by the local community – the Yishuv – or by Jewish philanthropic institutions abroad.

The Jewish school system began with the kindergarten for three- to five-year-olds. In addition to preparing their charges for school, the kindergarten exercised (as they still do) important social functions. They permitted mothers to go out to work and, by teaching the children not only the Hebrew language but also the standards and habits of the westernized community, they began blending together the disparate immigrants into an Israeli nation.

From kindergarten, the children moved on to elementary schools from the age of 6 to 14. These schools introduced a note of division for, by the time the community council took over the schools in 1932, they were already segregated into three types – what were known as the 'trends'. The General Zionists who were the mainstream of the Zionist movement in pre-State years, were responsible for schools of the 'general trend'. These offered a general educational course, including Jewish subjects, but without any emphasis on religious observance, which they regarded as the concern of the home rather than the school. At the end of the Mandate, more than half the children within the Jewish school system attended general trend schools.

Opposed to the exclusion of religion from the classroom, Mizrachi, the religious Zionist party, had created its own schools. Secular education was not neglected and similar standards to the general schools were maintained. but the teaching of Judaism played an important role. To ensure the influence of religion by example as well as by tuition, the Mizrachi schools employed only religious Jews as teachers and supervisors. By 1948 these schools catered for about 25 per cent of pupils.

The third and newest of the trends was Labour. The kibbutzim and cooperative settlements of the Labour movement had, from the very outset, established schools for their own children, emphasizing social issues and socialist ideology. As the movement grew, Labour schools were also founded in the towns, and in 1924 the Zionist Organization recognized this network as the Labour trend. Affiliated to the Histadrut, it expanded to cater for another 25 per cent of the elementary school population.

A fourth group of schools, outside the national school system, included those belonging to the separatist, super-orthodox Jews of Agudat Israel, together with a handful of independent orthodox schools founded by the old Yishuv. All these concentrated almost exclusively on religious studies with only a smattering of secular education. Steering clear of the non-religious organization of the Jewish national school system, the ultra-orthodox schools constituted a *de facto* fourth trend.

The creation of a comprehensive state system of education out of this *mélange* took a little time, but the first major step came quickly after independence. The Compulsory Education Law of 1949 made education free and compulsory both in Arab schools and in the existing three Jewish trends, financial responsibility being assumed by the Government and local authorities. Any child could attend any school, but in practice neither Arabs nor Jews went outside their own school systems. The free and compulsory schooling began with one year in kindergarten at the age of 5 (a recognition of its unique importance in Israel) followed by eight grades in elementary schools belonging to one of the trends, from the age of 6 to 14. A peculiarity of the law attributable to Israel's special situation was the provision that children who had not completed eight grades (mainly immigrants who had come from countries where these facilities were not available) were required to remain at school until the age of 17.

In those early years of mass immigration, the educational trend system operated to the distaste of many members of the public. The Education Law gave parents the right to choose the trend in which they wanted their children to be educated, but in practice the situation was quite different. Rivalry between the trends led to competition for pupils among the new immigrants. In part, it was caused by genuine ideological zeal; the Socialists and the orthodox had confidence in the ideas they were promoting and were eager to spread the message. But party political interests were also involved, each trend seeing the parents of its pupils as potential voters for their party. In response to criticism of what was often described at that time as 'body snatching', the trends shared out residential areas among themselves, in the result denying parents the right of choice.

The situation became so unseemly that a Government enquiry was instituted and a second basic Act, the State Education Law, passed in 1953, abolished the trends – but not entirely. Mizrachi was unwilling to abandon its own school system, the instrument through which it hoped, in the long run, to be able to ensure the future religious orientation of the State. By making it a condition for participating in the Government coalition, the religious party insisted on a parallel system – which exists today – of State schools and State religious schools. The ultra-orthodox Agudat Israel schools, which had opted out of the State system, were accorded the classification of 'unofficial recognized schools'. This meant that they would receive government grants and loans for running costs and development, provided that they taught an approved secular education as well as their own religious programme.

Later changes extended the school-leaving age to 15 and amended the structure by following six years of elementary education with two years of 'intermediate' classes in junior high schools. Pupils with good grades could continue their education at a high school until the age of 18. Secondary schools were fee-paying institutions administered by a medley of non-government institutions and, although the national education authorities were unhappy with the system, they could do little about it because of the cost of taking them over. Gradually the benefits of secondary education were made available to more children whose parents could not afford to pay for it by granting them free or subsidized places paid for by the Government. By the end of the '70s, about 500,000 pupils were being educated in the Hebrew part of the State system, some 70 per cent of them in the non-religious schools, about 20 per cent in the religious stream, with the remainder at independent schools, including the Agudat Israel institutions.

In Israel today, compulsory education begins at the age of 5 with a year in kindergarten, and at the age of 6 parents have the choice of sending their children to elementary schools of either the religious or non-religious variety. The syllabus in both includes tuition in Hebrew language and literature, the Bible (interest is enhanced by school visits to biblical sites), history, geography, science, mathematics, a foreign language in the higher grades (English, Arabic or French), arts and crafts, and physical training. In addition, the religious schools teach Talmud, religious laws and prayer. In March 1978 the school-leaving age was raised to 16, and secondary education up to the age of 18 was brought into the free State system. Only two private fee-paying high schools remained, the Herzlia Gymnasium in Tel Aviv and the Reali School in Haifa.

The object of secondary education in Israel is to obtain the Bagrut, matriculation – the passport to university or other institutions of higher learning. Those who leave before the age of 18 receive the lesser diploma of a school-leaving certificate and similar leaving certificates are available for graduates from vocational and agricultural schools.

Pupils at high schools are required to perform some national service and many do volunteer work on kibbutzim for a week or ten days a year. Others receive elementary military training as members of Gadna, a para-military youth organization, which provides high school pupils with a weekly lesson from one of the school teachers specially trained in the work. Toughening 'hikes' in the countryside and school visits to places of historical interest break the monotony of the classroom. The school year runs from the beginning of September to mid-June, with holidays at the Jewish festivals. Hours of tuition at elementary schools are from 8 a.m. to 1 p.m., with handwork or social activities in the afternoons, while high school hours are from 8 a.m. to 3 p.m. Standards of teachers and teaching vary widely. Not all teachers are graduates of teacher-training institutions; demand exceeds supply and in development towns and remote areas the number of unqualified teachers is high and standards correspondingly lower.

The integration of culturally deprived (generally Oriental) children in the school has, in the opinion of many teachers, reduced standards, as teachers gear their courses to a lower level. Moreover, only a fraction of Oriental children receive any secondary education; they are in fact over-represented in the vocational training programmes, while the Jewish 'wasps' go on to higher education. In 1980, fewer than 10,000 of Israel's 60,000 University students were of Oriental origin.

A further division is created by the dual system of religious and non-religious schools at a time when attitudes are formed and friendships made. For most schoolchildren contacts outside school are restricted, and they tend to continue their social lives in the 'trend' in which they were educated. Furthermore, religious schools discourage intermingling. One teacher at a non-religious high school who was supervising a national service project for pupils of both school systems was told not to organize any discussion groups or classes including both categories of pupils. She could act only as their tour guide.

The Ministry of Education and Culture has been fortunate in being headed by a series of Israel's most enlightened politicians. The first incumbent was Zalman Shazar, a scholar, writer and journalist who later became President of the State. His successors, who included Abba Eban and Yigal Allon, were all Labour adherents until 1977, when, with the change of Government, the National Religious Party received the valued prize of the Ministry of Education. The new Minister, Zvulun Hammer, was known as a religious militant, and secularists were alarmed at the prospect of increasing religious influence in the non-religious schools.

Religion in the schools

When the trend system was abolished and the two school streams replaced them, control of the religious schools was vested in a fourteen-member council for Religious State Education, nine being nominees of Mizrachi, now the NRP. The law provided that this Council's approval was required for any changes in the supplementary religious programme of the religious schools.

All State primary education, in both school systems, was to be based on the values of Jewish culture and the achievements of science, love of country and loyalty to the State and the Jewish people. For the teaching of 'the values of Jewish culture' the Ministry of Education provided a syllabus for all schools which included the Bible, Hebrew language and literature and

Jewish history. That was augmented in the schools in the religious stream by a supplementary programme of studies defined as 'comprising the study of the written and oral law and aimed at a religious way of life.' The supplementary syllabus could not occupy more than 25 per cent of the time devoted to all tuition.

While the Bible was studied in the secular schools as the source of Jewish culture and of ethical ideas, the religious schools stressed the rules of religious observance and avoided Bible criticism. No less important to orthodox Jews than the syllabus was the character of the teachers. The Council for Religious Education was given power to disqualify teachers on religious grounds and it laid down precise rulings as to the degree of religious commitment required.

Zvulun Hammer, in an interview he gave in 1978, forcefully justified both curriculum and staffing in the religious schools. He pointed out that for thousands of years, the Jews had survived on a diet of Bible, Talmud and Halacha (rabbinic law). The children in the religious schools were being taught values ultimately more useful for day-to-day life than any academic subject. Such teaching was positive and valuable and the independence which assured its curricular preeminence was worth maintaining. He continued: 'Religious children should be taught only by religious teachers. A non-religious teacher in the secular subjects would ultimately plant seeds of doubt in his pupils' minds through what he teaches. And even in the sciences, conflict between teachers' premises and the pupils' faith would arise. Say, a biology teacher would teach that man descends from the apes and was not created . . . in the image of God.'

The Jewish studies curriculum in the religious schools can point to considerable success in nurturing a commitment to Judaism among its students. In particular the youth movement, Bnei Akiva, which draws its members from the religious schools, is widely regarded as the best of all Israeli youth movements. But the effectiveness of the 'values of Jewish culture' classes in the secular schools, notwithstanding Ben-Gurion's efforts after the Eichmann trial to instil 'Jewish consciousness', has been continually doubted. Critics claim that pupils in secular schools learn little or nothing of Jewish history or the Jewish tradition, and that this gap in their education has led to ignorance of Zionism as well as of Judaism. That ignorance, they argue, is at the root of the decline in idealism in the country so that the rigours and sacrifices entailed in the Jewish renaissance are not now readily accepted. Although the diagnosis is open to debate, the existence of the ailment is unquestionable.

Soon after becoming Minister of Education, Hammer appointed a special assistant to undertake the revitalization of Jewish religious studies in the State schools. He was a young man in his thirties, Dr Daniel Tropper, who had emigrated to Israel from New York ten years earlier (the number of American-born Jews prominent in all Israel's orthodox movements is remarkable). Despite the budget cuts which had, since 1976, compelled schools even to reduce the hours of tuition, Hammer disclosed his priorities by providing almost $1 million in 1979 for the introduction of an optional religious course for boys and girls in the 7th grade (approximately 13 years old). In 1979, Dr Tropper's programme was being taught experimentally in 80 selected schools all over the country and, if adjudged to be successful, would be extended to 400 elementary and 100 junior high schools in 1980.

Based on four attractive and stylishly produced booklets prepared by a group of religious educationalists, the course is planned to occupy no more than two hours each week. There is no requirement that the course be taught only by religious teachers and, in practice, it rarely is. Experience so far suggests that when the subject is taught by people who have no religious axe to grind, it does not provoke the resistance offered to more obvious attempts at indoctrination. With its emphasis on ethical and moral issues relevant to contemporary life, the new course seemed to be making an impact. A representative view expressed by a non-religious teacher was: 'It strikes a responsive chord among my pupils, [the booklets] touch topical, actual interests and concerns and do not give an impression of proselytizing.'

The influence of a religious Minister of Education has been felt in other ways. At the secular schools, the start of Jewish studies in the second grade (ages 7–8) has always been marked by a celebration, the continuation of an ancient tradition. At this party, each child is given a personal copy of the Bible, and all take part in tableaux, plays or presentations, so that their introduction to the cultural heritage of their people is made into a joyous event. It has always been a secular ceremony performed in the schools but, under the new influences from the Ministry, it is now often transferred to the synagogue and made into a religious occasion, emphasizing the link between the Torah scrolls in the synagogue Ark and the Bibles placed into the hands of the children.

Literature syllabuses in schools have been amended to given them some religious content by including examples from the works of religious writers and of Chassidic and other moralists. In the teaching of history, more emphasis is being placed on Jewish history at the expense of general history and orthodox religious themes have been introduced into a variety of pedagogical material. A children's play book, for example, in a description of a simple do-it-yourself recipe, introduces a reference to the religious dietary laws, of which most of the children from non-religious households are likely to be ignorant. Subtle introduction of religious concepts occurs in material on contemporary issues. A teacher's outline on the concern about the plight of the Kampuchean children quoted texts of rabbinic and other religious source material dealing with the Jewish values of compassion and charity.

Many teachers complain that, because of unfamiliarity with this new material, their jobs have become more difficult. The need to attend refresher courses has also been added to their burdens and has fortified their demands for better pay and conditions. But few secular school teachers object to the more religious orientation, seeing it as a positive element which, unless taken to extremes, could be beneficial in Israel's evolving educational process.

Outside both the State system and the 'unofficial recognized schools' of Agudat Israel, a fringe educational system of religious elementary schools is maintained by Chassidic sects concentrated mainly in Jerusalem. Catering for some 6,000 children (12 per cent of the local school population), these schools impart Jewish learning to their pupils for some eight hours a day, six days a week, fifty-two weeks a year except for religious holidays. Only one hour a day is devoted to secular subjects and Yiddish is the language of instruction (Hebrew, as the holy tongue, is profaned by common use). Although their principles forbid them to accept aid from the Zionist State, many of these schools have now succumbed to temptation and have become beneficiaries of the funds for religious schools paid out by the Begin Government as the price of the continuing support of the religious parties.

Seven universities

Israel's institutions of higher learning, all of them autonomous bodies, grew rapidly after the establishment of the State to meet the demand for teachers at all levels and for trained personnel for the burgeoning activities of Government and private enterprise. Before 1948, only two institutions of university standard existed: the Technion in Haifa, which opened in 1924 and had 700 students in 1948, and the Hebrew University in Jerusalem, which began to function in 1925 and had a student body of 1,000 in 1948. Since then, five other universities have been established. First came the Weizmann Institute of Science at Rehovot in 1949, followed by Bar Ilan University (1955), Tel Aviv University (1956), Haifa (1970), and the Ben-Gurion University of the Negev (1973). The number of students working for recognized degrees in Israel's institutions of higher learning rose from 1,635 in 1948–49 to 54,000 for the 1977–78 academic year. The latter figure is augmented by thousands of other students not included in the official statistics because they are engaged on diploma or other non-degree courses. About half the students are women and about the same proportion are working their way through university.

Today's seven universities all possess distinctive features. Jerusalem is the Oxbridge of Israel. Tel Aviv has the largest student body. The Technion is the engineering and technological mecca, while the Weizmann Institute, with more scientists than students, constitutes a research community. Bar Ilan, on the outskirts of Tel Aviv, emphasizes religion, while the two newest, Haifa and Ben-Gurion, were set up mainly to meet regional requirements.

Different though they are, all these institutions were founded by the same process and their administrative structures are more or less identical. They all came about as cooperative endeavours between Israel and the Jewish diaspora communities, and their Boards of Governors are composed of both Israelis and diaspora Jews, the latter being eminent scholars, large contributors or fund-raisers. Each Board of Governors meets only annually when reports are presented and discussed, the annual budget debated and approved, and major policy decisions taken. Between Board meetings, an Executive Committee is responsible for the management of affairs. The usual procedure is for an Executive Committee to be made up of equal numbers of Israelis and overseas representatives, but additional local representation ensures that the Israelis retain effective control.

The academic affairs of the institutions are the exclusive responsibility of the Senate, which is composed of the deans of the faculties, the full professors and the elected representatives of the other academic ranks. The academic head of each university is the Rector, who is one of the full professors elected by the Senate, while the administrative head is the President appointed by the Board of Governors.

In creating this structure, Israel's other universities followed the example of the Hebrew University, thus perpetuating on their campuses one of the conflicts inherent in the administrative scheme devised in Jerusalem. The Hebrew University's first head was Judah Magnes, an American Reform rabbi, who was scholarly and impressive, but was not accepted as an academic by the academics. Appointed in 1925 with the title of Chancellor, he exercised overall authority, academic as well as administrative, but his conduct of academic affairs was persistently criticized by the faculty which, within a decade, persuaded the governors to make a change. Magnes was given the title of President while academic direction was transferred to a Rector appointed by the Senate. That division of responsibilities was adopted by all the other universities, except the Technion.

The situation created frictions from the outset. Professor Selig Brodetsky, a British academic and Zionist leader, who succeeded Magnes as President in 1949, suffered acutely because of it and ultimately resigned for that reason. In a brief but bitter account of his Hebrew University experience in his memoirs, Brodetsky quoted a letter he had sent to all Governors after a series of frustrating events in which he had been ignored or overruled by the faculty. In that letter he urged – vainly as it turned out – that the President should possess complete authority, and that the Rector should be no more than his academic adviser. The difficulties became muted during the tenure of the three Presidents who followed Brodetsky, two Israeli academics and an ex-Ambassador, but flared up again under another, the English-born President, Avraham Harman, who was appointed in 1968 after his retirement as Israeli Ambassador in Washington.

Harman made no secret of his support for a unitary system of authority with the President in control. Tensions became more acute as the economic situation grew more difficult and the Government reduced its financial support. The administrators who, in these circumstances, had to make cuts and tighten procedure, fell foul of the academics who wanted complete control of the academic budget. Harman, unwilling to continue in office, proposed that he be succeeded by an academic President with wide authority, but failed to win enough support. It remains one of the unresolved problems of all Israeli universities; the faculty possess all the authority, while the administration bears all the responsibility.

The bulk of the finance for the universities comes from the Government and from the Jewish Agency out of funds collected abroad for general Israeli purposes. The Agency's allocation to the seven universities for 1978–79 amounted to almost $50 million, which, together with Government aid, covered about 70 per cent of their budgets. The rest was made up of students' fees and direct contributions from abroad. In each university, a public relations and fund-raising department is responsible for soliciting gifts and organizing societies of 'friends' throughout the world. It is an extremely competitive business, in which the Hebrew University was first in the field and is still the most successful. But the others are now trying harder.

Students and teachers

Most students in Israel enrol for university places only after completing their military service, which means, in most cases, at about the age of 21. A limited exemption applies to the most promising high school pupils, who may be placed in the 'academic reserve', thus deferring their service until they have graduated. High schools and technical schools are given a quota, and principals recommend which pupils should be granted deferment within the limit of the quota given. In the case of technical schools, the deferment is two years and medical school six. When the members of the 'academic reserve' are eventually called up, they serve for four years instead of the usual three, with the fourth on full pay.

Because of their prior military service, students are older and more heavily burdened when they begin their three undergraduate years than their counterparts in other countries. Military service takes further toll of the continuity of university education by interruptions for reserve duty – generally for several weeks every year – both for faculty members and for students.

In 1979, there were about 60,000 university students in Israel, a large number for so small a population. They made up about 15 per cent of the 18–24 age-group. No fewer than 40 per cent of them were married, and at least half combined some gainful employment with their studies. On the one hand, this produces a more mature, more highly motivated student body. On the other, Israel's students find little joy in their studies, and their university years are rarely the best years of their lives. Many university teachers report that their students are serious and hard-working but virtually impervious to the intellectual stimulus generally associated with the idea of a university. They want to acquire their qualifications as quickly as possible and get out.

For all these reasons, students' campus activities are far less intense than in most Western universities. The students have neither the time nor the inclination for intellectual relaxation or for politics and even during the widespread student turbulence at the end of the 1960s, Israel never experienced a student revolt. In some universities, notably Jerusalem, small minorities of Arab and left-wing students have attempted campus demonstrations but these have been frowned on by the authorities. Leaflets and posters are permitted, but public meetings or demonstrations are not regarded as a function of being a university student and are prohibited. Student activists are told that they may demonstrate in the same places as all other citizens but not on campus.

Student unions in each university are affiliated to the National Union of

Israeli Students, whose main function is to offer practical assistance, although the universities themselves help in many ways. Money is generally the most urgent of the students' needs and the best of them are awarded scholarships and fellowships. In other cases, fees are reduced in relation to students' means and, with the assistance of the banks, cheap loans are obtainable to be repaid by instalments beginning a year after graduation. As an indirect subsidy to students, the cafeterias provide inexpensive meals and, for some, inexpensive accommodation is available in dormitories.

Since 1973, the number of post-graduate students working for higher degrees has declined in most of the universities. The drop coincided with the beginning of cuts in university budgets which brought about a reduction in the number of new teaching jobs. In 1979, the Hebrew University had 1,300 doctoral students, a drop of 10 per cent since 1973. Tel Aviv University, with a larger student body than Jerusalem, had 700. The number of undergraduates has also begun to decline, as suitable job opportunities become harder to find. On 'employment day' in May 1979, 112 firms sent representatives to the Tel Aviv University campus offering jobs, but the students were unenthusiastic, complaining that the majority were routine clerical and administrative appointments. What was the point, they asked, of the years of study and the expense?

Israel's university explosion provided great opportunities for young academics. No longer did they have to wait to acquire enough seniority to gain promotion. However young, they were now sought after and competed for by Haifa, Beersheba, Tel Aviv and others. Jobs and rapid promotion were available and academic staff throughout Israel increased from 193 in 1948 to a total of no fewer than 9,000 in the 1975–76 academic year (the latest for which official statistics are available).

University appointments in Israel are not advertised. The system, described by one professor as 'faculty nepotism', and by another as an 'academic mafia', amounts to a closed guild in which teachers recommend their favourite pupils. A departmental head will recommend a candidate to the Dean, who takes it to the university's appointments committee. If a budgetary slot already exists for the appointment it is generally approved, but if the appointment is a new one, a budget will have to be found, either by the departmental head who is pushing for it or by the university administrators. A shrewd departmental head will try to bring in somebody from abroad for a new appointment, because the Government offers some financial help to new immigrants and, for the first two years, the university can have him cheaply. After the two-year inaugural period, a retirement may occur or another budgetary slot may become available enabling the immigrant to continue in the post.

On the whole, the system of 'faculty nepotism' appears to work, and all seven universities have on their faculties teachers of great standing and international repute. But one of its negative aspects has been the ability of the closed circle of the scholarly power-brokers to block appointments or promotion. There are many examples of outstanding scholars who have left Israel for this reason.

On the national level, a considerable degree of coordination among the seven universities is achieved through the Council for Higher Education, a statutory body created by the Knesset in 1958. Headed by the Minister of Education and Culture, the 23 members of the Council are appointed by the President who is required by law to ensure that at least two-thirds are academics of standing. For some years the Chairman of the Council has been Professor Natan Rotenstreich, who has occupied the chair of philosophy at the Hebrew University since 1955 and is probably the most highly respected of Israel's academics. The Council is enjoined not to limit the independence of the universities, which are all entitled to conduct their affairs as they see fit within the limitations of their budgets. However, the Council for Higher Education has considerable influence over their budgets.

Formally, the functions of the Council are to grant recognition to institutions of higher learning, to approve the degrees they may award (it is an offence in Israel to give unauthorized degrees) and to advise the Government on its financial assistance to the recognized institutions. In practice, the Council has established the procedure that its approval must be obtained for each university's itemized budget before it recommends the Government grant. Any new development appearing in an itemized budget, such as a new research project, will be subjected to careful scrutiny. The Council may decide that it is not necessary or that it duplicates an existing facility. Ben-Gurion University, for example, has not set up its own school for social work, because the Council pointed out that the Hebrew University's school for social work did not have its full complement of students. Beersheba acquiesced, because disregard for the Council's opinion could have affected its Government grant.

Had it been established earlier, the Council for Higher Education could have avoided considerable duplication. No fewer than six universities maintain expensive chemistry departments, by no means all necessary to meet Israel's need for chemists. In 1979 the Technion Chemistry Department had only about a dozen students, said the Rector of the Hebrew University, while Jerusalem received only 120 applications for its 80 places, 'inevitably lowering the level of our chemistry students'. By way of comparison, the medical school, with an annual intake of 90, receives about 800 applications.

Attitudes to higher education

Pioneering Zionism called for a return to the soil. The abnormalities imposed by the centuries of diaspora living had forced the Jews to abandon the good and natural life on the land in favour of either trade or intellectual occupations. The early Zionist ideologists were intellectuals, but the ideal they propounded was that of the cultivated Jew ploughing the fields or milking the cows. The Land of Israel was to be rebuilt by agricultural pioneers, not by university graduates.

This attitude existed side by side with the more ancient and deep-rooted Jewish attachment to intellectual values and admiration for scholars and scholarship. The result was that, as Zionism grew, institutions of learning were created as well as kibbutzim. Scholars were honoured. Dr Weizmann, the first President of Israel, was a scientist and most of his successors were men of learning. Israel's fourth President, Professor Katzir, was also a scientist and President Navon, the fifth, is the first to have come from the ranks of the active politicians.

However, the number of academics involved in Israel's public life is surprisingly modest. The Knesset includes several scholars. Yigael Yadin, a Deputy Prime Minister, is a Professor of Archaeology, while his associate in the formation of the DMC was another professor, Amnon Rubinstein. Three dynamic scientists are Likud MKs, and Abba Eban taught at Cambridge University before being recruited for Zionism. Professor Shlomo Avineri of the Hebrew University served for a while as Director-General of the Foreign Ministry. Another Professor, Yuval Ne'eman, founded the Tehiya Party in 1979, adopting the hard-line position occupied by Herut before it came to power. Academics have been influential spokesmen for the nation's conscience. Professor Dan Patinkin, a highly regarded economist, headed a group of 'doveish' academics who, in 1971, urged that Israel should make more concessions on the occupied territories – to the annoyance of Golda Meir. Another Prime Minister, the great Ben-Gurion, was also called to account by academics, among them Jerusalem's eminent historian, Professor J. L. Talmon. Their accusations of absolutism were unnerving and unsettling, and probably contributed to his political decline. The Patinkin and Talmon precedents were followed more recently by the academics who urged peace policies after the Yom Kippur War.

But on the whole, Israel's academics prefer to stand aside from the decision-making process and content themselves, on occasion, with expressing consternation. The politicians tend to dismiss academics as unrealistic and indecisive because, like Eban, they are capable of looking at more than one side of the question. Golda Meir often dismissed an argument to which she could not find an immediate reply with, 'That's just like a professor.'

Israelis are less academically orientated than diaspora Jews, for in Israel a university education is not a *sine qua non* for career advancement as it generally is in the West. Apart from the professions, Israelis can succeed without a degree. Their attitude to universities is also affected by their cynicism towards experts who have so often been contradicted by events. Instead, they place great store on self-education. Ben-Gurion never attended a university and proudly described how he had taught himself Greek, so that he could read Plato in the original.

Suspicion of higher education and academics invariably surfaces in Knesset debates discussing cuts in higher education. Even during the growing inflation from 1977 to 1979, Ministers were able to resist cuts in their own Ministries' expenditure – but made them on higher education. Between 1972 and 1978. when the national Budget grew in real terms by about 30 per cent, the only sector to be cut back was higher education, which decreased by 20 per cent over the same period. A question frequently asked by the critics of higher education is, 'How many academics do we need?'

Perhaps this tension between the intellectual and anti-intellectual influences in Israel is ultimately a constructive one for there are few countries where academics, particularly in the sciences, have contributed so much to the public weal. Educated and highly trained manpower has become Israel's major national asset.

Culture

The Frederick Mann Auditorium in Tel Aviv on the first night of a subscription concert series could easily be confused with the Philharmonic Hall in New York or London's Royal Festival Hall on a gala night. Not a seat is unoccupied, the audience is elegantly dressed and their appreciation of music is patent. The only substantial difference between opening night and one of the routine performances is a reduction in sartorial quality, but the hall is always crowded, and only high-level connections can produce a ticket. The Tel Aviv concert hall bears the name of a Philadelphia philanthropist, one of the many examples of the alliance between wealthy diaspora Jews, who have provided the means for culture, and the Israelis who provide the content.

The Israelis, with their roots in Western culture, brought to their new land their intense cultural interests, apparent not alone in the Tel Aviv concerts of the Israel Philharmonic Orchestra, but in every aspect of cultural life. Jerusalem has its own Symphony Orchestra (which is also the orchestra of the Israel Broadcasting Authority), and numerous chamber ensembles, choirs and individual instrumentalists make music for eager listeners all over the country. The Spring festival of music at the Kibbutz of Ein Gev, on the shores of the Sea of Galilee, attracts thousands of Israelis. The marvel is that the thirty years of war and threat of war, which constituted Israel's history until the peace treaty with Egypt, should have left time and concern for other than the martial arts. But perhaps the Israeli devotion to the arts and culture is a similar reaction to that of Londoners who packed the National Gallery's concerts during World War II. Likewise, the fact that the country devours poetry – Israel's major literary achievement – may be a consequence of the stress under which it exists, for poetry has always specially lent itself to the expression of the deepened thoughts and emotions aroused in times of war.

When the Jews began their return to Palestine, they hoped to find a new cultural identity as part of the Middle East. Writers, musicians and artists experimented with the introduction of Oriental themes, and the early shomrim (guards), the armed protectors of the Jewish settlements, usually dressed like Arabs. But in the tug-of-war for supremacy, European culture won and even the mass immigration of Oriental Jews, now 60 per cent of the population, did not change the situation. Both Jews and Arabs from the Middle East possessed ancient cultural traditions, but they had stagnated for centuries, and the cultivated sector of the North African immigration brought with it not Sephardi or Arabic but French culture. The Habima Theatre came from Russia with its emphasis on heavy drama and heavy make-up. The formative influence on Israeli ballet was Martha Graham and it became an extension of American ballet. Writers like Bialik and Agnon brought with them the style and interests of East European Jewry.

In time, the emphasis changed, but not the basically Western approach. The new writers address themselves to contemporary issues. They write about Israeli themes and, to be able to do so, have transformed the language from the literary Hebrew of their East European mentors into the practical, down-to-earth language of the street. Under the influence of Yosef Milo, a capricious but talented impresario, the Cameri Theatre has shifted the repertoire of the stage from Eastern to Western Europe, and the Jewish ingredient from the shtetl to Israel.

But the main influences have remained European, and an indigenous culture based on an organic creation of the environment has not yet emerged. What is distinctive about culture in Israel is that, because of the peculiarities of the Israeli background, it comes closer to the mass of people than perhaps anywhere else in the world. As readers of books and newspapers, the Israelis probably hold the world record. They buy about ten books per person per year, about 25 million annually in all, which is said to be the highest number of books sold *per capita* in the world. Museum attendance is the highest in the world in proportion to population. As theatregoers, too, the Israelis claim a world record. In England, the proportion of theatregoers is about 5 per cent of the adult population, while the figure for Israel is about 50 per cent, making the theatre a non-elitist cultural activity. Israel's theatres are in almost perpetual motion, touring in towns and in rural areas, and they have exercised a decisive influence on the taste of the people.

One of the consequences of the Israeli theatre's popularity with the mass of the population is its conservatism. A popular audience is not attracted by the avant-garde, and the theatre of alienation makes no appeal to an unsophisticated and often uneducated audience, who will avidly follow Shakespeare, but experience no self-identification in *non sequiturs* and intellectualizing.

In terms of influence on life, literature occupies pride of place in Israeli culture. Historically, Israeli writers can be conveniently divided into the old school of Zionist intellectuals, nearly all immigrants, and the contemporary literary establishment. The early literary figures bridged the Jewish intensity of Eastern Europe and the Zionist renaissance. They included Chaim Nachman Bialik, the greatest Hebrew poet of his generation, and the novelist S. Y. Agnon, a graphic chronicler of the departed world of the East European ghetto. But probably the most influential today of those literary figures of the past is Yosef Chaim Brenner, who came to Palestine as a teacher in 1909 at the age of 28. His own life ended in tragedy (he was a victim of the Arab riots in 1921) and his constant themes were indictments, not only of the doomed Jewish life he had left in Europe, but of the Hebrew rebirth in Palestine.

Revered but rarely read, his popularity in Israel suddenly reached almost fad proportions among the country's intellectuals after the Yom Kippur War. In the prevailing sombre mood of the people, the pessimism of his writing and the fact that he was one of the first casualties of the Arab-Israel conflict, struck responsive chords. Some of Brenner's works have been republished, and Israel television has transmitted a new production of his most famous play. He seems to have a message for the times. Ironically, under the heading of 'We are all brothers', Brenner had published an emotional appeal in the Hebrew press calling for Arab-Jewish understanding only a few weeks before he was murdered.

The new and contemporary Israeli writers seldom hark back to the ghetto. The theme on which their novels, poems, essays and articles are based is the country's distinctiveness. All of them have been profoundly influenced by the Holocaust, by the necessity to define the nature of the Jewish State, its relationship with the Arabs and the problems of the underprivileged elements. Of these, the writer most appreciated by the other writers is Yoram Kaniuk, a left-wing, politically engaged novelist, who lives in a slum in the Oriental part of Tel Aviv.

More popular are two other novelists, A. B. Yehoshua and Amos Oz. Both were born in Israel in 1939 and both received higher education abroad, Oz at Oxford and Yehoshua at the Sorbonne. Both have written best sellers. The English version of Oz's *My Michael* sold 250,000 copies, while Yehoshua's novel, *The Lover*, was a best-seller in the USA and even sold 35,000 hard cover copies in Israel. Oz lives on a kibbutz and is politically active as a left-wing publicist with extremely 'doveish' views on the future of the occupied territories. But he is very much a thinker's writer, influential in kibbutz circles and among the young left-wingers of the cities, but too much of a European, too cerebral, to touch the masses of Oriental Jewry with whom Yehoshua, a Sephardi, identifies himself. Yehoshua's involvement in drawing attention to the disparity between the 'two Israels' has had practical effects on Ministry of Education programmes designed to raise the level of education for the Oriental communities.

The impact of these two writers on the Israel scene in general, not merely the literary scene, has been enhanced by their qualities as radio and TV personalities. Both are articulate, fluent and photograph well; and their public appearances, particularly Yehoshua's, are frequent. Their styles vary. Oz tends to be cool, deliberate and penetrating, while his contemporary is voluble and sometimes emotional. They, together with Amos Elon, and Shabtai Tevet, Israel's most thoughtful and distinguished journalists, and Yehuda Amichai and T. Carmi, its outstanding poets, constitute Israel's most quoted and most widely respected literary figures.

If they are not wealthy in the Harold Robbins range, they are all reasonably affluent. Not so the average Israeli writer, although he will find it easier to start in Israel than his equivalent in Europe, since publishing costs are lower and publishers are more inclined to take a risk. But the price structure of the Israeli book trade is such that, unless he is published abroad, an Israeli writer cannot expect to make any money. A best-seller in Israel, which would mean sales of 50,000 copies or more, would produce a maximum of $3,000 for the author – and this only happens to two or three books a year. Paperbacks account for the major part of these big sales and they are on a particularly low royalty scale.

Generally, the visual arts are in the mould of Western culture and the Jews from Asia and North Africa have not yet made their mark. The well-known Israeli painters were all products of the European art movements in which they were trained, and some, like Agam, though remaining Israelis, spend most of their lives in Europe or America. What is Israeli about Israeli art is that it is created by artists living in Israel. But some of the best have been affected by the physical circumstances of the country, in particular the special light. Reuben Ruben was fascinated by the ancient, gnarled olive trees so characteristic of the Israeli landscape, while the black and white drawings of the Judean hills by the veteran Anna Ticho (who died in 1980 at the age of 86) have something of the mystical flavour of Jerusalem itself. Artists who have settled in Israel, it has been noted, often use more yellow or white in their paintings and sculptors are influenced by the rock formations and the grandeur of the mountain and desert configurations.

Some artists, on the whole the less well regarded, have tried to introduce Oriental or Jewish motifs within the Western form. Pictures of this kind are frequently seen in the tourist art galleries catering to visitors who want to buy something from Israel that looks Jewish. The fact that these objects are often expensive does not affect their lack of artistic merit.

Good artists in Israel find it relatively easy to exhibit in commercial galleries, which abound in Tel Aviv, Jaffa, Jerusalem and Safed. Some of them are more pioneering and are prepared to accept young, promising unknowns, and all benefit from the distortion of the art scene caused by the ethnic interest of the free-spending tourist. Art exhibitions in non-commercial galleries and museums are much more difficult and very limited. The Israel Museum in Jerusalem – a combination of the National Gallery and the British Museum in London – has hitherto given only limited display to the work of Israeli artists, but in 1980 fund-raising began for a special wing for this purpose. Tel Aviv Museum, which is an art gallery, had a long tradition of neglect of Israeli artists in favour of imports, an emphasis which has departed along with Dr Haim Gamzu, the Museum's first Director.

The vibrant and prolific art scene encompasses all its forms. The Israel Philharmonic Orchestra is considered the most important and most representative arts institution and, in its tours abroad, acts as one of Israel's more effective ambassadors. Israeli theatre was long dominated by Habima (The Stage) formed in Moscow in 1918, which came *en bloc* to Palestine in 1931 and has become the national theatre. As is frequently the case with venerable artistic institutions, Habima has become too conservative and limited and ultimately its productions suffered considerably in quality.

Its place as a contemporary theatre has been taken by the Cameri, which has been willing to stage experimental and even controversial plays. One of them, a play called *Queen of the Bath Tub* by Hanoch Levin, who is Israel's most defiant and irreverent satirist, created such a violent public reaction that it was unceremoniously withdrawn. Levin, now in his 30s, bitter and misanthropic, is Israel's only original theatrical talent. A gifted playwright, he is spiritually shallow but dramatically powerful and his simplistic but allegorical and often obscene plays seem inevitably to create controversy, which Israel's theatre damagingly lacked.

The iconoclasm of Levin in the theatre is paralleled by the irreverence of the pop arts and, in particular, pop music. Probably its most admired exponent in Israel today is Danny Sanderson, who heads a group called 'Gazoz' (fizzy drinks). He led a reaction to the conventional folk-singing of Israel by introducing light-hearted social criticism into his contemporary pop sound and his shows are a synthesis of the current international idiom with a special irony which is the Jewish-Israeli contribution.

In Israel the dance is arguably the art form which manifests the greatest interaction between the imported and the indigenous. The story of its development illustrates many of the singularities of Israel's cultural growth.

Terpsichorean Rothschild

The name Rothschild is a revered one in Israel. Baron Edmond de Rothschild, who lived in Paris between 1849 and 1935, is generally recognized as the father of Jewish Palestine. He gave vast sums and incalculable encouragement to the ideal of the return of the people to its ancestral soil. Known as Hanadiv (the Benefactor), he bequeathed his devotion to the cause of the Jewish renaissance to his son, James. These two were followed by other scions of Jewry's 'royal family'. One of them, Baroness Bathsheba de Rothschild of the French branch, was the first to make her home in the State and, following family tradition and her own interests, became a benefactor of the arts.

Two different incidents are frequently quoted to explain her creation of the Batsheva Dance Company. One was a comment said to have been made to her by Anton Dolin during a visit to Israel in 1962: 'Those kibbutzniks', he told her, 'don't quite have ballet dancers' legs.' She herself once explained that she had started the company because 'there were two or three modern dancers around here with nothing to do'. Whatever the catalyst, the Baroness embraced the idea with enthusiasm and became the adviser to the new group which was founded in 1964. Bathsheba paid all the bills, but was said to be cheese-paring, resenting the cost of a taxi for a ballerina when a bus was available.

The Batsheva Dance Company was fortunate in its two principal dancers – Rina Shenfield, to this day Israel's queen of the dance and one of the world's outstanding modern dancers, and Ehud Ben-David, who remained with the company until his death in a car crash some ten years later. The company was greatly helped by the goodwill of Martha Graham, a friend of the Baroness, who permitted it the use of her repertoire – the only company other than her own to be given this privilege. (Her permission was withdrawn in 1977.) Within a few years, Batsheva was winning plaudits on European stages. Awards followed and critics predicted an important future for this vigorous new dance company which combined modern dance techniques with new creative talent.

But the promise was never fulfilled. With the early success of Batsheva, other companies were formed. The Baroness herself founded the Bat Dor

group in 1968, with a greater emphasis on classical ballet, and that was
followed by the Kibbutz Company (folk dance), the Israel Ballet (classical)
and Inbal (folksy). There were too many of them and too thin a spread of
the available talent produced mediocrity, a common occurrence in Israel.
The decline was aggravated when an attempt at militant trade-union
action by Batsheva's dancers in 1974 caused the company's founder to end
her association with it. She then concentrated on Bat Dor.

The Batsheva company, now the recipient of Government aid and with a
supply of new young dancers from its own school, has begun the pirouette
back to its original aspirations and standards. Aided by the Baroness'
generosity, it has never had to worry about attracting audiences. Nor, in its
emphasis on imported works, has it become sufficiently Israeli by using
native choreographers and themes unique to Israel. The assumption that
imported was synonymous with good was a reaction against the 'Levantini-
zation' of the arts – the introduction of superficial and shoddy gimmickry, a
lack of subtlety and precision which, in Israel, often destroys the fragile
illusion on which ballet, theatre and opera are so dependent.

In 1971, the Baronesss provided the Bat Dor company with its own small
but opulent theatre and dance school in Tel Aviv's fashionable Ibn Gvirol
Street. Bathsheba de Rothschild personally directs the affairs of the
company, theatre and school, which has become Israel's main dance
academy. Its daily classes are held at six different levels, and the teaching
staff includes both residents and guests, among the latter being some of the
best known figures in the world of dance. The company has a permanent
complement of between 20 and 25 dancers and, under the benevolent
dictatorship of its principal dancer, the Baroness' close friend Jeanette
Ordman, is setting high standards of precision and technique.

With this experience – and similar histories exist in almost all the other
artistic forms in Israel – a new realism is making itself felt. A greater degree
of confidence has led to a diminution of the fear of becoming Levantine or of
losing Western or European roots. Many in Israel accept the idea that it is
preferable for Israeli art to be a creation of the Israeli experience rather
than an import. It is being reluctantly accepted that an original production,
even if provincial, will do more for the development of the arts and culture
than a reliance on the products of other cultures.

Managing the arts

Israel's preoccupation with the basic necessities of survival left few public
resources available for the encouragement of the arts. That some Government funds are applied for this purpose is largely due to the former cultural
overlady of Israel, Lea Porat, the first Director of the Cultural Department
of the Ministry of Education. She wore an additional and similar hat as
Chairman of the Israel Council for Culture and the Arts. Her power in this
area of national life and the authoritarian manner in which, some critics
complain, she exercised it led to her being dubbed the 'cultural commissar'.

Lea Porat began working for the Palestine Broadcasting Service as a part-timer in the news department while still at university. She had just arrived in Jerusalem in 1935, a young girl from Czernowitz in Romania, and attended high school and the Hebrew University. After graduating, she began working full-time in broadcasting, then still controlled by the Mandatory authorities. She became a Hebrew announcer, a job in which she was highly successful, thanks to her excellent Hebrew, her diction and delivery (at one time she was considering becoming an actress). When Kol Israel (the Voice of Israel) began operating as the broadcasting authority of the new State, she headed the radio station in Tel Aviv and in 1961 was promoted to the influential post of Director of Programming for the Israel Broadcasting Authority. After a brief diversion as Israel's Counsellor for Cultural Affairs in Boston, she returned in 1968 as head of the Ministry of Education's cultural department when Yigal Allon became the Minister. Although never active politically, she had been a member of the left-wing Achdut Avoda Party of which Allon was the leader. That Party is probably the most closely knit nepotic group in Israeli politics. They help and are loyal to each other in an outstanding way and Lea Porat remained very loyal to Allon.

In her new post, she was in a key position to encourage the arts and influence them through the allocation of Government funds. Her Chairmanship of the Arts Council came later and, in any event, its resources were trifling compared with the more than $10 million which the Education Ministry in 1979 distributed to artists and cultural institutions. (The Ministry of Education and Culture spends more than any other Government department, with the exception of Defence.) The Advisory Boards for literature, theatre, music and other fields set up by the Ministry were frequently consulted by her, but Lea Porat exercised the power.

The world of the arts appears singularly susceptible to controversy and she became a permanent target of critics who assailed either her choice of beneficiaries or her alleged high-handedness. But few challenged her great contribution to cultural pursuits, for she has shaped the institutional landscape for the arts. One project, likely to have the most far-reaching effect, was her 'Arts for the People' programme, which brought theatre and music to remote areas and development towns. For many of the Oriental immigrants, this was their first encounter with these arts. She made culture a major concern of Government and instituted an organized pattern of distribution and budgetary control.

Married to a successful Tel Aviv optician, Itzhak Gur, and the mother of two children, Lea Porat lives in the affluent township of Savyon. She is an opinionated and articulate lady, but can be diplomatic or manipulative general, has absorbed culture rather than studied it. In 1980 she was succeeded by Moshe Shalev, then in his forties and the former Chief Education Officer of the IDF. But, until her successor makes his mark, Lea Porat will undoubtedly continue to be a major figure in cultural politics, not alone through her own talents, but also because there are today no other outstanding figures in the Israeli arts world.

Perhaps the largest single Government subsidy goes to the theatre, namely the Habima National Theatre. In the past, substantial sums were also granted to the Israel Opera, thanks to pressure by influential supporters. This was against the advice of Lea Porat, who thought (rightly) that it was inferior and badly managed. The opera eventually ran into insurmountable problems and, to her satisfaction, the grant ceased.

In Britain and the USA, the directors of the major art galleries, as well as art writers and critics, exercise considerable influence and frequently become public figures. Since the departure of the controversial, dogmatic and influential Haim Gamzu, who was both the Director of the Tel Aviv Museum and a prolific writer on the arts, no single figure of his eminence has emerged in Israel's art world. The gallery directors do not, as a rule, assert themselves. Yona Fischer is the Senior Curator of Contemporary Art at the Israeli Museum but the power in the museum (as in everything else connected with Jerusalem) resides in the Mayor, Teddy Kollek. When the Museum opened in 1965, Kollek refused to hang a painting by Joseph Zaritsky, leader of the older generation of Israel's abstract painters, because he did not like its modernity, but his taste later became more eclectic. He is also important in the running of the Jerusalem Music Centre, where the artistic influence is that of Isaac Stern, the American virtuoso violinist.

The Ministry of Education and Culture and the Arts Council are not the sole patrons of the arts in Israel. The Jewish Agency has helped to fund arts for the people and supports immigrant artists. The Histadrut and the main municipalities subsidize kibbutz and local artistic endeavours. Institutions like the Jerusalem Foundation also make their contribution. From the US, the American Cultural Foundation has given aid to almost every expression of the arts and has encouraged and supported young artists of talent.

In no artistic field has the Israeli genius shown itself to better advantage than in music. It has produced young virtuosos like Daniel Barenboim, Itzhak Perlman, Pinchas Zuckerman and a promising younger group, outstanding among whom is Shlomo Mintz. Many of them are now international rather than Israeli personalities.

The preeminence of music in Israel is symbolized by the status accorded to the Israel Philharmonic Orchestra. A cooperative, managed by a committee of members of the orchestra, the IPO is co-owner with the city of Tel Aviv of the Mann Auditorium in Tel Aviv. Its prestige has given the orchestra a certain self-importance and arrogance, which came to the fore when the Israel Chamber Orchestra acquired the distinguished Russian conductor, Barshai, as its musical director. The IPO felt that the Chamber Orchestra was becoming too symphonic and competitive, and used its weight to deny the smaller group the use of the auditorium – except on one occasion, when Isaac Stern, whom they did not wish to offend, was the soloist. The Knesset Education and Culture Committee gave notice that it would press for a reduction of the Government subsidy to the IPO if it continued its obstruction of the Chamber Orchestra. The threat worked and the popular Israel Chamber Orchestra has been given a qualified promise of the use of the main concert hall 'from time to time'.

Politics are never far from any major Israeli preoccupation and the arts are no exception. The main reservoir of funds, the Ministry of Education and Culture, is now under religious leadership in the person of Zvulun Hammer. Possibly because of the powerful presence of Mrs Porat, he pledged no political interference with the arts and, apart from introducing a religious panel on the Arts Council, he has so far not involved himself or his political and religious attitudes in the affairs of the Cultural Department. But the changes to follow the departure of the Director could tell.

Chapter ten

Applied Socialism

Collective settlement

'Kibbutz' (meaning gathering, plural kibbutzim) has entered the international vocabulary and, in word association games would probably be linked with 'Zionism'. The kibbutz is indeed synonymous with the highest socialist-Zionist ideal. Throughout history, groups of individuals have tried to create utopian societies, communities in which social justice and equality would prevail, in which efforts and reward would be fairly shared, where the best aspirations of human dignity and comradeship would be applied in daily living. The kibbutzim are the Israeli version of this utopia and they are unique in having retained their essential principles for seventy years despite a general diminution in idealism and the compromises which had to be made in response to practical necessities.

In her autobiography, Golda Meir* wrote: 'The kibbutz is the one place in the world where people are judged, accepted and given a chance to participate fully in the community to which they belong, not in accordance with the kind of work they do or how well they do it, but for their intrinsic value as human beings.'

The kibbutz is a collective unit of which each member owns an undivided share of the whole; in this respect it differs from a cooperative, in which individuals own a divisible share. The first kibbutz, Degania, was founded in 1909 and today there are some 250 of them with a membership of over 70,000 and, with dependants, comprising a total population of approximately twice that size.

Degania was the organic succesor of the kvutzva (commune), some of which had been created by idealistic pioneers at the turn of the century. To these visionaries, a commune, generally consisting of 12 to 15 members, was not simply a method of working a farm; it was also an end in itself, the end being the establishment of a humane and progressive society. The Jews were returning to Palestine not only to solve the Jewish problem but to pioneer a truly socialist way of life. But the small kvutza was not really adequate for the scale of operations necessary to set up viable farming units, and it expanded into the kibbutz. The kibbutz, in turn, expanded further so as to be able to incorporate industry with agriculture.

---

* She and her husband, Morris Myerson, arrived in Israel in 1921 and, committed Zionist-socialists that they were, settled on a kibbutz. But Morris Myerson was not happy with kibbutz life and moved to Tel Aviv and, later, Jerusalem, preferring to work in an office. Golda herself worked in a local trade union office and entered politics through that route and not via the kibbutz.

The founders of Degania applied basic socialist principles in its constitution. All the members were equal, and men and women shared all the
duties and work. Because all were equal and all work was equal, no classes
existed; the status of the man or woman who performed the menial tasks
was no lower than that of the administrator or teacher. Equality was
applied to the material standards of life, because no member received any
pay and all shared equally what was produced. The kibbutz furnished them
with their material needs, housing, furniture, clothing and the food which
they ate together in the communal dining hall.

Kibbutz management was by direct participatory democracy, all decisions being taken at weekly meetings attended by every kibbutz member.
These decisions were not limited to those of communal importance but
extended to the personal requests of its members. Would the kibbutz agree
to send a particular child to the university? Should a member be seconded
for an overseas mission? They were all subjects for general decision because
kibbutz members, apart from a small amount of pocket money, had no
capital of their own. If a member needed money for a necessary purpose, it
would have to be provided by the kibbutz as a whole. The general meeting
was also required to approve the admission of new members, generally after
one year's probation – though a member could leave at any time and
without the approval of the general meeting.

The original kibbutzim were not religiously observant. As Marxists, the
kibbutzniks (as members are called) rejected religion. There were no
religious ceremonials, and a marriage was determined not by an inscription
on a piece of paper, but by the decision of a couple to share their lives.
Children were encouraged and nurtured – but since the parents were not
regarded as necessarily competent for this expert job and, in any case, could
not be spared from their full-time work, the children of the kibbutz were
accommodated in a separate house and cared for by trained personnel. Not
that parental love was rejected, for the children spent their evenings and
other non-work periods with their parents.

Education was something of a fetish in all kibbutzim and every effort was
made to give the children the best possible intellectual foundation. Since
the kibbutz movement was very conscious of cultural and political needs,
children were reared in an environment in which there were books, talk
about books, talk about politics and government. Their teachers were
carefully selected and trained in the kibbutz movement's own training
college. As a result, the children received an above-average education
which produced an above-average standard of conduct. On the seventieth
anniversary of the foundation of Degania, one of its oldest inhabitants
claimed, 'By and large, our children grow up honest. I don't know whether
it is the environment, the schooling or something innate. But they're
honest.' This is a view in which most citizens of Israel would concur.

The tranquil and comfortable kibbutz of today, with its gardens,
swimming pool and general atmosphere of relaxed well-being (the bomb
shelters are well-placed and camouflaged), is a far cry from the conditions
under which the pioneers of the movement laboured. Many of them died of
malaria or other diseases as they worked in the unsalubrious, infested

swamplands. At the same time, they were called upon to defend themselves against Arab marauders and suffered regular casualties. Some who could not meet the physical and psychological demands had to leave. Those who stuck it out and stayed were the fittest, physically and spiritually.

Retaining and attracting the best elements, the pioneers created an elite. Gerald Kaufman* compares the influence of the kibbutz in Israel to that of Eton, the great British public school, in the Conservative Party. Just as Eton has been the training ground for a high proportion of Conservative Cabinet Ministers, so the kibbutz has contributed, with similar disproportion, to Israel's ruling elite – at least during the formative years of Labour Governments.

One-third of the members of Israel's first constitutional assembly of 1948 came from the kibbutzim, although at the time, kibbutz members made up less than 5 per cent of the population. According to Amos Elon,** at the peak of the kibbutz strength the proportion of members or former members of kibbutzim in positions of national leadership was seven times as great as their proportion of the population. Today, although their influence has declined, the figure is still something like four times as great. Between 1949 and 1967, one-third of all Israel's Cabinet Ministers were products of the kibbutz.

Their disproportionate power was equalled only by their disproportionate contribution to the country. In the Six Day War, 200 of the 778 fatalities and 25 per cent of all the casualties were kibbutzniks who, at that period, constituted only 4 per cent of the population. Nearly a quarter – 22 per cent – of all officers came from the kibbutzim. The kibbutz, to this day, provides some of the best personnel for the most dangerous assignments, ready and willing to be mobilized for everything useful to Zionism and socialism: open and clandestine missions abroad, as well as defence at home.

After the War of Independence, mass immigration brought with it new realities. Most of the new immigrants were more concerned with making a living and advancing in a capitalist society than creating an idealistic communal existence. The kibbutz was no longer the spearhead of the new society but an enclave, still admired and respected, but no longer epitomizing the aspirations of the nation as a whole. During the 1960s, almost half of the kibbutz-born youngsters did not return to kibbutz life after their army service.

That decline reflected the adaptation of the kibbutzim to capitalist society, and the dilution of their pure socialist ideology. In the early days, the principle of 'no hired labour' was an article of faith in the kibbutz movement. Egalitarianism demanded that there be neither employers nor employed – all were owners and workers. But as they expanded from agriculture into industry, their labour requirements outpaced the supply of kibbutz members. At the same time, there was a social obligation to offer work to the new immigrants. The combination of both factors was too great

* *To Build the Promised Land* (London 1973).

** *The Israelis: Founders and Sons* (London/New York 1971).

to be resisted, and the kibbutzim, with much misgiving, began hiring labour.

The employment of hired labour remains a troublesome problem. Some of the kibbutzim, in an effort to reduce their dependence, limit the number of employees, while others believe that automation will eventually remove the need for extra labour. The more realistic argue that the solution is to create a partnership with urban workers, but they have not yet come to grips with the contradiction such a relationship would create between the dual status of the kibbutz members as socialist workers and as 'bosses'.

Material growth and success brought the good life to the kibbutzim as well as to society generally. Their prestige also diminished as a succession of wars replaced the kibbutzniks with soldiers and generals as the hero figures of Israeli society. Yet, despite all their problems, the kibbutzim remain a more value-orientated society than the nation as a whole. They cling to idealistic concepts in education and in standards of conduct. Each member still contributes as much as he can, so that the needs of all can be more fully met. The work ethic still counts.

The kibbutzim are again growing, and some even have waiting lists. New ones are being created (an innovation in recent years has been a kibbutz in the Negev founded by Reform Jews) and, while their major activity remains farming, industry is increasing. As a reflection of the high quality and the motivation of the work force, kibbutz productivity is about 25 per cent higher than the average in Israeli industry as a whole.

Because kibbutz members today live longer and are healthier than their predecessors, the percentage over the age of 65 is rising. In the older kibbutzim, it accounts for about one-third of the total work force. The older members remain the repositories of the traditional kibbutz values and, though the more active roles have been taken over by their successors, they still exercise their influence in political orientations.

Kibbutz living

There are as many singularities in the range of kibbutzim as there are differences between cities, but a particular pattern of daily life is common to them all. In appearance, too, they present a common style – a cluster of white single-storey houses set among trees, shrubs and flowers. Verdant paths intersect the housing area and converge on the communal buildings, usually also one storey. Most dining halls used to be austere sheds furnished with long tables and benches, but some of the wealthier kibbutzim now have well-equipped restaurants. The Bet Tarbut (cultural building) which, in the smaller and poorer kibbutzim generally doubles up with the dining hall, is the most impressive of the public buildings. Schoolrooms, children's houses and playgrounds, sports grounds for the adults, a swimming pool – all or some – complete the kibbutz residential complex. Contiguous or close by are the farms, cattle sheds and factories where the kibbutz members work.

All work – men and women, young and old, even the children – for the work ethic is fundamental. The working day for adults is eight hours, six days a week. But the arrangement is a flexible one, particularly in agricultural work where the seasons and weather determine the working hours. When men reach the age of 55 and women the age of 50, their working day may, at their option, be reduced but they can carry on working for as long as they wish. Children begin to work from the age of ten as an essential ingredient of the carefully planned educational system; they start with one hour daily increasing to four hours for the top classes.

Women in the kibbutzim are full and equal partners, although they have not so far made any appreciable dent in male domination. They are theoretically free to do so, but very few kibbutz women have aspired to leadership positions either in kibbutz administration or politics, locally or nationally. The male kibbutz leaders reply that this phenomenon is not unique to the kibbutzim but applies to national life as a whole and to other countries as well. While they have a wide range of options as to the work they can do, most women in kibbutzim appear to prefer (or, possibly, have been conditioned to prefer) working in the kitchen, the dining hall, the children's home or the school.

Apart from the children, whose work may range through all kibbutz activities, the other workers are expected to specialize. Every kibbutz discusses and agrees an economic plan for the year ahead, and the workers in each branch of activity arrange the schedule which will be necessary to achieve the desired target. Each year, too, the kibbutz draws up a budget allocating its financial resources between investment in agriculture and in industry, and improvement in living standards.

Responsible for all the planning, and reporting regularly to the weekly members' meeting, are two administrative organs, a council consisting of 15 to 21 members and an executive of five to seven. They are elected annually, as are the full-time administrators like the secretary, the treasurer and the works director. Most kibbutzim also appoint numerous committees to supervise education, cultural activities, sports and a wide range of other kibbutz pursuits. It has been estimated that about a third of the kibbutz membership gives spare-time service on these committees.

There is much else to do in spare time. After working hours, parents of young children spend time with them, usually in their own apartments which have cooking facilities for light meals – main meals are taken in the dining hall. The library, reading room and club room in the cultural building are available for evening and rest-day entertainment while physical recreation facilities are there for the active. Many kibbutzim present a weekly film show, some have live or recorded concerts and any kibbutz member interested in self-improvement can take a variety of adult education courses or attend lectures. Everyone has enough to do and at a far less frenetic pace than the residents in the city jungles.

The children of the kibbutz live in children's homes until they are about 15 or 16, when they are given their own homes. Despite the headshaking and forebodings of the older and more dogmatic critics, there is no evidence to suggest that bringing up children apart from their parents has had any damaging effect on the parent-child relationship. In fact, the kibbutz system seems to benefit both sides because children can share the parents' relaxed leisure instead of making importunate demands on their attention when they are otherwise occupied.

All the large kibbutzim have their own schools with twelve classes or grades, up to the age of 15, while smaller kibbutzim combine to form regional schools. Standards of education are high, even when the additional kibbutz workload is added to the Ministry of Education syllabus. Teachers are kibbutz members themselves and, since strikes are inconceivable and, unlike many of their city counterparts, they do not need to take part-time jobs, they can concentrate on their duties. At the age of 18 the children of the kibbutz (like all Israeli youth) enter their compulsory military service and, on their return, those who would benefit from higher education are sent at the expense of the kibbutz to universities or technical establishments.

Every basic need of kibbutz members is supplied from general kibbutz resources. These basics are housing, dining hall meals, children's care and education, medical and health service, clothing repairs and laundry. Other needs like clothes, furniture, holidays and small consumer items are either met out of a personal allowance given to each member or are collected, as required, from stocks held by the kibbutzim. The more sophisticated kibbutzim have hairdressing and beauty-care establishments, although attention to grooming was not a traditional concern of kibbutz ladies, who generally disdained the fripperies. Every kibbutz member and his family is insured for life and provided permanently with all the material necessities – and that extends to the maintenance of aged parents whether inside or out of the kibbutz.

Kibbutzniks, as a group, tend to preserve their distinctiveness. Most of them marry within the group, though rarely in the same kibbutz. Apparently the intimacy of their upbringing in the same children's house seems to militate against the emergence of romantic relationships. As a group they tend to maintain characteristically kibbutz social and cultural attitudes which set them apart from the general, materialistic society. Also, because all their commercial dealings are with the institutions of the kibbutz movement, they have become economically divorced from the environment. The kibbutzniks are indeed a peculiar people within a peculiar people.

Politics of the kibbutz

The founders of the kibbutzim and of the national kibbutz movements all came from the political hothouse of Eastern Europe. They were workers creating their ideal society in their own kibbutzim but, at the same time, determined to make their political mark on society generally. They were all socialists, Marxists of varying emphases; and being Jewish added extra force to the intense disputatiousness general among East European socialists at that time. From the beginning, ideological controversy was a feature of socialist Zionism. Differences of approach created different streams in the kibbutz movement mainly between the doctrinaire Marxists and the social democrats. At times, conflicts between them ran

extremely deep, creating powerful personal and organizational antagonisms.

In 1979, a merger took place between two of the three main national
kibbutz movements: Kibbutz Hameuchad (United kibbutz), which has
links with the Achdut Avoda group in the Israel Labour Party, and the
Ichud Hakvutzot v'Hakibbutzim (Union of Kvutzot and Kibbutzim),
which is close to the Mapai group, by far the largest section of the party.
Mapai and Achdut Avoda have been united in the Israel Labour Party
since 1968, but their kibbutz movements remained separate for eleven more
years – it took a little longer for old animosities to die down in the kibbutzim
than in the political machines.

Kibbutz Hameuchad was born in 1927, when a number of kibbutzim
broke away from the existing central organization, which had become too
doctrinaire for them. Hameuchad consisted of the more social-demo-
cratically minded who wanted a more pluralistic and flexible organization
than their Marxist colleagues would allow. Twenty-four years later, in
1951, Hameuchad itself split over the issue of acceptance of the Soviet
Union as the leader of the international class struggle; the breakaway group
of the more middle-of-the-road socialists eventually became the Ichud.

The intensity of the passions which accompanied the great 1951 split
(*pilug* in Hebrew) still accounts for residual suspicion and bitterness
between the two movements, even though they are now merged. During the
pilug, kibbutzim literally divided in two. The minority in a number of
kibbutzim actually moved out and established their own new kibbutz near
the old one. Within many kibbutzim, partisan feelings ran so high that even
the members of the same family did not speak to each other and took their
meals at opposite ends of the communal dining hall.

The breakaway Ichud was at pains to avoid total identification with any
political party so as to prevent any repetition of the bitterness of the pilug.
Most of its leaders were, in fact, members of Mapai but the new
organization permitted its members political independence, and some of
them supported Ben-Gurion when he broke away from Mapai and formed
Rafi. Hameuchad continued as before, tightly controlled, more to the left
politically and totally identified with Achdut Avoda.

The 1979 merger between these two groups to form a powerful new
organization, the Tenua Hakibbutzim Hame'uhedet (United Kibbutz
Movement) succeeded because a new generation, not personally involved
in the 1951 split, had arrived in leadership positions. Both movements were
led in 1979 by young and forward-looking leaders: Ichud was headed by
Moshe (Musa) Harif, and Hameuchad by Ya'acov Tsur. Both agreed that
separate movements were, as they put it, 'quite irrelevant to contemporary
reality'. A catalyst was undoubtedly the election of a right-wing Government in 1977, which encouraged socialist unity in the face of the common
threat.

In the kibbutz tradition, the merger was preceded by months of intensive
debate at meetings of the general membership. Many of the veterans, still
suspicious, opposed the move but, in the end, youth and logic prevailed. In
the course of the long debate, the basic issue, endlessly discussed, was the

differing concepts of the nature of kibbutz political programmes. That debate has not been resolved, but what is certain is that the kibbutz of the future will be politically more flexible and less ideological, reflecting the changes of the past thirty years, which have brought them prosperity and security. Harif, who took the leading role in the merged organization, has commented: 'The kibbutz isn't a party, but a way of life. It's broader than a party. Politics for the kibbutz members means the sum of their activities to affect the world around them.'

The remaining independent kibbutz movement is Kibbutz Artzi (National Kibbutz), connected with Mapam, the Marxist party which joins the Israel Labour Party in a united electoral list but otherwise retains its separate party existence. Artzi Kibbutzim number 77, with a population of 41,000. This compares with the new united movement's total of 154 kibbutzim and 72,000 population. But Artzi remains a strong, tightly knit and efficiently structured organization, resolutely independent. During the merger negotiations, repeated appeals were made to it to join, but to no avail. Artzi still relishes its present political affiliation with the more leftish ideological approach of Mapam.

These two major national kibbutz movements include all Israel's kibbutzim except the dozen or so religious kibbutzim with their own federation, Kibbutz Dati, to represent their interests, and a further handful of kibbutzim which maintain a sturdy, unaffiliated, independence.

The kibbutz movement had to take a new look at itself in the light of the Labour Party's defeat in 1977. It had been strongly critical of the circumstances which led to the elections and of the unending series of internal dissensions within the Labour Party, and the newly united and strengthened organization came about in part because of what had happened. It intended to use its weight to institute a revival within the party, in terms both of policies and of personnel; to restore it as the party of government. In any case, ideology apart, the kibbutz movement had no love of a government which was denying it the favoured treatment it had always received from Labour and which it regarded as a right.

Amos Oz, a distinguished novelist and a serious thinker within the kibbutz movement, is one of the few to have formulated principles which the kibbutz movement should be applying in its changed role as a political opposition. He sees this period as an opportunity to restore the platform of democratic socialism to its original pride of place in kibbutz ideology. He has denounced the compromise of the secular principle implicit in the approval which has been given by some kibbutzim to the religio-national-istic policies of the Likud and the clericalists. He concluded an article in the literary forum of the kibbutz movement: 'We, the kibbutz movement, are under siege within a siege; a minority within a minority. What does a minority within a minority do? It is clear that the small minority of the kibbutz movement is the heart of the orchestra and is, intellectually, the sole group of musicians within the orchestra still capable of producing a clear and possibly attractive melody.'

For some others, however, the question is whether the kibbutz can any longer claim to be a working-class enterprise. It may be coming to the end of its historic and elitist phase and could well be transformed into a farmers' party or special interest group. Like the rest of Israel, the kibbutz is in a state of transition as the nation works out its social, political and economic priorities.

The moshav

Since the return to Zion was also a return to the land, the Zionist movement has always given the greatest support to those engaged in agriculture. The kibbutz was their pride but many of those who wanted to make their living on the land, including socialists, were unable to adjust to kibbutz conditions. One of their main difficulties seemed to be the lack of privacy. Others found the kibbutz uncongenial because they wanted scope for individual enterprise and earnings.

The moshav ovdim (workers' cooperative) was the answer. While the character of the kibbutz evolved gradually, the moshav idea was formulated first in theory and then applied concretely to the first village established on those lines in 1921. Those principles, still the basis for all moshavim, were propounded in a pamphlet published in 1919 by the founder of the movement, Eliezer Yoffe, and they were simple. The farmers would settle on nationally owned land, buy their own equipment and sell their produce cooperatively; they would do their own work, live with their own families and keep what they earned.

For the first decade of their existence, because the Zionist institutions gave a much higher priority to the kibbutzim, the progress of the moshavim was slow, and when the State came into existence, only 59 moshavim had been established. But the movement came into its own during the first years of statehood in response to mass immigration. The immigrants came in families, generally large ones which included elderly parents as well as children, and they wanted to live together as families. The moshav, with its family orientation, was ideal for them and, with veterans of the existing moshavim to lead and guide them, for they knew little of farming, hundreds of new moshav villages were created. Today they number almost 350, with a total population of more than 125,000.

Soon after their first ten years, the moshavim came together to found their own national organization, Tenuat Hamoshavim (Moshav Movement), which was closely associated with the Labour Party. It set up its own bank, pension fund and insurance company, as well as regional purchasing and sales organizations. Later it developed educational, social and cultural activities. The Tenuat Hamoshavim was followed by other national organizations linking like-minded moshavim with other political or religious organizations, while a number remained unaffiliated.

Each moshav elects its governing bodies at an annual meeting and, because their affairs have become increasingly complex, their management and accounts have been regulated by government legislation. The functions of the moshav have been extended to take in education and medical care, while instruments have been created for the protection of their members' interests in questions of taxation and social security. Moshavim have become the major agricultural producers in the country, most of them mechanized and sophisticated.

But, as with the kibbutz, growth has brought with it an assault on some of the fundamental principles of the moshav. Labour shortage brought about the introduction of hired labour, generally Arab. This is today the most serious of the issues debated in the moshav movement. The Secretary of Tenuat Hamoshavim summarizes the dilemma: 'I see the increase of hired labour in all its forms, including organized and unorganized Arab labour, as portending inestimable dangers to the state and the moshav. But, to my regret, I do not believe, as so many other people do, that the solution will come through decisions prohibiting such labour. There is no power in the world that can stand before the need to supply the lack of hands in the moshav economy. Therefore, in my humble opinion, the only way is to introduce new and appropriate mechanization systems into organizing work in the farm branches.' But that remains an aspiration.

An interesting variation of the moshav idea which incorporated features of the kibbutz is the moshav shitufi, the co-partnership moshav. About 40 of them exist now, the villages, land and equipment being owned and operated collectively as in a kibbutz. The whole of the moshav economy, whether based on farming or, as in most instances, industry or services, is owned jointly by all the members, among whom the profits are distributed. Like a kibbutz too, the general meeting determines the monetary allocations and elects the management.

In respect of housing, education and health services, the moshav shitufi also operates like a kibbutz, the difference lying in the attitude to private property, which the moshav permits. Each family runs its own house, maintains the home out of its own income and, if it can, accumulates capital, too. Politically, only about one-quarter of these moshavim belong to the Labour-affiliated moshav national movement. The rest are connected with other parties or movements, but a degree of coordination has been introduced through an inter-movement committee.

Religion and the kibbutz

The utopianism of the kibbutz drew inspiration not only from nineteenth- and twentieth-century socialism, but also from the age-old messianism which occupied a central place in Jewish belief. The early kibbutz thinkers translated their messianism into secular terms, and made it a point of principle to reject religious belief and observances. Nevertheless, their history was Jewish history while the calendar of the Jewish State included the Jewish Sabbath and festivals.

Saturday, the Sabbath, is the Jewish rest-day in Israel, which has a working week of six days. From the earliest days of the kibbutz, a running discussion has been concerned with the creation of a non-religious content for the Sabbath. It was not enough for it to be merely a respite from work. Kibbutzniks made efforts to introduce new emphases, expressions and forms. Today, in most of the non-religious kibbutzim, the Sabbath is the day for cultural activity, concerts, exhibitions, displays and group activities. The religious festivals have been given national or agricultural forms of expression. Passover has been transformed from a religious festival into an occasion for the historical and secular re-enactment of the flight of the Children of Israel against oppression, and of their struggle for freedom. Pentecost and Tabernacles are commemorated as agricultural festivals, when kibbutzim present pageants and displays of their own produce.

The new national search for historical and cultural roots stimulated by the Six Day War also affected the kibbutzim. Articles in kibbutz publications and debates at meetings expressed the need of non-observant Israelis to fill a spiritual void and restore some religious traditions and practices, though, as secularists, they cannot base them on faith. That void was felt all the more in the socialist kibbutzim as the appeal of socialism waned or disappeared. In some kibbutzim, synagogues have been built since the Six Day War, ostensibly for parents of members. They remain a minority and no clear direction has emerged in this search, but groping towards a more positive attitude towards the Jewish tradition, if not religion, is a feature of many kibbutzim today.

A best-selling book after the Six Day War recorded interviews with young soldiers. One of them, a secularist kibbutz member, was quoted as saying: 'No, I am not religious, but the Western Wall spoke to me . . . I felt for the first time, not the Israeli side but the Jewish side of my people.'

Much more spiritually secure are the thirteen kibbutzim that belong to the Kibbutz Dati (Religious Kibbutz) movement, as well as the two belonging to the more rigid Poalei Agudat Israel. Kibbutz Dati, with a total membership of about 4,000, is affiliated to the National Religious Party. It has exercised an influence in the party out of all proportion to its numbers both because of the personal example of its members, who live by their principle of Torah ve Avoda (Torah and Labour), and because of their comparative liberalism in a climate of extremism in Jewish orthodoxy.

Official orthodoxy in Israel, for a variety of reasons which are discussed elsewhere, expresses the most conservative attitudes. The National Religious Party finds it expedient to work closely with the rabbinate and to do so maintains an uncompromising posture in managing the orthodox establishment. Only the Kibbutz Dati in the religious sector has the temerity regularly to criticize the rabbis, propounding religious ideas which official orthodoxy has denounced as dangerously 'free thinking' and 'disloyal to the law of Moses'. Many of the religious kibbutz leaders oppose the policy of their parliamentary party in promoting legislation to enforce religious observance, and the movement as a whole supports compulsory military service for Yeshiva (religious school) students as well as for girls, contrary to the firmly held policies of their elders. In fact, Kibbutz Dati members accept their national military service in all respects and have won general approbation for their bravery and leadership in action. Moreover, Kibbutz Dati, against the wishes of orthodox leadership, maintains a dialogue with the non-orthodox, though it still opposes any form of recognition for any non-orthodox denomination of Judaism.

Their more flexible approach has come about because, unlike the cloistered rabbis, the kibbutzim are faced with the practical problems of maintaining agricultural and industrial communities while observing the orthodox codes. To avoid some of the most restrictive prohibitions, some kibbutzim have applied and extended a general rabbinic doctrine that even the most stringent of religious laws can be displaced by the over-riding necessity to save life. Application of this principle permits religious Jews to perform vital services on the Sabbath. Re-interpretation of other ancient laws tries to ensure that the spirit of the religious law is maintained, while avoiding the intolerable rigours of its strict application. But the kibbutzim are still struggling with problems in the face of the intractability of the leading rabbis and the pusillanimity of the party political leadership.

Every religious kibbutz has its own synagogue, observes the dietary laws and the traditional celebrations of the Sabbath and festivals; otherwise they are run on the same lines as their much more numerous non-religious counterparts. Some are showplaces much favoured by religious tourists, or by others who enjoy vicariously the nostalgic experience of traditional observance. Kibbutz Lavi, not far from Tiberias, is one of the most popular. It runs a profitable hotel and maintains a particularly attractive synagogue, in which tourists may celebrate their familial religious occasions with traditional *éclat* and with traditional kosher cuisine. The kibbutz has introduced the manufacture of synagogue furniture as a kibbutz industry, though agriculture remains its mainstay.

The religious kibbutzim are marginal to the kibbutz movement as a whole and to religious life in Israel. But at a time when the secularists are showing interest in a return to tradition, and the religious establishment remains unenlightened and uncompromising, the Kibbutz Dati movement may well have a crucial mediating role to play in the future of Judaism in Israel.

The capitalist union

A vast solid building set back on a tree-lined Tel Aviv boulevard, and known by the locals as 'the Kremlin', houses the empire of the Histadrut, Israeli socialism in practice. The boulevard, Rechov Arlozoroff, is named after a labour leader, a founder of the Histadrut, whose assassination in 1933 was believed by his supporters to have been committed by right-wing extremists. The event deepened the already bitter conflict between Israeli socialists and the Revisionists, and the trauma can still be detected in the more-than-political hostility between Labour and Herut.

Second only to the government in power and influence, the Histadrut is a uniquely Israeli phenomenon. Its full name was Hahistadrut Haklalit Shel Ha-Ovdim Ha-Ivriyyim Be-Eretz Israel, the General Federation of Jewish Workers in the Land of Israel, and even when it was founded in 1920 it was not simply a trade union federation like the Trades Union Congress in Britain or the AFL-CIO in the United States. At the heart of the Histadrut concept was the aim of the Jewish workers of Palestine to achieve the creation of a socialist society in the Jewish homeland. The 87 delegates to the first general conference of workers which gathered in Haifa in December 1920 produced a constitution which declared that the Histadrut 'unites all workers in the country who live on the fruits of their own labour without exploiting the labour of others for the purpose of arranging all the communal, economic and cultural affairs of the working class of the country for the building of the Labour society in the Land of Israel.'

David Ben-Gurion, who became the first Secretary-General of the Histadrut, may have been overstating the case when he later claimed: 'Without it, I doubt whether we would have had a state,' but it is beyond question that the contribution of the Histadrut in creating institutions and services and in providing trained personnel was of incalculable value when, in 1948, the structure of a new State had to be created virtually overnight.

At the start, most of the workers who joined the new federation were members of kibbutzim or moshavim engaged in agriculture, and one of the Histadrut's first functions was to create jobs on the land for new immigrants. Having found them jobs, some of them as direct Histadrut employees, the federation turned to organizing the workers both on the land and in urban areas, where the newcomers were being exploited by small private employers. It began to organize unions for unskilled and skilled workers and also set up labour exchanges for those who were seeking employment.

During the slump in the 'thirties, jobs became difficult to find, and the Histadrut organized cooperative groups of workers to undertake building and public works. In a short time, that developed into a Histadrut Office for Public Works and Building which received government and private sector building contracts. As early as 1921, the Bank Hapoalim (Workers' Bank) was founded as the credit institution for these operations.

And so it grew, from the one-room office shared in 1920 by the first seven members of the Executive to today's giant. Ben-Gurion described the development graphically: 'We created something new in labour organization. The Histadrut did not confine itself to improving conditions of work. In the absence of adequate social services under the Mandatory Government, the Histadrut initiated them for its members. . . . It ran schools. It made itself responsible for the welfare of the workers. And then it took a big step farther. To widen the opportunities for work for the new immigrants – shut out for the most part from government projects and completely from the Arab economy – the Histadrut created jobs, by going into the business of building and contracting which they were later to extend to heavy industry.'*

It went beyond work and welfare. The creation of the Histadrut coincided with serious rioting and attacks on Jews by the Arabs. Some of the Histadrut leaders set up an underground self-defence organization called Hagana (Defence) which, for the first decade of its existence, was supervised and led by Histadrut officials. The membership of this force was recruited almost exclusively from the Histadrut membership and it was directed from an office in the Histadrut building. When the State came into existence, the office of the Hagana was a ready-made Ministry of Defence.

The decisive move to take the Histadrut beyond the boundaries of a trade union federation and to lay the foundation of a workers' economy took place

* Moshe Pearlman, *Ben Gurion Looks Back* (London 1963).

in 1924 with the foundation of Hevrat Ovdim (Workers' Society) which has
the English title of General Cooperative Association of Labour in Israel. Its
membership is identical with that of the Histadrut and its function is to act
as the owner of the organization's assets. The labour economy which it
controls falls into two groups, cooperative societies started by their
members, and enterprises started and controlled by the Histadrut. Among
the former are included the bus service, kibbutzim and moshavim, while
Histadrut-controlled enterprises amount to about one-quarter of the total
national assets of Israel, employ one in four of the working population and
70 per cent of those engaged in agriculture.

Most important of all the welfare activities of the Histadrut is its sick fund
– Kupat Holim – which offers a comprehensive medical service to its own
members as well as to those of other organizations affiliated for this purpose
– in all, some 70 per cent of the total population. Among the other social
services pioneered by the Histadrut were schools (later merged in the
national system); provident and pension funds; sports (the Hapoel organization with its football teams in every town, was established by, and is still
part of the Histadrut); workers' colleges and vocational training schools. It
publishes *Davar*, one of the major daily newspapers, and owns its own book-
publishing house.

The growth of the Histadrut into the giant of the Israeli economy gave it
equally giant powers which have, on occasion, been ruthlessly employed.
Strikes by Histadrut employees were sometimes followed by an offer from
Hevrat Ovdim to purchase the business involved. Protests were heard that
its friends in government had sold to the Histadrut valuable areas of
abandoned Arab property, without any competitive tenders being requested. Foreign investors selling to the Histadrut a substantial share,
preferably a controlling interest, in their business, often did so in the
expectation of easier access to government favours. On the labour front, so
powerful were the Histadrut unions and the closed-shop agreements they
negotiated, that employers were frequently supplicants rather than
negotiators.

Its vast stake in the Israeli economy has also given the Histadrut a
substantial share in the responsibility for the country's economic ills. It has
done much for the workers of Israel, but in making it virtually impossible to
dismiss them for inefficiency or incompetence, the Histadrut has harmed
industry and encouraged the proliferation of a sluggish bureaucracy. The
year after the State was created, the Government entered into an agreement
with its *alter ego*, the Histadrut, in which it practically abdicated all its
responsibilities in the employment of the civil service to workers' committees operating under the Histadrut banner. With the Government's
authority over the workers lost, not even the most conscientious and
efficient Minister could ensure the efficiency of his staff.

The Histadrut is not quite a monopoly. In 1934, the conservative
Revisionist party founded its own trade union organization, the Histadrut
Ha-Ovdim Ha-Leumit (National Labour Federation), because it believed
that the Histadrut had prejudiced its role as a trade union by its concurrent
status as an employer. The other, newer, Histadrut acts as a trade union

only, opposes socialism and advocates a national institution for compulsory arbitration. The successor of the Revisionist Party, Herut, subsequently organized its own group of supporters within the Histadrut, and the National Labour Federation became non-party. Today it claims a membership of 100,000 and provides similar services to those of the Histadrut.

Histadrut organization and leadership

The Histadrut became strong because its founders, with experience of the divisive potentialities of party politics, decided that it should not be allowed to become the instrument of any single one of the numerous socialist factions it embraced. Nor, they insisted, should it become merely a federation of unions depending on the approval and, therefore, control of all the participating bodies. All the founders had the foresight to recognize that a strong labour federation depended on its ability to take decisions free from the endless bargaining that would ensue if they were dependent on the approval of all the political parties involved.

As a result of these decisions of principle, the Histadrut was – and remains – a self-governing body, with the parties represented on its administration according to their proportion of the vote at the Histadrut's own general election every four years. It was, moreover, constructed in such a way that the central body, the Histadrut, and not any subsidiary trade union, should receive the first loyalty of its members, for it was the Histadrut alone which provided the benefits. Finally, the organizational structure was so planned that the relationship of the Histadrut is with the party machines directly, so that its organization will not be weakened should an irremovable representative lose the confidence of his own party.

Members of the Histadrut (the total is almost one and a half million, 63 per cent of the population) vote in a general election once in four years for the delegates to the Histadrut convention. As in national elections, they vote for party lists. Theoretically, any group of members may put up a list, but in practice only the national political parties do so and, as in national elections, the voters have no say in the choice of the individuals elected to represent them. The 1,501 delegates to the convention will be selected by the parties in the proportion of the votes their lists received.

All the power inside the Histadrut works down from the convention. With its party composition determined by the convention election, the convention will itself elect a Council of 501 members with the same party proportions as the convention. The same representation is accorded to the parties on the Central Committee of 179 members nominated by the Council. But the rules change for the election of the real governing body, the Executive Bureau. Its 30 members are elected by the Central Committee, but the 'party key' stops there. This working group does not contain representatives of all parties but, for all practical purposes, is controlled by the majority party, so far always the Israel Labour Party.

Whether it be the Convention, Council, Central Committee or Executive Bureau, the choice of individuals to serve on them is invariably made by the party, and the party can at any time replace one of its nominees who rejects party discipline – or for any other reason that satisfies the party. A dramatic example occurred in 1961 when Pinhas Lavon (charged by Ben-Gurion with responsibility for a 'security failure') was dismissed from his post as Secretary-General of the Histadrut by the Central Committee of Mapai, the labour faction which was then the dominant party in the Government. Within the Histadrut organization, all the forms of democracy are sedulously observed, but the real control lies with the party leadership.

Israel Kaisar, Deputy Secretary General since 1977, has explained, turgidly, that 'the advantage of this method is that it preserves the general agreement of the parties to function within the Histadrut and not outside it or in opposition thereto; and to ensure its cohesion and prevent control by groups of workers enjoying power who might act in their own interest, neglecting the collective social objectives for the attainment of which the Histadrut as an entity regards itself responsible.'

Most of the 30 members of the Executive are on the Histadrut's full-time payroll. Twelve of them are chairmen of departments (they are described as 'holding portfolios') of which the most important are Trade Unions (Chairman, Israel Kaisar), Finance (Chairman, Natan Almozalino) and Hevrat Ovdim, the workers' commonwealth whose chairman is Moshe Bankover. A recent addition to the top echelon of the hierarchy of portfolios is Naftali Ben-Moshe, a member of the left wing of the Israel Labour Party, who heads the Industrial Democracy Department, the object of which is to gain worker participation in management.

Membership of the Histadrut, carrying with it the right to vote in the general election for the convention, is open to all men and women over the age of 18 who work for a living. Housewives and students, regarded as self-employed, are also eligible. The fee in 1979 for a single worker was 3.75 per cent of his monthly earnings up to a ceiling of I£9,000 per month (a maximum monthly payment of about US$10). A married worker paid over 4.5 per cent of his monthly earnings (maximum $12 per month), subject to the same ceiling which rises regularly, being linked with the cost-of-living index. About 75 per cent of members agree to have their dues deducted by their employers. The Histadrut uses about two-thirds of the membership dues it receives for its health service, with the remaining third applied for general trade union and cultural purposes. Having joined the Histadrut, the worker may then join any one of the forty-two Histadrut trade unions without paying any extra fee.

The two top managers of the Histadrut are its Secretary-General, Yeruham Meshel, and his deputy, Israel Kaisar. Worlds apart in appearance and background, they form an effective and complementary combination. Meshel could be the prototype of an Israeli Labour leader, Russian-born, socialist, former member of a Zionist youth movement. Kaisar, on the other hand, came into the Histadrut via academic studies and specialist service in the Labour Party.

Meshel could have been Secretary-General in 1969 when the post became vacant but Golda Meir, then at the height of her power, used her influence to favour her friend, Yitzhak Ben-Aharon, a former Minister of

Transport. It was an unusual appointment, for Ben-Aharon was a member of Achdut Avoda, whereas all his predecessors had belonged to Mapai, the largest component of the Israeli Labour Party. Ben-Aharon's tenure was not altogether happy. He fell out with the Finance Minister, Pinhas Sapir, who regarded him as irresponsibly left-wing, and antagonized his mentor, Golda Meir, by intemperate criticism of her Government's policies. When his term expired in 1974, the Labour leaders decided to return to the traditional qualifications for this post and Meshel, a sound Mapai man, was appointed. He had been a skilled and patient negotiator, a sober and responsible pillar of the establishment.

Meshel was born in Pinsk in 1912, a predominantly Jewish town with a strong Zionist tradition in the area of Czarist Russia called the Jewish Pale of Settlement. Chaim Weizmann, the outstanding figure in Zionism until the foundation of the State, was himself educated in Pinsk and described it affectionately in his autobiography as a 'city and a mother in Israel'. Meshel, as was almost inevitable for a young, thinking Jew in those days and in those places, became a Zionist, joined a Zionist youth movement and emigrated to Palestine in 1933 as an agricultural worker. But it was difficult to find agricultural work at that time, and after a year of unemployment, Meshel became a building worker in the El Arish-Rafah area of Sinai. He became interested in his trade union and was elected to the works committee. His ability brought him rapid promotion to the secretaryship of the Tel Aviv branch of the Metal Workers Union in 1943.

In 1947, he was nominated by Mapai to the Histadrut Executive Bureau, where he held the portfolio of Industrial Relations and then the major department of Trade Unions, representing the Histadrut in all labour negotiations. He was a conspicuous success, gaining the confidence of the workers for the gains he achieved, and the respect of employers for insisting that labour had obligations as well as rights.

Six weeks after the 1977 General Election which resulted in Labour's fall from power, the Histadrut's own election took place. By that time, the Herut Party, the main component of the Likud which had gained power in the General Election, had its own list in the Histadrut and was contesting that election with the hope of repeating its national election success. If that had happened Labour would have lost control of this vast source of political and economic power – almost a greater catastrophe for the party than the loss of the General Election. The alarming prospect jolted the Labour politicians from the state of shock in which the General Election had left them. Meshel led the recovery and, immersing himself in the campaign, rapidly organized brigades of workers' committees to canvass and bring in the vote. Shimon Peres and the other party leaders recruited the kibbutz resources for the same purpose and the frenzied activity was successful. Labour retained control, but the Herut minority grew to about 30 per cent.

Meshel was the ideal man on the spot in the unprecedented situation in which the Histadrut now found itself. The Histadrut was for the first time identified with the Opposition and not the Government, but Meshel assured the new Prime Minister that he would not seek to use the Histadrut as an anti-government weapon. At the same time, he gave a warning that

his organization would fight to the end to prevent any attempt by the
government to take over any of its services, particularly the sick fund. That
could be the Achilles heel of his organization, and he is determined to
protect it.

Nearing his seventies, Meshel is an active man, physically and intellectually. Grey-haired and portly, he looks older than his years. He beams
benignly on all around him and his loquacity never seems to lead to
indiscretion for he clearly knows exactly how much or how little to say. He
enjoys his membership of the Knesset, where he is a popular figure; his
progress in the cafeteria is usually interrupted by greetings from practically
every table, to which he responds with practised, cheerful repartee. In his
open shirt and safari jacket, he could not be other than a Zionist pioneer
become labour politico.

The Deputy Secretary-General, Israel Kaisar, slight and swarthy, brisk
and decisive, looks the technocrat. He was born in the Yemen in 1931 and
came to Palestine with his parents and six other children in 1933. At first
they lived in an Arab house in conditions of some adversity on the slender
earnings of the father, a labourer. But, slowly, conditions improved. The
family moved to Jerusalem, where Kaisar attended school, and they settled
on a moshav near the Arab town of Tulkarem. After the War of Independence, the bright boy attended a labour college for the study of economics
and sociology run by the Histadrut, following it with a degree course in the
same subjects at the Hebrew University.

His background in the Yemenite community and his academic studies
(he later gained another degree in labour studies at Tel Aviv University)
made him an ideal recruit for the department of the Ministry of Labour
dealing with the absorption of new immigrants. He remained there for six
years, making the easy transition in 1966 to the Executive Bureau of the
Histadrut, where his first portfolio was as Chairman of the Youth and
Sports Department.

Energetic and shrewd, he progressed through the hierarchy, Chairman
of the Manpower Department, Treasurer, Chairman of the Trade Union
Department and, since 1977, deputy to Yeruham Meshel. Kaisar is the first
Yemenite to have risen so high in the Histadrut, but other Oriental Jews are
making their way up the ladder, and seven are today members of the thirty-
member Executive Bureau.

Trade unions

Before the formation of the State, the Histadrut performed many functions
which would normally have been the responsibilities of the State. Among
them were the creation of new settlements, setting up of a defence body and
the organization of clandestine immigration to beat the restricted quotas
imposed by the Mandatory Government. It regarded these services as far
more important than the sectional interest of achieving better pay and
conditions for workers. But, with the creation of the State and the
assumption by national institutions of the broader functions, the Histadrut
returned to the tasks of a normal trade union movement.

In the process something was lost. The unity of purpose and sense of high achievement had encouraged altruism and idealism. These qualities were hardly applicable, and certainly became less dominant, as the organization changed to the pursuit of advantage for its members. The decline in the spirit of idealism in the organization as a whole brought with it a weakening of workers' solidarity too, as groups within the Histadrut became militant in the pursuit of their own interests. What the bureaucrats of the Histadrut refer to as the 'formal and legitimate centre of power', by which they mean the Histadrut's centralized power machine, was challenged by local workers' groups intent on going their own way.

Worried debate in the organization has not yet brought about a solution to the problem of the rejection of discipline on the shop floor. Constitutionally, the Histadrut may expel a member in breach of discipline, but this remedy has never been applied to a group. An alternative sanction is the suspension of medical services but that too, though permissible, has never yet been applied, since it would be likely to harm the families rather than the erring workers themselves. On the other hand, however defiant groups of workers have been towards the Histadrut's 'legitimate centres of power', very few have left the organization and so remain, to some degree, susceptible to central influence.

Local militancy has inevitably led to a weakening of central authority, a new and uncomfortable situation for the all-powerful and often dictatorial officials at 'the Kremlin'.

Once every two years the Trade Union Department produces the wage structure and labour relations policies for the entire labour force. They are defined in general principle, while the wages structure is presented in ranges and classification varying with increases in productivity, the economics of a particular industry and any special considerations that may apply to a particular group of workers. It constitutes the framework within which the Histadrut trade unions are supposed to engage in negotiations with employers. Not all do, however, and some, employees in the public service particularly, are prone to breaches of discipline and wildcat or unofficial strikes. Unions have their own strike funds, but the Histadrut also operates its own central strike fund which, since it is not available to unofficial strikers, serves to some extent to bolster its authority. But not appreciably for, in recent years, the number of work days lost in strikes has grown:

1974	51,333
1975	164,509
1976	308,214
1977	416,526

Of the 1977 figure, no less than 42 per cent of the days lost were accountable to the public services, while 75 per cent of the days lost were due to short, generally unofficial, strikes of between two and six days.

National trade unions number 42, ranging from the small union of pharmacists with a membership of 1,000 to the National Federation of

Clerical Workers which claims 120,000 members. The union of workers in the Histadrut has a membership of 30,000.

The local unions branches, called works committees, to which union power has been steadily moving, do not follow the Histadrut system of voting for party lists and proportionately dividing up the places according to the votes. Candidates for election to works committees are put up for election on a personal basis. They owe nothing to parties and, if they wish to be re-elected, will have to please their fellow-workers, not the party managers; so that, in a conflict with headquarters, the members of the works committees are much more likely to be susceptible to local than to national influence. Some Histadrut leaders, aware of the growing gap between the rank and file and the centre, have made the revolutionary proposal that election to the central institutions should include some personally nominated candidates as well as the party list. This might bring about a closer relationship between the workers and the impersonal bureaucracy, but something will have to be changed if the trade union power of the Histadrut is not to be rendered completely nugatory by the breakdown of discipline and lack of a common policy.

A singular problem for the Histadrut has been its relationship with Arab workers. It was originally conceived as an organization only of Jewish workers – that was its title – and was strongly Zionist in ideology. Arab workers were therefore unable to join, a situation which embarrassed the socialist leaders, who accepted the principle of the common cause of the labouring classes in a class society. At its third convention in 1927, the Histadrut therefore decided to establish a Confederation of Palestinian Workers, a roof organization of autonomous Arab unions.

It was not a tenable solution. The patent discrimination suffered by the Arab worker in wages and social benefits gradually impinged on the Histadrut, particularly when, after statehood, the burgeoning national economy created opportunities for Arab employment in Jewish enterprises. When Arabs began receiving the same wages and working under the same conditions as Jewish labour, their segregation in their own labour organization became increasingly anomalous. In 1953, they were admitted to the Histadrut Sick Fund and all its other mutual aid institutions, while a special section for Arab workers was formed in its Trade Union Department. The process of integration was completed in 1959, when Arabs were admitted to full membership and the name changed to General Federation of Labour in Israel. Arab membership increased rapidly, rose to about one-third of the total Arab population and was extended to East Jerusalem after the Six Day War.

Workers' Commonwealth

Hevrat Ovdim, literally Workers' Society, but more generally known as Workers' Commonwealth, is the division of the Histadrut which owns a wide range of commercial enterprises employing about 250,000 workers who constitute some 23 per cent of the total national work force. It was set up in 1924 with two main objects. The first was the need to find work for immigrants since private enterprise could not offer enough jobs. Secondly, the socialist ideology of the Histadrut's founders prescribed that agriculture and industry should be owned and controlled by the workers, whose interests were more important than profits.

The largest of all the components of the Workers' Society are its kibbutzim and moshavim, accounting for some 60 per cent of the country's agricultural products and some 70 per cent of the total agricultural labour force. With the growth of industry in kibbutzim, Hevrat Ovdim created the Kibbutz Industries Association, which finances and organizes 300 industrial enterprises in 170 kibbutzim. They range from food processing, the manufacture of musical instruments, and fashion wear to sophisticated electronics and plastics, the largest of all the industrial divisions being metal-working, which accounts for almost one-third of all kibbutz industries.

Marketing both agricultural and industrial products is kept within the Histadrut 'family' through two cooperatives, Tnuva for farm products and the Israel Cooperative Wholesale Society for consumer goods. Histadrut-managed cooperatives include the two major bus companies, Egged and Dan, now merged. In Israel, public transport is almost exclusively by bus – the railways are negligible – and these two companies, with a virtual monopoly of travel within the country, offer essential services which have resulted in high pay for the drivers, the elite in the hierarchy of Israeli workers.

Koor Industries Limited is the industrial conglomerate of the Histadrut. It owns about one hundred manufacturing plants throughout the country and employs more than 23,000 workers, producing chemicals, food and consumer goods, steel and metals, glass, ceramics and cement. Tadiran Electronics Industries, an important producer of defence equipment, constitutes a division on its own in the company while the Koor group of trading companies operates from Israel, New York, Hong Kong and Amsterdam. Almost half its business consists of joint enterprises with private entrepreneurs and it has recently opened a subsidiary in Cairo in cooperation with an Egyptian company. Trade in 1977 was worth some 1.2 billion US dollars with exports accounting for about half this sum. The Board of Directors of Koor consists of thirteen nominees of the managing committee of Hevrat Ovdim, together with a token workers' representative. This vast operation was the first industrial group in Israel to introduce profit-sharing, and in 1977 some three million US dollars was distributed to the staff.

Profits in 1978 of this Histadrut giant leapt to approximately seventy million dollars, an increase of no less than 35 per cent above the previous year and a substantial achievement, well above the inflation rate. Most of it was due to higher sales in the home market, a reflection of the inflationary buying spree.

Solel Boneh (Paver and Builder), Israel's largest construction company, was founded by the Histadrut in 1920. Intent on providing more jobs, it expanded more rapidly than its enthusiastic but inexperienced management could cope with and, seven years later, went bankrupt. For a while it

was replaced by local operations undertaken by the Histadrut as it sorted
out the mess, reappearing in 1935 and growing to become one of the major
building and civil engineering contractors in the whole of the Middle East.
A reorganization in 1958 hived off its overseas activities into a subsidiary
company called Solel Boneh International Ltd which carried out contracts
in 1978 worth some 400 million US dollars.

During the heyday of Golda Meir's policy of leapfrogging over Israel's
hostile neighbours and establishing links with the Third World, Solel
Boneh was in the van of Israeli projects, aid and advice to African countries.
Although most of the African countries joined the Arab boycott of Israel
after the Six Day War, some of Israel's achievements still survive. Solel
Boneh's buildings abroad include the Hilton Hotel, International House
and other major buildings in Nairobi's city centre, the Ife University and
Lagos City Hall in Nigeria, the Tehran Hilton, two 400-bed hospitals in
Tanzania, and a 30-million-dollar commercial centre in Venezuela. Its
public works and housing projects in those countries and in Argentina,
Uganda, Ivory Coast, Ethiopia, Kenya and Thailand amounted to hundreds of millions of dollars. In Israel, some of its notable constructions are
the Knesset building and the Hebrew University campus in Jerusalem,
Ashdod harbour, and countless houses, factories and public buildings.

Of enormous assistance to all these Histadrut commercial activities is
access to the pension and welfare funds from which long-term loans are
available through the Histadrut's main financial arm, Bank Hapoalim,
which operates under Hevrat Ovdim and is now competing with Bank
Leumi for the distinction of being the largest Israeli banking operation.
Bank Hapoalim has advanced dramatically in the past few years by
investing in industry. It has always been at pains not to compete with
Hevrat Ovdim enterprises and therefore restricts investments to services
rather than industry or insurance, in which Hevrat Ovdim is involved.

The Bank was started in 1921 and capitalized in Egyptian currency
since, at that time, the British had not yet introduced the Palestine pound.
Its Board of Directors is elected by shareholders (it is a public company),
but since the founders' shares owned by Hevrat Ovdim give it a decisive
vote in the elections, the Directors are actually Histadrut nominees. They
decide major policy, while the day-to-day running is in the hands of a
ten-man Board of Management appointed by the directors and consisting
of full-time employees.

Jacob Levinson, Chairman of Bank Hapoalim's Board of Directors and
the architect of its impressive development, attributes its success to what he
describes as 'the kibbutz spirit' and, in fact, three of the ten managers are
former kibbutzniks. Directors are not paid and the members of the Board of
Management earn no more than the ordinary salary for their jobs as
employees of the Bank. The excellence of staff relations may be due in part
to Levinson's care to be present at all staff meetings to discuss and explain
any problems raised. Almost alone among Israeli businesses, the Bank has
never experienced a strike.

As employers, all Hevrat Ovdim enterprises deal with the claims of their
staff through the trade unions of which they are members, in exactly the

same way as their privately owned competitors. For a long time, the anomalies inherent in this situation, where the employees were also the nominal owners, were theoretical rather than real. The trade union wage rates and policies laid down by the Histadrut would automatically be implemented in the Workers' Commonwealth. Not only were their wages always in line with the private sector, but Histadrut employees enjoyed additional fringe benefits and were therefore reluctant to put their jobs at risk by militancy. Moreover, in the early days, the emphasis was on egalitarianism, when a manual worker on a university campus earned as much as a professor, and the driver of a Cabinet Minister's car took home as much as his boss. When that ideal faded in the flush of the affluent society, Histadrut employees began to behave towards their employers just as their colleagues did in the private sector. They all wanted more, so the unthinkable happened – strikes took place in Histadrut enterprises.

Nevertheless, on the whole, a balance is struck, and the majority of Histadrut's labour force is loyal and responsible, though some are restive at the refusal of Yeruham Meshel to pay Histadrut employees the wages Histradrut trade unions are demanding from private enterprise. The Histadrut points to the fringe benefits and greater security its employees enjoy. As a Histadrut spokesman said bitterly after a 1979 demonstration: 'The workers have short memories. During the building slump from 1975 to 1978, whoever worked for the capitalists went home the day there was no work.' But the leader of the construction workers' union, while acknowledging the greater security of Solel Boneh workers, responded: 'With such inflation, the workers look at pay more than at job security.'

Increasingly, the managements of the Workers' Commonwealth occupy the role of a normal employer, concerned more with efficiency and profits than political ideology. For their part, the workers relate to their employers no differently from their counterparts in the capitalist economy. Indeed, as far as profits are concerned, Histadrut enterprises are no less eager for them than capitalist concerns. They seek profits to pay dividends to investors and for profit-sharing with employees. Hevrat Ovdim's contribution to the national economy is immense and the asset value of all Histadrut enterprises – wholly or partly owned – amounts to almost one-quarter of the total national assets.

Working with the Likud

The Histadrut has always been the real power base of the Labour Party. Its economic enterprises provided the funds for the party organization and 'jobs for its boys', while the party workers who brought in the votes at elections came from the rank and file of union members. In return, Labour governments have protected the interests of the Histadrut in a cosy, symbiotic relationship which ended with the 1977 General Election. For the first time in Israel's history, a non-socialist Government, owing nothing to the Histadrut, took office.

While it groped towards a reassessment of its role in this unprecedented situation, the Histadrut made soothing noises to the effect that it would not seek confrontation with the Likud Government. At its 13th Convention, six months after the elections, it remained conciliatory announcing that wage claims would be moderate to avoid damaging the Government's efforts to achieve economic stability. But as the Government followed free enterprise policies, and the freeing of the economy accelerated inflation, the Histadrut's obligation to protect the living standards of the workers inevitably brought about a change.

The Histadrut charged that the cancellation of controls, the attempts to introduce a pay freeze, the abolition of food subsidies and roaring inflation had 'turned Israel into a paradise for currency speculators and the get-rich-quick boys. It has worsened the distressed situation of so many working people while opening up new prospects and vistas for the wealthy.' The Histadrut declared war against the government's economic programme and the first engagement was a one-hour stoppage in all factories in July 1977 when the first currency devaluation was announced. Meshel forecast more aggressive action and declared that 'the time for a confrontation with the government has arrived.' More strikes followed, more declarations of the incompatibility between a right-wing Government and the interests of the workers as represented by Histadrut.

At the same time, the Histadrut was fighting an intercine war, too. The Herut faction, which had secured almost one-third of the votes at the 1977 election, had also taken control of many local works committees. The increasing independence of the local committees – not all of them Herut-controlled – was a growing problem. The Histadrut claimed that the problem was aggravated by Government attempts to make its own direct contacts with the workers and to bypass or even undercut the Histadrut. Dov Ben-Meir, a Tel Aviv Labour Party and Histadrut leader, accused the Likud of being intent on breaking the power of organized labour and converting the Histadrut into a fragmented trade union federation.

The atmosphere was hardly improved when, at the 1979 Herut convention, the Deputy Defence Minister, Mordechai Zipori, referred to the Histadrut as 'a Mafia which gives backing to parasites'. He later withdrew the remark, but did little to mollify his furious opponents by endorsing the general purport of his statement that 'the organization which is supposed to look after the interests of the working man gives support to those who do not lift a finger, but cannot be fired because of Histadrut protection.' Later, Prime Minister Begin, while deploring the use of the word 'Mafia', objected to the situation where the Histadrut was the nation's largest industrialist 'while, at the same time, it is supposed to look after the workers' interests.'

Potentially the most serious clash between the Histadrut and the right-wing Government was about power. The Histadrut had often been at loggerheads with Labour government but the differences were about methods. No Labour Government wanted to weaken the Histadrut, from which it had so much to gain. True, the Histadrut had lost many of its functions to the new State – its school system was absorbed into the national school organization in 1953, and a few years later its labour exchanges were nationalized. That had not been accepted without heartsearching, because the exchanges had brought into the Histadrut the new recruits for whom jobs had been found. They were an important instrument of power, and their loss was keenly felt by the Histadrut bureaucracy. That made them determined to oppose Ben-Gurion's statist principles and prevent further nationalization of their institutions.

The Likud has every reason to welcome the weakening of the Histadrut and is well aware that, were its Sick Fund to be absorbed in a national health service, the result would be a drastic drop in Histadrut membership. With the loss of members would come fewer jobs, less money, less patronage and less power. A similar threat exists to the Histadrut's pension funds. These funds are an important capital resource for all Histadrut enterprises, and their transfer to the National Insurance Institute – as some Likud supporters have proposed – would be an immense blow to the workers' organization.

The Likud would love to be able, at a stroke, to perform what would be a logical rationalization in transferring essentially government functions from the Histadrut to the State, while simultaneously inflicting serious damage to its main opponent, the Israel Labour Party. The strength and diversity of the problems faced by the Likud Government on a number of fronts and, in particular, the perilous economic situation, have militated against its capacity to take on so tough an opponent, or to find the vast sums of money required to nationalize the Sick Fund. But Begin and his supporters have undoubtedly been awaiting their opportunity.

Chapter eleven

Judaism in Practice

Religious influences in Zionism

Even the secular Zionists never envisaged Israel solely as a haven for homeless Jews. It was also to be a *Jewish* state, and the degree and extent of its Jewishness have been the subjects of continuing debate from the very start of the Zionist movement. The religious Jews who joined the movement were positive that the land of Israel should be reconstructed under the rule of the Torah, the laws of Moses contained in the Pentateuch and developed and interpreted by rabbis of authority up to the present.

The political Zionist movement only developed in the late nineteenth century, but ever since the Jews had lost their national homeland (after the Roman conquest of the Holy Land in the first century) their religion had kept alive the hope of a return. The destruction of the Temple in Jerusalem in AD 70 had brought about a radical transformation in the nature of Judaism. The Temple ritual around which it had revolved was replaced by a philosophy and liturgy which reconstructed Jewish living based on the synagogue and the home. In practising their religion in dispersion, Jews applied a fiction, the 'as if' theory – as if they were living in their own land.

They prayed for rain or dew, not when they needed it in Poland, Germany or France, but at a season when it was vital for agriculture in Palestine. They prayed for the return of the Jews to the Promised Land and for the restoration of the Temple. Jews physically turned to Jerusalem in prayer and regarded it as the highest aspiration to live in the Holy Land, even though in most cases they went there to die. The observance of the Jewish religion kept alive the spirit of Jewish nationalism during the very long dark ages of antisemitism and persecution.

There was never a time when Palestine was devoid of Jews, although the numbers were often small. They began to grow under Turkish rule, which started in the sixteenth century, and by 1880, before the Zionist movement had been born, the total Jewish population was 25,000. Those who lived there devoted themselves to Jewish study and a life of religious observance, subsisting on the charitable contributions of Jews from abroad.

This life of piety might have been expected to engender tranquility, but in fact the Jews of Palestine were rarely free from conflicts and internal stresses. Those following the rituals of Spain and Portugal, the Sephardim, quarrelled with their Western co-religionists, the Ashkenazim, about the allocation of the charitable takings, and were also involved in endless doctrinal controversies between the different sects to which they belonged. Palestine Jewry was divided and fractious, but practically all its members lived lives of undeviating orthodoxy, vying with each other in meticulous observance of the rabbinic applications of the Divine Will. This was the 'Old Yishuv' (Yishuv means settlement), so described to distinguish it from the 'New Yishuv', the Zionist settlers. Its descendants remain a separate enclave in Israel to this day.

The Russian pogroms after the assassination of Czar Alexander II caused the mass emigration of Jews from Russia. Some of the hardier and more idealistic among them began a movement for settlement in Palestine called Lovers of Zion, and from 1881 to 1903 about 25,000 of them arrived in the desolate, neglected country. They bought land, farmed and traded and, from the start, were shunned by the old Yishuv for their irreligion.

Yet, much as they would have preferred to do so, the Lovers of Zion could not altogether avoid involvement in religious concerns. In 1889 they found themselves in the middle of an intense controversy, when the obscurantist rabbis of old Jerusalem insisted that, in accordance with biblical law, the land was to lie fallow during that sabbatical year. Diaspora Jewry took sides, and the pressure on the farmers to comply with Jewish law was unrelenting. Nevertheless, they insisted on tilling their soil. It was the first major clash between the needs of a modern, productive community and the dictates of an ancient, unchanging faith.

The Zionist movement was launched in 1896, when Dr Theodor Herzl, an assimilated Viennese journalist, published Der Judenstaat (The Jewish State), in which he advocated the re-creation of a Jewish sovereign state to solve the Jewish problem which, to him, was one of homelessness. He was emphatic that it was not to be a theocracy and proposed the separation of church and state: 'We shall keep our rabbis within their synagogues just as we shall keep our army within their bases.'

In its early years, the Zionist movement encountered opposition from both extremes of religious Jewry. Reform Judaism was hostile because Jewish nationalism conflicted with its belief in the religious mission of dispersed Jewry. The orthodox right wing, on the other hand, was shocked by the pretensions of these Westernized, secular Jews in trying to achieve a return to the Holy Land; that could only come about with the advent of the Messiah. Herzl, gaining experience of the realities of Jewish life, of which he knew little when he began his movement, realized that it was essential to mollify religious Jews. At the second Zionist Congress in 1898 he supported a resolution which defined Zionism as aiming at 'not only a political and economic revival of the Jewish people, but at a spiritual revival as well, founded on modern culture and its achievements. Zionism will not undertake anything contrary to the injunctions of the Jewish religion.'

Although the near-fanatical far right of orthodoxy continued to oppose the new movement, it attracted the East European Jewish masses, including many who were religiously observant. In 1902 the religious Jews formed their own party in the World Zionist Organization and called it Mizrachi, an abbreviation of two Hebrew words, Mercaz (centre) and Ruchani (spiritual). Its slogan was, 'The Land of Israel for the people of Israel, according to the Law of Israel.'

The Mizrachi Party made itself part of Palestine Jewry by creating a network of practical enterprises, including capitalist businesses, socialist kibbutzim, a newspaper and a separate religio-orientated school system. Under the impact of the Nazi Holocaust, many members of the anti-Zionist orthodox Jews also found a haven in Palestine while the Old Yishuv, still inflexibly opposed to Zionism and the creation of a Jewish state, continued the uneven tenor of their disputations. But when the State was proclaimed in 1948 the total of all religious Jews amounted to a minority of the Jewish population of 650,000.

The State of Israel was declared a secular state with no established religion and its Declaration of Independence guaranteed religious freedom. But problems connected with religious law have continued to divide the nation.

When the Knesset in 1953 confirmed the powers of Israel's rabbinical courts over marriage and divorce (see the discussion of the system in Chapter 4), it was well aware of the problems. In introducing the measure, the then Prime Minister, Moshe Sharett, said: 'We cannot ignore the fact that the acceptance of this law involves concessions in principles and basic concepts concerning an advanced society for many people. Therefore the test of the law will be its execution. The authority which will enforce this law – the Israeli Rabbinate – will be facing a test. The stability of the law will depend on a certain flexibility in its application. The longevity of the law will depend on the ability to adapt it to concepts of equality and a respect for man and his individual rights which exist in the modern societies today.'

The hopes of rabbinical flexibility and the adaptation of religious concepts to a modern society have not been realized.

Judaism in society

The roots of Israel, as we have seen, lie deep in the Jewish tradition, but the society which was created, largely by the twentieth-century immigrants, owed more to the political ideologies of the socialist movements in the East European countries from which they had come. Palestine was an escape from the ghetto and, in rejecting what the ghetto represented, these people were also rejecting the Jewish religion which many of them saw as the heart of the ghetto way of life. Yet they were also, many of them, idealists and romantics and they could not wholly abandon the traditional background from which they had come, nor the inspiration of their biblical past. This ambivalence accounts in large measure for the anomalies in the position of Judaism in Israeli society today.

The religious section of the community (they call themselves dat'iim – religious ones – and can be distinguished from the rest of the population by their 'kipot' (skull caps)) has tended to keep itself socially and residentially apart. Their degree of self-ghettoization varies. At the extreme are the successors of the Old Yishuv, augmented by the post-Hitler chassidic zealot immigrants who came mainly from Hungary. They deliberately set themselves apart from the State. They live in totally segregated areas, wear distinctive clothing (men in black and wearing sidecurls; females in shapeless and voluminous dresses; married women covering with wigs the hair which may be seductive to men) and do not recognize the authority of the Government.

These ultras are an anachronism, but attract attention in inverse proportion to their exiguous numbers. Their unmistakable appearance and the violence of their reaction against modernity have made them prime targets for the cameras of the newspapers and television. But, in fact, they are little more than a bizarre fringe of Israeli society, a few thousand in number, concentrated mainly in the Mea Shearim district of Jerusalem. The disproportionate public attention paid to this minority arises from their exotic appearance and the nuisance they are prone to create.

They throw stones at vehicles which desecrate the Sabbath peace near their homes. To protect it, they have erected barriers across roads to the danger of road users (the Israeli sculptor, Palumbo, was killed when his motorcycle hit a chain stretched across a road in Jerusalem), and they have demonstrated violently against such 'profanities' as a mixed swimming pool and a sports stadium in Jerusalem. They pronounce excommunications, imprecations and intemperate threats. But tolerance has been wearing thin and the Mayor of Jerusalem has appealed to the police to treat these zealots in the same way as other lawbreakers. They have so far been handled carefully, partly because of some residual respect for religious feelings and partly because the (religious) Minister of Police was thought to be worried at the possibility of trouble with his own party if he took tough measures.

Except on Saturday, the Jewish Sabbath, visitors to Israel are not likely to find themselves unduly affected by any manifestations of Judaism. They will generally be made aware, particularly in Jerusalem, of the presence of orthodox Jews by their dress. They may also have seen young men, in uniform or in normal civilian clothing, demonstrating their religiosity by wearing abbreviated crocheted kipot. Visitors who entertain an overwhelming desire to enjoy bacon, pork chops or shellfish will probably experience some difficulty in finding a restaurant or hotel which will serve them, but they exist almost everywhere.

On the Sabbath, from Friday evening to Saturday at sunset, the visitor will be aware that this is a Jewish State. Most shops, places of entertainment and restaurants are closed; public transport (except in Haifa) does not run and most hotels will not serve freshly cooked food. But most Israeli Jews do not attend synagogue on their rest-day; they are more likely to be seen thronging the streets, parks and beaches.

Non-religious Israelis experience some inconvenience caused by Sabbath observance and the application of the dietary laws, but this is hardly intolerable and, as a result, little opposition has been generated. Bodies such as the League against Religious Coercion have been largely ineffectual, because the majority of Israelis, while not themselves religious, are ready to accept some degree of official recognition of the Jewish religion, provided that it does not impinge on them too uncomfortably.

In practice, the only occasions on which the average Israeli may be seriously affected is if he becomes involved in a problem concerned with

marriage, divorce, or any other matter of personal status within the jurisdiction of the rabbinical courts. Difficult issues have arisen in these areas of
Jewish rabbinic law, but they directly affect only a few people. In the
absence of civil marriage, most Israelis will go through a religious
ceremony, but some decline on the ground that such a ceremony would be a
sham for an unbeliever. In such cases they can live without benefit of clergy
(a 'common law wife' has now been given virtually all the rights of a legal
wife) or go abroad for a civil marriage. Another problem is that Jewish
religious law contains various restrictions, such as the prohibition of
marriage between a Cohen (a descendant of the ancient priestly tribe) and a
divorcee. Such was the situation of Supreme Court Justice Haim Cohn. His
solution was a civil marriage in Cyprus, which Israeli Law recognizes
because it is a valid marriage in the country in which it was contracted.

Israeli synagogues, with very few exceptions, have no aesthetic merit.
The larger ones in the cities are undistinguished architecturally, often little
more than shabby halls with, at one end, an Ark containing the scrolls of the
law and in the centre, a reading plaform, the bima. Women are segregated
in a gallery or some other sequestered adjunct. But the majority of
synagogues – Jerusalem has some 800 and Tel Aviv 600 – are small and
intimate, catering for local residents, members of the same sect or from the
same place of origin. The Sephardi and Ashkenazi synagogues can usually
be distinguished by the seating. The Sephardi seating generally goes round
the walls, while in Ashkenazi synagogues the worshippers are accomodated
in conventional rows of seats or pews. The range of synagogues, especially
in Jerusalem, is enormous, preserving the rituals, customs and traditions of
Jewish communities from every corner of the Middle East, the Far East,
North Africa and Europe.

With few exceptions, synagogues in Israel are neither built nor maintained by their members, but through subventions from the Government
via the local religious councils. This does not apply to the non-orthodox
synagogues, which are not recognized by the State and are thus not eligible
for aid from the Ministry for Religious Affairs. Synagogues are free for all,
and there are no privileges of synagogue membership. The Western-style
rabbi as pastoral minister caring for his flock is unknown in Israel, where
nearly all the practising rabbis are either District Rabbis performing
various ritual functions, Judges of the Rabbinical Courts, or teachers. The
few rabbis who serve synagogues in the manner familiar to Jewish
communities elsewhere, do so by individual private arrangement.

The gap between the religious minority and the population at large has
widened as orthodox attitudes have moved to the right and have concentrated almost exclusively on ritual observance. Establishment Judaism
has nothing to say about moral or spiritual issues. Petty squabbling within
the religious hierarchy, the resentment felt towards the clericalist politicians, the exemptions that have been secured from military service by their
youth and the almost total absence of religious leadership have all widened
that gap.

In Israel, as in world Jewry generally, the orthodox religious tone is set
by the most conservative of the rabbis, the principals of the great Talmudic

schools, the Yeshivot. So profound is the respect of the orthodox rabbinate for these Torah scholars (and so acute their fear of being smeared as 'reformers') that they have all become hostages of the religious diehards. Anti-intellectualism is an essential element in their outlook, for they see secular scholarship as inevitably leading to doubts and eventual heresy. Consequently, very few leading rabbis in Israel are university graduates* and immigrant rabbis from the West who possess university degrees find it almost impossible to secure official appointments.

Israel does not have a rabbinical school or theological seminary similar to the great institutions which existed in pre-war Europe or to those in the United States today. The training of Israeli rabbis is limited to the narrow Yeshiva curriculum, which concentrates on study of the Talmud, ignores modern scholarship and precludes the spirit of free enquiry. Not only is pastoral work unknown as part of the rabbi's activities, he is not even expected to deliver sermons to a congregation; his sole formal duty is to conduct a class in Talmud for those who want to learn. The District Rabbi has no responsibility for educating the young, does not visit the sick or bereaved (unless there is a personal reason) and is not called upon for, nor does he offer, any form of public leadership.

Little wonder that Rabbi Adin Steinsalz, one of the few independent and thoughtful voices in Israeli orthodoxy has written: 'Israel is one of the States in the world in which religion has relatively little influence in culture or politics. The rabbis, as clergymen, do not constitute a factor in the lives of the great majority of Israelis. Even the word "religious" has become a blameworthy epithet . . .'. He might have added that the rabbis cannot escape responsibility for the complete separation between orthodoxy and morals. One orthodox rabbi said to me, with some bitterness: 'If a man wears his kipa, his prayer shawl and phylacteries, he is accepted as an orthodox Jew. It makes no difference how he conducts his life. You don't even hear the question asked.'

Institutional structures

The religious political parties (see chapter 4), because of their access to the Government source of power and finance, have become the all-pervasive influence in Israel's religious establishment. They exercise their power through the Ministry for Religious Affairs which, since the beginning of the State, has (apart from a very short break) always been headed by a nominee of the National Religious Party.

The Ministry is there to look after the concerns of all four recognized religious communities: Jewish, Moslem, Druze and Christian. This involves two main functions. The first is providing financial assistance towards the maintenance of religious institutions and activities, and the second is responsibility for the ecclesiastical courts of law through which each community handles its personal status affairs. Jews constitute the

*The last was Chief Rabbi Isaac Herzog who went to Palestine from Eire in 1935. A distinguished scholar, he held a doctorate from the University of London. Israeli right-wing rabbis were in the habit of referring to him as 'Doctor' and not as 'Rabbi'.

large majority of the population of Israel and the Ministry for Religious
Affairs is therefore mainly occupied with their religious affairs. These are
controlled through three interlocking structures, the Chief Rabbis and the
rabbinate, the ecclesiastical courts (Bet Din – plural Batei Din) and a
national system of local religious councils.

The idea of a hierarchy of rabbis is unknown in the Jewish tradition. All
rabbis are equal in status, their prestige deriving solely from the respect
accorded to the individual's learning or piety. The institution of senior, or
chief, rabbis came about in diaspora communities only because of the
practical need to nominate one rabbi, selected for his qualities of personality rather than rabbinic competence, to represent the Jewish community
in its external relations. When the British took over the Mandate for
Palestine after World War I, the Jews living there had no central religious
authority. A representative Sephardi rabbi had been appointed by the
Sultan but he was not recognized by the Ashkenazim.

To remedy this situation, the British convened an assembly of rabbis and
laymen which elected a Rabbinical Council of eight – four Sephardi and
four Ashkenazi rabbis who elected from among themselves one Ashkenazi
Chief Rabbi and one Sephardi Chief Rabbi. The two had equal status. The
Chief Rabbinate Council was recognized by the Government as the sole
authority in matters of Jewish law and, with some modifications, the system
was continued after the State of Israel was established.

While the Chief Rabbinical Council remains the supreme Jewish
religious authority for the Israeli Government, the Chief Rabbis are not
recognized by the Agudat Israel Party, which accepts only the religious
authority of its own Council of Torah Sages. Nor are they recognized by the
even more orthodox groups of the Old Yishuv. Today, Israel continues to
have two Chief Rabbis, but the Council has been changed, consisting now
of ten rabbis elected under a complicated system involving District Rabbis
and local religious councils, designed to ensure fair representation of both
Ashkenazim and Sephardim. All the members of the Rabbinical Council
hold office for five years as do the Chief Rabbis, but this has rarely been
strictly adhered to. Habitual disagreements between the religious
managers have led to frequent election extensions. The precedent was set
when the first Rabbinical Council, which was elected for three years, stayed
on for twelve because the religious groupings were unable to reach agreement on the procedure for new elections.

In 1972, Chief Rabbis Goren and Yosef were elected by an electoral
college of 150 members – all male since women have no role in the public
affairs of orthodoxy. Eighty of them were rabbis, nominees either of the
major communities or of the Minister for Religious Affairs. The other 70
consisted of the Mayors (or their delegates) of the twelve largest local
authorities, and lay representatives of local religious councils.

The major cities – Tel Aviv, Jerusalem, Haifa and Beersheba – each have
two local Chief Rabbis (Sephardi and Ashkenazi), while the smaller towns
have one Chief Rabbi only. The other categories of rabbis in the system are
the District Rabbis or local rabbis, and the rabbi responsible for the
supervision of kosher food. Appointments of District rabbis are made by the

local religious councils and require the approval of the Chief Rabbinate; their salaries are paid by the local religious council out of funds supplied by the Ministry.

The second element in the religious institutional structure is the Ecclesiastical Courts, the Batei Din; in 1979 there were 24 of them throughout the country, including 8 in Tel Aviv and 3 in Jerusalem. Each Bet Din consists of three rabbinical judges called Dayanim (singular Dayan) and its jurisdiction is, for all practical purposes, limited to adjudicating on questions of marriage and divorce. An appeal from a Bet Din lies to the Rabbinic Court of Appeal, the Supreme Bet Din* which is headed by the two national Chief Rabbis.

Dayanim are formally appointed by the President on the recommendation of an appointments committee and with the approval of both Chief Rabbis. This requirement has presented problems in recent years when the two Chief Rabbis have been at loggerheads. In 1979, twenty vacancies on the rabbinic bench were unfilled because the Chief Rabbis refused to approve each other's nominations. The new Minister for Religious Affairs, Aharon Abuhatzera, taking an overdue strong line which previous Ministers had shirked, asked each Rabbi for his list, made his selection and *ordered* both Chief Rabbis to sign. Awed by such uncharacteristic forcefulness, they complied.

Before being considered by the appointments committee, the prospective Dayan, who must be an ordained rabbi, is required to pass written and oral examinations conducted under the auspices of the Chief Rabbinate. Most of the candidates are practising rabbis, but some have come directly from Yeshivot. The posts are much sought after, for they are life tenures, pensionable at the age of 70 and with the same salary scales as civil judges.

Local religious councils, a system originally instituted under the British Mandate, complete the religious institutional structure. They exist side by side with the secular local government institutions and act for the Ministry for Religious Affairs. The Minister appoints 45 per cent of the members of each local religious council, the local authority a further 45 per cent and the local rabbinate 10 per cent. The result of this system is that they are totally under the influence of the National Religious Party. Each religious council prepares its own annual budget which has to be approved by the local authority. One-third of it comes from the Ministry, an agreed amount (negotiated by the local coalition) from the local authority, and the remainder from fees received for such services as the supervision of kosher catering establishments.

The sums involved are substantial. In 1979, the total Ministry grant to all religious councils amounted to some $8 million, which means that their overall expenditure was about $24 million. But, despite the size of the budget, there is less difficulty in obtaining the approval of the municipality than might be thought because it has usually already been bargained for by the NRP in the coalition agreement setting up the local authority. As on the

* In Jewish law, the judgment of a Bet Din is final. A rabbinic Court of Appeal exists only in Israel because the British Mandatory Government, on grounds of natural justice, insisted on it.

national level, proportional representation at local elections produces coalitions, and the NRP, as the price of its participation, calls for various undertakings, one of them being concerned with the amount of money to be paid to the religious council.

The turbulent priests

A lofty, impressively domed building on one of Jerusalem's main boulevards bears the inscription (in commendably small letters) 'Hechal Shlomo. The Seat of the Chief Rabbinate of Israel'. On the side wall of what was originally the main entrance, an engraved panel records that this centre 'erected to the glory of God and His Holy Torah was dedicated to the memory of the late Shlomo and Necha Sarah Wolfson by the Wolfson family, London, England.'

What was formerly the spacious, marble entrance hall is now a permanent synagogue replacing the original beautiful Italian sanctuary. That became too small to hold all the residents and visitors who flocked to it because, when opened in 1958, it was that rare phenomenon – an orthodox Jerusalem synagogue where decorum prevailed. Israel's orthodox synagogues continued the tradition of the intimate houses of worship of East European Jewry, which were notable for their total informality. Worshippers – possibly that is not the aptest of descriptions – attended as much to talk with their friends as to communicate with their Maker, with the result that the hubbub would frequently blot out the recital of the prayers. Because of the English atmosphere created by its ex-Mancunian executive, Maurice Jaffe, the Hechal Shlomo Synagogue, with its decorum and melodious cantor, became an attraction.

The building houses the Chief Rabbinate – another instance of the interlocking of private benefactions and Government services – and is also the seat of the Supreme Rabbinical Court, which hears appeals from the local religious courts.

In creating the two-headed Chief Rabbinate, Sir Herbert Samuel, who was the British High Commissioner at the time, bequeathed a baneful legacy. What else could have been expected by appointing two religious leaders possessing equal authority and standing? In the absence of a single decisive voice, friction inevitably developed between the two equals, and warring Chief Rabbis have become a permanent feature of Israel's religious life. It hardly affects the Israeli man in the street, but the continuation of this strife over a long period has damaged the morale of Israel's rabbis and has brought them and the religion they profess into ridicule or disrepute.

Differences arise between the two Chief Rabbis not only because they are predictable between two people of equal authority, but also because the two men come from totally different backgrounds, the one being Ashkenazi and the other Sephardi. During the many centuries of separate development, the Sephardim in the backward countries of North Africa and the Middle East and the Ashkenazim in Europe created very different life styles. Their rituals vary and their intellectual approach to Judaism follows different lines. In addition their rabbis, in interpreting and applying Jewish law, have often reached different conclusions influenced by the widely different conditions of life between the two geographical areas. Personality clashes have added to the disagreements, and never have they been greater than between the present incumbents, Shlom Goren, the Ashkenazi Chief Rabbi of Israel, and Ovadia Yosef, his Sephardi analogue.

Chief Rabbi Yosef was born in Baghdad in 1921 and his career followed the traditional, unspectacular path. He was brought to Jerusalem at the age of 5, showed ability in Talmudic studies and received rabbinical ordination at the age of 20. Soon afterwards he took up a rabbinical appointment in Egypt but returned to Israel to become a Dayan of Jerusalem's Rabbinical Court. His progress continued with his election as Sephardi Chief Rabbi of Tel Aviv in 1968 and then as Rishon L'Zion (First in Zion, the official title of the Sephardi Chief Rabbi of Israel) in 1972. His reputation for mildness and humility encouraged many to hope that Chief Rabbi Yosef would be successful in achieving an amicable relationship with his Ashkenazi counterpart, particularly as they had cooperated for sixteen months as the two Chief Rabbis of Tel Aviv. However, it took no more than a few days for these hopes to be dashed.

Immediately after the Chief Rabbinate elections in October 1972, Goren announced, with characteristic ebullience, a grandiose plan to convene an assembly of all the Chief Rabbis of the world, to try to solve 'world wide Jewish problems'. The assembly was to be followed by the establishment of a world rabbinical committee as a permanent organization. Within days, Yosef issued a statement that he was 'puzzled' by Goren's failure to consult him about these proposals. 'He is not the sole Chief Rabbi. I would have thought that for something out of the ordinary like this, he would have seen fit to consult his colleague.'

The first brush set the pattern which the passage of the years has intensified. The two Chief Rabbis have barely been on speaking terms, and have avoided meeting each other as far as possible even when it meant paralyzing the machinery of the religious establishment. If one Chief Rabbi made a pronouncement, the other, almost totally irrespective of the merits of the issue, pronounced the converse. When a mother in Britain gave birth to a baby after a womb implant, Yosef's comment that it was permissible according to Jewish law was published first. Immediately, Goren declared it to be forbidden, although many of his rabbinic colleagues were of the opinion that, had it not been for Yosef's earlier ruling, Goren would have approved of it as being consistent with his general approach to these problems.

Goren sanctions a new Army prayer book, Yosef rejects it. Goren says that it is contrary to Jewish law to relinquish territory included in the biblical promise to the Children of Israel; Yosef says that according to Jewish law, the preservation of life through peace was a higher priority than territory. When Goren ruled that it was permissible to pick and eat capers growing on the Western Wall, Yosef said that it was not.

Everyone was aware of the growing hostility and divisions between the two religious heads, but new elections, which might resolve the issue were repeatedly delayed in the absence of any consensus about changes in the electoral law. A new Chief Rabbinical Law passed in 1980 now provides that the two Chief Rabbis will be elected for a ten-year term (instead of the present five), after which they will not be eligible for re-election. To avoid clashes, their functions will be divided. One will be the acting Chief Rabbi of Israel and the other President of the Supreme Rabbinic Court, and they will alternate in the posts. Rabbis Goren and Yosef will continue in office until the first election under the new dispensation, scheduled to be held not later than 15 March 1983, but neither will be a candidate. Given the rate of postponement of rabbinical election dates in the past, there can be no certainty about the new one. Nor, given the history of these offices, is it certain that the new conditions will ensure a better relationship between these two equal, but hitherto very separate, authorities.

Chief Rabbi Shlomo Goren

The Ashkenazi Chief Rabbi is the most dynamic and controversial figure in Israel's religious establishment. His short, stocky figure is dominated by an oversized bushy beard, which seemingly reaches halfway down his body. He is a man of boundless energy and enthusiasm, though both have become subdued by the cares and trials of his present office. He smiles rarely, but when he does, his eyes brighten as his features soften. Except at times of weariness, he speaks rapidly and with vigour.

Goren regards himself as a modern orthodox Jew, but he accepts modern scholarship solely to confirm his orthodox convictions. He has the strength of his rigidity. To him, the halacha, the rabbinic corpus of law which regulates the Jewish way of life, is divinely ordained and therefore unchangeable. But he is a humane man and will use every device of legal interpretation to avoid harsh consequences from the application of the law.

Typical of his approach was his role in the Langer case. According to the halacha, children born to a married woman and a man other than her husband, known as 'mamzerim' (singular, mamzer), may only marry another mamzer or a proselyte. In 1971, a brother and sister, Chanoch and Miriam Langer, both serving in the IDF, had met partners they wanted to marry. Their mother had at one time been married to a Polish gentile who had converted to Judaism, but she left him when she fell in love with a Jew by birth named Langer, with whom she emigrated to Israel. Only after she had given birth to Chanoch and Miram did she obtain a divorce from her first husband. When this history became known, the rabbis refused to permit the marriage of the children on the ground that they were mamzerim.

The case aroused a public storm. Moshe Dayan, then Defence Minister, outraged by the situation, called for the introduction of civil marriage – anathema to the orthodox – and he was supported by many Labour and Liberal Members of the Knesset. The then Ashkenazi Chief Rabbi resisted all appeals to reverse the decision of his rabbinical colleagues. 'The feeling of compassion', he said, 'must not permit the citadel of Judaism to be shaken.' That statement did not end the controversy, and feelings became so intense that the much dreaded 'kulturkampf', a confrontation between religious and non-religious Israelis, seemed about to break out.

Controversy over the issue continued to simmer until Goren became Chief Rabbi one year later. As Chief Rabbi of the IDF he had been quoted earlier as saying that 'those who fought and died for Israel should not be debarred from the religious community if the halacha can be bent to accommodate them'. He was as good as his word. With the speed, surprise and precision which were the hallmarks of the Israeli army, Goren convened a 'drum-head' Bet Din which, after less than one hour's deliberation, ruled that the first marriage had been invalid, since the husband's conversion to Judaism had been 'questionable'. Mrs Langer was not, therefore, a married woman when the children were born and they were, consequently, not mamzerim. In a second preemptive strike, Goren himself participated the same day in the double wedding of the Langers, with Moshe Dayan present as one of the guests.

The Chief Rabbi was born in Poland in 1917 and brought to Palestine at the age of 8. His brisk and decisive method of handling affairs is the result of his long service as Chief Rabbi of the IDF, and he was reputed to have been somewhat bewildered to find, on entering civilian life, that his orders were not carried out as rapidly or as efficiently as those he had given in the army. Appointed to his IDF office when the state began in 1948, he held it for no less than 23 years. With practically no experience of the civilian rabbinate but with the support of the National Religious Party and Moshe Dayan, he became first, Ashkenazi Chief Rabbi of Tel Aviv and, sixteen months later, Ashkenazi Chief Rabbi of Israel.

He rose to the rank of Major General in the IDF and achieved the respect of his peers by his fearlessness in risking his own life to retrieve bodies from the battlefield; he saw it as his duty to ensure that the dead received a Jewish burial. He became a paratrooper and proudly wore the wings on his battledress. That came about as the result of his long campaign to persuade the paras to observe the Sabbath and the dietary laws, as did all other units of the Israel Defence Forces. But this elite company trained seven days a week, their kitchens were not kosher and they had no synagogue. All Goren's remonstrances met with the response that, since there were no religious paratroopers, these facilities were unnecessary. When Arik Sharon took command of the unit, Goren lost no time in repeating his request. Sharon's reply was that, when the first religious para arrived, it would all be done. Goren personally volunteered and, after his first jump, Sharon kept the promise.

Goren played a key role in keeping religious politics out of the army. When compulsory military service was introduced in May 1948, the religious parties asked for separate units to be created for the orthodox conscripts so that they could maintain their religious obligations. Goren thought it would be disastrous were the army to be divided in this way. What kind of national unity could be created if the religious personnel were to eat in one mess and the non-religious in another? With his backing, Ben-Gurion directed that only kosher food was to be supplied throughout the forces, that Saturday was to be the rest-day and that synagogues were to be available for all fighting units. That situation still prevails.

The capture of the Old City of Jerusalem in June 1967 was for Goren an event of the greatest drama and excitement – almost a messianic portent. He hurried to the surviving Western Wall of the ancient Temple and sounded a ringing blast on a ram's horn, a feature of the Temple service at the Jewish New Year, as a demonstration of deliverance. In the ensuing years, he became a profound believer in Israel's duty to retain the biblical lands taken in the Six Day War and has declared that, according to Jewish law, it is forbidden to relinquish them.

He is keenly aware of the problems of relating the ancient faith to the necessities of a modern state, but believes it can be done by a process of re-interpretation within the existing framework of Jewish law. He opposed the idea of reviving the Sanhedrin of rabbis, which had last existed as a legislative authority on Jewish religious law in the fourteenth century. Goren does not believe that such a body today would be able to change any laws or dogmas but, given the present climate of orthodoxy, would only issue further prohibitions. In any case, no doubt recalling his own abortive attempt to set up a world council of Chief Rabbis, he is doubtful whether there would be any agreement among leading rabbis as to the composition of a Sanhedrin. 'It would be harder to bring about than to bring the Messiah,' he has concluded.

For Goren, the main religious problem in Israel today is the widening gap between the religious and non-religious Jews, exacerbated by the increase of extremism. He would like to strengthen middle-of-the-road Judaism, a prescription viewed with great suspicion by the diehards. Despite his own strict orthodoxy (he will not shake hands with a woman, in obedience to the laws of separation during the menstrual period), he is looked on as a dangerous radical by the heads of the Yeshivot – the spiritual leaders of the ultra-orthodox – and they have made his tenure of office difficult and unhappy.

As a result, Goren is a sadder man than during his ebullient years in the IDF. He can still wax rapturously enthusiastic, but the occasions have become rarer and he is increasingly thinking of returning to the less exposed and less political world of study and writing. Because of the various pressures on the Begin Government, the introduction of the new Chief Rabbinate laws has been repeatedly delayed, so Goren soldiers on, still pugnacious, at loggerheads with his Sephardi colleague, resentful at the very idea of standing for re-election ('The Archbishop of Canterbury doesn't, the Pope doesn't'). Whatever assessment may eventually be made of his Chief Rabbinate, Goren's abiding monument in Israel will be the pattern he established for religion in the forces, a positive contribution both to his nation and to his faith.

Who is a Jew?

In the State of Israel, this seemingly innocent question has given rise to a running political, legal and religious controversy which at times exploded into major government crises. At issue are two factors of considerable political importance. The first is the Law of Return, enacted in 1950, to demonstrate Israel's role as the home of the Jewish people. This law, in conjunction with a later Nationality Law, gives every Jew the right to 'return' to Israel and there acquire instant automatic citizenship. Other immigrants go through the process of naturalization. In applying this law, a definition of a Jew had to be given.

The second factor relates to personal status. The Ministry of the Interior maintains a national register which includes religion, and the religious authorities have access to it to ascertain whether a couple seeking to marry (the ceremony must be a religious one since there is no civil marriage) are Jews. A Jew had also to be defined for the purpose of entry in this register.

The religious authorities insist that only a person regarded as a Jew under orthodox Jewish law, the halacha, should be accepted as one. The halacha lays down that a Jew is a person born to a Jewish mother or one converted to Judaism by a recognized orthodox authority. Reform Judaism will accept as a Jew the child of a Jewish father and a non-Jewish mother, while Conservative and Reform Judaism's conversion procedures are not acceptable to the orthodox. If people in either of these categories were to be registered as Jews, they could marry an orthodox Jew and, apart from the breach of the halacha involved, all sorts of personal status problems could be created for the child of such a marriage.

Before statehood, the matter had not been serious, because individual problems had, on the whole, been dealt with compassionately and flexibly by orthodox rabbis in the diaspora. In Israel, however, the most rigid and uncompromising elements in orthodoxy have taken command, placing the Israel Government in a serious quandary. It was reluctant to offend the orthodox, yet the interests of the new State could best be served by a more flexible approach which, in particular, did not question the Jewishness of large numbers of Reform and Conservative Jews, most of them in the United States. The majority were committed supporters of Israel and some of them actual or potential immigrants.

Controversy was compounded into political crisis because of a threat by the religious parties to leave the Government – thus bringing about its fall – if a definition of a Jew not acceptable to them were adopted. On the registration question, the issue also came into the political arena, because the Ministry of the Interior, which maintains the national register, has traditionally been headed by a member of the National Religious Party, who has applied religious, rather than national, criteria for registration.

The Supreme Court was brought into this minefield in 1962 over the case of Brother Daniel. This Carmelite monk, who was born a Jew in Poland, embraced Christianity during World War II. He joined the Carmelites because he felt deeply drawn to the Holy Land where they maintained a centre. Eventually he achieved his desire, arriving in Israel in 1958 and applying for citizenship under the Law of Return and for registration as a Jew. He claimed that he was a Jew in accordance with strict orthodox Jewish law, since he had been born of a Jewish mother, and also that his conversion to Catholicism was irrelevant according to rabbinic doctrine.

The decision of the Court that Brother Daniel was not a Jew (although he could remain in the country and go through the normal naturalization procedure) was significant, because it offered a secular answer and not one based on Jewish religious law, under which Brother Daniel's submission was in all probability correct. The Supreme Court was giving notice that it did not consider itself bound by orthodox Jewish law.

Continued agitation both in Israel and among Jewish communities overseas, together with another decision by the Supreme Court in 1968 in a case involving the Jewishness of the children of a mixed marriage, finally induced the Cabinet gingerly to grasp the nettle. It asked the Knesset to approve an enactment that, for the purpose of the Law of Return, the word Jew 'means a person born to a Jewish mother, or who has been converted to Judaism and is not a member of another religion'. This led to a vigorous national debate, culminating in two days of discussion in the Knesset, and ended with the passage of the legislation.

The significance of the new definition lay less in the words used than in those omitted. The NRP and other religious parties were pressing for the words 'in accordance with the halacha' to be added after 'converted to Judaism'. This would have meant that Reform, and possibly, also Conservative converts would not have been recognized as Jews in Israel. But they reluctantly accepted the final text because Golda Meir, then Prime Minister, was adamant.

But that has not been the end of the matter. Recurrent crises and threats of crisis have continued over the issue of conversion, and the orthodox have never abandoned their intention to change the law to restrict recognition only to their converts. They seemed to be on the brink of success when, as the price for their support of his new Government, the two main religious parties persuaded Begin to promise in the written coalition agreement (see Chapter 4) to 'make every endeavour to mobilize a parliamentary majority' for two private Bills to be tabled by the religious parties. One would declare that conversion, for the purposes of the Law of Return, would be recognized only if it had been carried out according to the halacha, and the other that the official Israeli rabbinate would be the only body to determine the validity of conversions performed abroad. Almost three years later, this legislation had not yet been proposed, but more will certainly be heard of it, because the principles involved are a major concern of orthodoxy and because the Israeli clericalist politicians will fight grimly to protect their religious monopoly in Israel.

The Sabbath

The day of rest, the Sabbath, occupies a unique place in Judaism. It dates from the biblical account of the Creation, 'And the Lord blessed the Sabbath day and sanctified it, for on that day he rested from all the work he had done.' The Sabbath is the only day ordained in the Ten Commandments, 'Remember the Sabbath day to keep it holy,' and the Jewish people, throughout their history, have indeed treasured this day as one of rest, reflection, study and domestic felicity. It was a cornerstone of the faith, and the statement by the philosopher of Zionism, Achad Ha'am: 'More than

Israel has kept the Sabbath, the Sabbath has kept Israel,' has become accepted as a truism by all Jews whether religious or not.

Work of any kind is forbidden on the Sabbath. The bible itself attempts no definition of what constitutes work, and makes only two specific prohibitions. But, over the course of centuries of rabbinic legislation, a vast body of detailed regulations has grown up, specifying what may not be done. On the Sabbath, an observant Jew is not permitted to pursue his normal occupation, use money, travel, prepare food, write, or carry any object outside his house. He may not light a fire (or turn on electricity), play a musical instrument or even handle an object whose normal use is forbidden on the Sabbath. Yet it should not be thought this accumulation of prohibitions was a burden to the religious Jew. They created the framework within which he could experience spiritual reinvigoration and, in the diaspora, any intolerable consequences of strict observance of the Sabbath laws could be mitigated by employing a gentile, a 'shabbos goy', to perform essential tasks forbidden to him, like lighting fires on a cold day.

The problem of Sabbath observance was the first religious issue which faced the new State. For the first time for nearly 2,000 years, Jews now had the responsibility to provide essential services for themselves, as well as to defend their country. Water, power, and health services had to be available on the Sabbath; the security services could not rest. The religious parties could not raise any objection to the principle that this work had to be performed by Jews – they only insisted that it should not be performed by orthodox Jews. In the police force, for example, the small number of orthodox Jews in the service are permitted to take the day off, and Sabbath exemption for orthodox Jews employed in essential services in the private and public sectors alike has become the general and accepted rule.

Many orthodox Jews are uncomfortable about this situation. One of them, Professor Isaiah Leibowitz, a scientist at the Hebrew University and an unconventional orthodox Jew, has made a scathing comment: 'Orthodoxy', he has written, 'has knowingly given up the idea of a Sabbath for the State and people in favour of a Sabbath for a section of Sabbath observers within a society of Sabbath violators who, by their work, provide for the needs of the sect. Orthodox Jews do not deprive themselves of water or electricity on the Sabbath, provided that other Jews operate them on the Sabbath. Orthodoxy is interested in the operation of a police force on the Sabbath, provided it is other Jews who perform police duties. It is also interested in the existence of a Jewish merchant marine, provided other Jews serve as sailors. Orthodoxy has become reconciled to girls serving in the army, so long as religious girls are exempted.'

By law, the Sabbath is the rest-day for Jews in Israel (non-Jews have the right to their own Sabbath days) and legal authorities regulate the opening of places of business and entertainment on that day. The degree to which they enforce orthodox attitudes depends on the strength of local orthodox opinion and its leverage in the bargaining for local government coalitions. As a result, practices vary. In Bnei Brak, an orthodox township near Tel Aviv, the Sabbath is very strictly observed and a ban is imposed on both private and public transport. In Tel Aviv itself, restaurants are open and private cars mill about, though public transport stops. In Haifa, where orthodoxy has never been strong, both public and private transport are permitted and many places of business and recreation are open.

Jewish employees are guaranteed their Sabbath rest-day by a 1951 law which also empowers the Minister of Labour to give exemption from this provision in cases where the public interest makes Sabbath work essential. But, at orthodox insistence, a general permit for exemption can only be given by a Ministerial committee which includes the Minister for Religious Affairs.

One of the rulings of this committee was that El Al aircraft are not permitted to land or take off on the Sabbath, with the exception of the so-called 'pilgrims' flights' whose passengers are presumed to be all gentile. However, other carriers may land at Israel's airports and use the services provided by Jewish personnel, for this is accepted as an essential task in the national interest. Newspapers do not appear on the Sabbath, but radio and television function; telegrams are not delivered and no trains run, but the telephones work.

The control of Sabbath observance in hotels rests with the official rabbinate. Left to their own devices, most of the hotels would be ready to provide all normal services on Saturdays, but they have not been left to their own devices. Most of the Jewish-owned or Jewish-patronized hotels regard it as commercially necessary to serve kosher food, certified as such by the rabbis, so what the rabbis have done is to demand some degree of Sabbath observance as a condition for granting their certificate. An attempt was made in the Knesset in 1966 to prohibit the rabbinate from imposing such conditions, but the opposition of religious MKs effectively killed the proposal. Today, the conditions imposed by local rabbis who grant certificates to kosher hotels vary. Some hotels are required not to admit new guests on the Sabbath, or to refuse monetary payment on that day and, usually to prohibit writing and smoking in public rooms.

On the whole, the Israeli public appear to accept the orthodox contention that, in the public domain, Sabbath observance should be enforced by law. In some particular instances, conflicts have been avoided by a certain amount of compromise on the part of the religious authorities – particularly when they are reasonably confident that the case will not become public property and open them to attacks by their own zealots.

Religious revival – Yeshivot old and new

The capture of Adolf Eichmann by Israel's Secret Service and his trial in Jerusalem in 1961 were portentous events in Israel's history. Eichmann was the Nazi SS officer with responsibility for implementing Hitler's 'Final Solution', and his trial made a profound impact on every generation of Israelis. As evidence continued to be presented, remorselessly, week after week, the older generation recalled the Holocaust and fortified their determination that, in Israel, the Jewish people would survive. Younger Israelis, it soon became apparent, knew little of these events or of modern Jewish history generally. Ben-Gurion, then Prime Minister, was shocked at their ignorance. He decided that steps had to be taken to make young Israelis aware of the history of their people, their roots, if for no other reason than to teach them the causes and ideals of the Jewish State. He initiated courses of instruction in the non-religious state schools on 'Jewish Consciousness', which included Jewish history and laid emphasis on the nationalistic aspects of Judaism. It turned out to be a pallid and vague substitute, however, incapable of arousing anything like the depth of feeling which religion could inspire. The courses made little impact, except to prepare the way for the reaction to the shock of the Six Day War and the exhilaration of the capture of the Old City of Jerusalem.

Both these events drew Israelis towards their Jewishness. In the long drawn-out prelude to the war, Israelis had felt themselves isolated as never before. The guarantors of their security, the United States, Britain and France, all showed themselves irresolute; the United Nations proved itself to be powerless. Only their co-religionists in the diaspora had given them unqualified support. This identification with the Jewish world acquired a further dimension through the Israeli presence at the Temple Mount, the site of Abraham's trial by ordeal and of the holy Temple. It reunited Israel with its spiritual past.

Young secularists who had fought in the war felt for the first time that they were Jews as well as Israelis; they all flocked to the Western Wall for inspiration. To some, all that emerged was a kind of religious sentimentality, a nostalgic affection for the traditions and rituals they no longer observed, but remembered from the homes of their parents or grandparents. But it also encouraged others, to whom the salvation of Israel after the threat of another Holocaust appeared as a supernatural event, to return to the Jewish faith. Some described this phenomenon as a religious revival. This was probably an overstatement, but 1967 was undoubtedly something of a climacteric in Israel's spiritual odyssey.

The religious establishment, which had completely equated religion with ritual, was incapable of responding or offering anything which even sounded like religious or spiritual inspiration. The Yeshivot, the traditional source of Jewish learning, were no less uncomprehending. That tight little world of some five hundred schools exercises a dominating influence in orthodox Judaism. Fundamentalist in their approach, they isolate themselves and their families from the modern world, for fear of contamination by it. They are enabled to exist and thrive through the material support of religious believers and through the massive financial support of the State, to which the Yeshiva world, as it is called, is at best only semi-attached.

Money comes through the Ministry for Religious Affairs which, in 1979, provided each institution with a grant of approximately $320 for each student. Every Yeshiva requesting this aid sends a list of its students to the Ministry, where some checks are made. In 1979, 47,000 Yeshiva students were approved for grants, totalling $15 million. Additionally, in the same year, Yeshivot received from the Ministry some $10 million in contributions and grants for development. Full-time married students receive monthly welfare stipends and supplementary benefits like rent subsidies and health fund contributions. As nearly all the Yeshivot are backed by the

NRP or Aguda, successive Governments have paid these sums as the price of political support or the avoidance of religious criticism. The financial contribution from the Israel Government to the Yeshivot has been increasing, in real terms, over the years and never more so than under the Begin regime.

Treasured by the religious right wing as citadels of Jewish learning and fortresses of tradition, the Yeshiva world with its own sub-culture has placed the real world out of bounds and, by so doing, has had little to say to the non-orthodox seekers after Judaism in the aftermath of 1967.

An attempt to fill this gap was the creation of a number of new Yeshivot geared to the needs of those who were searching for a religious faith but lacked even the minimum basic knowledge. The philosophy, standards of learning, and the intensive curriculum of the old Yeshiva world made little or no appeal to this new type of prospective student. In the main, they were young Jews from the West who came to Israel in the swell of emotion after the Six Day War to identify themselves with their people. The Yeshivot for Ba'alei T'shuva (penitents) were launched by an American born Rabbi, Mordechai Goldstein, who in 1967, with the approval of the Ministry for Religious Affairs, occupied a derelict building on Mount Zion for his novel institution.

Then in his thirties, Rabbi Goldstein was a mixture of religious mystic, evangelist and huckster. He was attracted to Mount Zion because legend foretells that it is the spot where the messianic age will be inaugurated, and he saw the appeal that particular location would make to the, mainly American, young students then arriving in Israel. He called it the 'Diaspora Yeshiva on Mount Zion' and began to recruit his students by approaching likely looking prospects at places like the Western Wall or the bus station. Many of them were in the process of 'finding themselves', while others were drop-outs, hippies, pot-smokers to whom the idea of living at a Yeshiva was as exotic as a sojourn with a guru in India. It was a time when young America was intent on 'doing its own thing', the time of the Vietnam draft from which 'divinity students' were exempted.

Today some fifteen of these institutions exist and their total compliment at a given moment is likely to be about 2,000, a fluctuating figure which includes transients. All the rabbis who started these Yeshivot and lead them are strong personalities; yet, although the cult of personality is not entirely absent, they bear little similarity to the cult leaders in America or the Far East, for the rabbis are themselves subject to the discipline of Jewish law. Each Yeshiva has an individual flavour, even to the style of dress. Some are formal and dignified, one is entirely blue-jeaned, while a third insists on the ubiquitous Mea Shearim black. They are all places of learning, but on a much lower level than the traditional Yeshivot and emphasising personal piety and living a good life rather than the grind of scholarship.

Only one of the new Yeshivot concentrates on Talmud, the main subject of study of all the old ones – that led by Rabbi Chaim Brovender, a graduate of New York's Yeshiva University, who has a Ph.D. in linguistics. He excludes students he does not regard as serious, and prefers Yale and Harvard men. Another, the Jerusalem Academy of Jewish Studies, has a strong English flavour, emanating from its founder and principal, Rabbi Baruch Horovitz, formerly of Manchester. It conducts its courses in Russian, Spanish, English and French as well as Hebrew.

All these Yeshivot offer one-year courses and, for beginners, the main subjects are bible and prayers. A few use psychological counselling, while others have adopted encounter techniques. They all clamp down now on pot-smoking, if for no other reason than its effect on fund-raising. Some of the Yeshivot have instituted four- to six-weeks cramming courses, and a few have added departments for girls. The goal of all of them is the prevention of assimilation and their means of achieving it is to expose these searching and impressionable young people to a kind of 'instant Judaism' in the hope that something will stick. Most students live in. Women are separately accommodated in apartments for 4 to 6, while boys who are considered unsuitable to live in the Yeshiva, because they either do not observe the dietary laws or may have live-in girl friends, are also housed in apartments.

Most of the students move on after a year – back to their secular education or to work. But before they leave, many of the Yeshivot try to marry them off to orthodox girls in an effort to ensure that they will maintain orthodox homes. One of the distinctions between the Yeshivot and the cults is that the former prefer the students not to stay on for too long; their aim is to process them into good Jews and then send them out. One rabbi has described these Yeshivot as 'religious supermarkets'.

The movement initially received adverse publicity in Israel; but when it reached its first decade, attitudes began to change. It gained respectability and prestige when Uri Zohar, an admired television celebrity and no 'kook', gave up the world of entertainment and entered one of the new Yeshivot as full-time student. That was further enhanced when the sons of two popular non-religious generals joined. Even Yitzhak Rabin, under the influence of Zohar, was toying with the notion of entering one of them after his fall from power, but abandoned the idea after press publicity.

All these Yeshivot receive the same *per capita* student grants from the Ministry for Religious Affairs as the established institutions. They also receive support from the Ministry of Immigration and Absorption, since about 60 per cent of the students are American. Most ask the students for fees, but will allow them to stay even without payment. Their major source of revenue, however, is private benefactors, and more than half of the new Yeshivot employ one or more rabbis who work exclusively on public relations and fund-raising. The Yeshiva principals or fund-raisers make regular, generally annual, visits to the United States and other Jewish communities to solicit contributions.

The movement has now settled down and shows signs of growth, which seems to be coming more through the creation of additional small Yeshivot than through the expansion of those which already exist, for the principals fear loss of control if they grow too large. No studies have been made to ascertain what effect these institutions have had on the thousands who have passed through them, but if the Yeshivot for penitents do exercise any long-term influence, it is less likely to affect Israel than the American Jewish community to which most of the students return.

The non-conformists

Orthodoxy is the only officially recognized form of the Jewish religion in Israel, but, over the past two centuries, Jewish communities in different parts of the world have created different religious trends. One of them, the Reform movement, was originally hostile to Zionism and took little part in the creation of the Jewish State, while Conservative Judaism only became a major force in American Jewry after the Zionist movement had settled into its hidebound party structure. The only organized religious force involved in the formative period of the Zionist movement and, subsequently, in the State of Israel, was therefore orthodoxy.

So far it has retained its religious monopoly in Israel. Reform and Conservative Jews are recognized, accepted and even welcomed as individuals, but the movements to which they belong are anathema to orthodoxy and have been given no kind of recognition as legitimate trends in Judaism.

This situation has been a permanent embarrassment to successive Israeli Governments. Between them, the Conservative and Reform movements account for the great majority of religiously affiliated American Jews, and their political and financial support has been invaluable for Israel. But when they complained of discrimination against their brands of Judaism in Israel, Ben-Gurion and Golda Meir could only tell them that their movements would be accepted in Israel if enough of their members settled in the Jewish State.

But the reception afforded to those who did come offered little hope of even the minimum of religious pluralism. The first significant immigration of Reform Jews was from Germany, the birthplace of Reform Judaism, in the years following Hitler's rise to power in 1933. Among them were several Reform rabbis and one of them founded the first Reform synagogue in Haifa in 1935. Two years later, another was established in Jerusalem. Conservative Judaism also arrived in Israel at the same period and its first congregation was founded in Jerusalem in 1937. But all these synagogues were small, maintained a low profile, attracted little attention and made no claims on the public purse.

Hebrew Union College (HUC) in Cincinnati, Ohio, is the central theological seminary for the Reform rabbinate in the United States. Its President in the early years of Israel's statehood was Nelson Glueck, a Zionist and archaeologist. He was eager to combine both interests by establishing an HUC school of archaeology in Jerusalem and, inspired by his enthusiasm, the Israeli Government contributed a plot of land in a central area of the city. On this site, HUC planned to build its school and, attached to it, a chapel for students and visitors.

The orthodox rabbis and the religious political parties were aghast. They saw this chapel as the thin end of the wedge. It would, they were convinced, undoubtedly be followed by more non-orthodox synagogues, would encourage demands for reform and would constitute a 'moving-staircase' (as one rabbi described it) from Judaism to Christianity. The Reform movement was assailed as a danger to Judaism and the State, the controversy, which continued from 1955 to 1963 when the school was opened, provoking a heated debate on the place of non-orthodox Judaism in Israel.

The then Sephardi Chief Rabbi, Itzhak Nissim, was unambiguous. 'Freedom of religion,' he declared, 'is intended for members of all religions, including the minorities, to enable them to pursue their own faith [but] it is not intended to achieve the opposite objective with the result that the dominant religion in the state, Judaism, be jeopardized and torn asunder . . . Reform is not a religion.' In an attempt to soften this approach, which was not always easy for Israel's politicians to explain to their American friends, it was later suggested that if Reform and Conservative Judaism were to accept the status of religions other than Judaism, they would be entitled to the same recognition and state aid as was accorded to Christianity and Islam. The offer was not accepted.

The non-conformists grew slowly, despite regular attempts by the orthodox to obstruct their progress. In 1962, a small Reform congregation near Tel Aviv, which had been started by some resident ex-Americans, among them Meyer Levin, the distinguished novelist, arranged to use a hotel for their New Year service. A few days before the event, the hotel manager withdrew the facility. The local religious council, he explained, had threatened to cancel his kosher food certificate, which would drastically have affected his business. The congregation arranged for the use of a municipal building, but that too was withdrawn under pressure from local rabbis. Eventually High Court proceedings were taken which ended in a victory for the reformers.

Other similar and well-publicized attempts at obstruction eventually aroused public opinion and the press, hostile to both the form and substance of the orthodox attitude, which on balance seems to have aided the non-orthodox groups by attracting to them publicity and sympathy. Important sections of diaspora Jewry also took up the cause and made known to the Government their view that this harassment was a violation of religious freedom. Slowly, a better climate developed. Some State help began to be given, quietly, to non-orthodox congregations for the building of places of worship and for the acquisition of religious appurtenances. With a little political pressure, the Ministry for Religious Affairs gave a grant of $35,000 towards the building of a Conservative synagogue in the French Hill district of Jerusalem. Elsewhere land was contributed for new non-conformist places of worship. But everything was given ex gratia and not as of right.

By 1979, there were 13 synagogues affiliated to the (Reform) Israel Movement for Progressive Judaism and 28 constituent synagogues of the (Conservative) United Synagogue of Israel. None of them received the same Government aid as orthodox synagogues and their rabbis were not recognized for the performance of marriage or any other religious functions recognized by law.

Non-orthodoxy in action

The Hebrew Union College School of Archaeology is a small complex of rectangular white marble buildings close to the King David Hotel in Jerusalem. Its controversial chapel is a large, almost square room, simple and uncluttered. The walls of cement blocks are pale grey, the floor is of beige marble, and the long wicker-work pews add an ingredient of openness to the total effect of coolness and light. The ceiling of slatted wood completes a subdued colour scheme of beige, brown and grey.

On Saturday mornings, a congregation of about one hundred comfortably fills the chapel. Israel's relaxed attitude to punctuality appears to have influenced the usually precise Reform movement, for the service sometimes starts late. The majority of the congregation are young American men and women, informally dressed in jeans or shorts, who are augmented by a sprinkling of older American tourists. Most males wear kipot and prayer shawls and some of the girls wear them too, which is not the case in orthodox synagogues. The officiating rabbis are distinguishable from the congregation only because they wear dark suits, shirts and ties.

One of the innovations of Reform Judaism in the diaspora was that a language understood by the congregants was used for prayer, instead of Hebrew as in orthodox synagogues. In Israel the vernacular is Hebrew, and Reform services, to the discomfiture of the tourists, are conducted in that tongue. However, to help them along, page numbers are given in English and the Hebrew sermon is followed by an abbreviated English version. Only the brevity of the service, its start at the reasonable hour of 10 a.m. (orthodox services begin much earlier and are much longer) and the accompaniment of instrumental music, proclaim it a Reform service.

The instrumental music, a most attractive element of the service, is not provided by the organ customary in American Reform synagogues, because in Israel organs are identified with churches. Instead, the HUC service is mellifluously accompanied by harpsichord and flute. The music tends to be jolly and Chassidic rather than the conventional solemn cadences. Yet, despite the influence of the Israeli environment, the synagogue remains very much an American institution. Its proximity to the King David Hotel has almost turned it into an annexe for the hotel's guests, while the nucleus of worshippers is made up of the very American HUC students.

Dr Ezra Spicehandler heads the HUC activities in Israel. Portly, relaxed and accessible, he is both scholar and administrator. He concedes that some of the attraction of the Reform movement in the diaspora is its convenience, the comprehensibility of its services and the inconsiderable demands it makes on its adherents. None of these, he says, applies in Israel, where reform will become accepted only through belief in its ideology, a difficult task because, so secularized have the non-religious become, that they are unlikely to return to any aspect of the Jewish faith.

He and his colleague, Rabbi Richard Hirsch, who heads the World Union of Progressive Judaism, have laid to rest the image of Reform Judaism as anti-Zionist. The founders of the movement could never have imagined, so strong was their opposition to Zionism, that one day their international headquarters would be located in Jerusalem and that their organization would actually become a constituent of the World Zionist Organization. Today, Israeli emissaries to Reform communities in the United States are paid for by the WZO, and a Reform kibbutz, founded in 1976, and doing well, is a symbol of the movement's commitment to the Jewish State. In 1980 the first Reform Synagogue purpose-built in Israel was opened in Haifa. It is to be a place of experiment, and from the beginning unusual musical instruments were introduced including electric guitars and drums.

The Israeli reformers would like to merge with the faster growing and more popular Conservative group in Israel, with which they have occasionally cooperated for specific purposes. They claim there are no important ideological differences between them and that a combined non-orthodox religious movement could make a greater impact than either of them individually. But the Conservatives have resisted. They feel their own standing might suffer by the association and, in any case, regard the ideological differences as substantial.

The United Synagogue of Israel is an offshoot of the American Conservative movement and an affiliate of the World Council of Synagogues, the movement's international organization. Conservative Judaism developed in the United States as a reaction against the radical changes that had been introduced by the reformers and, in practice, Conservative synagogues differ from Reform in using more Hebrew in the services and in laying greater stress on the dietary laws, the Sabbath and a range of other traditional observances. Theologically, the substantial distinction between them is their attitude to the halacha. To the orthodox it is sacred and unchangeable. Conservative Judaism regards itself as bound by the halacha but is prepared to introduce changes within the principles of rabbinic interpretation, while Reform Judaism rejects the halacha as a binding authority.

Although Conservative synagogues were introduced into Israel at about the same time as those of the Reform, they attracted less hostility. Not only did Conservative Judaism have a far superior record in support of Zionism, but the spiritual leaders of the movement tended to be cautious, avoiding actions or the raising of issues which might draw attention to themselves and antagonize orthodoxy. While this policy has avoided many of the public conflicts in which Reform Judaism has been involved in Israel, it has not gained the Conservatives any greater official recognition.

Most of the 28 Conservative synagogues are led by American rabbis who, in the main, emigrated from the United States to Israel after retirement. Their membership varies between a few score and a few hundred, and is predominantly American, although some of the younger congregations outside the big cities have attracted sizable numbers of Israelis. They nearly all have full-time rabbis, a tribute to their dedication, since the rabbis have to be maintained without the state aid which the official rabbinate receives.

Sometimes, a practical accommodation is reached with the orthodox authorities. In 1973, the Conservatives were able to conduct weddings at their Jerusalem central synagogue by a tacit agreement with the local religious council, which sent along an official rabbi to stand by as the service was conducted by Conservative officiants. But all such informal arrangements are dependent on the goodwill of individuals, and when a new, overzealous Chief Rabbi was appointed in Jerusalem a few years later, the concession was abruptly withdrawn.

The spiritual and organizational headquarters of the Conservatives is a fine old building on a prime corner site in Jerusalem, piquantly facing the Hechal Shlomo, centre of the orthodox rabbinate. An American rabbi, breezy, engaging and efficient, Dr Pesach Schindler, heads an enthusiastic staff, mainly American, in directing a varied programme of religious, cultural and social activities. His budget and those of the constituent synagogues are met by grants from the World Council of Synagogues and other Conservative institutions in the United States, supplemented by local community fund-raising efforts.

Both non-conformist movements claim encouraging prospects for growth, although the actual performance of the Conservatives in congregational development is the more impressive. But they face the same difficulties in a country where Judaism has long been synonymous with orthodoxy and for whose residents the choice has long been all or nothing. But Reform and the Conservatives in Israel set themselves similar aims: to reach out to Israelis with a growing interest in their Jewish identity and to persuade public opinion, the government and the important non-governmental institutions to support them as legitimate expressions of Judaism. Success would produce valuable material aid as well as the removal of their disabilities, but they have a long way to go, for the acceptance of Jewish religious pluralism in Israel is not yet within sight.

Chapter twelve

Social Services

Fragmented evolution

Israel is a welfare state with a mass of social services involving no fewer than eight Ministries, all the local authorities and numerous public institutions and private charities. It is a gallimaufry of a system, owing its complexity to the variety of strands which went into its making.

The oldest of them were the institutions evolved by the religious groups which made up the Jewish population of Palestine before Zionism. Maintained by the charitable donations of their more affluent co-religionists abroad, they solicited gifts for the sick, the needy and the aged and they developed institutions for the distribution of these funds. These philanthropic activities continued after the creation of the State. The uncompromising ultraconservatives were opposed to the new secular Israel, rejected any association with it and continued their own educational and social welfare network.

Based mainly in Jerusalem, their welfare agencies have none of the outward trappings. It is, indeed, rare for any of them to have identifiable offices or permanent officials. Most of them operate from private homes, shops or places of worship, are administered by volunteers and are difficult for outsiders to locate. But the communities they serve know where to find them and the dispensers of tzedaka (Hebrew for the religious obligation to give charity) know where to find their beneficiaries. These small and highly personal philanthropies of the separatist orthodox help members of their own communities with interest-free loans, food for the needy for the Sabbath or the festivals, dowries for brides and maintenance for those engaged in religious study. The intimacy of these services brings with it obvious advantages, but Israel's social workers point out that it has encouraged hawking from one charity to another, while the absence of any professional study of case histories often produces inadequate or harmful results.

Historically, the second ingredient in Israel's melange of social services came with the arrival in Palestine of the early groups of Zionist pioneers in the first decades of the twentieth century. They brought their own political ideologies which, as we have seen, provided the seeds from which Israel's present political structure has grown. Basic to their approach was the work ethic and the ideas of self and mutual help rather than the acceptance of philanthropy. They created the Histadrut, the General Federation of Labour which, as early as 1911, instituted a Sick Fund (Kupat Holim), which is still the health service for a majority of Israelis. Other welfare schemes followed to such effect that, for Israel's working population, a welfare state virtually existed before any state was formed. Some of these functions were later taken over by the Government, but many remain with the Histadrut.

Not all the necessary services were provided by the Histadrut, nor were their facilities available to the whole Jewish population. The Palestine Jewish community, itself almost a Government in embryo during the Mandatory period, set up in 1931 a department for welfare and social services. Its first director was a dynamic and compassionate Zionist leader from Baltimore in the USA, Miss Henrietta Szold. A trained social worker, she brought to Israel the concept that welfare work was a profession, and she founded a school to train social workers. Being outside the Labour Party and the Histadrut, the new community service provided relief for the unemployed and needy without becoming involved in socialist theories about philanthropy. The policies Henrietta Szold devised and implemented created the foundation for the national welfare systems of the future state.

All these services, private charity, Histadrut and community, faced their greatest tests in the first four years of Statehood. Between 1948 and 1952 the population doubled. Over 600,000 Jews arrived. Survivors of the concentration camps, rootless, sick and with lasting scars from the Holocaust, were matched with a mass of destitute, underprivileged, often primitive families from Moslem lands. An inexperienced new Government, helped by voluntary organizations funded from abroad, had to assume the heavy responsibilities of this massive immigration. The new citizens had to be registered, taught, housed, fed, employed – all with the country in a state of siege.

The extensive, but complicated and fragmented, social services that exist in Israel today are the consequence of this history.

Health

Israel possesses the highest ratio in the world of doctors to population: in 1978 it was approximately one to five hundred. Most are employed by Kupat Holim, which provides a comprehensive health service for about 70 per cent of the population. Three other, smaller, funds offer a similar service to another 20 per cent. Every member of the Histadrut is automatically a member of the Sick Fund, which is financed by membership dues calculated as a proportion of the member's income. Although the Histadrut itself has always been closely linked with the Labour Party, other party groups are permitted to associate themselves with the Sick Fund.

The benefits embrace the complete range of medical care for the members and their families. General practitioners employed by the fund will see patients at home or at clinics; specialist and nursing services are provided; members have the free use of hospitals, free medicines, X-ray and all other treatments. Dental and optical care are available at reduced rates.

With the major responsibility for health services in the hands of the private funds, the Ministry of Health adopted the policy of filling any gaps left by the non-governmental institutions. Consequently, in the area of direct medical services, the Ministry has provided, and maintains, almost half of the hospital beds in the country. For many years, Kupat Holim received a hidden subsidy since its members were accepted in Ministry hospitals at a reduced rate. But that has been changed and they are now required to pay the same fees as other hospital users. The other main areas of Ministry activity are the supervision of medical standards and the provision of the principal public health services.

The hospitals of the Sick Fund and Ministry are powerfully augmented by those sponsored by voluntary organizations. In fact, all the general hospitals in Jerusalem are philanthropic foundations – Hadassah, the largest with 800 beds, Shaare Zedek and Bikkur Cholim. Each receives substantial support from its fund-raising organizations in the Jewish communities abroad, but they also benefit from Government subsidies. The Jerusalem hospitals all have agreements with the Sick Funds to take their members, since none of them has any hospital in the city.

Free hospital care is available for all confinements. So popular has this been that, in 1976, all Jewish women and 98 per cent of non-Jewish women had their children in hospital, according to official figures. Partly due to the large number of maternity cases, every hospital tends to be overcrowded and occupancy in many is as high as 120 per cent of the official capacity – beds in corridors are a common sight. The Sick Fund hospitals fare the worst, particularly since the loss of cheap access to Government hospitals.

Out-patient departments are always overcrowded and service is slow; they have become little more than classification centres. The quality of general practitioners has declined with the absorption of doctors who have recently immigrated from Eastern Europe where training is poor by Western standards, but that is a transient phase. Four excellent medical schools in Israel take in annually over 300 highly motivated students. Competition for these places is keen, and the standard of the domestically trained doctors is high.

A new phenomenon, out of harmony with the egalitarian ideals of Israel's founders but a product of affluence, has been the development of private medical services. Doctors employed in the Ministry hospitals and those of the Sick Funds are permitted to practise privately in the afternoons. The fees are, so far, low: a consultant normally receives about $15 a visit, roughly one-third of comparable charges in Britain. In addition, private hospitals have become more numerous, and in 1977 accounted for some 6,000 hospital beds – 25 per cent of the national total.

In almost every town and village in Israel, mother and child health centres have become a significant element in Israel's preventative health services. The first of them was opened in 1921 by Hadassah, the powerful American Women's Zionist organization, and they have been developed by the government and local private institutions. Today, about 750 of these centres provide pre- and post-natal care and supervise the health of children up to adolescence for families in all economic and social groups. The Government operates about 65 per cent of them; the remainder are run by private organization and municipalities.

Though the services provided are comprehensive, the system is uneven. The high doctor-patient ratio, for example, is misleading in some respects. Doctors are concentrated in the main population centres and shortages exist in rural areas. Far too little is spent on preventative medicine, while the multiplicity of organizations involved in the patchwork of health service has brought about considerable waste in unnecessarily large bureaucracies and in overlapping.

To remedy the situation, it has been regularly proposed that all these separate facilities should be coordinated and rationalized into a National Health Service providing equal treatment for the whole population. In 1950, a Government committee in fact recommended this, but no action followed. In 1972, a proposed law was presented to the Knesset, but got no further. The new Government elected in 1977 also proposed introducing a new health law which would have had the effect of making all present facilities available to the population at large, to be financed by the Government through a new health tax.

None of these proposals has so far made any headway against the opposition of the Histadrut and the Israel Medical Association. Dr Ram Yishay, the President of the IMA, claims that the Likud-proposed National Health Law would cost the public more and provide an inferior service. Echoing his colleagues in Britain thirty years ago and in the USA today, in opposition to a national health organization, Yishay says, 'Let the patient choose. All Israelis must be enrolled in some sort of health service, but let them decide which.' He believes that the Government should concentrate on the prevention of disease through improved sanitation, help the young and aged, and leave the present system of treatment alone.

Dr Yishay's view was not shared by the Likud Minister of Health, Eliezer Shostak. In a report presented to the Knesset in June 1979, he drew attention to what he described as a paradox in Israel's health services: 'On the one hand, the conditions exist for giving medical service that could be the best in the world, the high level of doctors, enough buildings, and equipment . . . On the other hand, the service given is not good and it is expensive. It is clumsy, uncoordinated, slow . . . it steals the patient's time, makes him stand in queues and takes repeated and superfluous tests.'

The Histadrut has continued to fight grimly for the survival of its Sick Fund. With the ideological appeal of its socialist approach waning, and with growing cynicism by the public towards the powerful entrenched institutions, the Sick Fund has become the main inducement for Histadrut membership. That trade union and labour fortress in Israel would undoubtedly suffer a crippling reduction in membership and influence were the Kupat Holim to be taken over. But the Begin Government, concentrating on the peace process and intent on cutting public spending, showed no immediate enthusiasm for a battle with the Histadrut or the expenditure of the massive funds which a take-over would involve.

The poor

With the arrival of statehood, the Social Assistance Department of the

Jewish Community Council was transformed into the Ministry of Social Welfare. The Ministry determines national policy on matters of public service, although the actual administration is in the hands of the local authorities. So, for example, the Ministry will determine the scale of various forms of financial assistance but the grants themselves are made by the local welfare offices administered by the local authorities.

This division is a continuation of the 'Ottoman approach' perpetuated by the Mandatory Government and designed to keep local authorities under the strict control of the central Government. In the welfare services it is the locals who do the work and are expected to know and understand local needs but, in determining policy, they are totally dependent on the government which supplies some 70 per cent of their budgets. During 1978, something like 10 per cent of all families in the country were receiving regular or occasional relief, or supplementary benefits for specific needs from the local welfare offices, while another 5 per cent received services.

The 'income maintenance' provided by almost two hundred local welfare offices throughout Israel is calculated so as to ensure that 'welfare families' receive 50 per cent of the officially announced national average family income (until 1971 it was only about 25 per cent). This figure rises with the increase in the cost of living, and so does the welfare payment. Households with no other income receive the full grant, while those with incomes lower than the relief rate are 'topped up' to the calculated figure. Appeals by applicants for relief go first to an officer of the Ministry and, if required, to local independent appeal boards. The fact that only a very small number of complaints received by the Ombudsman relate to welfare payments suggests that the appeal system must be working satisfactorily.

But the Ministry of Social Welfare is not the only Governmental department concerned with welfare assistance. Disabled military personnel, their families and the families of fallen soldiers are served by a special organization in the Ministry of Defence. Today, after five wars in thirty years, this is a voluminous category, whose needs are income maintenance, rehabilitation, medical services, educational services for children – in fact the whole range of welfare services. Social workers refer to this category as the 'aristocratic' class of clientele, for which the standard of services provided is higher than for the other categories.

In the middle of this stratified system, below the 'aristocrats' and above the welfare office clientele, are the new immigrants. For their first three years, they are the responsibility of the Ministry of Absorption. They have the same needs as all the others, but for those three years they are 'respectable' clients and are serviced by the Ministry of Absorption with greater consideration than they are likely to receive later. After three years and one day – nothing has changed for them – they come under the aegis of the welfare offices of the Ministry of Welfare. They lose their middle status and become members of the stigmatized lower class who are 'on relief'. This kind of class system which has grown up in the organization of welfare is the consequence of administrative decisions which determine whether an individual comes under this or that Ministry or resource. All have the same needs, but they go to different places and receive varied treatment. The result of this segregated structure has been to create and perpetuate differing social status for welfare clients.

National insurance

All permanent residents of Israel, whether citizens or not, whether employed or self-employed, are members of a compulsory national insurance scheme. As in the British counterpart, the contributions of employees (in 1979 about 5 per cent of salary) are deducted by their employers, whose contribution is approximately 20 per cent. A ceiling on these payments is twice the national average wage. Self-employed individuals make payments directly to the body which administers the scheme, the National Insurance Institute.

In the hierarchy of Israeli institutions, the Institute is second only to the State Comptroller in the respect it enjoys from the public. Its spirit is that of the school of labour leaders who believed in socialism and the virtues of work, thrift and self-help. Its virtual independence and excellent administration are the creations of the man who built it, Dr Giora Lotan, a German Jew, the archetype of the incorruptible and meticulous 'yekke'. The National Insurance Institute is linked with the Ministry of Labour, but to avoid any danger of political meddling with its substantial funds, it was constituted, and has remained, a semi-independent body, and its funds are kept separate from state funds.

The Begin Government did suggest in 1979 that the Treasury take over the task of collecting national insurance, on the ground that the tax-payer should pay both taxes and insurance to one government agency which would then make distributions internally to its various departments. But the proposal sank without trace, so strong was the feeling in the Knesset that, not only did the NII perform an excellent job of collecting and disbursing (whereas the Treasury has been far less efficient), but also that it was important to protect the national insurance system from the vicissitudes of the economy.

The national basic pension, which varies with the family situation, is between 20 and 30 per cent of the national average monthly wage. Those entitled to it are insured men of 65 and women of 60 who have stopped working and have a low income. At the age of 70 for men and 65 for women, all insured people receive the basic pension whatever their income. For about 75 per cent of the working population, the basic pension, which is minimal, is substantially augmented by the Histadrut social security scheme, which includes pensions among its benefits. Government employees are covered by their own pension scheme to supplement the basic payment.

Since 1975, the NII has taken over the payment of children's allowances, which are uniform and paid to the whole population. Israel's need for population growth is expressed not only in its promotion of immigration – but also in the encouragement of what is called 'internal immigration' – an increase in the birth rate. A tax-exempt allowance is granted for every child. Moreover, it is directly linked with the consumer price index to ensure that it keeps pace with inflation. Figures issued by the NII show that, at the beginning of 1978, a family with three children received allowances totalling 17 per cent of the average monthly wage, a family with five, 37.7 per cent and one with nine children, 82.1 per cent. In addition, maternity benefits include up to 75 per cent of the wage of working women for the three months of leave they are required to take by law.

In 1973, legislation made it compulsory for employers also to deduct at source the health insurance payments for Sick Funds, and the NII was made responsible for the collection of these dues from employers, which it then passes on to the fund. When the four Sick Funds were doing the collection themselves, they employed 150 people for the job; these became redundant when the NII took over. But the Institute did not have to increase its own staff at all – it merely added another line to the forms which go to all employers.

Unemployment is one of the less demanding responsibilities of the NII, since Israel has always kept firmly to a policy of full employment. Even at times of economic recession, the number of recipients of unemployment benefit has rarely risen above 15,000 for any period of time. In all these cases of income maintenance, whether it be pensions or unemployment benefit, further assistance is available to those in need through a supplementary benefits system totally funded by the Government. This additional form of public assistance is at present run by the local authorities, but plans have been made for it to be administered nationally by the Institute.

As its reputation for efficiency grew, the NII was charged with additional functions. One of the most recent is the payment of alimony or maintenance to wives with children. In the past, the wife needed to apply to a court for an order, which she then had to enforce – often unsuccessfully – against a husband who had disappeared. Now the woman applies directly to the NII, which pays immediately and is empowered to obtain reimbursement from the husband or ex-husband.

Insurance against injury at work, also within the purview of the NII, covers employees and the self-employed who make national insurance contributions. Coming under the rubric 'only in Israel' is an amendment to the National Insurance Law which was passed by the Knesset in July 1979. The original law provides that, if an insured person is injured in an accident on his way to work, this shall be considered an accident while at work, for which he will be compensated. The amendment now protects the worker who stops off at synagogue on his way to work. If he suffers an injury while at his devotions, that will also be deemed to be an accident at work and he will be eligible for compensation.

The old and the young

The mass immigration into Israel during its early years made a considerable impact on its age structure. The pioneers who laid the foundations of the new State were a youthful group and, immediately before 1948, less than 4 per cent of the population was over 65. Their own youth and immense preoccupations with political and economic problems gave them little time or inclination to consider making provisions for the ageing and the aged. Before the establishment of the State, therefore, the only facilities were a few homes for the aged, maintained either by religious groups or the organized Jewish community.

The immigrants after 1948, preponderantly from North Africa and the Near East, included substantial numbers of ageing or aged members of family groups, who were either unproductive or needed medical or nursing services. The Government had too many other problems on its hands at the time and left the solution of this one to that great philanthropic institution of American Jewry, the Joint Distribution Committee (JDC). In 1949, the JDC set up an organization called Malben which, in a short time, provided thousands of beds for the aged in institutions and nursing homes. The policy of the JDC has always been to initiate programmes and then to have them continued by local enterprise. So, in 1975, in pursuance of this policy, Malben went out of business and transferred its institutions and services to the Ministry of Health. But the JDC has continued its activity in a new joint venture with the Government to plan and develop services for the aged.

Because of the close family relationships of Jews generally and, in particular, of the large multi-generational families who came from the Afro-Asian countries, few of the ageing members were placed in institutions. They stayed with their families. Today, of about 300,000 Israeli Jews over the age of 65, only about 8,000 live in institutions. According to estimates, by the end of 1980 the 65+ age group will number 317,000 and, in 1985, about 350,000.

Institutions or homes for the aged can be broadly divided into three groups: those run by Government or government-associated bodies, those operated by non-profit organizations, and some thirty private institutions – these last are mostly small and costly, and account for a small proportion of the demand. In the first category are thirteen institutions with approximately 3,500 beds open to all and charging fees adjusted to means. The non-profit organizations, the largest being the Histadrut and the Association of Immigrants from Central Europe, maintain high-quality institutions (six Histadrut and five Association) but they are restricted to their members and, generally, for the ambulatory aged. Some of the private homes for the aged are used by the Ministry of Social Welfare for welfare cases for whom there is no place in other institutions. The serious shortage lies in beds for the aged sick.

Provision for the needs of the aged, other than homes, is still in process of development. The local authorities of the main cities either maintain a department for services to the aged, which include providing a club or day-care centre, or help to fund private organizations performing these functions. Voluntary organizations all over the country offer recreational and work programmes for the aged and the Ministry of Labour runs a special unit to find part-time work for them.

All the Ministries concerned, as well as the voluntary organizations, recognize the need to improve and develop facilities. The American Brookdale Foundation recently established an Institute for the Study of Geriatrics and Human Development with support from the JDC and the government. The study of geriatrics in Israel, as elsewhere, is likely to be given a higher priority in the future than has been accorded to it in the past.

In marked contrast to the deficiencies with regard to the aged has been the provision of services for children and youth. Israelis have continued the Jewish tradition of devotion to their children who, from the earliest Zionist days, have been high on the list of both national and family priority. The educational system, ten years of compulsory, free schooling, is a comprehensive one, with loving care and expertise lavished on the pupils. Standards are variable and so is the involvement of the'pupils; and there has been a worrying increase in truancy. Education in Israel starts early. Almost all the children attend pre-kindergarten activities in nursery schools or programmes offered by voluntary organizations. With Government aid voluntary organizations have established a national network of hundreds of day-care centres for the young children of working parents.

More unexpected is the extent to which Israeli parents send their children to boarding schools. A small proportion are delinquent children or welfare cases, but the majority of the approximately 50,000 children in boarding institutions of various kinds, almost 20 per cent of the 13–17 age group, have been placed by their own families. Some are children from rural areas where there are either no secondary schools or inadequate ones. Others are placed in theological boarding schools (Yeshivot) or in kibbutzim. A special case is that of Youth Aliyah. Founded to look after children who were brought to Palestine without their parents, Youth Aliyah constructed its own youth villages and institutions to house and educate them. The post-statehood immigration, mainly from the Afro-Asian countries, consisted of large families and the Youth Aliyah institutions came to be used for their children. Today they serve thousands of underprivileged children and young people, housing them in their educational villages and in kibbutzim.

The non-boarding 80 per cent of schoolchildren, when they are not working at their demanding homework, can join a wide range of youth movements of which probably the largest is the Scouts. This is a non-political youth movement and includes Arabs, but the others are generally sectarian, political or religious. The youth movement of the latter, called Bnei Akiva, is generally conceded to be one of the best. But most Israeli children prefer to organize their own social lives in informal neighbourhood groups.

Juvenile delinquency is dealt with in the Juvenile Courts and by the juvenile probation service. Serious crime among juveniles has decreased in recent years; from a high peak figure of 5,282 convictions in 1970, the numbers declined each year until, in 1977, it was reduced to 2,755. But the total of all juvenile cases heard rises constantly – from 1,833 in 1955 to 7,061 in 1977. Delinquent or deprived children, such as those in need of care and protection, and the mentally and physically handicapped, are serviced by a bewildering variety of agencies formed by local authorities, various Ministries and voluntary organizations. Social workers would like to see a comprehensive child welfare law to rationalize the present imperfect distribution of responsibilities.

The second Israel

Jews who were born in Afro-Asian countries, or whose parents came from these countries, constitute a majority of Israel's Jewish population. They are generally referred to as the Edot Hamizrach (Eastern or Oriental Communities), Sephardim or Orientals. In many respects, their social and economic situation is analogous to that of the Blacks in the United States in relation to their white compatriots. The Orientals in Israel come from poor, often primitive material conditions and from environments which, though devoutly religious, lacked educational and cultural resources. What they did bring with them, their simple piety and their closely knit families, was undermined by the open and secular society they found in Israel. Deprived of their traditional values, lacking any substitutes, living in overcrowded slums, unable to compete successfully at school or at work with their far more advantaged Ashkenazi fellow citizens, they have become the second Israel.

Some progress has been made. A Sephardi has become Israel's President, two North African immigrants became members of Begin's Cabinet, improvements have been effected in education and housing, and the incidence of intermarriage between Sephardim and Ashkenazim is rising. But the Orientals remain Israel's underprivileged ethnic group, well below the Ashkenazim in material and social position and most directly affected by galloping inflation. The concentration of successive Israel Governments on security has led to the neglect of social problems. With this background, it is little wonder that many Orientals have been drawn into the seamier aspects of Israeli life.

The eruption in 1971 of a group of young Oriental militants who called themselves 'Black Panthers', after the Black group in the USA, brought about a greater awareness of the social problem of the second Israel. Golda Meir, then Prime Minister, set up a Commission on Disadvantaged Youth which blossomed and proliferated into Ministerial Committees, inter-Ministerial committees, task forces and teams, sub-committees and advisers. The Ministry of Social Welfare was one of the few administrative arms to make changes as a result of investigations into the special requirements of the Orientals, but the post-1977 concentration by the Government on peace and national security destroyed the sense of urgency that once briefly existed.

The deteriorating economic situation which brought about the removal of food subsidies resulted in special hardship for the poor, whose income has always lagged behind the rise in the cost of living, and led to a re-emergence of the Black Panthers towards the end of 1979. Following an earlier precedent, demands were again being made on the Government to do more by way of education and social services to improve the situation of the underprivileged Orientals, if for no other reason than to avoid the weakening of the country through internal dissension. At the root of the grievances of the Government's critics is the fact that the Ministry of Finance, which has the last word on welfare (as on other) expenditure, is concerned with money and not social problems.

In particular, far too little has been done to cope with the growing problem of drug abuse in Israel, although an Inter-Ministerial Committee on Drugs has three sub-committees, and the Ministry of Health has its own Drugs Committee. The extent of the problem, mainly in the second Israel, was described in the 1978 Shimron Report on crime (see Chapter 7): about 10,000 regular hashish smokers and an estimated 4,000 users of hard drugs. These figures exclude the army, whose authorities have not revealed the scale of the drug problem in the services and tend to play it down. The Shimron Committee found that drug abuse was increasing, and recommended that the Ministries of Education, Health and Social Welfare should embark on a comprehensive information campaign against it, especially among the youth. It also came to the conclusion that 'de-criminating' the use of 'soft' drugs would be against the public interest both because they are harmful in themselves and because they lead to 'hard' drugs.

In 1978, however, Israel had only sixteen beds for drug addicts in all its psychiatric hospitals. A 1979 investigation at the Hadassah Hospital revealed that about 75 per cent of drug addicts were Orientals, and a Social Welfare Ministry estimate in the same year concluded that there were 'at least' 5,800 addicts. But the Ministry of Health runs only two experimental drug treatment centres although it has also contracted with practitioners, medical and psychological, for the treatment of some addicts. The Ministry of Health has not yet created a regular service for addicts nor has the Ministry of Education yet defined what its policy should be on teaching about drugs in schools, while the Ministry of Social Welfare – which has done very well with the treatment of alcoholics – has not yet instituted its own programme for drug addicts.

The volunteer services have made a very useful contribution in this area, as in others concerned with social welfare. One youthful volunteer told me of his experience working in a development town with street gangs and drop-outs. They smoke hashish, steal and roam the streets, having persuaded themselves that crime is the only way they are likely to get what they want. The personal counselling given by the young members of voluntary organizations is probably more likely to produce some degree of success than institutionalized governmental programmes.

Chapter thirteen

Business

The sad state of the economy

Milton Friedman, the Nobel Prize-winning economist and apostle of the free economy, was invited by the Begin Government to advise on how Israel's economy could be put right. Not unsurprisingly, he proposed that public spending be reduced and unemployment increased. His views were listened to with the respect due to so eminent a friend of Israel, but he was telling the Government policy-makers what they and their predecessors already knew, and they patiently explained to him why it was impossible to accept that prescription.

Israel, they told him, has a Zionist mission. It involves the encouragement of immigration and the creation of conditions which inhibit emigration. Jobs have to be available for immigrants even if they have to be created, and full employment must be maintained to keep them there. Moreover, every able citizen serves 30 to 60 days in the reserve forces. If the reserve soldier were not sure that his job would be there when he returned, he might have other things on his mind than the country's defence as he watches the borders.

Politicians in both government and opposition have ruled out the creation of unemployment as a solution to Israel's economic headaches. Nor, for the same reason, has it been possible to make substantial cuts in the costly welfare state; it had to be maintained to absorb new immigrants and give them a minimal standard of living.

In addition to the economic burden of full employment and the welfare state, Israel's economy is also weighed down by the costs of its defence. Because of the constant threat of war since its creation, Israel spends proportionately more on defence than any other country in the world – close to 30 per cent of its Gross National Product (in the USA the proportion is 6 per cent). When Menachem Begin became Prime Minister he told his then Finance Minister that neither the defence nor the social welfare budgets could be cut, and the result has been progressive inflation, moving to an annual rate of over 100 per cent by the end of 1979.

A combination of inflation with a virtual absence of economic growth, over-full employment and expensive welfare schemes ensure that Israel lives beyond her means. The resulting deficit had been met by massive aid from the USA – about half of it in non-repayable grants – and by the fund-raising efforts of Jews throughout the world.

One of the ways in which public spending could have been cut would have been to permit rising prices to reduce consumption. But political considerations almost invariably prevented this course of action, and wages have risen faster than the rate of inflation. Because wages, pensions, social security payments and interest on Government bonds are all linked to the rising cost-of-living index, the effects of inflation were hardly felt. One of Israel's leading bankers was reported early in 1979 as saying: 'The public here doesn't pay the price of inflation. The United States and the Jewish people around the world do that.'

In the early years after the creation of the state, Zionists on fund-raising tours in the Jewish diaspora frequently encouraged the generosity of their audiences by assuring them that their sacrifices were required only to set Israel on her feet and enable her to absorb mass immigration. Within a foreseeable period, audiences were confidently informed, Israel would become economically self-sufficient. And indeed from 1953, when the immigration flood had subsided, until the Six Day War of 1967, a period of fourteen years, Israel made uninterrupted economic progress. The rate of economic growth was about 10 per cent, comparable with the achievement of Japan and Korea, and the national deficit was being steadily reduced. At that rate of growth, economic experts were unanimously predicting that the balance of payments deficit would end by the early 'seventies.

That prospect was destroyed by the 1967 war which diverted production from exports to military equipment and necessitated vast expenditure on importing armaments. The Yom Kippur War six years later compelled further massive rearmament at a time when the world inflation of 1974 and 1975 had sharply increased the cost of most of the imported raw materials on which Israel depended.

Successive Governments were unable to achieve any radical improvement of the situation. Recession, unemployment, and cuts in public spending were not only unacceptable since they would have harmed the Zionist ideal, but were electorally unpopular – and this was a period when all Governments were acutely aware of their slender majorities. In addition, all Governments were coalitions, a fact which entailed compromise decisions to keep everyone happy. Two years after he became Finance Minister, Simcha Ehrlich was reported as saying: 'Inflation is preferable to unemployment, and it's possible that inflation is actually good for the people under some circumstances.'

Until the appointment of Yigal Hurwitz as Finance Minister towards the end of 1979, the Likud Government was unable to apply painful remedies. It might, nevertheless, have made the attempt, had not Sadat arrived on his peace mission in November 1977. Now with peace in prospect, the Prime Minister and his Cabinet were unwilling to risk trouble at home. Instead they bought internal peace and a national consensus by continuing to print money.

Ministers agreed in Cabinet that cuts were essential – but for every Ministry other than their own. They fought fiercely to retain or even increase their own budgets. Some were successful. The religious parties, whose political support was essential for the coalition's existence, were paid off by increased subsidies to religious institutions. Vested interests were placated. In a TV speech before the meeting at Camp David, Begin attacked the damaging effect of the teachers' pay claim of 35 per cent – and then, when the teachers went on strike, applied pressure on the Cabinet to accept a compromise, which turned out to be an increase of 37½ per cent.

After two years of the Begin Government, the rise in public expenditure had brought with it an increase in the maldistribution of the labour force. Why should a worker undertake a strenuous job in industry when he could have a comfortable, secure and undemanding office job which also (were he so minded) gave him both the time and energy to take on a second job and make more money?

In 1979, only 32.3 per cent of the work force was engaged in productive labour. The remaining 67.7 per cent were in service occupations, the majority of them bureaucrats. Only 25 per cent were engaged in industry, while the comparable figure for West Germany was 41.5 per cent. A combination of union power and ineffective government had brought about a shortage of labour for industry and low productivity. Shlomo Lahat, the Mayor of Tel Aviv, would have liked to dismiss some 5,000 municipal office workers but failed to gain sufficient support in the face of a threatened general strike.

When he reported on his own Ministry's activities and plans in the 1979 Budget debate, the Minister of Trade, Industry and Tourism, Gideon Patt, told the Knesset that the failure to attract labour was the main limitation on the expansion of industrial production and, therefore, of exports. 'Serious efforts', he said, 'must be made to reduce the number of workers in service jobs, so as to make manpower available for the productive branches of the economy.' But subsequent speakers in the debate, sadly or gleefully – depending on party allegiance – noted that the Minister had failed to put forward any specific proposals on how to achieve that objective. One of the speakers in that debate broke a taboo by referring to the economic losses caused by the black economy, a rare subject for public discussion.

The black economy

Diamonds are Israel's best friends. She exports over a billion dollars' worth of polished gemstones a year, more than the combined total of her other industrial exports. The international diamond trade has been very much a Jewish affair, and it was natural that Jewish diamond craftsmen and merchants should have brought their expertise to the Jewish state. About a half of the world's annual supply of rough diamonds are cut and polished in Israeli workshops and factories, which employ a work force of 25,000. A visible sign of the success of the industry is the high rise block of Israel's Diamond Exchange in Ramat Gan near Tel Aviv, the world's largest centre for the diamond industry. It is all a far cry from the cowshed in Petach Tikva where, in 1937, Jewish refugees from Holland and Belgium opened the first diamond-cutting workshop in the country.

As in the Antwerp Diamond Bourse, Hatton Garden in London and the Diamond Exchange in New York City, deals are based on mutual trust and go unrecorded by any accounting devices. A transaction which may involve millions of dollars is (metaphorically) signed, sealed and delivered by a handshake and the words 'Mazal Uvracha' (Luck and Blessing). To attract the diamond cutters and merchants to settle in Israel and bring their industry, Israel accepted their contention that, by the nature of their trade, they could not be expected to keep books, because many customers would refuse to buy or sell if their transactions were recorded. One of the results of this concession was that it was difficult to recover tax, and large sums in cash floated around – in addition to the money the diamond people left abroad in foreign currency, even though it was, at that time, illegal.

Despite efforts initiated in 1977 to fight tax evasion and improve collection, the diamond industry belongs to a considerable extent to Israel's underground economy which, a distinguished Tel Aviv accountant claimed in August 1979, made up one-third of the total national economy.

The tax deficiencies of the diamond business might have been tolerable as a very special case, but other businesses were not slow to follow the precedent. One of the first and most substantial boosts to the black economy followed the 1967 victory. Israel could not spare the men required for a large army of occupation and, to enable a small force to hold Sinai, a series of fortifications were built (they were either blown up or removed when Sinai was returned to Egypt in 1979). This Bar Lev Line, as it was called (it failed ignominiously when Egypt invaded in 1973), cost hundreds of millions of dollars and, to encourage work in the uncongenial desert, the Government offered tax inducements to capital and labour. Getting the work done was far more important than wasting time on meticulous book-keeping. The Government did not deduct tax at source, contractors bought material without payment of tax and paid in cash, while Government accounting procedures were lax or non-existent.

More fuel for the black economy was produced by the development of extensive and intimate trading relations with the Arabs of the occupied West Bank. Israeli merchants bought goods for cash and sold them for cash. The Arabs who sold to them did not pay any taxes or keep books, nor did their customers.

By the very nature of the subject, hard facts are difficult to come by, but Israelis are generally aware that hundreds of self-employed professionals, craftsmen and shopkeepers also participate in the black economy by receiving cash payment for unrecorded transactions. Only occasionally do examples become public. Many dentists are commonly believed to have amassed large sums by cash payments (usually in dollars) for the more expensive forms of treatment. One of them, a Professor at the Hadassah Hospital and a practitioner of considerable distinction, was found guilty of tax evasion on large cash payments and received a prison sentence.

In addition to the accumulation of undeclared income, the black economy is substantially augmented by the proceeds of crime. The Shimron Committee on crime, in its report published in 1978, was 'shocked' to learn that, in addition to the billions of black money originating from legitimate businesses whose owners evaded income tax, 'there are additional billions of black money whose source is illegal businesses such as drugs, extortion and smuggling.' The Committee recommended the adoption of a law on the reporting of cash transactions, not only to yield more income tax, but as a weapon against crime.

The effect of this black money on the economy has been to increase the rate of inflation. Some of the cash is undoubtedly 'laundered' and finds its way into legitimate business, but some goes on expensive cars, villas, travel and other forms of conspicuous consumption. It has been argued, on the other hand, that earning untaxed income has helped thousands of crafts-men and small traders from the 'second Israel' (the underprivileged immi-grants from the Middle East and North Africa) to improve their economic – and therefore social – standing in a society dominated by their European co-religionists.

But whatever the arguments about the black economy's possible benign consequences, the post-1977 Government, more than any of its pre-decessors, fought back against the tax evaders with considerable effect – even requiring the diamond dealers to keep books. The new tough approach, including surprise raids and the confiscation of books, has been widely approved – particularly since it affects only a small minority of Israelis. The overwhelming majority of the population, salary- or wage-earners, pay their income tax by deduction at source.

Living with inflation

When it took office in 1977, the Likud Government inherited a 35 per cent inflation rate. Committed to the idea of a free economy, the new Govern-ment almost immediately abolished currency controls and variable ex-change rates. Israelis were now free to buy foreign currency on the basis of a free floating Israeli pound whose value was determined by the market. The value of the dollar immediately soared, and the many Israelis who brought in money from abroad found that they had far more Israeli pounds to spend. They could also now borrow dollars from abroad at lower interest rates than in Israel and spend or invest them.

This growth in purchasing power was powerfully augmented by a rash of Government spending which pumped more money into the economy. Very high on the list were the hidden subsidies which all Governments of Israel had given to agriculture and industry in the form of cheap loans, either as working capital or for investment. The low interest rates on these loans were not linked to the cost-of-living index, nor was the capital. The result was that, at a time of rapid inflation, the loans turned out to be virtually outright gifts, for the money that had to be paid back in two, three or five years was, in real terms, only a fraction of the amount initially borrowed.

The Central Bureau of Statistics estimated that, in 1978, the subsidy element in cheap government loans and grants to industry and agriculture was in the region of $1 billion – about 11.5 per cent of the Gross National Product and almost 100 per cent higher than in the previous year. The recipients of this largesse were accused of using their loans to buy index-linked bonds on the Tel Aviv Stock Exchange, thus bringing in a tax-free income keeping pace with inflation – a risk-free profit totally at the tax-payers' expense.

The final contribution made by the Government to the inflationary spiral (which was running at more than 100 per cent by the end of 1979) was to freeze prices for a period in 1978 without, in deference to the Histadrut, freezing wages. This meant further subsidies to the producers of the 'frozen' goods, while the wage growth made more money available to chase other goods.

Unfortunately, the direct and indirect (hidden) subsidies were only part of the Government's massive overspending. More money was spent on El Al, the national airline, because it was an essential service – military, as well as civil – and it had to have money to purchase new equipment. The attachment to education is deep-rooted in Israel and urgent demands for new school buildings were not resisted. The support of the religious parties was essential to keep the ruling coalition in power, and it could only be bought by increased contributions to their institutions. More money had to be spent on the police to fight the growth of crime and the Government's policy of settlements in the occupied territories also had to be paid for.

The money could, in theory at any rate, have been found by increasing taxation and improving methods of collecting it. But an increase of taxation to the necessary heights would have been an electoral disaster, and the improved collection which did take place was only marginal in its economic effects. Cuts in public spending were talked about, but the most that was achieved in practice, a reduction of approximately $300 million in 1979, merely cut the *rate* at which the Budget expenditure was expanding. By the end of 1979, new loans to farmers and businessmen were index-linked, but the existing unlinked loans remained (because of galloping inflation) hidden and valuable gifts.

Israelis learned to live with this new phenomenon. Most observers marvelled at the rapid adjustment Londoners made during the blitz – the abnormal soon became normal. Such was the reaction in Israel to inflation. Complaints were, of course, to be heard, but nearly everybody seemed to be managing. Wages were linked to the cost-of-living index and so, until Yigal Hurwitz ended the subsidies on basic foods late in 1979, increased wages took care of all necessities. (In fact only 70 per cent of wages or salaries were index-linked. The government offered to increase it to 100 per cent but this was declined by the Histadrut for the – undeclared – reason that the trade union division would then have nothing further to fight for. As it is, the fact that only 70 per cent is linked still leaves opportunities for continuing wage negotiations.)

Not only are the salaries linked, but so are borrowing and saving. When inflation puts prices up, everything else goes up in the same proportion. The only snag, and one which affected principally the lower-income groups, was the time-lag, because adjustments to wages in consequence of the cost-of-living increases are made only every six months. The Governor at the Bank of Israel, Arnon Gafny, told a reporter in 1978: 'Nobody suffers much from inflation, so it is hard for us to argue the need for restraint.'

And there was little restraint. As prices rose and more money entered the domestic market, buyers hurried to the shops. 'Buy now because tomorrow the price will be higher,' was the general maxim. No visitor to Israel in 1978 and 1979 could be unaware of this buying spree. Colour television sets were being bought feverishly, despite the fact that all local programmes were broadcast in black and white (the Broadcasting Authority used colour cameras, but wiped out the colour on transmission so as to avoid fuelling an inflationary demand for colour sets). The price being paid for these sets in mid-1979 ranged between $1,500 and $3,000, and this was being paid readily. Customers paid the price asked because it was important to convert money (going down in value) into goods (going up in value). Nor did they shop around for competitive offers, for by the time the round was completed the prices would probably have risen. The rush for TV sets was paralleled by a similar demand for other consumer durables.

Home owners – about 75 per cent of Israelis own their own flats – saw them appreciate rapidly in value, while those in the process of buying a flat with low interest mortgages were receiving the same kind of subsidy as the industrialists and farmers. Merchants were happy with their burgeoning sales and profits, and criticism was rare, except in some newspapers. During this inflationary period, the Israelis maintained and even improved their standard of living (wages in 1978 rose by an average of 3 per cent in real terms); yet uncertainty about the future created a widely felt, though little articulated, apprehension that encompassed the rulers as well as the ruled.

The price of inflation between 1977 and 1980 was being paid by the Americans. But how much longer would they be prepared to pay and what price Israel's political independence as a remittance state? Israelis learned to live with spiralling inflation, but the anxieties it created added to the spiralling national malaise. The President of the Manufacturers Association admitted in 1979 that 'inflation – at least at this stage – is good for the people living in the country, but it will lead to a national catastrophe eventually.'

The manufacturers

The Manufacturers Association is the spokesman of the private sector of industry, the capitalist entrepreneurs who, even under socialist Governments, were encouraged to make their particular contribution to the creation of a stable and productive Jewish State. It consists of over 1,200 privately owned enterprises which include a few owned jointly by the Histadrut and private investors with private participation over 50 per cent. Maintained by the subscriptions of its members, the Manufacturers Association is a formidable representative body for private industry which accounts for about 70 per cent of the country's industrial production.

Housed in a modern building in Tel Aviv's commercial centre, the Association employs a staff of about seventy-five. The members are organized into industrial and local groupings, paralleled by departments of the Association's administration, which carry out the policy decisions of the various committees. A Board of Directors of sixty, elected by Association members, meets monthly to consider policy, but the day-to-day administration is controlled by a Presidium of fourteen, elected by the Board of

Directors and meeting weekly. At the pinnacle of the pyramid is the President, Avraham Shavit, known familiarly throughout Israel as 'Booma'.

Tall and burly with strong, heavy features and steel-grey hair, Shavit is young by the standards of Israeli leadership, having been born in Tel Aviv in 1927. He and his three brothers were born into industry and all joined the electrical appliance business founded by their father and successfully expanded into one of Israel's larger enterprises. 'Booma' still works in the family business from about 8 a.m. until noon, after which he repairs to his fashionably contemporary office at the Manufacturers Building in Montefiore Street. His energy and powerful personality have projected both the Association and himself as important elements in Israeli life, and his talent for expressing his views in clear and forceful images ensures that he is frequently quoted. An example in 1979 was: 'The only genuine overtime being done today is at the Mint where they keep on printing more money.'

He was a vociferous supporter of Government subsidies to industry, justifying the handouts to manufacturers as essential backing for the expansion of exports. At the same time he saw no inconsistency in attacking Ministers for refusing to accept Budget cuts and charged them with placing their vested interests before national needs. But then Shavit's strength lay less in his logic than in the combined power of Israel's manufacturers and his own brashness.

He blames the public sector for the problem of low productivity and argues that, until 1967, business was run primarily for what he terms the 'social' reason of providing jobs for newcomers. Israel at that time created labour-intensive industries which are now in the process of being converted into sophisticated labour-restrictive industries. He proudly claims that total exports of $87 million in 1948 have been transformed to almost $7 billion in 1978 and that Israel, now exporting high-quality sophisticated goods and technology, is eighth in the world list of exporters *per capita* of population.

Shavit is unhappy with Israel's situation as the recipient of charitable funds from Jews abroad, and believes that the millions of dollars from US Jewry do Israel more harm than good. What incentive is there for people to emigrate to Israel, he asks, when, for the purpose of fund-raising in America, it must project itself as run-down and needy? He also feels that it damages Israelis' self-respect – makes them feel like beggars. Yet, he cautiously concedes that the fund-raising programme does create involvement with Israel and should not be abandoned until another form of involvement has been developed to replace it.

At the end of 1979, Shavit was appointed Chairman of the Board of El Al, which was economically ailing. The post was non-executive and Shavit was not expected to give it his full time. It gave him the opportunity to show whether he could apply the business principles he had been advocating and end the losses of millions of dollars which this badly managed national asset had been incurring. His immediate impact was striking. Within a month of his appointment, he had given El Al a new lease of life by persuading the union to accept not only mass dismissals but also, almost incredibly, substantial wage-cuts. His job at El Al was Shavit's political ordeal by fire. If he succeeded, it would open the way to the political career which was, for him, the obvious next step.

Industrial achievement

The Government sector of the economy includes the nation's largest industrial enterprise, Israel Aircraft Industries. Because it is Government-owned, the normal test of profitability hardly applies, but IAI, employing over 20,000 workers (17 per cent of Israel's industrial workforce), is described by normally cynical economists, as well as economic defence correspondents, as a model of efficiency and productivity. It is the heart of Israel's thriving arms industry, vital to national defence and important as a major exporter. Israelis themselves are amazed that their small new nation now supplies sophisticated technology and aerospace components to no fewer than forty-three countries.

IAI has other activities outside the production of military equipment. It services Boeing airliners belonging to seventeen countries, completely runs the fleets of four national airlines and manufactures the civilian Westwind/Arava executive jet (which also has military uses). But the bulk of its production is arms – fighter aircraft (particularly the Israeli developed Kfir), missiles and missile boats, guns and radar equipment. Other Israeli industries also produce weapons systems, and it is estimated that altogether half of Israel's industrial workers are engaged in the production of armaments.

The development of so powerful an arms industry has been a painful necessity for Israel. The succession of wars, the continual threat of attack and the unreliability of arms supplies from abroad (Israel will never forget the ban suddenly imposed in 1967 by France, at that time her major arms supplier) forced Israel to divert much of her national effort into achieving self sufficiency in weapons. Many thoughtful Israelis are not only unhappy at this distortion of national creativity into armaments, but they are embarrassed by some of the customers for their products.

In the early 1960s it was revealed that Israel had sold a considerable supply of her novel and efficient machine guns to West Germany. The *Jewish Chronicle* published a leading article expressing repugnance at the fact that, so soon after the defeat of Nazism, the Jewish State should be selling such weapons to Germany, of all countries. When we met in Israel shortly afterwards, Ben-Gurion, who was then Prime Minister, chided me, as the editor of the *Chronicle*, for this comment. He explained that an armaments industry was vital and that no country, let alone a small and poor Israel, could cover the high costs involved unless some of the vast expenditure was recouped from export sales. And, he concluded, customers did not grow on trees.

As weapons systems have become even more costly, Ben-Gurion's successors have had to look even harder for customers and accept business from far less acceptable regimes than West Germany. Israel has become an arms supplier to South Africa and a number of dictatorial governments in Latin America. Israelis are miserably resigned to this, explaining that it is an unavoidable necessity in the fight for national survival.

In 1979, Defence Minister Ezer Weizman estimated that Israel's arms exports that year would reach a record $600 million. But he could not look farther ahead, because of considerable uncertainties, primarily due to political factors. The decision to suspend supplies to Nicaragua brought about a loss running into millions of dollars and, although arms trans-actions are generally not publicized, it was reported that two missile boats ordered by that country from IAI had been returned together with their sea-to-sea missiles. Another arms deal which failed at about the same period was the sale of 70 IAI-overhauled Skyhawks to Malaysia. Iran was yet another market lost in 1979.

Exporting arms is becoming an increasingly competitive business, with shrinking markets, while the increase in labour costs is making Israel's prices less attractive. The industry may be facing a slump although efficiency, particularly in electronics and other areas of supertechnology, is likely to ensure that Israel will not only be able to take care of her own needs, but continue to find markets for defence supplies.

A more aggressive selling programme was evident in Israel's major display at the 1979 Le Bourget air show in Paris. IAI's pavilion, designed to represent a huge flying saucer, offered a selection of integrated systems including the Sea Scan, Arava and Westwind jets, two effective naval systems, the Gabriel radar homing sea-to-sea missile and the Dvora missile patrol boat. Land systems and air systems included a new product from the electronics division of IAI that enables tank commanders to communicate with their drivers without speech. In addition to IAI, six other Israeli manufacturers of aerospace and related equipment exhibited marvels of modern science at the show. Rafael, the Israel Armament Development Authority, displayed electronic intelligence and special computer and communications systems. The Bet Shemesh works showed its new gas turbine engines, while Iscar Blades exhibited its high-precision jet engine blades, already used by four of the largest jet engine manufacturers in the world.

The Government sector of industry also includes Israel Chemicals, combining the mining, extracting and processing of minerals; El Al, the national airline; and 40 per cent of Zim, the shipping line.

The two other sectors of the Israeli economy, the Histadrut and the private sector, are more affected by economic factors which, in the Government sector, may have to take second place to vital national necessities. In the case of the Histadrut, as we have seen, considerations of ideology led to the establishment of substantial commercial and industrial enterprises more to provide jobs than to make money, but the private sector has had to develop with an unashamed emphasis on the profit motive, although Israel's entrepreneurs have not hesitated to seek, and secure, valuable Government support.

Apart from diamonds (the greatest single export), defence and related industries and agricultural produce, next on the list of Israel's industrial successes comes textiles and clothing. Polgat, a textile group, is claimed by one of its customers, Marks & Spencer – no mean judge of these matters – to be the most efficient clothing manufacturing plant in the world. The story of its beginnings and growth offers an enlightening illustration of the problems and achievements of Israel's industrial private sector.

The Pollock family (Pol of Polgat) was involved in the textile business in Czernovitz, Romania, before World War II, where the grandfather of the present generation built the first knitting factory. In 1940 the Russians took it and Dov Pollock, who now coordinates Polgat group operations, started his working life in the ghetto at the age of 9. When the war ended, he and his brother Yossi made their way to Palestine. Their 'illegal' ship was intercepted by the British and they were detained in Cyprus, eventually reaching their destination during the War of Independence in 1948. Almost simultaneously, their uncle, Israel Pollock, who was to become the founder and dynamo of Polgat, emigrated to Chile. There he joined another brother and began a textile business which achieved considerable success.

Public-spirited Israel Pollock became a leading member of the Santiago Jewish community and President of the Zionist Organization in Chile. In that capacity he welcomed Pinhas Sapir, then Israel's Minister of Finance, on one of his regular fund-raising and general scouting expeditions among the prosperous Jews of Latin America. A visit to the Pollock factories convinced Sapir that Israel Pollock had to be persuaded to build a factory in Israel – and Sapir was a forceful persuader.

In 1961, when Pollock started in Israel, the town of Kiryat Gat in the arid Lachish region just north of the Negev had a population of 4,000 and high unemployment. It had been started only a few years before with the intention that it should become the urban and economic centre of the group of agricultural settlements founded in the area in the mid-1950s. That did not work out because Tel Aviv, Jerusalem and Beersheba were too close and convenient. Kiryat Gat as a business centre languished.

Sapir was anxious to attract industry to this depressed township and invited Pollock to start up there. Advocating his cause with fervour, Sapir listed all the advantages of Kiryat Gat, including its proximity to Jerusalem. To make this point, Sapir offered to drive Pollock down, but on consulting his diary, found that the only time available was 5 a.m. They drove down together at that hour and, in the absence of other traffic, swept through the narrow road at a great pace. Only later did Israel Pollock realize that under normal traffic conditions the journey was a multiple of his original travelling time!

Cheap land, Government incentives and his own idealism combined to induce Israel Pollock to start. The Pollocks (by that time Dov and Yossi as well as other members of the family had joined their uncle) provided 40 per cent of the working capital, Government loans via the Development Bank a further 45 per cent and the Ministry of Development the remaining 15 per cent on condition that the greater part of production would be exported.

On this basis, Polgat opened a spinning factory employing 250 workers, most of them unskilled immigrants from twenty-four countries. For the first five years, until they produced the first trained workers and foremen, the going was hard. One of their greatest successes was to fire their Jewish workers with their own idealism, thus creating a productive work force. Borrowing from Marks & Spencer's experience and following the same lines as the British firm (which was to become its largest customer), Polgat gained the loyalty, almost devotion, of its employees by providing them with an extensive range of social services – kindergartens, high school grants and social workers.

As the business developed and labour requirements increased, Polgat recruited Arab workers from Gaza and the West Bank. When the Arab workers (now over 1,000 out of a total work force of 4,000) were brought in, the Pollocks explained to the Jewish workers the necessity for that step: to make the greatest use of the costly machinery, there had to be three shifts and there was simply not a sufficient supply of Jewish labour for the purpose. The integration of the Arab workers was smooth. All workers are paid on the same basis and the Arabs receive promotion on the same criteria as the Jews. They are trained within the regular Polgat training schemes and some, after training, have left to work as foremen in Kuwait and other Arab states. Above all, the object of Polgat training schemes has been to maintain high-quality control and a fine finish. In 1979 Polgat exported products to the value of $28 million to the most developed countries in the Western world.

The factories in Kiryat Gat are staggering in their size and sophistication. Polgat Woollen Industries spins and weaves a variety of fabrics in vast, hangar-like workrooms, the heat and noise of the weaving and dyeing departments contrasting dramatically with the cleanliness and quiet of the almost entirely automated spinning process. An adjoining and connected plant houses the operations of an associated company, Bagir, which manufactures men's suits, blazers and trousers – hundreds of thousands of them, of which no less than 85 per cent are exported.

Polgat is an example of efficiency in industry in a country which, on the whole, has acquired no great reputation for efficiency. It is a success story on the social as well as the economic level achieved by a management which enjoys, as one of them put it to me, 'mixing computers with the human touch'.

Not that profits are scorned. Each part of the group is expected to pay its way, and does. The family still retains control, but 24 per cent of the shares were offered to the public in 1977 – 2.55 million at four times the nominal value (I£4). The increase in the price of Polgat shares, as in the group's profits, has been far higher than the rise in the general share index.

The banks

The main office of the Bank of Israel in Jerusalem's Jaffa Road could be a fortress, with its unrelieved walls and barred windows. Clearly no great trouble has been taken to maintain the buildings, for a new block is in course of construction in the Government office area close to the Knesset. The private office of the Governor is on the third (top) floor, spacious but utilitarian, with tiled floors and simple furniture. Large though the room is, it seems too small for its occupant, Arnon Gafny, who has been the Governor of Israel's central bank since 1976.

Created as recently as 1954 by the Bank of Israel Law, this is not only the newest of the major state institutions, but also the only one not directly answerable to the Knesset. Nor is the Governor a political figure in this over-political country. The first governor, David Horowitz – known throughout Israel as Dollek – was an immense power in the country. He shaped the new central bank, with which his name was synonymous for the first seventeen years of its existence, and gave it international respect-ability. Horowitz was invited by Sapir to succeed him as Finance Minister but declined because it was a party post and he had always kept clear of party politics.

Gafny, the third occupant, has been a member of the Labour Party since his youth, but was never an activist. His sole experience in electioneering took place in 1965, when he supported the campaign of Eshkol only because he was then being attacked by Ben-Gurion. The year after his appointment, which carries with it the title of 'Economic Adviser to the Government', Gafny became the first Governor to work with a Cabinet which did not appoint him. In this unprecedented situation, he continued to fulfil the role which Dollek Horowitz had once described as 'constructive persuasion' – if he failed to persuade the government to follow the course of action he advocated, he felt free to make his own views public. Gafny has not hesitated to make his views on economic policy public, even when they are critical of Government policy.

Such an occasion was the liberalization of the economy undertaken by the Likud Government in October 1977. Foreign exchange control was abolished, the lira was floated, and import levies and premiums were discarded. Gafny was apprised of the government's intentions some three months in advance and, with his expert economic staff, studied the proposals and suggested limits, conditions and techniques. He recom-mended tight monetary and fiscal policies to avoid spiralling inflation, but when the 1978 Budget appeared, he was appalled that three billion lira of expenditure had been added in response to pressures from departmental Ministries. Gafny protested and argued and, when he failed to change the policy, attacked it before the TV screens. Begin was furious and condemned his action, but there was never any suggestion that the Governor of the Bank had not acted within his rights, or that any disciplinary action should be taken against him.

Governors hold office for a five-year term, and the appointment is made by the President on the recommendation of the Cabinet. He could be dismissed by the same procedure, but that has never happened. Neverthe-less, to ensure that the Governor feels himself to be independent and not inhibited by the threat of sacking, the Bank of Israel Law provides that if a Governor is dismissed, he will still receive his full salary and pension provisions for the balance of his term. The independence is real and has made the Bank the voice of economic realism against the political compromises of embattled ministers. Within the Bank, relations with the politicians are primarily the task of the Governor, but he is supposed to be aided by an Advisory Board, the members of which are appointed for two years by the Government. The new members appointed by the Likud changed the political complexion of the Board from its former Labour hue, but since the Board is only an advisory body without authority, it hardly troubles the Bank's officers.

The Bank, like other central banks, is the Government bank and the bankers' bank. It has the power to order the commercial banks to deposit with it a certain proportion of their own liquid cash in order to control the flow of money into the economy. It also handles the country's foreign exchange reserves, which it invests to the country's profit, and lends the country money in return for Treasury bills. It handles the issue of state loans, and in its reports tells the nation what any bank manager will tell his customers about the prudent conduct of their financial affairs.

Arnon Gafny was born into the world of finance and economics. His father was the Inland Revenue Commissioner for Palestine under the British Mandate, and he himself was Director of the Budget division of the Ministry of Finance, eventually becoming Director-General. He was the second choice for the Bank; Prime Minister Rabin's first nominee for the post, Asher Yadlin, was arrested on corruption charges before he was installed. Gafny was loath to leave his job at the Ministry. He regarded it as a greater centre of real power in the country's economic affairs, the place where the economic policy of the country was made. But at the Bank, he has more time for basic thought, and is aided by an economic research department which is easily the best in the country. For a professional economist, the post is the peak of a career but Gafny is too young (he was born in 1933) and too able not to be considered for further advancement.

Commercial banking is dominated by the big three – Bank Leumi, Bank Hapoalim and the Discount Bank. Their branches are everywhere; Leumi alone has more than 250. But it is not only the boom in banking business which has induced the proliferation of branches. The acquisition and development of property is seen by them as the best hedge against inflation.

All the commercial banks wield more power and influence than their counterparts in most other countries, primarily because of their large investments in all sectors of the economy. The pioneer in this expansion was the Discount Bank, the newest of the big three, founded in 1935 by an immigrant from Salonika, Leon Recanati. It began investing in shipping, insurance, property and industry, and the others followed. The Discount Bank today controls a shipping business, is closely connected with Phoenix Insurance and has a 20 per cent holding in Property and Building Corporation. The Recanati family is still prominent in the management of the Bank and is its major shareholder, but in recent years talented outsiders have been brought in. One of them, ex-General Dan Tolkowsky, is a mechanical engineer and an enthusiast for technological progress. Through his initiative, the Investment Corporation of the Bank (of which he is Managing Director) acquired a 38 per cent interest in Elron Electronic Industries, which made profits of nearly $20 million in 1978–79.

Bank Leumi – the largest (though Bank Hapoalim challenges the distinction) – is also the oldest, being the successor of the Anglo-Palestine Bank, which was the Government Bank before the formation of the Bank of Israel. Founded in London in 1902 as a subsidiary of the Jewish Colonial Trust Ltd, it opened its first branch in Palestine in Jaffa the following year. It grew with the growth of immigration into Palestine during the British Mandate, and transferred its board from London to Tel Aviv in 1931. Growth was rapid as it profited from the influx of capital into the country with the German immigration after Hitler. The Zionist Organization and the Jewish Agency used the bank for their activities, and set up the General Mortgage Bank together in 1924. (Each of the major banks has a controlling interest in a mortgage bank, the Israeli equivalent of a British building society or a Savings and Loan Bank in the United States).

Because of Bank Leumi's special position, its chief executive officer is *primus inter pares* of Israel's commercial bankers. The present incumbent, Ernst Japhet, was appointed in 1970 and is a member of the distinguished banking family of that name. Japhet prefers to stay within the traditional boundaries of banking and has been reluctant to develop Leumi's industrial and commercial interests. Nevertheless, it has, like its peers, connections with an Insurance Company, Migdal, and owns a majority shareholding in Africa-Israeli Investments, a large property and building company. Shares in the bank are publicly quoted and the Jewish Agency retains considerable control, though Japhet has been successful in keeping his bank clear of involvement with the Government or politics.

The most progressive of the big three in recent years has been the Histadrut-controlled Bank Hapoalim. Its rapid advance under the direction of its present Managing Director, Jacob Levinson, has been mentioned in the account of the activities of the General Federation of Labour. Purely in the field of banking, it is Israel's number one in size and profitability, and the largest single tax-payer. It does not invest in insurance or industry – to do so would be to compete with its parent, the Histadrut. Instead, it has invested in services like computers and communications. Owned by the Histadrut through its commercial holding group, Hevrat Ovdim, Bank Hapoalim nevertheless acts as a totally independent bank. The only links are the founders' shares of the bank, which Hevrat Ovdim owns and which give it a 50 per cent say in the appointment of directors. Levinson concedes that a 'certain rapport' with the Histadrut may be assumed.

Apart from the strength of the commercial banks through their involvements in all branches of the nation's commerce and industry, they have acquired additional importance as channels for the massive (subsidized) loans which governments have long given to agriculture, industry and tourism. The commercial banks have been responsible for checking borrowers' collateral and for collecting repayments. All the big three participate as shareholders and directors of the Bank of Industrial Development, which considers applications for Government loans.

Not less important is the function of Israel's commercial banks as brokers on the Tel Aviv Stock Exchange and as advisers to private investors. They are in a good position to know, for the shares of the banks and their various subsidiary or associated companies form a substantial portion of all shares traded on the Stock Exchange.

Chapter fourteen

Jews Outside; Arabs Inside

The Jewish Connection

A considerable literature discusses whether the Jews constitute a religion, a race or a nation, for they do not fall conveniently into any of these categories. Many committed Jews are not religious believers; Jews belong to a variety of races; and while Israel is a Jewish State, Jews outside it are citizens of many nations. To talk of the Jews as a people begs the question in the absence of a generally accepted definition of peoplehood. But, though it is difficult to define the Jews, the Jewish State is capable of precise definition. It is a sovereign state, a group of people with certain common characteristics living together in a territorial area, governing themselves in their own way and accepted as a state by the comity of nations (with the exception of the Arab 'rejectionists').

But it is a state with a difference.

The distinctiveness of Israel does not lie in the fact that it has a large diaspora – for so have, for example, Ireland and Italy. It lies in the relationship between the State and the diaspora. In no other country does any particular group of non-citizens possess rights of an exceptional nature granted them by law. Israel's Law of Return, symbolizing its existence as the Jewish national home, declares that every Jew has the right to live in the Jewish State and to acquire instant citizenship. All diasporas have evolved by a centrifugal movement of population away from an existing state; but only in the case of Israel was a state created by a centripetal ingathering of a diaspora.

Israel was created through the instrumentality of the Zionist movement, a world-wide organization that had grown from very small beginnings among the oppressed and persecuted Jewish masses of Eastern Europe towards the end of the nineteenth century. An assimilated Viennese Jew, Theodor Herzl, built a political movement out of disparate groups of philanthropists, idealists and revolutionaries, and set it on course as a national solution to the Jewish problem of homelessness. Its first major success came during World War I in 1917, when the British Government issued what became known as the Balfour Declaration. So portentous a commitment took a peculiarly prosaic form. It was made in a brief letter signed by Arthur James Balfour, then Foreign Secretary, which stated that His Majesty's Government viewed 'with favour the establishment in Palestine of a national home for the Jewish people.' The letter was addressed to Lord Rothschild, then President of the British Zionist Federation.

World War I ended with the Middle Eastern Ottoman empire in the hands of the victorious allies. After earlier wars, victors had simply taken whatever they wanted of the territories they had gained by force of arms, but in the more enlightened twentieth century such flagrant land-grabbing was no longer acceptable. Something had to be done, however, about the parts of the Ottoman empire which were obviously not going to be returned to Turkey. The solution reached was to vest ownership in the newly founded League of Nations, which then delegated the actual administration of particular areas to one or other of the Allies. Britain accepted such a 'mandate' for Palestine, and the terms under which it was granted were contained in a legal document.

That document required Britain to secure the creation of the Jewish National Home by, among other things, facilitating Jewish immigration; and it was to present an annual account of its custodianship to the Permanent Mandates Commission at the League of Nations. The Mandate also authorized the setting up of a 'Jewish Agency' to cooperate with Britain in the performance of the purposes of the Mandate. Provisionally, the agency was the Zionist Organization, but in the course of time a separate institution was created representing both Zionist and non-Zionist Jews. The latter, while they were not Jewish nationalists, were ready, for philanthropic reasons, to assist Jews who wanted to settle in Palestine.

Although the Mandate has long since gone (Britain relinquished it in 1947) the Jewish Agency, still retaining the same name, persists. So does the World Zionist Organization. By the time of statehood, the two organizations were virtually synonymous, for the old distinction between Zionists and non-Zionists had lost its meaning. With the exception of a fringe of diehards, the overwhelming majority of the fifteen million Jews in the world, Zionists and non-Zionists, had tacitly reached a remarkable degree of unanimity on two propositions. The first was that the Jews living in the free world did not consider themselves in exile, so that few emigrated to the State. Secondly, nearly all Jews felt a strong emotional, religious or humanitarian obligation to support Israel. It existed as a nation, and arguments about Jewish nationalism were academic.

The Jews who lived in Palestine (not, of course, the diaspora Jews) became nationals of the new sovereign state but they were anxious to maintain ties with the diaspora. Ideals and emotions aside, they also recognized that they needed the material and political support of their co-religionists to sustain the fledgling new state. Every Israeli leader talked of partnership with world Jewry. In a formal sense, that partnership was cemented in a 1952 enactment of the Knesset called the 'Zionist Organization – Jewish Agency for Palestine Status Law', which gave a special status and special rights and obligations to a non-Israeli entity purporting to represent the Jewish people.

The following paragraphs from that law are of importance because they set out the concepts and the division of functions between Israel and the diaspora:

1. The State of Israel regards itself as the creation of the entire Jewish people, and its gates are open, in accordance with its laws, to every Jew wishing to immigrate into it.

2. The World Zionist Organization, from its foundation five decades ago, headed the movement and efforts of the Jewish people to realize the age-old vision of the return to its homeland, and with the assistance of other Jewish circles and bodies, carried the main responsibility for establishing the State of Israel.

3. The World Zionist Organization, which is also the Jewish Agency for Palestine, takes care, as before, of immigration and directs absorption and settlement projects in the State.

4. The State of Israel recognizes the World Zionist Organization as the authorized agency which will continue to operate in the State of Israel for the development and settlement of the country, the absorption of immigrants from the Diaspora and the coordination of the activities in Israel of Jewish institutions and organizations active in those fields.

5. The mission of gathering in the exiles which is the central task of the State of Israel and the Zionist Movement in our days, requires constant efforts by the Jewish people in the Diaspora. The State of Israel, there-fore, expects the cooperation of all Jews, as individuals and groups, in building up the State and assisting the immigration into it of the masses of the people, and regards the unity of all sections of Jewry as necessary for this purpose.

6. The State of Israel expects efforts on the part of the World Zionist Organization for achieving this unity; if, to this end, the Zionist Organization, with the consent of the Government and the approval of the Knesset, should decide to broaden its basis, the enlarged body will enjoy the status conferred upon the World Zionist Organization in the State of Israel.

Jewish Agency/WZO

A large, well-maintained building surrounded by a tall security fence on King George V Boulevard in Jerusalem houses the Jewish Agency. Its confident, powerful appearance symbolizes the strength of the organiza-tion, whose importance in the country is only less than that of the Govern-ment and the Histadrut. The centre block of the complex is occupied by the Jewish Agency itself: on each side, curved wing buildings bear lettered signs – Keren Hayesod (Foundation Fund) on one, and Keren Kayemeth (Jewish National Fund) on the other – the names of the two main funds created by the Zionist Organization to channel the financial contributions of world Jewry towards the rebuilding of a Jewish nation.

The Agency is not the only recipient of financial contributions to Israel. Innumerable other institutions make individual appeals. But the Agency derives its power from the size of its budget – $350 million in 1979. It comes from two sources, the United Israel Appeal in the United States and the Keren Hayesod; the funds raised by the United Israel Appeal, Inc. in America go directly to the Agency for distribution – the estimated total for 1978–79 was $227 million. Money given by the Americans directly to the Israeli Government would not be regarded as charitable contributions under the laws of the USA and could therefore not be set off by donors against their income tax liability – a most vital consideration in fund-raising. Given to the Jewish Agency to be used exclusively for the settlement of refugees, it is recognized as a legitimate charitable contribution. The second major source of funds for the Agency, the Keren Hayesod, is the fund-raising arm of the WZO, and the recipient of donations from the Jewish communities of some sixty countries. In 1978–79, the estimated income from this source was $57½ million.

The WZO disposed of a separate budget of over $50 million in 1979. This budget, although distinct from the Agency budget, was administered by the same officials. In some departments, like those dealing with immigration, immigrant absorption and settlements, the WZO performs functions which the tax structure of the Agency precludes. The departments dealing with these areas are therefore administered by two co-chairmen, one each from the Agency and the WZO.

A reconstruction of the organization in 1971 returned the Agency and WZO to their original status as separate organizations. The WZO is the political, cultural and information entity, while the enlarged Agency is the money-raising body. The 'new' Agency consists of nominees of the WZO, the American United Israel Appeal and diaspora communities outside the USA in the ratio of 50–30–20. More diaspora Jewish organizations have been encouraged to affiliate to the WZO, thereby gaining representation on the Agency and a share in the control of the large funds. However, the real authority has remained in Israel, and the top posts continue to be apportioned in accordance with the 'party key', the proportion in which Israel's political parties are represented in the Knesset.

The organizational structure of the Agency consists of an Assembly which meets annually and selects a Board of Governors, not at random, but with fixed proportions for its three constituent groups. Most important of the functions of the Board is the election of an Executive, based in Jerusalem, which does the work and constitutes the 'cabinet', whose members are paid on the same scale as Israeli Cabinet Ministers. The 'Prime Minister' of the Agency is the Chairman of the Executive. That post (as well as the Chairmanship of the WZO Executive) has been held since 1977 by Aryeh (Leon) Dultzin, a member of the Likud. Born in Minsk in 1914, he emigrated with his family to Mexico in 1929 and went to live in Israel when he was in his thirties. Multilingual, suave, relaxed and gregarious, he is universally popular, and his election, unprecedentedly, received the unanimous support of all parties. His career in Israel has been almost exclusively within the ranks of Zionist officialdom.

Approximately half a million Israelis received help from the Agency in 1979. Most were either new immigrants or former immigrants still in need. The most central of the various Agency departments is that of Immigration and Absorption which, with an expenditure in 1978–79 of more than $65 million, accounted for 19 per cent of the total Agency budget. That expenditure covered the operations of offices and transit centres abroad, the activities of immigration emissaries; the transport of immigrants and shipment of their belongings to Israel and, when they reached Israel, all the necessary services to help them to settle in comfortably.

The existence of a Ministry of Absorption with essentially similar objectives has led to a tug of war between the two authorities in recent years. In 1979, Begin proposed the establishment of a unitary immigration and absorption authority under the control of the Agency. Dultzin naturally welcomed the plan but it ran into heavy weather when David Levy, the influential Minister of Absorption (which he doubled with the Ministry of Housing), objected on the grounds that the Agency had been unsuccessful in the past and that the plan would only lead to a repetition of the failure. Backed by the 500 employees of the Ministry, Levy was also supported by the Herut party leaders who took the view that absorption was a Government responsibility which should not be delegated to a non-state body. With a plethora of other conflicts and problems facing the Government, the proposal was quietly shelved, and Government employees have not been dismissed.

Second only to immigration and absorption in its expenditure is the Agency's department for higher education, which provides substantial financial support to the seven Israeli university institutions – nearly $50 million in 1978–79. In addition, the Agency itself operates a number of educational programmes, like language centres for immigrants, aid for immigrant students and scholarships for secondary school pupils. Some $2 million is expended for 'intensification of Jewish education abroad'.

Possibly the most efficient and certainly the most highly regarded of the all the Agency departments is that dealing with rural settlements. Its co-chairman, Ra'anan Weitz, is one of the great world authorities on this subject. He is a member of the Labour Party and is responsible for settlements other than those in territory occupied during the Six Day War. That more limited settlement activity is under the control of his co-chairman, a Likud nominee.

Other portfolios cover youth work, information, organization and education. There are two for education, because the National Religious Party was not content with non-religious control over education and the compromise solution was the setting up of another department for religious education which, naturally enough, was to be under its direction. In all, twenty-two portfolios of ministerial rank are divided among nominees of the Israeli political parties. In 1979, the Likud held the portfolios of the Chairmanship (Dultzin), Immigration and Absorption, General Education, one of the youth departments and half of the settlements department, as well as several minor offices. Labour held the treasureship, the major half of the settlement department and the chairmanship of, among others, the important Organization Department. The NRP held the Religious Education Department, a youth department and the department which supplies religious functionaries abroad.

So widespread are the activities of the Agency and so large its budget that it has spawned an overblown bureaucracy and a system of patronage rivalling as well as supplementing that of the Government. Party workers for whom no post can be found in the Government have often been placed in the Agency. It possesses one of the most attractive forms of patronage in Israel, an official mission abroad.

As the organization linking Israel with the diaspora, the Agency necessarily employs representatives to perform various tasks in Jewish communities abroad. In 1979, the Agency had on its payroll no fewer than 460 emissaries operating all over the world, together with 800 part-timers engaged locally, and frequently, also, Israelis living abroad. Most of the emissaries are occupied in encouraging and helping actual or potential immigrants, working with Jewish youth groups and engaging in educational activity. They generally serve a two-year term abroad, and many perform an invaluable service in helping to maintain Jewish consciousness and advance Jewish learning in communities threatened with disintegration because of their inability to provide teachers and other services from their own resources. In this respect the Agency performs a dual function, helping Jewish life in the diaspora to resist the erosion of assimilation while, at the same time, helping Israel by strengthening its most loyal ally.

In an operation on this scale, abuses are bound to occur and the institution of 'emissaries' has not been immune. So attractive is a stint abroad that these posts have not infrequently been used as payoffs to political allies. The nominees may (but not invariably) possess the necessary qualifications, but they are political appointees. The present administration of the Agency, very conscious of the damage caused by political nepotism, has been working towards a reduction in the number of emissaries – and of staff in general. The total staff of the Agency and the WZO amounts to over 3,500 and, as is the case in Israel generally, they are virtually undismissable. Reductions were planned by filling vacant jobs only when essential. This seemed to be working. In 1978, 600 staff left and only 180 were replaced.

Allegations of extravagance and waste have been levelled against the Agency and the WZO for so long and with such persistence that, largely through the prodding of diaspora leaders, measures have been taken to streamline the organization and trim expenditure. In 1979 special equipment was installed in the offices to monitor telephones, with the object of eliminating wasteful or unauthorized long-distance calls. The extensive and abused car pool has been abolished; the official cars provided for department heads and their Director-General are made available for other staff when not in use by these senior officials. The patronage element of the 'party key' is diminishing and today the new party appointments are limited to the departmental heads, the Directors-General and possibly a few other top jobs.

Both the functions and the organizational structure of the Agency/WZO are in the process of change as the partnership between Israel and the diaspora evolves. The re-creation of the Jewish State after almost 2,000 years was so unprecedented an event in Jewish history that its effects on Jewish life generally will take generations to unfold. As those changes occur, the institutions should adjust to them, but they have been laggard in doing so up to now. Nevertheless, the Agency/WZO remains a potent force in Israel's constructive endeavours and a focus for the efforts of diaspora Jewry. Whatever doubts are entertained about the functioning of the organization, there is little question that its fund-raising campaigns are the

biggest single factor activating Jewish life in the sixty countries in which
they are conducted. Giving money is an act of Jewish identification and
raising money is a Jewish commitment. Contributors and fund-raisers alike
in the diaspora, by learning something of the purposes in Israel to which the
funds go, are also engaging in a Jewish educational activity.

Fund-raising and the fund-raisers

In his indispensable anthology, *The Zionist Idea*, Arthur Hertzberg quotes
an illuminating passage from the diary of Moshe Leib Lilienblum, one of
the intellectual fathers of the Zionist movement. In an entry of 1883,
Lilienblum set the stage for what has become the greatest Jewish activity in
the diaspora: 'Whoever wants to support the national idea', he wrote, 'will
contribute a kopeck a week, to be saved for a given period in special boxes to
be placed in every house, for the settlement of Eretz Israel. In a year this
will add up to thousands of rubles. It is also possible to earmark given
percentages of the sums donated in the synagogues, at weddings, at funerals
of the rich, etc. Perhaps too a Jewish lottery can be set up so that there will
be no more need to talk about the sale of shares in stock companies and the
like.'

The Agency/WZO receives by far the largest share of funds collected
abroad. But other Israeli institutions engaged in fund-raising activities in
the diaspora are legion, and the public announcement of benefactors is
ubiquitous.

An ambulance parked on a Jerusalem street will have painted on it
almost as much reading matter as a Chinese wall-poster. Apart from the
obvious indication of its purpose, lengthy inscriptions on the doors and side
panels record for posterity (at least until the vehicle is scrapped) such facts
as that it has been donated via the American Friends of Magen David
Adom by Mr Jacob So-and-so of Oshkosh, Wisconsin, together with his
brother-in-law, Mr Joseph Such-and-Such of Oakland, California, in
memory of their respected late father and father-in-law, Mr Isaac So-
and-so.

Not merely ambulances, but practically every non-Government public
building is either named (in large letters) after a contributor, or bears
plaques and inscriptions recording the names of givers. Nothing escapes.
Gardens, parks, park benches, theatre seats, synagogues, synagogue seats,
trees, every kind of vehicle and every kind of building bear visible
expressions of Israel's spectacular success in the field of fund-raising. There
can be no other society anywhere in the world into which so much
philanthropy has been poured and in which fund-raising has been developed into such a fine art.

Innumerable institutions maintain fund-raising organizations and staffs.
At the lower and unsophisticated level, the long-established institutions of
orthodox Judaism despatch impressively bearded representatives to the
homes of the pious all over the world, replete with a much rubber-stamped
letter of authorization and a book of receipts. Whether it be in Johannesburg,
Melbourne, London or New York, the envoys have addresses and, with the

minimum of organization, collect money and live off the land. At the other end of the spectrum is the highly professional machinery of the major fund-raising institutions, chief of which is the Keren Hayesod – United Israel Appeal. Its present chairman, Avram Avi Hai, was appointed in 1978. Born in Toronto in 1931, he worked in the Prime Minister's office from 1960, later becoming Associate Dean of overseas students at the Hebrew University. A full-time fund-raiser, he has been active in reorganizing and modernizing his large machine.

All the major fund-raising institutions go about their tasks along lines which have by now become standard. Meetings of (preferably) prosperous Jews are organized in cities, towns and hamlets, wherever they can be found. These can be breakfast meetings, lunches, dinners or cocktail parties. Sometimes they even take place without the accompaniment of food. The groups are either geographical or, in the larger centres, broken up in accordance with their scale of giving, or by trade and profession. In the USA particularly, dinners may be held in honour of worthies to which their friends are invited and are expected to contribute (or buy Israel Bonds) as a tribute to them. The despatch to Israel of 'missions' made up of groups of actual or potential contributors has become a growth industry in recent years.

Taking care of the missions or study groups to ensure that they see the country generally and the particular institutions under whose aegis they are visiting Israel, is an important task of fund-raisers. In addition to groups, thousands of individual visitors arrive during the year, and dozens of religious institutions, charitable organizations and schools are only too eager to demonstrate their good works to them. Individuals, groups and conferences generally pay their own way but the local fund-raisers incur expenses, sometimes considerable, in shepherding them around and in offering hospitality.

Increasing vigilance by donors and the overseas fund-raising agencies is succeeding in reducing expenses of this nature in Israel. Yet, if diaspora Jews are to be encouraged to visit the country and attend meetings and conferences, these have to be made attractive – which costs money. The 1978 annual assembly of the Jewish Agency cost almost $175,000 and one of the most expensive single items was a festive concert in Jerusalem at which some $12,000 were spent on an orchestra and a popular singer. Conferences also involve the preparation of expensive documentation for the partici-pants, only a part of the mountain of educational and promotional material of all kinds generated by the fund-raisers of every Israeli institution.

Jewish life in the diaspora is an annual round of fund-raising events for Israel. The central appeals – Joint Israel Appeal in Britain, the United Israel Appeal and Israel Bonds in the USA – have the highest priority. They are followed by a plethora of institutional appeals. Every institution of learning, though receiving substantial finances from the Government and the Jewish Agency, maintains its own fund-raising apparatus and operates world-wide. The pioneer and the most experienced is the Hebrew Uni-versity, whose fund-raising staff in Jerusalem totals about forty, including secretaries. At its head is Bernard Cherrick, the University's Vice-Presi-dent, Dublin-born, English-educated and a confirmed bachelor. A graduate of the Liverpool Yeshiva, he ministered to a congregation in London with considerable success, served as a chaplain with the British forces in World War II and emigrated to Palestine in 1947.

Cherrick himself spends an average of four months a year 'on the road'. In January 1979 he visited Mexico, Venezuela and the USA. May saw him in Norway, Denmark, Belgium and England. In August he toured South Africa, Argentina, Uruguay and Brazil, and in November, the USA and Canada. Some of his time is spent organizing the groups of 'Friends' that exist all over the world, but most of it is devoted to fund-raising. Cherrick is good at it, both the private discussions with the big donors, and the speeches he makes at public gatherings. He and the President of the University, Avraham Harman, have been its most effective fund-raisers. Ben-Gurion and Tel Aviv Universities, both new and exciting, have recently been doing exceptionally well at fund-raising and are beginning to challenge the supremacy of the Hebrew University.

For the big general Israel appeals, the most popular speakers have been Cabinet Ministers, with Abba Eban the star followed by Yosef Burg, the Minister of the Interior. Eban impresses with his polished oratory, while Burg attracts audiences by his warm personality and fund of Jewish stories.

Of the more specialized funds and institutions raising large sums in the diaspora, one of the most successful has been the Jerusalem Foundation. In the twelve years from 1966 to 1978, it collected $50 million for specific projects to improve the city's facilities and preserve and enhance its historical sites. No visitor to the golden city can be unappreciative (or unaware, because they are all designated) of the gardens, the restoration and the beautification for which the Jerusalem Foundation has been responsible. In Israel, it is headed by a distinguished Board of Directors and equally honoured names grace its associated foundations in Canada, England and Germany. But the driving force in creating it, raising the large sums of money and directing how they are spent, is Teddy Kollek, the indefatigable Mayor of Jerusalem. He does not shine as an after-dinner speaker, but his almost demonic energy, his connections with the rich and famous all over the world, his patent love for the city and his practised charm have made him a near irresistible fund-raiser.

If there is anyone in the long, skilful and ingenious history of Zionist fund-raising more successful than Teddy Kollek, it must be the late Meyer Weisgal, creator of the Weizmann Institute in Rehovot. Describing himself as a purveyor of immortality to millionaires, he was successful in attracting munificent contributions for the construction and endowment of the splendid buildings of the Institute. Weisgal always thought big. To a tycoon whom he entertained lavishly in the expectation of a large gift. Weisgal is reputed to have handed back a cheque for a few thousand dollars with the comment, 'We don't charge for meals here.'

Some Israelis, while acknowledging the benefits which philanthropic contributions have brought to the country, are uneasy about some of its effects on Israel attitudes. In the 1960s, a disaffected Labour intellectual, the late Eliezer Livneh, broke away from the party and formed a new political group, one of whose slogans was: 'Not another sou from the UJA [the

American United Jewish Appeal].' Livneh claimed that the receipt of so much unearned income was a disincentive to local effort and encouraged corruption and the growth of what he termed 'an expense account morality'.

Those fears have not been allayed, but the needs of Israel in its abnormal situation are so vast, that the charitable contributions of the diaspora are indispensable in enabling the country to absorb immigrants and to maintain institutions essential to the quality of life.

Universities, religious schools and similar institutions offer their services not only to Israelis, but to Jews from abroad, in this way making important contributions to the preservation of Jewish life. As far as the contributors are concerned, their charity, like the quality of mercy, is twice blessed. Certainly, it benefits the recipients, but Israel's fund-raisers give to the Jewish world as well as take. In their travels to the major – and minor – centres of Jewish population, these itinerant Israelis give their listeners a sense of identification and spiritual uplift. In trying to arouse support they serve an educational purpose, talking about Jewish tradition, expounding on Jewish values, recalling Jewish history. The most skilled and experienced of the fund-raisers aim to leave the community they have visited feeling better about Jews. Their theme has always been, 'Don't give until it hurts – give until it feels good.'

The Arab minority

The Arab citizens of Israel (the population of the occupied territories is outside the scope of this work) number about half a million, compared with the 156,000 who remained in what became the Jewish State after the War of Independence. A population growth of this magnitude in just thirty years was due in the first place to the high rate of natural increase, the highest in the world, and secondly to the sharp decline in infant mortality. In addition there was a certain amount of immigration, permitted under a scheme for the reunification of families, which brought in about 40,000 Arabs. As a result of the abnormally high rate of natural increase, the Arabs of Israel are a young minority with a median age of 15.5.

The law gives Israeli Arabs full civil and cultural rights. They can vote (and in General Elections the proportion of those voting is higher than among the Jews), can sit in the Knesset, and can organize their own political parties. They can publish their own publications, utilize all Israel's public services, send their children to state-financed Arab-speaking schools and exercise religious autonomy on the same basis as the Jewish community. In one area alone do they not have the same duty as their Jewish fellow citizens, the duty to serve in Israel's armed forces – an exemption which symbolizes their ambivalent situation. They are a minority regarded by the majority as not completely trustworthy, a security hazard.

Whether or not the Arab minority would have reacted positively to the declaration of confidence implied by permitting them to participate in the defence of their country will remain an academic question. But there can be no doubt that Israel's Arabs do not share the national aspirations of Israel's

Jews. A survey of Israeli Arabs by the Haifa University Arab Centre, funded by the Ford Foundation, was undertaken in 1979. It found that 60 per cent of Israeli Arabs did not recognize Israel's right to exist and that 64 per cent regarded Zionism as racist. Some 75 per cent supported the creation of a Palestinian state, and 64 per cent wanted to see Israel's Law of Return (the fundamental commitment to Jewish immigration) abolished. The only satisfaction that Israel could glean from the report were its findings that more than half those surveyed classified themselves as Israeli Arabs rather than as Palestinians and confirmed that even if a Palestinian state were to be established, they would prefer to remain in Israel.

It was probably inevitable, given the conditions of minority status, of the continuing war between Israel and her Arab neighbours and of the inferior status accorded to Jews by Islam, that Israeli Arabs should identify themselves, and be identified, as separate and apart from the majority. Separateness, rather than the development of a common Israeli identity, has been fostered by the education system, in which the Arabs are provided with an Arabic, rather than Israeli, education. Arabic is the language of tuition in all subjects, with Hebrew as the second language. The emphasis in studies is upon Arabic literature and history with a natural identification with the Arab world and Arab nationalism.

The abolition in 1966 of military government in the areas in which most Arabs lived, the payment of compensation for expropriated land, the acceptance of Arabs as full members of the Histadrut and other similar measures have not produced any apparent improvement in the attitude of Israeli Arabs towards Israel. The reverse has been the case and, particularly since the Six Day War, which made contact possible between Israeli Arabs and their West Bank compatriots, their Arab nationalism has been encouraged and radicalism intensified.

The 156,000 Arabs who became Israelis in 1948 were on the whole a rural and backward element of the population. Fewer than fifty of them were university graduates and no more than three hundred had even gone through secondary school. Nazareth was the only Arab town, although Arab minorities persisted in the mixed towns of Jaffa, Haifa, Acre, Ramle and Jerusalem. The majority of Arabs remaining in Israel were peasants, living mostly in villages in the north of Israel and in what was called the 'triangle', a group of farm villages adjacent to the Jordanian border.

Their economy was based on primitive farming, which was constantly plagued by the chronic disadvantages of lack of water for irrigation and divided plots of land due to the inheritance laws. There was no organized marketing and, with the exception of the Karamans, a Moslem family living in Haifa, no industry or financiers. An attempt in the 1950s to create an industrial plant in the Arab sector failed. Faris Hamdan, an MK and former landowner who died in 1966, was persuaded to build a food-canning industry by his friends in the Government and Histadrut, eager to industrialize the Arab sector. The experiment proved that an ex-landowner, lacking in managerial know-how, was out of his depth in such an enterprise. The unfortunate result of the Hamdan failure was that it inhibited further industrial experimentation for the following decade.

Confiscation by the Israeli Government in 1948 of over 40 per cent of the land belonging to the Israeli Arabs forced many of the dispossessed farmers to leave their villages in search of work. Most of them found jobs in building construction and, thirty years later, hundreds of wealthy Arabs in Israel are operating successful building firms. Two of the most prosperous are the Boulos brothers from the village of Baaneh in Western Galilee, and the Druze Kadamani family. The Boulos brothers began as stone cutters. Originally the work was done by hand, using the methods employed by stone cutters from time immemorial. Now they sell Galilee marble and Negev stone in Italy, France, Germany and Japan. They employ hundreds of people and skilled Arab labour operates the modern machinery they have installed. The six brothers of the poor Kadamani family in the Druze village of Yarka found work as welders in two nearby kibbutzim in 1950. Today, they own a prosperous steel plant and a textile factory and are engaged in construction enterprises all over Israel. These success stories are paralleled by many others.

A major Arab economic activity in Israel is in the tourist industry, particularly transportation and catering. Many of Israel's 'Oriental' restaurants are run and owned by Arabs, and Nazareth, Israel's Arab capital with some 500,000 residents, is the base for three tour operators and travel agencies, four hotels and a score of church inns to welcome pilgrims and visitors. The Nassars, a group of cousins who started working as waiters, have built a chain of about twenty successful restaurants all over the country.

But most of Israel's Arabs have remained on the land, and their farming has been transformed by the introduction of new techniques. In many cases they are organized into cooperatives to bring water to irrigate their fields. Ministry of Agriculture experts have introduced new crops with an eye to the Arab 'strong point' – large families which provide cheap labour. Most of Israel's strawberries are produced in Arab villages, especially in Tira in the triangle. The Arabs work on Jewish farms producing other highly sophisticated agricultural products like winter vegetables, flowers and turkeys, but many more are starting their own glasshouses for winter products. Two new agricultural schools for Arab students have been built by the Government in Ramel and Beir al-sekkeh, and their graduates will certainly accelerate the creation of new farming enterprises.

Outside the farm, Arab labour is employed in garages, furniture shops and in some Israeli labour-intensive factories. One of the pioneers in this sphere, Gibor, a large textile enterprise, was the first to make use of the hitherto unemployed reserve of Arab 'woman power'. Because of their conservative tradition, these women were unable to leave their villages, so Gibor brought a plant to them. Other Israeli concerns followed Gibor's example, and Arab entrepreneurs have combined with Israeli manufacturers to create dozens of factories in Arab labour centres.

The more highly educated Israeli Arab has a more difficult time of it. Outside the Ministry of Education, few Arabs are employed in government offices. Students tend to study medicine, law, accountancy or engineering because in these occupations they can be self-employed.

Arab leadership

Today, as in 1948, most Arabs live in villages. For the purposes of local government, there are two Arab towns (Nazareth and Shfara'am), forty-six villages with local councils and twenty-seven villages within larger regional councils. Distinctions seem to be arbitrary. Shfara'am, with a population of 15,000, is a town, while Um el-Faham and Tiybeh, each with populations of about 18,000, are classified as villages, the classification determining the type of local government. Towns have mayors and municipal councils, while villages have only local councils. No doubt the growing 'villages' will eventually be reclassified as towns.

Elected local governments operate in some 70 out of the 110 places in which Israeli Arabs live. They have responsibility for a variety of local services, which include the school system. Local taxes finance most of these services, but the Government generally contributes about half of the cost of development projects like road construction, the installation of electricity or school building. In the course of planning and executing these projects, the National Committee of Arab Heads of Local Councils, founded in 1974, has begun to establish itself as the nucleus of an Israeli Arab representation.

Israeli Arabs, as Israeli citizens, have the right to enter the country's universities on the same terms as their fellow citizens. Approximately 2,000 attend at any given moment, with the largest concentrations at Haifa (10 per cent) and Jerusalem (5 per cent). Their relationship with the Jewish majority is an uneasy one. The young Arabs arrive from, on the whole, culturally deprived backgrounds – from communities lacking in libraries and qualified teachers and from homes with little intellectual content. The Jewish students, on the other hand, have generally come with greater advantages and after their military service necessitated by the state of war with the Arab countries.

An additional source of conflict is that many, probably the majority, of Arab students come from the villages, and the upheaval caused by their move away from a closed environment and its replacement by the openness of the campus has encouraged radicalism. The nationalistic activities of the Arab students constitute an additional barrier to any friendly relationship with the Jewish student body, and the result has been an almost complete segregation. Every institution of higher learning has an Arab students' committee and, while its formal functions are to assist the Arab students in the solution of personal problems, they have almost all become the focal point of radical political views. As a result, the encounter between Arabs and Jews on the university campuses has been a hostile one. It has tended to radicalize Arab students who, in turn, have influenced the radicalism of the Arab minority as a whole.

During the first sixteen years of Israel's existence, the Arabs had no significant political party of their own and supported Mapai, then Israel's main Labour party. Under Mapai's banner, Arab lists for the Knesset received some 60 per cent of the Arab vote, with the next highest proportion for the Communists. The six or seven elected Arab MKs were complaisant and accommodating to Mapai, voting in accordance with the party line and, in return, securing Government support for improvements in the Arab sector.

Demographic and political changes brought about a shift from this cosy arrangement. By 1967, more than half of the Arabs living in the Jewish State had been born there. They were unaffected by comparisons between their situation and the poverty-stricken lot of the Arabs in the pre-State period, but pointed instead to the present contrast with their Jewish fellow-citizens. Improvements in the Arab educational system served to raise their critical faculties and the level of their expectations. At that time, the Soviet Union was giving strong support to Nasser and to the Arab cause generally, raising the prestige of communism and attracting more Israeli Arab votes. Rakah, the predominantly Arab Communist party, grew steadily, increasing its share of the Arab vote from about 22 per cent in 1955 to almost 50 per cent in the 1977 election, while Mapai's share fell from over 70 per cent in 1955 to 27 per cent in 1977.

After the 1977 election, the total number of Arab MKs remained at seven but their party affiliation was now changed, so that three of them represented the Communists, while two Druzes (an Arab non-Moslem minority loyal to Israel) were elected on the list of the Democratic Movement for Change and one on the Likud list. The Arab list supported by the Israeli Labour Party won only one seat.

Since the mid-1950s and the Soviet Union's involvement in the Middle East, the Israeli Communist Party became particularly attractive to the Arabs. It was the only party which propounded a non-Zionist ideology, and the growing number of literate young Arabs, infected by the rise of Arab nationalism, voted Communist less because of a belief in the party's political outlook than because it was the only party they could vote for which was hostile to Jewish nationalism. The Communist Party, now re-named the Democratic Front for Peace and Equality, still seeks to present an Israeli, rather than exclusively Arab, image and, for that reason, Meir Wilner, a Jew born in Vilna, Lithuania, in 1918, remains the Secretary-General. He has been a member of the Knesset since 1948, and another of the party's five Knesset Members is also a Jew. But the election results demonstrated that more than 90 per cent of the Communist vote came from the Arabs.

In return, the Party helps the Arabs. More than 300 young Israeli Arabs are studying in Eastern Europe, the party paying the bills with the help of friendly Governments. The graduates come back to their villages, grateful for the benefits they have received, and become advocates for the twin causes of communism and Arab nationalism. Communist Party leaders have replaced the conservative 'notables' and they include Towfik Toubi, born to a Protestant family in Haifa in 1922 and active in Communist groups even before 1948. He has been a member of the Knesset uninterruptedly since 1952. Emile Habibi, another son of a Haifa Protestant family and one year older than Toubi, served in the Knesset until 1954, when he resigned to make way for his friend, Towfik Zyyad. Reelected to the Knesset in 1977, Zyyad is a Moslem born in Nazareth in 1929. He has been a political activist since 1949, describes his profession as poet and has been the Mayor of Nazareth since 1975.

Habibi is the most active and thoughtful political agitator of the party and an outstanding prose writer. He has published two novels, written in the sardonic and sarcastic style to which his Arab readers strongly respond. Zyyad is the only Moslem in the Communist Party leadership and represents the new Moslem converts to the party line. The nationalistic fervour of his poetry, rather than its literary merit, has made it widely known and appreciated in the Arab world.

The Communists publish a weekly Arabic-language newspaper, two monthly magazines and a quarterly, all potent instruments in advancing their cause among the frustrated younger generation of Israeli Arabs.

Herut integrated Arab candidates into its electoral list in 1973 when Amal Nasr el-Din, a Druze who lost his son in combat against Palestine Liberation Organization units in 1970, was elected to the Knesset. He was returned again in 1977, but his task of popularizing the Likud among his community has not been assisted by Prime Minister Begin who, in the first half of his term at any rate, failed to initiate or take part in one debate in the Knesset on policy towards the Arab minority.

The two Arabs in the Knesset on the DMC list are Shafik Asa'ad, a farmer from the Druze village of Beit Jan, born in 1937, and Zeidan Atsheh, a former television reporter and Information Counsellor at the Israeli Consulate in New York. Both were elected by Jewish voters (only about 10 per cent of their votes came from Arabs) and are unlikely to keep their seats when the voters have the opportunity to express their disenchantment with the DMC. The MK for the United Arab Party, the satellite of the Israel Labour Party, is a Beduin sheikh from the Negev, Hamid Abu Rabi'a.

The older generation, the settled and experienced, still turn for leadership to their religious authorities, who maintain the traditional posture of an insecure minority, seeking to attract support and protect their rights without antagonizing the Israeli authorities. The outstanding religious leader who followed this path was Archbishop George Hakim who was the head of the Melkite Greek Catholic community in Galilee up to 1967. His successor, Archbishop Maximos Salloum, maintains the same approach as do the other Christian religious leaders: Agostine Harfoush, the Maronite Vicar, and the Roman Catholic Bishop, Mgr Hanna Kaldani. The Greek Orthodox bishops in Nazareth follow a different policy. These two Greek nationals regard it as their duty to serve the faithful inside the Church only. They provide no special schools, raise no funds to encourage students at the universities and take little interest in the secular affairs of their Arab adherents.

Moslems face a different and more severe problem of leadership. They are a recognized religious community, so the salaries of the qadis (judges of the religious courts) and of those who lead the faithful in their prayers at the mosques come from the Israeli Government. This circumstance has resulted in a certain alienation by the clergy from the interests and concerns of their coreligionists. They have become functionaries rather than religious leaders, with the result that the Israeli Moslems, as well as the Greek Orthodox Christians, have no effective religious leadership.

The leadership of Israel's Arabs continues to move away from the notables to the Communists, the militant National Progressive Movement and the even more militant 'Sons of the Village'. At the beginning of 1978 a group of intellectuals, many involved in the Sons of the Village movement, published a manifesto which called both for a Palestinian state and the right of self-determination for Israeli Arabs. It has brought about a bitter conflict between the Communists and these new radicals. The Communist support for UN Resolutions 242 and 338 (which deal with the occupied territories and assert Israel's right to recognition and peace) has been denounced by the radicals, who see it as limiting Arab options, while the Communists, for their part, attack the radicals as unrealistic extremists.

It is one of the peculiarities of the Israeli Arabs' situation, that it is the Communist leaders, concerned with their status as a legitimate party operating within the law, who stand for comparative moderation. The radicals spurn the Communists for participating in Israeli elections and the fact that 92 per cent of the Arabs voted in the 1955 General Election and only 72 per cent in 1977 is mainly due to the influence of these extremists, who urge abstention from the polls.

Evidence began to accumulate in early 1980 that the Khomeini revolution in Iran had inspired an upsurge of Islamic fervour among some Israeli Arabs. A new organization called Young Muslims, which came into existence at that time and seemed to be gaining recruits, was opposed on Moslem fundamentalist grounds not only to Israel but also to the local Communist Party and the Arab nationalistic groups. It was a trend with potentially serious implications for the State, particularly if the economic conditions of Israel's Arabs were to deteriorate.

In the competition to fill the vacuum in the Israeli Arab leadership, a group of a thousand Arab socialists close to the Israel Labour Party have created a movement 'for Change and Co-existence'. Moderate though its members are, the group has also had to adopt a rhetoric of forceful nationalism, in order to avoid charges of disloyalty to the Arab cause. It is still far too soon to assess the potential of this new grouping, but the struggle for the leadership of Israel's Arabs is more likely to be affected by the overall Arab-Israeli situation than by any internal contests.

The intelligentsia

The majority of Palestine's Arab intellectuals left the country during the 1948 war, and the few who remained were cut off from the mainstream of the Arab cultural world. The present Israeli Arab intelligentsia were born and educated in Israel. They form a small group, products of Israeli schools and Israeli and foreign universities, and are estimated to number no more than 5,000 in all. The number is small both in absolute terms and in comparison with the educated proportion of the Jewish population, but it is significantly expanding with the number of Arab students at Israeli universities rising from 268 in 1965 to 2,000 in 1978.

The number of those who articulate the aspirations of Israel's Arabs as authors, journalists and poets is far smaller. Poets are the most numerous. Out of some 300 original works in Arabic published in Israel, about 250 were poetry. Short stories are the second most common form of expression, and novels and political works comprise the smallest segment.

Outstanding among the poets today are Jamal Qaa'mar, a school teacher from Nazareth, and Samih El-qasem, a Communist editor of Druze origin. Foremost among the short story writers is Mohammad Mannaa, who comes from the village of Beit Jan, while novelists include Atallah Mansour and Emile Habibi. Not all the literature in Arabic is political, but much of it is. Recurring themes are the ordeal of Arab refugees and the hardships and yearnings of those who have lost their homes. The feeling of alienation, which has gripped these Arab intellectuals at their separation from the growth of Arab nationalism, is apparent in most of their writings.

Mansour in his novels and autobiography vividly portrays the tragedy of the Israeli Arab intellectual seeking to find peace in the Israeli environment. The militant Arab nationalist looks upon him as having sold out to the Israeli oppressor, while the Israeli Jew regards him as suspect because he is an Arab. Above all he is agonized by what Mansour, in his autobiography *Waiting for the Dawn* describes as 'a deep bitterness and frustration caused by the humiliations of the present and the thought of past glories . . . the shame inferior children feel as they reflect on their great fathers. The Jews are suspicious of their very shadows, while the Arabs are still day-dreaming.' Fawzi el-Asmar, an Israeli Arab political journalist now living in England expressed similar sentiments in his autobiography *To Be an Arab in Israel*.

Another of the tiny group of Arab political writers is Emile Touma, editor of the Communist Party organ, a Cambridge graduate and possessor of a Ph.D. in History from Moscow University. The only real addition to this limited literary production are university theses in history or sociology, published in popular form by a handful of university graduates.

An invaluable function in interpreting Arab Israeli attitudes and views to Israel's Jews is being performed by a small group of Arabs working in the information field. Atallah Mansour in *Haaretz*, Towfik Khouri in *Yediot Aharonot* and Anan Safadi in *The Jerusalem Post*, write regularly on Arab affairs for their newspapers while Rafik Halabi and Bessam Jaber perform the same service for the Hebrew-language TV and radio. A dozen or so Arab journalists work for Israel's Arabic-language TV and radio, but none has any executive powers in the services which are all controlled by Israeli Jews. That fact, as much as anything else, epitomizes the position of Arabs as a suspect minority in Israel and is the source of much of their sense of grievance.

Dr Moshe Sharon resigned as Begin's adviser on Arab affairs in 1979. The subject, he complained, was being ignored. He came to this dispiriting conclusion about the position of Israeli Arabs: 'in the absence of any possibility of common identity, the maximum the State of Israel can demand from its Arab citizens is to be loyal, law-abiding citizens. No more. Their feelings, their aspirations, their emotional attachments, do not belong to Israel and cannot be taken as positive factors in regulating Jewish-Arab relations.'

Chapter fifteen

Defence Forces

The human face

Israel was never conceived of as a Sparta; nor did the Jews, without a state of their own for almost 2,000 years, regard themselves as a warrior people. The very notion of an army to defend the national home hardly entered the consciousness of the non-martial Zionist ideologues, and their writings and speeches during the early years of the movement have an air of unreality about them today. The controversies, exhortations and debates which pre-occupied them concerned the nature of the Jewish return to the ancestral soil, the rejection of Jewish assimilation, the place of religion and of political ideology, the methods of land acquisition, the organization and funding of the new movement. Almost everything was discussed except the local Arabs. It was assumed that they would benefit from the reinvigorating of Palestine's desolate soil and that they would entertain nothing but good will and gratitude to their benefactors.

Only when the settlers began arriving did the practical necessities of defence arise. The Turkish Government, which controlled the territory, possessed neither the resources nor the will to protect the new arrivals from the attentions of some of the local Arabs, less concerned at that time with the political implications of Zionism than with plunder through banditry. Arab nationalism, the seeds of which were sown at about the same time as those of Zionism, began to express itself in violent terms only after the Balfour Declaration of 1917. The makeshift, irregular self-defence groups of young armed Jews which then sprang up evolved, with the growth of Arab hostility, into the Israel Defence Forces, a citizens' army which has fought four wars (some add a fifth, Nasser's war of attrition which followed the Six Day War) and won them all, against the immense odds of 40–1 in terms of populations.

The nerve-centre of the IDF is not a Pentagon, or even a modern office block, but incongruously, a wide-spaced compound of low, white-painted, simple one- or two-storey buildings set among trees, shrubs and flowers. It still looks like the village it once was in the open country near Jaffa. Founded by German Templars and named Sarona, this colony became encircled as Tel Aviv, the first all-Jewish city, rapidly expanded to the north, south and east. The German colonists dispersed, and the neat orderly settlement became a barracks for the army and police of the British Mandatory authority.

The departure of the British left Sarona again uninhabited. It was eagerly snapped up by the new Government and, renamed Hakirya (The City), became Israel's Whitehall. To the disappointment of some local patriots, Jerusalem, not Tel Aviv, was named the capital of the new state. Tel Aviv was Israel's largest city, the centre of commerce and culture, the scene of action, but it could not possibly compare with the historic and emotional appeal of Jerusalem. By the end of the second decade of Israel's existence, most of the Ministries had moved to Jerusalem. But the Ministry of Defence remained in Hakirya, now a heavily, though unobtrusively, protected compound, teeming with casual, khaki-clothed, burly men and neat, charming, uniformed girls, and with every possible parking place occupied by a small camouflaged car.

No glittering horse guards or even rigid security procedures guard the entrances, and the informality that prevails, reflects the human face of this army. Higher ranks are saluted by their subordinates, but usually addressed by their first names, with a total absence of deference or obsequiousness. Brutality is non-existent with the IDF, for the intimacy of the small country has its counterpart in the intimacy of its band of defenders. They are all members of one extended family, offering each other the same mixture of frictions and basic understanding of needs and feelings as most families do.

The human face of the army extends to the planners. Unless military emergencies demand, soldiers are permitted to go home for the Sabbath, and every Friday afternoon bunches of uniformed young people clutching their Uzi guns wait on main roads, thumbing for the lifts that will take them home to their families. If their homecoming is delayed, a telephone call from HQ will generally reassure parents. Family needs are not neglected, even at times of high tensions, and an immediate priority after battle is establishing communication between the fighters and their homes.

On the wider national scene, the most important purposes that the IDF has served, beyond its essential function, are educational and social. The national educational system does not always ensure that, when the time for compulsory military service arrives, the young recruit has mastered the basic elements of education. Some either started school too late, or were hampered by the negative aspects of their environment. An educational programme in the army rectifies the omissions. The basic three-months course is an intensive immersion in study for 600 hours, in classes which generally number no more than ten pupils each.

The army has been a unique school, teaching not merely literacy but the basis of ordinary life in a modern society to many whose home background has remained that of the fairly primitive countries from which they came. Not only has the IDF been – as it continues to be – Israel's most successful educational organization, it is also the single most important instrument in creating a unified society from the variegated elements which have gone into its making.

Because the Israel Defence Forces are a cross-section of the country's citizens, the main component being the reservists called upon to serve for short periods during their normal civilian occupations, no military caste or junta has developed, and it is inconceivable that a military *coup d'état* could occur in Israel. Equally, the fact that it is an army of citizens defending their own homes and families and nation, has made it a formidable fighting force recognizing that, while its antagonists could afford to lose a war, it could not. The slogan of 'Ein Brera' – 'We have no alternative' – encapsulates the IDF's source of strength. But essentially Israel is not militarist, and the role which conditions have forced upon it is one the country would gladly relinquish. It could well be the greatest success of the IDF that the Arabs' recognition of their inability to defeat Israel in battle may finally bring them round to the idea of peace.

The shaping of the army

The army had its birth in Jaffa in September 1907 with a meeting of ten pioneers. Their leader, an intense young Russian Jew named Israel Shochat, argued that it would be impossible to achieve the Zionist ideal of reviving the nation unless Jews were prepared to undertake their own self-defence. He scornfully dismissed, as incompatible with the dignity of their aspirations, the existing practice of hiring Arab and Circassian guards. His listeners agreed, and the result of the meeting was the formation of a secret army of Jewish watchmen ready to assume guard duties whenever called upon. It had to be secret, because its existence was unlawful under Turkish rule. The name they gave their society was Bar-Giora, after a Jewish fighter against the Romans in the war which ended the last sovereign state of the Jews in the year AD 70.

Twelve months after the meeting, in 1908, came the Young Turk revolution and, concentrating much more on home affairs, the Turkish Government took little interest in ensuring law and order in Palestine. Banditry increased, and so did the number of Jewish watchmen. The secret society was replaced by an open movement called Hashomer (the watch-men), recruiting and training only volunteers of exceptional quality, committed to the three ideological essentials – self-defence, the Hebrew language and socialism. Hashomer grew, and though it never had more than a few hundred members, it established the idea that Jews could be fighters capable of effective defence of Jewish lives and property. Outlawed by the Turks during World War I, the society went underground; weakened by arrests and deportations, it barely survived the war and disbanded in 1920.

By that time, Jewish units had been formed to take part, together with the British forces, in the conquest of Palestine. Many of the young Zionists who were later to become leaders of the movement served in the Jewish Legion during World War I and gained experience of military affairs, one of them being David Ben-Gurion, Israel's first Prime Minister and Minister of Defence. After the war, Britain took over the administration under the Mandate and, with it, assumed responsibility for law and order. But the Jews of Palestine soon came to the conclusion that the British Army was not over-concerned to protect their settlements from Arab attack. Not long after its formation in 1920, the Histadrut (General Federation of Labour) created for that purpose a workers' militia called Hagana (defence). Starting in an office in the headquarters of the Histadrut, Hagana was the precursor of the IDF.

The small band of defenders was not taken too seriously by the British, the Arabs or even the Jews. Its first leadership training group of thirty was ridiculed by the members of the kibbutz where it conducted its activities and the trainee officers, trying hard to look military as they drilled, were derided as 'comedians'. But slowly an effective force grew, and its first valuable operation was the organization of 'illegal' immigration into Palestine. Arab rioting had succeeded in persuading the British to restrict the number of legal immigration certificates issued to Jews, and the Jewish response was to find all possible means of bringing them in without certificates.

Severe Arab rioting and atrocities in 1929, and the inability of the British authorities to provide effective protection for the Jews, resulted in a reappraisal of the scale of the Hagana. It had to be larger, every fit male had to be trained to bear arms, and far more weapons had to be acquired. The British, too, recognized that the Jews had to be helped to defend themselves. By 1936 some 3,000 authorized Jewish auxiliary guards had been armed with light weapons by the British and trained by a brilliant and eccentric British army officer, Captain Orde Wingate, in 'active defence'. In the meantime, some Jewish non-socialists, objecting both to the socialist domination of the Hagana and to what they regarded as its excessive caution, formed another defence organization called Irgun Zvai Leumi (National Military Organization).

On the outbreak of World War II, the Jews in Palestine allied themselves with the British in the fight against Nazism, and more than 100,000 volunteered for service within the first few days. For reasons of their own, the British were less than enthusiastic about active Jewish participation, employing the volunteers in non-combatant duty and describing them as Palestinians. Nevertheless, many leaders and members of the future IDF received some military training in this way.

While most able young Jews were thus occupied, the Hagana High Command decided in 1941 to organize a mobile field force for the defence of the Jews of Palestine in the event of invasion by the Nazi forces. Called Palmach from the initial syllables of Plugot Mahatz (Strike Companies), this eager and enterprising force became the elite defence group, outstanding in bravery as in military skill and intelligence. Dogged, like the Hagana itself, by pitifully small financial resources, inadequate and antiquated arms, and an almost complete lack of heavy weapons, they learned to improvise, setting up simple weapons workshops of their own until they were able to acquire arms from abroad.

At the end of the war, both the 'official' defence organizations, the Hagana and the Palmach, and the independent military groups (the Irgun had split, creating two independent bands of freedom fighters) cooperated intermittently in the struggle to permit the entry of survivors of the concentration camps against the opposition of the British. The departure of the British forces, when the Mandate ended, left the Jews to face alone an invasion by the Arab states – the War of Independence. An army came into existence under fire, its deficiencies in numbers, training and weaponry compensated by motivation, intelligence and improvisation. Ben-Gurion recognized that unity of command and the exclusion of politics were essential to its success, so, at the cost of lives and the creation of bitterness which endured for a generation, he forced the dissolution of the Irgun. The Palmach was also absorbed into the Israel Defence Forces (IDF), established by order of the Provisional Government on 26 May 1948 and consisting of ground, air and naval forces. The order instituted general conscription and prohibited the establishment of any other force.

Ben-Gurion, a powerful and decisive Prime Minister and Minister of Defence, bulldozed into operation all the concepts he considered essential. He set up a centralized command system and four regional commands, North, Central, East and South; issued standard uniforms and badges of rank; and, flexible even about the egalitarian principle in the interests of defence, ordered separate messes for officers. That was the basic structure of the IDF when the War of Independence ended with an armistice, but without peace.

In that situation, security was – as it continued to be – Israel's major concern, and a permanent force had to be constructed of sufficient strength to defend the country. At the same time, it could not be allowed to become so heavy a drain on Israel's limited manpower as to undermine her economic existence. The answer was a force made up of four components: 1) a small force of regulars; 2) conscripts; 3) reserves and 4) territorial defence based on the settlements.

Enacted by the Knesset in September 1949, the Defence Service Law provided for two years' compulsory military service from the age of 18, new immigrants being liable for conscription up to the age of 29. After their term of service, conscripts were assigned to reserve units, to which they could be summoned for additional training or service. The actual period of time for active service and reserve service varied with national needs but these provisions, amended and consolidated by later legislation, remain effective.

The new Chief of Staff in November 1949 was Yigael Yadin. As proved to be the case after subsequent wars, victory brought with it a certain decline in spirit and efficiency. Yadin's task was further complicated by the extreme strain on the economy brought about by the mass immigration of hundreds of thousands of poor and untrained North Africans and Asians. The army was deprived of essentials, and its morale was seriously affected. Yadin, overcoming these obstacles, directed its rehabilitation, in the process creating the structure which prevails today. The four commands of 1948 were reduced to three: North, Central and South. Commanders of the Air Force and Navy became members of the unitary General HQ, which also included the heads of the three administrative branches. At the top of the military pyramid was the Chief of Staff, with the rank of Rav Aluf (Lieutenant General), the only officer with that rank. The other senior officers were Aluf (Major General), Tat Aluf (Brigadier) and Aluf Mishne (Colonel).

The intensification of Arab incursions and the growing threat of further hostilities led to an expansion of military intelligence, which later became an independent branch of GHQ. Yadin's appointment of Haim Laskov as commander of the then puny Air Force set it on the road to its later brilliance. No less important were the plans being prepared and implemented by the Chief of Staff for training officers and conscripts, and the systems employed for training and employing the pool of reservists.

Moshe Dayan, who succeeded Yadin as Chief of Staff in 1953 at the age of 38, made his own, very personal imprint on the IDF. Impatient of committees, procedures and establishments, and brushing aside formalities and ceremonies, he set out to develop a tough and individualistic force of fighters. He created a special paratroop unit, headed by Major Ariel Sharon, to carry out the reprisal raids which the Government had accepted as the policy for responding to the increasingly troublesome Arab attacks, and pushed on with the formation of the amoured units started by Yadin. But above all, Dayan is credited with inspiring what has become the characteristic boldness of Israeli officers who, he directed, 'do not *send* their men into battle. They *lead* them into battle.'

The Sinai campaign of 1956, though it failed in its political aims, was the first intimation to the world of the achievement of the IDF. In one hundred hours of operations, the IDF armoured columns had taken the whole of the Sinai Peninsula and destroyed the Egyptian forces there. The lessons of the Sinai Campaign brought about a new and stronger emphasis on combined operations between armoured brigades and the Air Force, and led directly to the strategy which was to secure such overwhelming and rapid military victories eleven years later, in the Six Day War. The armoured corps was expanded to become the spearhead of all the forces. The Air Force received a very high priority and its head, Ezer Weizman, forged it into a deadly striking force.

By the time of the 'anticipatory counter offensive', the official Israeli euphemism for the preemptive strike which launched the 1967 war, Israel was believed to be spending no less than 14 per cent of its Gross National Product on defence. The standing army numbered about 50,000 men and women and 250,000 reserves. It possessed about 900 tanks and about 500 planes. The military leaders, headed by Yitzhak Rabin as Chief of Staff, all stressed resilience and initiative in the field. The skill of these fighters, their comprehension of the technology of the equipment they employed, and their high motivation in fighting for survival, all contributed to the remarkable military victory of the Six Day War, which had been assured by the precision of the Air Force in destroying on the ground within a few hours practically all the aircraft the enemy possessed. Having thus gained air supremacy, armoured forces first attacked Egypt and routed its Sinai forces within three days, then turned on Jordan and Syria with equally devastating results.

In the economic boom which followed the war, the budget of the IDF expanded; but at the same time the complacency to which the new prosperity gave rise had its effect in the forces too. The near-disaster in the Yom Kippur War of 1973 when, on the Day of Atonement (Yom Kippur in Hebrew), President Sadat launched a surprise attack across the Suez Canal, owed much to the looser, more lax and casual attitudes of the defence establishment and the Israeli soldier.

1973 and its consequences

The Suez Canal had become, in the words of Rabin, 'an important obstacle in our system of defence', when Nasser proclaimed a war of attrition against Israel after 1967. A chain of concrete forts was constructed by the Israelis along their side of the Canal, originally only to provide cover for the troops, but heavy artillery barrages from the other side, together with commando incursions and the concentration of Egyptian troops and equipment, led Israel to strengthen what became known as the Bar Lev Line, named after the then Chief of Staff, its initiator. By 1973 it looked as if an impasse had been created. President Sadat's 'year of decision' had passed without war and he had expelled his Soviet advisers. Neither Israeli nor American Intelligence considered that the Egyptians were in a position to exercise a credible war option. The Bar Lev Line, originally manned by some of the best regulars, was now held by a small number of members of the reserve on their annual tour of duty.

On 6 October 1973, the Egyptians and Syrians began the Yom Kippur War. After air strikes against Israeli targets, the Egyptians crossed the Canal while Syrian tanks moved down from the north. The Israelis were unprepared. Their Intelligence assessment had discounted the probability of war; the reservists in Sinai and on the Golan Heights were as relaxed and complacent as the Intelligence and, indeed, as the national mood. Delays and uncertainties led to mobilization orders going out as late as 9.30 a.m. on the Day of Atonement itself when a high proportion of the population was already in synagogue on the holiest day in the Jewish calendar.

The war lasted just under three weeks. For the first few days, the Israeli situation was desperate and the IDF suffered heavy losses. The initial counterattacks after full mobilization were not successful. A turning point was the repulse by Israel on 14 October of the major Egyptian tank offensive. This provided the opportunity for an Israeli counterattack, which took the IDF across the Canal a few days later. When the cease-fire came, the Israelis were occupying hundreds of square miles of Egyptian territory on the west bank of the Canal and had surrounded the Egyptian Third Army. In the north, the Israelis had crossed the border with Syria. They had averted a disaster, but had lost 2,812 dead in the process.

Dissatisfaction, both with the military performance and with the political outcome of the war, led to an intense national debate which impelled Golda Meir's Government to set up a commission of enquiry headed by Shimon Agranat, president of the Supreme Court. It included another Supreme Court Justice, Moshe Landau, Yitzhak Nebenzahl, the State Comptroller, and two former Chiefs of Staff, Yigael Yadin and Haim Laskov. Its preliminary report appeared on 1 April 1974, and the final one on 30 January 1975. The latter consisted of more than 1,500 pages, of which only 42 were published. But enough is known to enable a reasonably accurate assessment to be made of the performance of the IDF in that war.

The first and fundamental cause of the initial disadvantage suffered by the Israelis was the series of errors of evaluation made by Military Intelligence. Because of the strongly held concept that the Arab armies

were in no position to wage war, all the new data brought in by the
Intelligence services were considered within the framework of that concept
and not independently evaluated. The complete dependence of the Prime
Minister and the Cabinet on the Intelligence evaluations of the military
alone meant that they were deprived of the opportunity to balance Military
Intelligence assessments with those made by the Foreign Ministry and the
other departments of Israel's extensive Intelligence community.

The Agranat Commissioners pronounced shattering judgment on some
of the military leaders. The Chief of Staff, General David Elazar, was
charged with uncritical acceptance of Intelligence assessments, with not
having acted quickly enough when war began, and with failing to ensure
that there should be a contingency plan for the kind of attack Egypt had
launched. General Gonen, who headed the Southern Command, was
charged with serious errors of judgment and was disqualified from future
high military office. He later resigned, as did General Elazar, who died two
years later. But while attaching this blame to Elazar and Gonen, the
Commission offered no criticism of Moshe Dayan, the Minister of Defence,
who had, in fact, delayed general mobilization against Elazar's recommendation. Despite his vindication by the commission, criticism continued
against Dayan and he joined the Prime Minister when she resigned in
1974.

On the positive side, even under the most adverse conditions that could
have been envisaged the mobilization system, applied in great haste, had
proved its efficiency. Coded messages on the radio, telephone calls and
personal visits combined to bring about the formation of fighting units out
of the civilian reserves within hours. Despite what was later revealed as the
over-enthusiastic rotation of senior military commands, with the result that
there were far too many inexperienced commanders in senior positions at
the same time, the combat resourcefulness of officers and men alike was
decisive in overcoming the initial reverses and pressing on to victory.

Controversy in Israel over the Yom Kippur War did not end with the
Agranat report. Many took the view that the nub of the problem was
neither the obvious Intelligence failings nor the faults and inexperience of
the commanders, but the inherent restrictions of a strategy based on
preemptive strike. The circumstances in which political realities permitted
the operation of the technique which had produced the stunning victory of
1967 did not prevail in 1973 nor were they likely in future; and the IDF had to
be changed to meet the new realities.

The new look

In March 1978, the IDF launched an attack in strength on Arab terrorist
bases across the River Litani in Lebanon in retaliation for a terrorist action
in Israel a few days earlier. The Litani operation, five years after the Yom
Kippur War, lifted the veil from developments during the intervening
period and prompted a severely critical report from the State Comptroller
(see Chapter 6). What was revealed gave small comfort to those who had
been hoping that the errors and omissions of 1973 had been rectified.

Improvements were on the way, however, particularly in the course of the redeployment made necessary by the peace with Egypt. A new infrastructure was created, so that the vast quantity of equipment would be immediately available and accessible if another war were to break out. In 1973, the tanks, for example, had to be collected from a depot in the heart of the country, while fuel and ammunition had to be loaded elsewhere. Only after this had been done could the tanks be loaded onto tank carriers and hauled to the front.

The changes in this field alone since 1973 give an indication of the new look in all army departments. What was done with the tanks marked a change in fundamental concept. Instead of concentrating them in a well-protected area, they were dispersed to the potential fronts. While this made them more vulnerable, they could be far more quickly and easily deployed. Ammunition and fuel were stored in the tanks themselves, again more of a risk but a great improvement in terms of speed of utilization, New roads were built to achieve effective dispersal and new bombproof 'shields' constructed for the tanks. The most innovative of the changes was the adaptation of a German process called 'dry storage' to enable the tanks, fully equipped with field rations, uniforms, ammunition and equipment, to be kept in a kind of mummified condition for long periods. It was achieved by placing the completely equipped tank into what has been described as a 'gigantic zipper bag' and then connecting the bag with an air-conditioning unit.

Quiet but fundamental changes have been made in a wide variety of army processes and procedures. The tank 'zipper bag' is one of the few instances where changes have been made public; most of the others remain on the secret list. Accompanying the technical changes was a plan for the reorganization of the army command which, after two years of gestation, was finally made public at the end of 1979 to the accompaniment of reports that it had created an 'earthquake among the General Staff'.

Soon after the Likud Government was elected in 1977, Ezer Weizman, the new Minister of Defence, asked General Israel Tal to prepare an organizational overhaul of the IDF for the first time since 1952. General Tal, who was then 54, had retired from active service with an excellent record as a tactitian and administrator. But what commended him most to Weizman for this purpose was his personal standing, the respect in which he was held by his fellow generals, and his disinterestedness. He was the kind of expert who could be expected to present a balanced, objective and thorough report with no suspicion of seeking personal advantage, and to see it through, doggedly and perseveringly. Tal had shown that he was capable of this perseverance in developing the first home-made tank, the successful Merkava, against the strong opposition of both the IDF and Government.

Tal's report (the text has been kept secret) was acted upon by Weizman more than two years after Tal's acceptance of the task. It called for a basic reconstruction of the General Staff by detaching from the responsibilities of the Chief of Staff the day-to-day operations of the IDF. The report recommended that they should be the responsibility of the Deputy Chief of Staff, who should be moved out of the operations branch. But such a crucial diminution of functions would have been too much to ask of the Chief of Staff, so Weizman left that proposal aside, and instead suggested implementing another of Tal's proposals for the establishment of a Ground Forces Command.

This new command would end the separate existence of the four corps that had existed up to this time – armoured, paratroopers, artillery and engineers. Weizman announced that all these would be merged into a new unified Ground Forces Command to be led by General Tal and that the new dispensation would come into effect within three months, i.e., before the end of March 1980. But there was considerable opposition among the General Staff to this proposal. It was reported in the American press, since military censorship in Israel prevented publication at home, that three senior Generals had resigned from the General Staff on the issue. After the announcement was made, it was revealed that implementation awaited a final feasibility study and that it was quite possible the Tal plan might be scrapped.

One of the side-effects of the Tal report and his appointment to the new command is that, if it goes through, it makes him, despite his age, a strong candidate for the top post of Chief of Staff when the present incumbent, General Rafael Eitan, retires in 1981. Eitan was described as a 'soldier's soldier' by Prime Minister Begin when he appointed him Chief of Staff in April 1978. He had indeed served in the forces since the age of 16 when he joined the underground army, subsequently serving as a paratrooper and rising to brigade commander in 1967.

'Raful' Eitan is an old-fashioned soldier, tough, taciturn and a strong disciplinarian (he directed widespread swoops by the military police to arrest sloppily dressed soldiers). His political views tend to be extremely conservative. He deplores the ways of contemporary society and longs for traditional values. On current issues, he is known as a territorial hard-liner, no doubt one of the reasons for his appointment by Begin. Having said on TV after his appointment that the West Bank should be held by Israel at all costs, his next major task was, paradoxically, to oversee the pullback from Sinai, which he performed stoically and efficiently.

Eitan also gave support to Gush Emunim, the religious group of West Bank settlers, who were later in conflict with the Government. But the most damaging publicity he received was that which followed three cases in which he commuted (as the Chief of Staff has the power to do) long-term sentences imposed by courts-martial on army personnel for offences involving loss of life, including two officers convicted of killing four Arabs during the Litani operation. These actions were the subject of violent criticism both at home and abroad. Eitan remained tight-lipped, offering neither explanation nor excuse for his controversial decisions. It was typical of the Chief of Staff: greatly skilled as a professional soldier, but failing to grasp the political implications of the decisions falling within his responsibilities. He is famous for his coolness in action. On 28 December 1968, he led forty paratroopers in a drop on Beirut Airport. While his men destroyed thirteen Arab aircraft on the ground, Eitan sat calmly in the airport bar sipping brandy.

Under the tough, no-nonsense direction of this soldier's soldier, the IDF has been greatly improved. Eitan accepted the Begin Government's position – that the IDF is there to execute orders and not to create policy. In past Governments, the Chief of Staff and Director of Military Intelligence sat in on key Government meetings and offered opinions. That situation no longer prevails.

Two of the regional commanders who were considered strong contenders for the succession as Chief of Staff before the Tal appointment were General Ben Gal, commander of the Northern Front, a bright young officer famous for his leadership of the Seventh Brigade in the Yom Kippur War, and the commanding officer of the Southern Front, General Dan Shomron, who was lionized for his leadership of the Entebbe exploit. The present Deputy Chief of Staff, General Moshe Levy – a solid officer without the flamboyance of his colleagues – could be a compromise candidate for Chief of Staff were Tal to be disqualified because of his age and Gal and Shomron because of their youth.

Nowhere else in the world is criticism of sacred cows more open than in Israel. Since 1973, the army has no longer been idolized, but because of its essentially civilian character, its activities and policies are followed with the most intense interest and with as much (some say too much) publicity as the secretive nature of security permits. For it touches the lives of the citizens from the start of their adult lives.

All males (with limited exceptions) are conscripted at the age of 18 for a three-year period, after which they serve in the reserves. The exemption now granted to girls on religious grounds is so extensive as to have made serious inroads into the whole general concept of conscription of women, but in theory, at any rate, it still applies. The pay the conscripts receive is nominal, but for the regulars it compares favourably with civilian occupations. A full colonel is paid at the same rate and subject to the same conditions as the Director-General of a Ministry. But comparisons of this kind are misleading. A top-grade journalist on a newspaper will earn about $850 monthly – about the same as a major. But a major may from time to time work twenty hours or more a day without payment of overtime, be away for weeks on end, live in the desert and be in danger.

The fringe benefits are few. Field officers are generally provided with a car, especially if they are married and need it to get home. HQ officers on the staff (Israel has no need of a special cadre of staff officers for they serve in rotation) share cars from the pool. From the rank of Lieutenant-Colonel and above, officers are provided with a car and driver. Additional benefits are a subsidized commissary store and, subject to specified conditions, subsidized housing.

In the early days of Israel, potential senior officers were sent abroad for training, but today there are two staff colleges. The National Defence Academy (Michlalat Bitachon Leumi) provides services for colonels and brigadiers as well as for Central Intelligence (Mossad) and the upper echelons of the civil service. The command and staff school (known as 'Pum' from the initials of the Hebrew title, Pikud Umateh) gives courses which are a requirement for promotion. It is an in-service training centre and officers in both the reserve and the regular army compete keenly for the available places.

Promotion brings considerable prestige and rewards. Officers from colonel (Aluf Mishne) upwards may retire any time after the age of 42 on full pension, but in general the upper echelons put in about twenty years of service before going on pension. When they leave the forces, they call on the army placement service to find civilian employment for them. There is no such creature in Israel as an unemployed ex-general. They are much in demand for management jobs, and several have entered commerce, industry (including the arms industry) and politics. But this has not created anything comparable to the 'industrial-military complex' in other states. That is primarily because even generals in Israel are essentially civilians. Like conscripts and reserves, they perform a military function not because they are militarists but because they are Zionists. When they leave the army, they tend to stay in their various top positions without creating any exclusive ex-army elite.

Intelligence

A new Director of Military Intelligence, Yehoshua Saguy, was appointed in 1979. He was the first Intelligence head to have grown up in the system in which, for twenty-seven years, he had served in every department before reaching the top; all former directors had been brought in from outside. Saguy was born in Jerusalem in 1933, and joined the army when he left school at the age of 18. At the end of his national service, he decided to make the army his career, and stayed in the Intelligence Corps in which he had been drafted.

He is known as a reticent man, somewhat lacklustre, but very ready to listen. One of his first acts in his new post was to tell all officers of the corps that they had the right and duty to disagree openly with any opinion or assessment of superior officers – right up to the Director himself. According to reports, this has worked well, and introduced a new openness into operations. But he has a long way to go to repair completely the internal loss of morale and the external loss of confidence after the Intelligence failure of 1973.

The three Intelligence services (military, Mossad and Shin Bet) co-ordinate their activities through an Intelligence Committee which includes the Director-General of the Foreign Office and the Chief of Police. Functions are divided. Military Intelligence deals with the military strength of the Arab world and is involved directly in any military activity originating in Israel but then crossing her borders. For example, if forces were to be sent into Beirut as in 1968, Military Intelligence would be involved.

The organization of the Israeli military Intelligence systems owes much to the British model, which was adapted for Israeli purposes by General Chaim Herzog between 1948 and 1950. The success of the Six Day War was a triumph of Military Intelligence, then under the leadership of General Aharon ('Arele') Yariv, who headed it for eight years until 1972. It was a misfortune for Israel that his successor, General Eliahu

Zeira, a protégé of Moshe Dayan, was so new to the job when the Yom Kippur War broke out. His failure led to further change, and the job was taken over by the brilliant General Shlomo Gazit who, in 1979, was followed by the professional Saguy.

The Mossad's full Hebrew title is Mossad Bitachon Leumi (Institute for State Security) and it is the Intelligence agency operating outside Israel. One of its main functions is the collection of military, economic and political information – basic Intelligence-gathering – like the CIA in the United States and MI5 in Britain. But it is far from limited to information-gathering and undertakes special operations, like the kipnapping of Adolf Eichmann from Argentina. It was also responsible for the operation which resulted in the killing of the wrong Arabs in Norway in 1973, and the information which emerged as a result of the Norwegian investigations shed much light on the Mossad's methods. On the other hand, one of its major successes was the dashing Entebbe rescue in 1976 which was based on Intelligence provided by the Mossad.

The head of the Mossad is chairman of the Intelligence (coordinating) Committee and reports directly to the Prime Minister. His name is an official secret and is never published in Israel, but *Time* magazine printed a story that he is Major General Yitzhak Hofi, Commander of the Northern Front during the Yom Kippur War. Before the outbreak of that war, Hofi, fortunately for Israel, did not accept the Military Intelligence view that the Syrian troop concentrations were merely routine, and maintained a high state of alert. He was also able to secure reinforcements and, by moving his forces into the Golan Heights, was in a good position to meet the Syrian attack when it came. His alertness and prescience on that occasion no doubt marked him out for higher things.

The third Israeli Intelligence organization is Shin Bet (the initial letters of 'Sherut Bitachon' – Security Service) which is responsible for internal security and counterintelligence within Israel and – since 1967 – also within the occupied territories. It has duties abroad, too, in the protection of Israeli installations. Like the Mossad, Shin Bet reports to the Prime Minister's office and the name of its head is kept secret.

Although the Intelligence Committee exists to bring all the various threads together, organizational interests and problems of conflicting personalities have led to friction from time to time. Isser Harel, the brilliant but jesuitical head of the Mossad in the early years of the State, was constantly at loggerheads with Military Intelligence in the struggle to establish prerogatives. His successor in 1961, General Meir Amit, who came from Military Intelligence, was more cautious and level-headed. He eased tensions and saw his role as a coordinator. With the opprobrium attaching to Military Intelligence after the Yom Kippur War failure, the Mossad and Shin Bet moved into positions of greater prestige and authority, both in Israel's Intelligence community and in the international Intelligence brotherhood.

Glossary

Agudat Israel (Association of Israel). The ultra-orthodox religious party, anti-Zionist in its origins. Won 4 seats in the 1977 election and joined the coalition led by Begin.

Achdut Avoda (Unity of Labour). Originally a faction within Mapai, the dominant Zionist socialist party, it became an independent party before statehood, joined in an electoral alignment with Mapai in 1965 and three years later merged with it and another party, Rafi, to form the Israel Labour Party. But Achdut Avoda still retains some independent identity and has strong support in the kibbutz movement.

Achdut (Unity). A one-member party whose Knesset representative elected in 1977 is Hillel Seidel. It joined the Likud coalition government.

Ashkenasi. Jews of Central and East European ancestry.

Aliyah. Immigration to Israel.

Bagrut. Matriculation.

Bar Giora. Name of a secret Jewish army formed in 1907 when Palestine was under Turkish rule.

Betar. Youth movement of the militant Zionist Revisionist Party which became the Herut Party after 1948.

Bet Din (House of Judgment; *pl.* Batei Din). Jewish ecclesiastical court mainly concerned with problems of personal status.

Bet Tarbut (House of education). The cultural building of the kibbutz.

Bnai Akivah (Sons of Akiba). Youth movement of the National Religious Party.

Cabbala – Cabbalist. A mystical interpretation of the Scriptures developed by some rabbis from the 7th century onwards.

Chassid; pl. Chassidim. Adherent(s) of a pietistic religious movement which began in the 18th century and made a special appeal to the Jewish masses of Eastern Europe.

Diaspora. Jews living in countries other than Palestine/Israel.

Dayan (Judge; *pl.* Dayanim). Judge of rabbinical court. *See* Bet Din.

Edot Hamizrach (Oriental communities). Jews born in Afro-Asian countries or whose parents emigrated to Israel from those countries.

Eretz Israel. Land of Israel.

Gahal. Abb. of Gush Herut Liberali (Herut-Liberal bloc). The electoral alignment formed by Herut and the General Zionist wing of the Liberal Party in 1965. In 1973 this alignment became the Likud.

Gush Emunim (Bloc of the faithful). Religious pressure group which advocates Jewish settlement within the Biblical boundaries of historical Israel. It has links with the National Religious Party.

Hadassah. American women's Zionist organization active in social work in Israel.

Hagana (Defence). The pre-State Jewish defence organization founded by the Histadrut in 1921 and the precursor of the Israel Defence Forces.

Halacha. Jewish religious law.

Hapoel Hamizrachi (Workers of Mizrachi). The socialist-oriented branch of the Mizrachi party, now the National Religious Party.

Hashomer (The watchman). A volunteer self-defence organization founded by Jewish settlers in Palestine in 1908, which was superseded by the Hagana.

Hatehiya (Revival). Right-wing political party founded by Professor Yuval Ne'eman in 1979.

Herut (Freedom). Israel political party of the right formed by the Zionist Revisionist Party in 1948. Merged with the Liberal Party in 1965 to form Gahal and became the strongest component of the Likud government coalition formed in 1977.

Hevrat Ovdim (Workers' society or commonwealth). The holding company for the commercial enterprises of the Histadrut.

Histadrut. Abb. of Histadrut haOvdim b'Eretz Israel (General Federation of

Labour in Israel), second in power only to the government.

Irgun Zvai Leumi (National military organization), otherwise described as IZL or Etzel. An underground fighting group of the Revisionist Party, the last leader of which was Menachem Begin. It was disbanded after statehood.

ILP. Israel Labour Party. The social-democratic party formed in 1968 by a merger of Mapai, Rafi and Achdut Avoda.

Kibbutz (Gathering, *pl.* Kibbutzim). Members of kibbutzim are referred to as kibbutzniks. A kibbutz is a collective settlement in which each member owns a share of the whole.

Kibbutz Artzi (National kibbutz). The kibbutz movement connected with the Marxist Mapam Party.

Kibbutz Dati. Religious kibbutz movement affiliated with the National Religious Party.

Kipa; pl. Kipot. Abbreviated skull-cap worn by religious Jews.

Knesset (Assembly). Israel's Parliament.

Knessia Gedola (Great assembly). The legislative convention of the Agudat Israel Party.

Kosher. Permissible food according to the orthodox Jewish dietary laws.

Kulturkampf (War of cultures). Particularly used in Israel to describe a confrontation between the religious and non-religious sections of the Jewish community.

Kupat Holim (Sick fund). The health service provided by the Histadrut.

Kvutza (Commune). The precursor of the kibbutz.

La'am. One of the four groups making up the Likud Party.

Likud (Gathering together). The right-wing electoral alignment of four parties, Herut, Liberals, La'am and Achdut. Formed in 1973 to oppose the left-wing alignment of the ILP, it gained power in the 1977 election.

Ma'arach (Alignment). The combined electoral list of the ILP and Mapam.

Mafdal. Hebrew acronym for National Religious Party.

Mapai. Abb. of Mifleget Poale Eretz Israel (party of Israel workers), the largest socialist party in Israel and the cornerstone of all Israeli governments until 1977.

Mamzer; pl. Mamzerim. A term in Jewish religious law for a child born to a married woman and a man other than her husband.

Mapam. Abb. of Miflegel Poalim Me'uchedet (United workers' party). The Marxist group which combines on a joint electoral list with Mapai and in 1977 had 3 members in the Knesset.

Mikva; pl. Mikvaot. A ritual bath used by orthodox Jews for purposes of religious purification.

Mizrachi. Abb. of mercaz ruchani (spiritual centre). Religious political party in the Zionist movement. Together with its socialist offshoot, formed the National Religious Party.

Moetzet Gedole Hatorah (Council of Torah Sages). The religious authority of the Agudat Israel Party.

Moshav; pl. Moshavim. Cooperative settlement of smallholders on nationally owned land.

Moshav Shittufi. A moshav incorporating collective features adapted from the kibbutz.

Mossad. Abb. of Mossad Bitachon Leumi (Institute for state security). Israel's central intelligence and security agency responsible for operations outside the country.

National Religious Party (NRP). Party formed through the merger of the Mizrachi and the Mizrachi workers' party which has been a partner in every coalition government in Israel since statehood.

Neturei Karta (Guardians of the city). A group of orthodox zealots in Jerusalem who do not recognize Israel as a secular state.

Palmach. Abb. of Plugot Mahatz (Strike forces). An élite unit of Hagana founded in 1941 and absorbed into the Israel Defence Forces after statehood.

Poalei Agudat Israel (Workers of Agudat Israel). The labour offshoot of the right-wing religious party.

Rafi. Abb. of Reshimat Poale Israel (Israel workers' list). A party formed by Ben-Gurion when he left Mapai in 1965. In 1968 it merged with Mapai and Achdut Avoda to form the Israel Labour Party.

Sabra. A person born in Palestine/Israel. Named after the fruit of the cactus – prickly outside, sweet inside.

Sanhedrin. The highest religious and secular tribunal of the Jews. It contained 71 members and ceased on the destruction of the Second Temple in AD 70.

Sephardi; pl. Sephardim. Descendants of Jews from Spain and Portugal.

Shelli. A loose alliance of left-wing groups which won 2 seats in the Knesset in 1977.

Shin Bet. Abb. of Sherut Bitachon Klali (national security and defence). The service responsible for security and counter-intelligence inside Israel and, since 1967, within the occupied territories.

Shinui (Change). Movement begun by Professor Amnon Rubinstein after the 1973 war. In 1976 it joined with the Democratic Party to form the Democratic Movement for Change. In 1978 it parted company with the DMC and was renamed Shai, abb. of Shinui v'Yosma (Change and initiative).

Shtetl. Jewish townships or hamlets in Eastern Europe. They all ceased to exist during World War II.

Talmud. Compendious collection of rabbinic interpretations of Jewish laws and traditions, completed *c.* AD 500.

Torah. The laws of Moses contained in the Pentateuch and interpreted by authoritative rabbis throughout the ages.

Torah v'Avodah (Torah and labour). The movement of religious pioneers associated with the Mizrachi Party; the principle by which religious kibbutz members live.

Tzedaka. Hebrew word for the religious obligation to give charity.

Va'ad Leumi (People's council). The representative body of the Palestine Jewish community under the British Mandate.

Yarmulka. See Kipa.

Yekke. Colloquial Israeli word for German Jews.

Yeshiva; pl. Yeshivot. Educational institutions mainly directed to the study of the rabbinic literature.

Yishuv (Settlement). Specifically the Jewish community of Palestine before statehood. The old Yishuv was the Jewish community before Zionism began. The Zionist immigration from the end of the 19th century is described as the new yishuv.

Selected bibliography

A very extensive literature has grown up on the State of Israel. Since a number of recently published books contain comprehensive bibliographies, I thought it more useful to list below only those books which I found of particular interest or relevance to my subject. For those who want to consult a larger list, I recommend the classified bibliography in Howard M. Sacher's *History of Israel*, which is mentioned below.

ABRAMOV, S. Zalman, *Perpetual Dilemma. Jewish Religion in the Jewish State* (New York 1976). Written by a distinguished Israeli lawyer and politician, this book examines all the problems created by the clashes between the ancient faith and a modern society. About a third of the long book is historical and the rest analyzes and sheds light on many religious issues still unresolved.

BELLOW, Saul, *To Jerusalem and Back* (London/New York 1976). A personal journal of a four months' stay in Israel sensitively recording thoughtful insights into Israeli attitudes and many shrewd observations on personalities.

BENTWICH, Joseph, *Education in Israel* (Philadelphia 1965). Many changes have taken place in Israel's educational system since this book was published but it remains a valuable reference work to the background of the subject which is necessary to an understanding of the present structure.

BRECHER, Michael, *The Foreign Policy System of Israel* (London 1972). In the course of a detailed and exhaustive account of how Israel's foreign policy is formulated and implemented, the author has included a wide range of information on other topics such as the political system, Israel's élites and the communications network.

EISENSTADT, S. N., *Israeli Society* (London 1967). Israel's leading sociologist has produced what is still, after more than a decade, the standard work on the subject. Particularly important on the class structure and the emergence of the élite groups.

ELIZUR, Yuval and Eliahu Salpeter, *Who Rules Israel?* (New York 1973). Two knowledgeable and experienced Israeli journalists wrote this chatty, gossipy and well-informed book about the various power structures of the country. Much of it is now dated and trivial, but there is enough useful information to make it a worthwhile as well as entertaining read.

ELON, Amos, *The Israelis: Founders and Sons* (London 1971). A portrait of national attitudes indispensable for an understanding of how Israelis think and act. The author is one of Israel's outstanding journalists and interpreters to the outside world. This is not an apologia but a passionate and honest presentation of the hopes, conflicts and realities which have produced the Israelis of today.

FISCH, Harold, *The Zionist Revolution. A New Perspective* (London 1978). The author believes in the purpose of the State of Israel as the fulfilment of God's covenant with the Jewish people. He supports Jewish settlement throughout the biblical promised land and sympathizes with the Gush Emunim. It is one of the few presentations of this point of view, which rarely attempts to explain itself to the non-religious public.

FREUDENHEIM, Yehoshua, *Government in Israel* (New York 1967). Though it is dryasdust and far from up-to-date, this is a useful and methodical compendium of the laws and regulations relating to the government and legal system of Israel. Many of the documents are not otherwise accessible to the English reader.

GILBERT, Martin, *Exile and Return: The Emergence of Jewish Statehood* (London 1978). The historical roots of Israel and the justification for the existence of the Jewish State. One of the features of this book is the inclusion of 28 maps which graphically illustrate the author's themes.

GOREN, Dina, *Secrecy and the Right to Know* (Tel Aviv 1979). A clear and well-informed account of the experiences of Israel with press censorship, all the more useful because of the comparisons made with Britain and the USA.

HALPERN, Ben, *The Idea of the Jewish State* (Cambridge, Mass. 1969). The second edition of a title in the Harvard Middle Eastern Studies, this is essentially a scholarly account of the origins, rise and fulfilment of Zionism. Although it takes the story only up to the Six Day War, I found the book particularly helpful on the struggles within Jewry on the issue of Zionism and Jewish nationalism.

HERTZBERG, Arthur (Ed.), *The Zionist Idea* (New York 1959). An anthology of the most influential voices in Zionism from the middle of the 19th century up to the founders of the Jewish State about a hundred years later. Fascinating texts and a valuable 100-page introduction by the editor which is itself a brilliant short history of Zionist ideology.

HERZOG, Chaim, *The War of Atonement* (London 1975). The Yom Kippur War of 1973 provoked fundamental re-appraisals in Israel which still continue. This is a straight and hard-hitting account of what went wrong, how the errors were overcome and who was at fault. Concentrating on the military side, it does not ignore the political aspects.

KATZ, Elihu and Michael Gurevitch, *The Secularization of Leisure: Culture and Communications in Israel* (London 1976). An empirical study of how Israelis spend their leisure. It discusses the supply and consumption of culture in Israel and is particularly interesting on the attitudes towards TV. It is a pioneer work on these aspects of the lives of Israelis.

KIMCHE, David and Dan Bawly, *The Sandstorm. The Arab-Israeli War of 1967: Prelude and Aftermath* (London 1968). The best account of the war which resulted in the Israeli occupation of the territories now at the centre of the conflict between the Jewish State and the Arab world.

KURZMAN, Dan, *Genesis, 1948* (London 1972). A massive work of some 700 pages describing in compelling detail the first Arab-Israeli war.

LAQUEUR, Walter (Ed.), *The Israel/Arab Reader* (London 1969). Contains all the essential documents from the beginning of Zionism to Abba Eban's brilliant speech at the UN General Assembly on the Six Day War. This documentary history is supplemented by a selection of addresses and articles from both sides on the prospects of war and peace in the Middle East.

LAQUEUR, Walter, *A History of Zionism* (London 1972). Written with this author's customary lucidity, this brings together, in a very readable way, all the strands that went into

the formation of the Zionist movement and its struggles up to the achievement of statehood.

MANSOUR, Atallah, *Waiting for the Dawn* (London 1975). The autobiography of a Christian Arab who is an Israeli citizen and writes in Hebrew for Israel's top newspaper, *Haaretz*. The deeply felt and honestly presented ambivalences of one of its most articulate representatives illumine the problems of Israel's Arab minority.

PEARLMAN, Moshe, *Ben Gurion Looks Back* (London 1965). A fascinating series of talks with Israel's first Prime Minister. What emerges is not only the turbulent and complicated character of the speaker, but graphic pictures of the ideals, achievements and conflicts of the fathers of the Jewish State.

PENNIMAN, Howard R. (Ed.), *Israel at the Polls. The Knesset Elections of 1977* (New York 1979). A detailed and unique examination of the political background, the issues and the conduct of the 1977 campaign. The contributors are all experts and this book ranges much wider than the campaign itself.

ROTHENBERG, Gunther E., *The Anatomy of the Israeli Army* (London 1979). An American Professor of Military History on the evolution of the Israel Defence Forces, with analyses of its performance in war and peace. The writing is not gripping but the book is well-organized and full of facts as well as interesting sidelights on the people who have shaped the special character of the fighting machine.

SACHER, Howard M., *A History of Israel from the Rise of Zionism to Our Time* (Oxford 1977). The most up-to-date history of Israel, concluding with an account of the situation after the 1973 war described as 'Aftermath of an Earthquake'. Though scholarly and detailed, the book is always readable. Its assessments of recent history will, I suspect, call for reconsideration when the events can be reviewed with greater perspective. The full index and bibliography are particularly useful.

Statistical Abstracts of Israel. Annual (Central Bureau of Statistics, Jerusalem). A best buy for anyone who is numerate and interested in hard, unvarnished facts about Israel. Almost 1,000 thin-paper pages contain every detail anyone would want to know about the population, society and economy of the State of Israel from its establishment. The hundreds of tables in this annual constitute a mine of information about issues great and small for the diligent researcher.

STEIN, Leonard, *The Balfour Declaration* (London 1961). A work of meticulous scholarship, this is likely to remain for a long time the definitive account of the origins of the British commitment to the Jewish National Home.

WEISGAL, Meyer and Joel Carmichael (Eds.), *Chaim Weizmann: A Biography by Several Hands* (London 1962). Distinguished by contributions from Isaiah Berlin (alone worth the price of the book), T. R. Fyvel and the late R. H. S. Crossman among others. The life of the first President of Israel is virtually the history of Zionism in the 20th century.

I also recommend the following:

ADAR, Zvi, *Jewish Education in Israel and the United States* (Institute of Contemporary History of the Hebrew University, 1977).

ALLON, Yigal, *The Making of Israel's Army* (London 1970).

ARENDT, Hannah, *Eichmann in Jerusalem* (New York/London 1962).

AVNERI, Uri, *Israel without Zionists* (New York 1968).

BAKER, Henry E., *Legal System of Israel* (Jerusalem 1968).

BEGIN, Menachem, *The Revolt: Story of the Irgun* (Tel Aviv 1964).

CURTIS & CHERTOFF, *Israel: Social Structure and Change* (New York 1973).

DAVIS, Moshe (Ed.), *World Jewry and the State of Israel* (New York 1977).

DAYAN, Moshe, *Diary of the Sinai Campaign* (London 1966).

FEIN, Leonard J., *Politics in Israel* (New York 1967).

HERMAN, Simon, *Israelis and Jews: The Continuity of an Identity* (New York 1970).

HOROWITZ, D., *The Economics of Israel* (London 1967).

KAHANA, K., *The Case for Jewish Civil Law in the Jewish State* (London 1960).

KOLLEK, Teddy, *For Jerusalem* (Jerusalem 1978).

Labour and Society in Israel (Department of Labour Studies, Tel Aviv University, 1973).

LESLIE, S. C., *The Rift in Israel* (London 1971).

MEDDING, Peter Y., *Mapai in Israel* (Cambridge 1977).

OZ, Amos, *My Michael* (New York 1972).

PRITTIE, Terence, *Eshkol: The Man and the Nation* (London 1967).

SCHAMA, Simon, *Two Rothschilds and the Land of Israel* (London 1978).

SIMON, Rita James, *Continuity and Change. A Study of Two Ethnic Communities in Israel* (Cambridge 1978).

SHAMIR, Moshe, *My Life with Ishmael* (New York 1972).

TALMON, J. L., *Israel Among the Nations* (London 1970).

Index